Microsoft®

Word 2010
for Medical Professionals

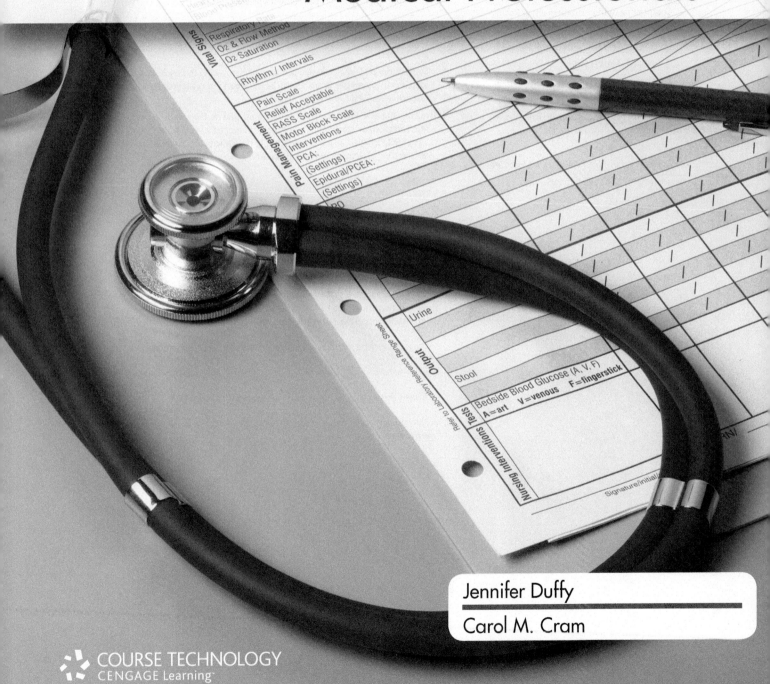

Jennifer Duffy

Carol M. Cram

COURSE TECHNOLOGY
CENGAGE Learning™

Australia • Brazil • Japan • Korea • Mexico • Singapore • Spain • United Kingdom • United States

COURSE TECHNOLOGY
CENGAGE Learning™

Microsoft® Word 2010 for Medical Professionals
Jennifer Duffy, Carol M. Cram

Vice President, Publisher: Nicole Jones Pinard

Executive Editor: Marjorie Hunt

Associate Acquisitions Editor: Amanda Lyons

Senior Product Manager: Christina Kling Garrett

Associate Product Manager: Kim Klasner

Editorial Assistant: Brandelynn Perry

Director of Marketing: Cheryl Costantini

Senior Marketing Manager: Ryan DeGrote

Marketing Coordinator: Kristen Panciocco

Contributing Author: Elizabeth Eisner Reding

Developmental Editor: Pam Conrad

Content Project Manager: Heather Hopkins

Copy Editor: Mark Goodin

Proofreader: Vicki Zimmer

Indexer: BIM Indexing and Proofreading Services

QA Manuscript Reviewers: Serge Palladino, Jeff
    Schwartz, Ashlee Weltz Smith

Print Buyer: Fola Orekoya

Cover Designer: GEX Publishing Services

Composition: GEX Publishing Services

Library of Congress Control Number: 2010943252

Trademarks:

Some of the product names and company names used in this book have been used for identification purposes only and may be trademarks or registered trademarks of their respective manufacturers and sellers.

Microsoft and the Office logo are either registered trademarks or trademarks of Microsoft Corporation in the United States and/or other countries. Course Technology, Cengage Learning is an independent entity from Microsoft Corporation, and not affiliated with Microsoft in any manner.

ISBN-13: 978-0-538-74947-3
ISBN-10: 0-538-74947-4

Course Technology
20 Channel Center Street
Boston, MA 02210
USA

Cengage Learning is a leading provider of customized learning solutions with office locations around the globe, including Singapore, the United Kingdom, Australia, Mexico, Brazil, and Japan. Locate your local office at:
international.cengage.com/region

Cengage Learning products are represented in Canada by Nelson Education, Ltd.

To learn more about Course Technology, visit **www.cengage.com/coursetechnology**

To learn more about Cengage Learning, visit **www.cengage.com**

Purchase any of our products at your local college store or at our preferred online store **www.cengagebrain.com**

Printed in the United States of America
4 5 6 7 8 9 19 18 17 16 15 14

Brief Contents

Contents

Office 2010

Word 2010

Web Apps

Preface

Welcome to *Microsoft Word 2010 for Medical Professionals*. This book is designed to meet the needs of students who are training for careers in medical office administration. What makes this book unique is that every lesson and exercise features a real-world spreadsheet or chart related to the medical profession. As they learn Word skills, students work with examples they are likely to encounter in a typical medical practice, clinic, or hospital.

If this is your first experience with this book, you'll see it has a unique design: each skill is presented on two facing pages, with steps on the left and screens on the right. The layout makes it easy to learn a skill without having to read a lot of text and flip pages to see an illustration.

See the illustration on the right to learn more about the pedagogical and design elements of a typical lesson.

What's New In This Edition

- **Fully Updated.** Highlights the new features of Microsoft Word 2010 including coverage on tools to create research papers, including adding citations, endnotes, and bibliographies. A new appendix covers cloud computing concepts and using Microsoft Office Web Apps. Examples and exercises are updated throughout.

- **Maps to SAM 2010.** This book is designed to work with SAM (Skills Assessment Manager) 2010. **SAM Assessment** contains performance-based, hands-on SAM exams for each unit of this book, and **SAM Training** provides hands-on training for skills covered in the book. (SAM sold separately.) See page xii for more information on SAM.

Each two-page spread focuses on a single skill.

Introduction briefly explains why the lesson skill is important.

A case scenario motivates the the steps and puts learning in context.

UNIT A — Word 2010

Saving a Document

To store a document permanently so you can open it and edit it at another time, you must save it as a **file**. When you **save** a document you give it a name, called a **filename**, and indicate the location where you want to store the file. Files created in Word 2010 are automatically assigned the .docx file extension to distinguish them from files created in other software programs. You can save a document using the Save button on the Quick Access toolbar or the Save command on the File tab. Once you have saved a document for the first time, you should save it again every few minutes and always before printing so that the saved file is updated to reflect your latest changes. You save your memo using a descriptive filename and the default file extension.

STEPS

TROUBLE
If you don't see the extension .docx as part of the filename, the setting in Windows to display file extensions is not active.

1. **Click the Save button on the Quick Access toolbar**
   The first time you save a document, the Save As dialog box opens, as shown in Figure A-5. The default filename, Memorandum, appears in the File name text box. The default filename is based on the first few words of the document. The default file extension, .docx, appears in the Save as type list box. Table A-3 describes the functions of some of the buttons in the Save As dialog box.

2. **Type WMP A-Staff Memo in the File name text box**
   The new filename replaces the default filename. Giving your documents brief descriptive filenames makes it easier to locate and organize them later. You do not need to type .docx when you type a new filename.

3. **Navigate to the drive and folder where you store your Data Files**
   You can navigate to a different drive or folder in several ways. For example, you can click a drive or folder in the Address bar or the navigation pane to go directly to that location. Click the double arrow in the Address bar to display a list of drives and folders. You can also double-click a drive or folder in the folder window to change the active location. When you are finished navigating to the drive or folder where you store your Data Files, that location appears in the Address bar. Your Save As dialog box should resemble Figure A-6.

QUICK TIP
To save a document so it can be opened in an older version of Word, click the Save as type list arrow, then click Word 97-2003 Document (*.doc).

4. **Click Save**
   The document is saved to the drive and folder you specified in the Save As dialog box, and the title bar displays the new filename, WMP A-Staff Memo.docx.

5. **Place the insertion point before** September **in the first paragraph, type** early**, then press [Spacebar]**
   You can continue to work on a document after you have saved it with a new filename.

6. **Click**
   Your change to the memo is saved. After you save a document for the first time, you must continue to save the changes you make to the document. You can also press [Ctrl][S] to save a document.

Windows Live and Microsoft Office Web Apps

All Office programs include the capability to incorporate feedback—called online collaboration—across the Internet or a company network. Using **cloud computing** (work done in a virtual environment), you can take advantage of Web programs called Microsoft Office Web Apps, which are simplified versions of the programs found in the Microsoft Office 2010 suite. Because these programs are online, they take up no computer disk space and are accessed using Windows

Live SkyDrive, a free service from Microsoft. Using Windows Live SkyDrive, you and your colleagues can create and store documents in a "cloud" and make the documents available to whomever you grant access. To use Windows Live SkyDrive, you need a free Windows Live ID, which you obtain at the Windows Live Web site. You can find more information in the "Working with Windows Live and Office Web Apps" appendix.

Word 8   Creating Documents with Word 2010

Tips and troubleshooting advice, right where you need it—next to the step itself.

Clues to Use boxes provide useful information related to the lesson skill.

Large screen shots keep
students on track as
they complete steps.

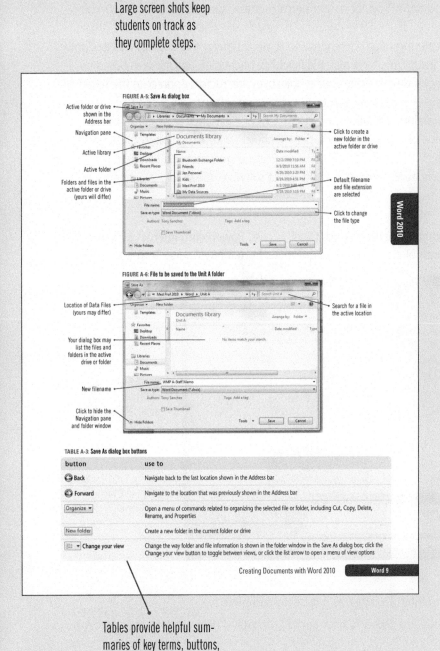

FIGURE A-5: Save As dialog box

FIGURE A-6: File to be saved to the Unit A folder

TABLE A-3: Save As dialog box buttons

button	use to
Back	Navigate back to the last location shown in the Address bar
Forward	Navigate to the location that was previously shown in the Address bar
Organize ▼	Open a menu of commands related to organizing the selected file or folder, including Cut, Copy, Delete, Rename, and Properties
New folder	Create a new folder in the current folder or drive
Change your view	Change the way folder and file information is shown in the folder window in the Save As dialog box; click the Change your view button to toggle between views, or click the list arrow to open a menu of view options

Creating Documents with Word 2010   Word 9

Tables provide helpful sum-
maries of key terms, buttons,
or keyboard shortcuts.

Assignments

The lessons use Riverwalk Medical Clinic, a fictional outpatient medical facility, as the case study. The assignments on the light yellow pages at the end of each unit increase in difficulty. Assignments include:

- **Concepts Review** consist of multiple choice, matching, and screen identification questions.

- **Skills Reviews** are hands-on, step-by-step exercises that review the skills covered in each lesson in the unit.

- **Independent Challenges** are case projects requiring critical thinking and application of the unit skills. The Independent Challenges increase in difficulty, with the first one in each unit being the easiest. Independent Challenges 2 and 3 become increasingly open-ended, requiring more independent problem solving.

- **Real Life Independent Challenges** are practical exercises in which students create documents to help them with their every day lives.

- **Advanced Challenge Exercises** set within the Independent Challenges provide optional steps for more advanced students.

- **Visual Workshops** are practical, self-graded capstone projects that require independent problem solving.

About SAM

SAM is the premier proficiency-based assessment and training environment for Microsoft Office. Web-based software along with an inviting user interface provide maximum teaching and learning flexibility. SAM builds students' skills and confidence with a variety of real-life simulations, and SAM Projects' assignments prepare students for today's workplace.

The SAM system includes Assessment and Training featuring page references and remediation for this book as well as Course Technology's Microsoft Office textbooks. With SAM, instructors can enjoy the flexibility of creating assignments based on content from their favorite Microsoft Office books or based on specific course objectives. Instructors appreciate the scheduling and reporting options that have made SAM the market-leading online testing and training software for over a decade. Over 2,000 performance-based questions and matching Training simulations, as well as tens of thousands of objective-based questions from many Course Technology texts, provide instructors with a variety of choices across multiple applications from the introductory level through the comprehensive level. The inclusion of hands-on Projects guarantee that student knowledge will skyrocket from the practice of solving real-world situations using Microsoft Office software. (SAM sold separately.)

SAM Assessment
- Content for these hands-on, performance-based tasks includes Word, Excel, Access, PowerPoint, Internet Explorer, Outlook, and Windows. Includes tens of thousands of objective-based questions from many Course Technology texts.

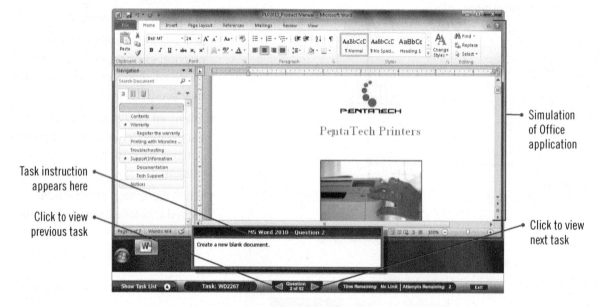

Task instruction appears here

Click to view previous task

Simulation of Office application

Click to view next task

SAM Training
- Observe mode allows the student to watch and listen to a task as it is being completed.
- Practice mode allows the student to follow guided arrows and hear audio prompts to help visual learners know how to complete a task.
- Apply mode allows the student to prove what they've learned by completing a task using helpful instructions.

SAM Projects
- Live-in-the-application assignments in Word, Excel, Access and PowerPoint that help students be sure they know how to effectively communicate, solve a problem or make a decision. (*Note*: There are no SAM Projects that are based on the content in this book.)

Instructor Resources

The Instructor Resources CD is Course Technology's way of putting the resources and information needed to teach and learn effectively into your hands. With an integrated array of teaching and learning tools that offer you and your students a broad range of technology-based instructional options, we believe this CD represents the highest quality and most cutting edge resources available to instructors today. The resources available with this book are:

- **Instructor's Manual**—Available as an electronic file, the Instructor's Manual includes detailed lecture topics with teaching tips for each unit.

- **Sample Syllabus**—Prepare and customize your course easily using this sample course outline.

- **PowerPoint Presentations**—Each unit has a corresponding PowerPoint presentation that you can use in lecture, distribute to your students, or customize to suit your course.

- **Figure Files**—The figures in the text are provided on the Instructor Resources CD to help you illustrate key topics or concepts. You can create traditional overhead transparencies by printing the figure files. Or you can create electronic slide shows by using the figures in a presentation program such as PowerPoint.

- **Solutions to Exercises**—Solutions to Exercises contains every file students are asked to create or modify in the lessons and end-of-unit material. Also provided in this section, there is a document outlining the solutions for the end-of-unit Concepts Review, Skills Review, and Independent Challenges. An Annotated Solution File and Grading Rubric accompany each file and can be used together for quick and easy grading.

- **Data Files for Students**—To complete most of the units in this book, your students will need Data Files. You can post the Data Files on a file server for students to copy. The Data Files are available on the Instructor Resources CD-ROM, the Review Pack, and can also be downloaded from cengagebrain.com. For more information on how to download the Data Files, see the inside back cover.

Instruct students to use the Data Files List included on the Review Pack and the Instructor Resources CD. This list gives instructions on copying and organizing files.

- **ExamView**—ExamView is a powerful testing software package that allows you to create and administer printed, computer (LAN-based), and Internet exams. ExamView includes hundreds of questions that correspond to the topics covered in this text, enabling students to generate detailed study guides that include page references for further review. The computer-based and Internet testing components allow students to take exams at their computers, and also saves you time by grading each exam automatically.

Acknowledgements

Instructor Advisory Board

We thank our Instructor Advisory Board who gave us their opinions and guided our decisions as we updated our texts for Microsoft Office 2010. They are as follows:

Terri Helfand, Chaffey Community College

Barbara Comfort, J. Sargeant Reynolds Community College

Brenda Nielsen, Mesa Community College

Sharon Cotman, Thomas Nelson Community College

Marian Meyer, Central New Mexico Community College

Audrey Styer, Morton College

Richard Alexander, Heald College

Xiaodong Qiao, Heald College

Author Acknowledgements

Jennifer Duffy Many talented people at Course Technology worked tirelessly to shape this book—thank you all. I am especially grateful to Pam Conrad, editor extraordinaire, whose dedication, wisdom, and precision are evident on every page.

Carol Cram This book is made possible through the combined efforts of many amazing people, most notably my developmental editor Pam Conrad, whose wit, wisdom, and patience are a constant source of wonder to me. I'd also like to thank my husband Gregg and daughter Julia who make everything I do possible.

Read This Before You Begin

Frequently Asked Questions

What are Data Files?

A Data File is a partially completed Word document or another type of file that you use to complete the steps in the units and exercises to create the final document that you submit to your instructor. Each unit opener page lists the Data Files that you need for that unit.

Where are the Data Files?

Your instructor will provide the Data Files to you or direct you to a location on a network drive from which you can download them. For information on how to download the Data Files from cengagebrain.com, see the inside back cover.

What software was used to write and test this book?

This book was written and tested using a typical installation of Microsoft Office 2010 Professional Plus on a computer with a typical installation of Microsoft Windows 7 Ultimate.

The browser used for any Web-dependent steps is Internet Explorer 8.

Do I need to be connected to the Internet to complete the steps and exercises in this book?

Some of the exercises in this book require that your computer be connected to the Internet. If you are not connected to the Internet, see your instructor for information on how to complete the exercises.

What do I do if my screen is different from the figures shown in this book?

This book was written and tested on computers with monitors set at a resolution of 1024 × 768. If your screen shows more or less information than the figures in the book, your monitor is probably set at a higher or lower resolution. If you don't see something on your screen, you might have to scroll down or up to see the object identified in the figures.

The Ribbon—the blue area at the top of the screen—in Microsoft Office 2010 adapts to different resolutions. If your monitor is set at a lower resolution than 1024 × 768, you might not see all of the buttons shown in the figures. The groups of buttons will always appear, but the entire group might be condensed into a single button that you need to click to access the buttons described in the instructions.

COURSECASTS Learning on the Go. Always Available...Always Relevant.

Our fast-paced world is driven by technology. You know because you are an active participant—always on the go, always keeping up with technological trends, and always learning new ways to embrace technology to power your life. Let CourseCasts, hosted by Ken Baldauf of Florida State University, be your guide into weekly updates in this ever-changing space. These timely, relevant podcasts are produced weekly and are available for download at http://coursecasts.course.com or directly from iTunes (search by CourseCasts). CourseCasts are a perfect solution to getting students (and even instructors) to learn on the go!

Read This Before You Begin

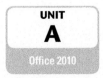

UNIT A
Office 2010

Getting Started with Microsoft Office 2010

Files You Will Need:

OFFICE A-1.xlsx

Microsoft Office 2010 is a group of software programs designed to help you create documents, collaborate with coworkers, and track and analyze information. Each program is designed so you can work quickly and efficiently to create professional-looking results. You use different Office programs to accomplish specific tasks, such as writing a letter or producing a sales presentation, yet all the programs have a similar look and feel. Once you become familiar with one program, you'll find it easy to transfer your knowledge to the others. This unit introduces you to the most frequently used programs in Office, as well as common features they all share.

OBJECTIVES

Understand the Office 2010 suite

Start and exit an Office program

View the Office 2010 user interface

Create and save a file

Open a file and save it with a new name

View and print your work

Get Help and close a file

Understanding the Office 2010 Suite

Microsoft Office 2010 features an intuitive, context-sensitive user interface, so you can get up to speed faster and use advanced features with greater ease. The programs in Office are bundled together in a group called a **suite** (although you can also purchase them separately). The Office suite is available in several configurations, but all include Word, Excel, and PowerPoint. Other configurations include Access, Outlook, Publisher, and other programs. Each program in Office is best suited for completing specific types of tasks, though there is some overlap in capabilities.

DETAILS

The Office programs covered in this book include:

- **Microsoft Word 2010**

  When you need to create any kind of text-based document, such as a memo, newsletter, or multipage report, Word is the program to use. You can easily make your documents look great by inserting eye-catching graphics and using formatting tools such as themes, which are available in most Office programs. **Themes** are predesigned combinations of color and formatting attributes you can apply to a document. The Word document shown in Figure A-1 was formatted with the Solstice theme.

- **Microsoft Excel 2010**

  Excel is the perfect solution when you need to work with numeric values and make calculations. It puts the power of formulas, functions, charts, and other analytical tools into the hands of every user, so you can analyze sales projections, calculate loan payments, and present your findings in style. The Excel worksheet shown in Figure A-1 tracks personal expenses. Because Excel automatically recalculates results whenever a value changes, the information is always up to date. A chart illustrates how the monthly expenses are broken down.

- **Microsoft PowerPoint 2010**

  Using PowerPoint, it's easy to create powerful presentations complete with graphics, transitions, and even a soundtrack. Using professionally designed themes and clip art, you can quickly and easily create dynamic slide shows such as the one shown in Figure A-1.

- **Microsoft Access 2010**

  Access helps you keep track of large amounts of quantitative data, such as product inventories or employee records. The form shown in Figure A-1 was created for a grocery store inventory database. Employees use the form to enter data about each item. Using Access enables employees to quickly find specific information such as price and quantity without hunting through store shelves and stockrooms.

Microsoft Office has benefits beyond the power of each program, including:

- **Common user interface: Improving business processes**

  Because the Office suite programs have a similar **interface**, or look and feel, your experience using one program's tools makes it easy to learn those in the other programs. In addition, Office documents are **compatible** with one another, meaning that you can easily incorporate, or **integrate**, an Excel chart into a PowerPoint slide, or an Access table into a Word document.

- **Collaboration: Simplifying how people work together**

  Office recognizes the way people do business today, and supports the emphasis on communication and knowledge sharing within companies and across the globe. All Office programs include the capability to incorporate feedback—called **online collaboration**—across the Internet or a company network.

Office 2010

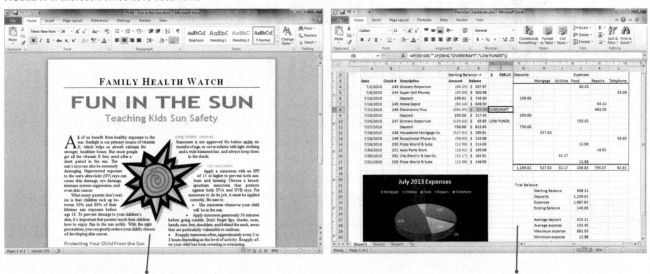

Newsletter created in Word

Checkbook register created in Excel

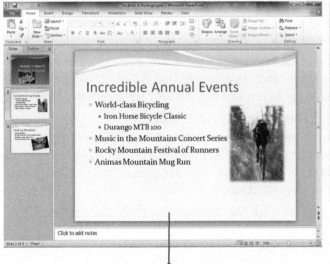

Tourism presentation created in PowerPoint

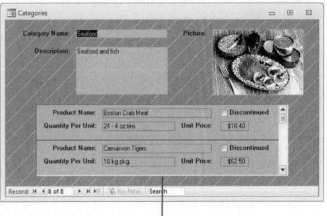

Store inventory form created in Access

Deciding which program to use

Every Office program includes tools that go far beyond what you might expect. For example, although Excel is primarily designed for making calculations, you can use it to create a database. So when you're planning a project, how do you decide which Office program to use? The general rule of thumb is to use the program best suited for your intended task, and make use of supporting tools in the program if you need them. Word is best for creating text-based documents, Excel is best for making mathematical calculations, PowerPoint is best for preparing presentations, and Access is best for managing quantitative data. Although the capabilities of Office are so vast that you *could* create an inventory in Excel or a budget in Word, you'll find greater flexibility and efficiency by using the program designed for the task. And remember, you can always create a file in one program, and then insert it in a document in another program when you need to, such as including sales projections (Excel) in a memo (Word).

Starting and Exiting an Office Program

The first step in using an Office program is to open, or **launch**, it on your computer. The easiest ways to launch a program are to click the Start button on the Windows taskbar or to double-click an icon on your desktop. You can have multiple programs open on your computer simultaneously, and you can move between open programs by clicking the desired program or document button on the taskbar or by using the [Alt][Tab] keyboard shortcut combination. When working, you'll often want to open multiple programs in Office and switch among them as you work. Begin by launching a few Office programs now.

STEPS

QUICK TIP

You can also launch a program by double-clicking a desktop icon or clicking the program name on the Start menu.

1. **Click the Start button 🏁 on the taskbar**

   The Start menu opens. If the taskbar is hidden, you can display it by pointing to the bottom of the screen. Depending on your taskbar property settings, the taskbar may be displayed at all times, or only when you point to that area of the screen. For more information, or to change your taskbar properties, consult your instructor or technical support person.

2. **Click All Programs, scroll down if necessary in the All Programs menu, click Microsoft Office as shown in Figure A-2, then click Microsoft Word 2010**

   Word 2010 starts, and the program window opens on your screen.

QUICK TIP

It is not necessary to close one program before opening another.

3. **Click 🏁 on the taskbar, click All Programs, click Microsoft Office, then click Microsoft Excel 2010**

   Excel 2010 starts, and the program window opens, as shown in Figure A-3. Word is no longer visible, but it remains open. The taskbar displays a button for each open program and document. Because this Excel document is **active**, or in front and available, the Excel button on the taskbar appears slightly lighter.

QUICK TIP

As you work in Windows, your computer adapts to your activities. You may notice that after clicking the Start button, the name of the program you want to open appears in the Start menu above All Programs; if so, you can click it to start the program.

4. **Point to the Word program button 📄 on the taskbar, then click 📄**

   The Word program window is now in front. When the Aero feature is turned on in Windows 7, pointing to a program button on the taskbar displays a thumbnail version of each open window in that program above the program button. Clicking a program button on the taskbar activates that program and the most recently active document. Clicking a thumbnail of a document activates that document.

5. **Click 🏁 on the taskbar, click All Programs, click Microsoft Office, then click Microsoft PowerPoint 2010**

   PowerPoint 2010 starts and becomes the active program.

6. **Click the Excel program button 📊 on the taskbar**

   Excel is now the active program.

TROUBLE

If you don't have Access installed on your computer, proceed to the next lesson.

7. **Click 🏁 on the taskbar, click All Programs, click Microsoft Office, then click Microsoft Access 2010**

   Access 2010 starts and becomes the active program. Now all four Office programs are open at the same time.

8. **Click Exit on the navigation bar in the Access program window, as shown in Figure A-4**

   Access closes, leaving Excel active and Word and PowerPoint open.

Using shortcut keys to move between Office programs

As an alternative to the Windows taskbar, you can use a keyboard shortcut to move among open Office programs. The [Alt][Tab] keyboard combination lets you either switch quickly to the next open program or file or choose one from a gallery. To switch immediately to the next open program or file, press [Alt][Tab]. To choose from all open programs and files, press and hold [Alt], then press and release [Tab] without releasing [Alt]. A gallery opens on screen, displaying the filename and a thumbnail image of each open program and file, as well as of the desktop. Each time you press [Tab] while holding [Alt], the selection cycles to the next open file or location. Release [Alt] when the program, file, or location you want to activate is selected.

FIGURE A-2: Start menu

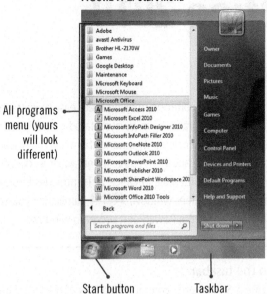

All programs menu (yours will look different)

Start button   Taskbar

FIGURE A-3: Excel program window and Windows taskbar

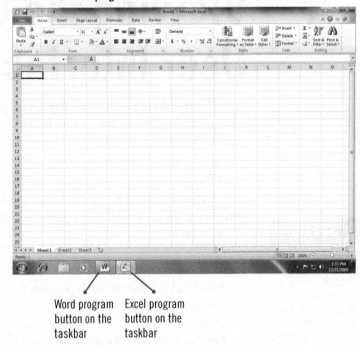

Word program button on the taskbar   Excel program button on the taskbar

FIGURE A-4: Access program window

File tab

Navigation bar

Exit command

Windows Live and Microsoft Office Web Apps

All Office programs include the capability to incorporate feedback—called online collaboration—across the Internet or a company network. Using **cloud computing** (work done in a virtual environment), you can take advantage of Web programs called Microsoft Office Web Apps, which are simplified versions of the programs found in the Microsoft Office 2010 suite. Because these programs are online, they take up no computer disk space and are accessed using

Windows Live SkyDrive, a free service from Microsoft. Using Windows Live SkyDrive, you and your colleagues can create and store documents in a "cloud" and make the documents available to whomever you grant access. To use Windows Live SkyDrive, you need a free Windows Live ID, which you obtain at the Windows Live Web site. You can find more information in the "Working with Windows Live and Office Web Apps" appendix.

Viewing the Office 2010 User Interface

One of the benefits of using Office is that the programs have much in common, making them easy to learn and making it simple to move from one to another. Individual Office programs have always shared many features, but the innovations in the Office 2010 user interface mean even greater similarity among them all. That means you can also use your knowledge of one program to get up to speed in another. A **user interface** is a collective term for all the ways you interact with a software program. The user interface in Office 2010 provides intuitive ways to choose commands, work with files, and navigate in the program window. ▰▰▰▰ Familiarize yourself with some of the common interface elements in Office by examining the PowerPoint program window.

STEPS

QUICK TIP
In addition to the standard tabs on the Ribbon, **contextual tabs** open when needed to complete a specific task; they appear in an accent color and close when no longer needed. To minimize the display of the buttons and commands on tabs, click the Minimize the Ribbon button ⌃ on the right end of the Ribbon.

1. **Click the PowerPoint program button 📷 on the taskbar**

   PowerPoint becomes the active program. Refer to Figure A-5 to identify common elements of the Office user interface. The **document window** occupies most of the screen. In PowerPoint, a blank slide appears in the document window, so you can build your slide show. At the top of every Office program window is a **title bar** that displays the document name and program name. Below the title bar is the **Ribbon**, which displays commands you're likely to need for the current task. Commands are organized onto **tabs**. The tab names appear at the top of the Ribbon, and the active tab appears in front. The Ribbon in every Office program includes tabs specific to the program, but all Office programs include a File tab and Home tab on the left end of the Ribbon.

2. **Click the File tab**

   The File tab opens, displaying **Backstage view**. The navigation bar on the left side of Backstage view contains commands to perform actions common to most Office programs, such as opening a file, saving a file, and closing the current program. Just above the File tab is the **Quick Access toolbar**, which also includes buttons for common Office commands.

3. **Click the File tab again to close Backstage view and return to the document window, then click the Design tab on the Ribbon**

   To display a different tab, you click the tab on the Ribbon. Each tab contains related commands arranged into **groups** to make features easy to find. On the Design tab, the Themes group displays available design themes in a **gallery**, or visual collection of choices you can browse. Many groups contain a **dialog box launcher**, an icon you can click to open a dialog box or task pane from which to choose related commands.

QUICK TIP
Live Preview is available in many galleries and menus throughout Office.

4. **Move the mouse pointer ⌖ over the Angles theme in the Themes group as shown in Figure A-6, but do not click the mouse button**

   The Angles theme is temporarily applied to the slide in the document window. However, because you did not click the theme, you did not permanently change the slide. With the **Live Preview** feature, you can point to a choice, see the results right in the document, and then decide if you want to make the change.

QUICK TIP
If you accidentally click a theme, click the Undo button ↺ on the Quick Access toolbar.

5. **Move ⌖ away from the Ribbon and towards the slide**

   If you had clicked the Angles theme, it would be applied to this slide. Instead, the slide remains unchanged.

QUICK TIP
You can also use the Zoom button in the Zoom group on the View tab to enlarge or reduce a document's appearance.

6. **Point to the Zoom slider ▽ on the status bar, then drag ▽ to the right until the Zoom level reads 166%**

   The slide display is enlarged. Zoom tools are located on the status bar. You can drag the slider or click the Zoom In or Zoom Out buttons to zoom in or out on an area of interest. **Zooming in**, or choosing a higher percentage, makes a document appear bigger on screen, but less of it fits on the screen at once; **zooming out**, or choosing a lower percentage, lets you see more of the document but at a reduced size.

7. **Drag ▽ on the status bar to the left until the Zoom level reads 73%**

FIGURE A-5: PowerPoint program window

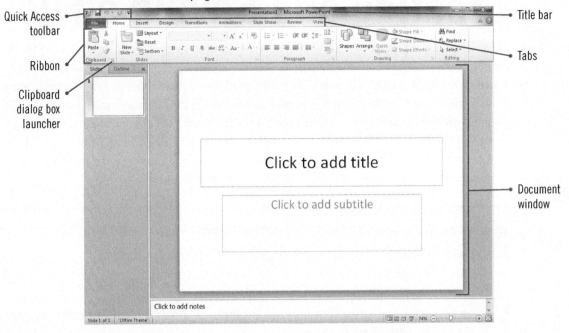

Quick Access toolbar

Ribbon

Clipboard dialog box launcher

Title bar

Tabs

Document window

FIGURE A-6: Viewing a theme with Live Preview

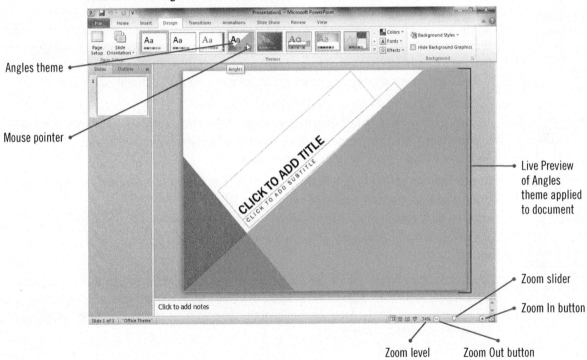

Angles theme

Mouse pointer

Live Preview of Angles theme applied to document

Zoom slider

Zoom In button

Zoom level

Zoom Out button

Using Backstage view

Backstage view in each Microsoft Office program offers "one stop shopping" for many commonly performed tasks, such as opening and saving a file, printing and previewing a document, defining document properties, sharing information, and exiting a program.

Backstage view opens when you click the File tab in any Office program, and while features such as the Ribbon, Mini toolbar, and Live Preview all help you work *in* your documents, the File tab and Backstage view help you work *with* your documents.

Creating and Saving a File

When working in a program, one of the first things you need to do is to create and save a file. A **file** is a stored collection of data. Saving a file enables you to work on a project now, then put it away and work on it again later. In some Office programs, including Word, Excel, and PowerPoint, a new file is automatically created when you start the program, so all you have to do is enter some data and save it. In Access, you must expressly create a file before you enter any data. You should give your files meaningful names and save them in an appropriate location so that they're easy to find. ⬛⬛⬛ Use Word to familiarize yourself with the process of creating and saving a document. First you'll type some notes about a possible location for a corporate meeting, then you'll save the information for later use.

STEPS

1. **Click the** Word program button 🖼 **on the taskbar**

2. **Type** Locations for Corporate Meeting, **then press [Enter] twice**
   The text appears in the document window, and the **insertion point** blinks on a new blank line. The insertion point indicates where the next typed text will appear.

3. **Type** Las Vegas, NV, **press [Enter], type** Orlando, FL, **press [Enter], type** Boston, MA, **press [Enter] twice, then type your name**
   Compare your document to Figure A-7.

QUICK TIP
A filename can be up to 255 characters, including a file extension, and can include upper- or lowercase characters and spaces, but not ?, ", /, \, <, >, *, |, or :.

4. **Click the** Save button 🖫 **on the Quick Access toolbar**
   Because this is the first time you are saving this document, the Save As dialog box opens, as shown in Figure A-8. The Save As dialog box includes options for assigning a filename and storage location. Once you save a file for the first time, clicking 🖫 saves any changes to the file *without* opening the Save As dialog box, because no additional information is needed. The Address bar in the Save As dialog box displays the default location for saving the file, but you can change it to any location. The File name field contains a suggested name for the document based on text in the file, but you can enter a different name.

QUICK TIP
Saving a file to the Desktop creates a desktop icon that you can double-click to both launch a program and open a document.

5. **Type** OF A-Potential Corporate Meeting Locations
   The text you type replaces the highlighted text. (The "OF A-" in the filename indicates that the file is created in Office Unit A. You will see similar designations throughout this book when files are named. For example, a file named in Excel Unit B would begin with "EX B-".)

6. **In the Save As dialog box, use the Address bar or Navigation Pane to navigate to the drive and folder where you store your Data Files**
   Many students store files on a flash drive, but you can also store files on your computer, a network drive, or any storage device indicated by your instructor or technical support person.

QUICK TIP
To create a new blank file when a file is open, click the File tab, click New on the navigation bar, then click Create near the bottom of the document preview pane.

7. **Click** Save
   The Save As dialog box closes, the new file is saved to the location you specified, then the name of the document appears in the title bar, as shown in Figure A-9. (You may or may not see the file extension ".docx" after the filename.) See Table A-1 for a description of the different types of files you create in Office, and the file extensions associated with each.

TABLE A-1: Common filenames and default file extensions

file created in	is called a	and has the default extension
Word	document	.docx
Excel	workbook	.xlsx
PowerPoint	presentation	.pptx
Access	database	.accdb

FIGURE A-7: Document created in Word

Save button

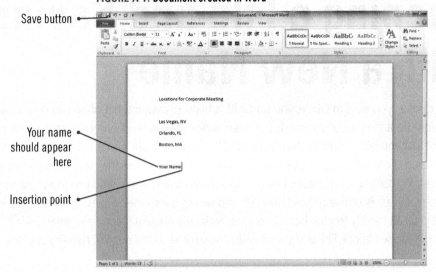

Your name should appear here

Insertion point

FIGURE A-8: Save As dialog box

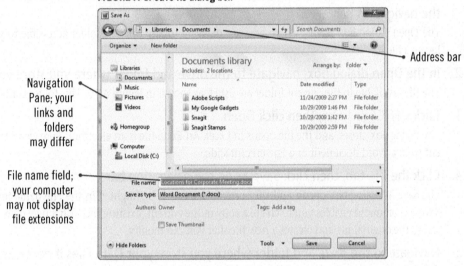

Address bar

Navigation Pane; your links and folders may differ

File name field; your computer may not display file extensions

FIGURE A-9: Saved and named Word document

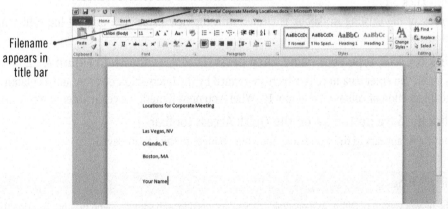

Filename appears in title bar

Using the Office Clipboard

You can use the Office Clipboard to cut and copy items from one Office program and paste them into others. The Office Clipboard can store a maximum of 24 items. To access it, open the Office Clipboard task pane by clicking the dialog box launcher [icon] in the Clipboard group on the Home tab. Each time you copy a selection, it is saved in the Office Clipboard. Each entry in the Office Clipboard includes an icon that tells you the program it was created in. To paste an entry, click in the document where you want it to appear, then click the item in the Office Clipboard. To delete an item from the Office Clipboard, right-click the item, then click Delete.

Opening a File and Saving It with a New Name

In many cases as you work in Office, you start with a blank document, but often you need to use an existing file. It might be a file you or a coworker created earlier as a work in progress, or it could be a complete document that you want to use as the basis for another. For example, you might want to create a budget for this year using the budget you created last year; you could type in all the categories and information from scratch, or you could open last year's budget, save it with a new name, and just make changes to update it for the current year. By opening the existing file and saving it with the Save As command, you create a duplicate that you can modify to your heart's content, while the original file remains intact. Use Excel to open an existing workbook file, and save it with a new name so the original remains unchanged.

STEPS

QUICK TIP

Click Recent on the navigation bar to display a list of recent workbooks; click a file in the list to open it.

1. **Click the Excel program button on the taskbar, click the File tab, then click Open on the navigation bar**

   The Open dialog box opens, where you can navigate to any drive or folder accessible to your computer to locate a file.

2. **In the Open dialog box, navigate to the drive and folder where you store your Data Files**

   The files available in the current folder are listed, as shown in Figure A-10. This folder contains one file.

TROUBLE

Click Enable Editing on the Protected View bar near the top of your document window if prompted.

3. **Click OFFICE A-1.xlsx, then click Open**

   The dialog box closes, and the file opens in Excel. An Excel file is an electronic spreadsheet, so it looks different from a Word document or a PowerPoint slide.

4. **Click the File tab, then click Save As on the navigation bar**

   The Save As dialog box opens, and the current filename is highlighted in the File name text box. Using the Save As command enables you to create a copy of the current, existing file with a new name. This action preserves the original file and creates a new file that you can modify.

QUICK TIP

The Save As command works identically in all Office programs, except Access; in Access, this command lets you save a copy of the current database object, such as a table or form, with a new name, but not a copy of the entire database.

5. **Navigate to the drive and folder where you store your Data Files if necessary, type OF A-Budget for Corporate Meeting in the File name text box, as shown in Figure A-11, then click Save**

   A copy of the existing workbook is created with the new name. The original file, Office A-1.xlsx, closes automatically.

6. **Click cell A19, type your name, then press [Enter], as shown in Figure A-12**

   In Excel, you enter data in cells, which are formed by the intersection of a row and a column. Cell A19 is at the intersection of column A and row 19. When you press [Enter], the cell pointer moves to cell A20.

7. **Click the Save button on the Quick Access toolbar**

   Your name appears in the workbook, and your changes to the file are saved.

Working in Compatibility Mode

Not everyone upgrades to the newest version of Office. As a general rule, new software versions are **backward compatible**, meaning that documents saved by an older version can be read by newer software. To open documents created in older Office versions, Office 2010 includes a feature called Compatibility Mode. When you use Office 2010 to open a file created in an earlier version of Office, "Compatibility Mode" appears in the title bar, letting you know the file was created in an earlier but usable version of the program. If you are working with someone who may not be using the newest version of the software, you can avoid possible incompatibility problems by saving your file in another, earlier format. To do this in an Office program, click the File tab, click Save As on the navigation bar, click the Save as type list arrow in the Save As dialog box, then click an option on the list. For example, if you're working in Excel, click Excel 97-2003 Workbook format in the Save as type list to save an Excel file so that it can be opened in Excel 97 or Excel 2003.

FIGURE A-10: **Open dialog box**

Available files
in this folder

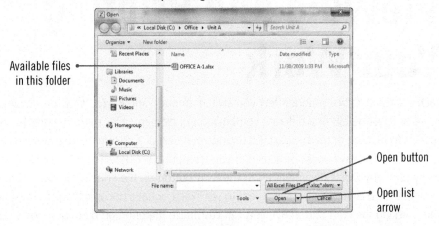

Open button

Open list
arrow

FIGURE A-11: **Save As dialog box**

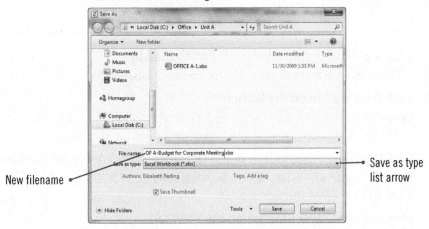

Save as type
list arrow

New filename

FIGURE A-12: **Your name added to the workbook**

Address for cell A19
formed by column A
and row 19

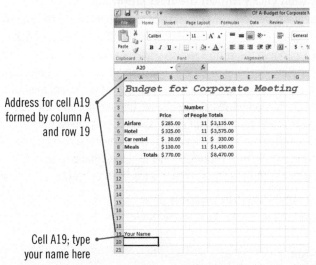

Cell A19; type
your name here

Exploring File Open options

You might have noticed that the Open button on the Open dialog box includes an arrow. In a dialog box, if a button includes an arrow you can click the button to invoke the command, or you can click the arrow to choose from a list of related commands. The Open list arrow includes several related commands, including Open Read-Only and Open as Copy. Clicking Open Read-Only opens a file that you can only save with a new name; you cannot save changes to the original file. Clicking Open as Copy creates a copy of the file already saved and named with the word "Copy" in the title. Like the Save As command, these commands provide additional ways to use copies of existing files while ensuring that original files do not get changed by mistake.

Viewing and Printing Your Work

Each Microsoft Office program lets you switch among various **views** of the document window to show more or fewer details or a different combination of elements that make it easier to complete certain tasks, such as formatting or reading text. Changing your view of a document does not affect the file in any way, it affects only the way it looks on screen. If your computer is connected to a printer or a print server, you can easily print any Office document using the Print button on the Print tab in Backstage view. Printing can be as simple as **previewing** the document to see exactly what a document will look like when it is printed and then clicking the Print button. Or, you can customize the print job by printing only selected pages or making other choices. Experiment with changing your view of a Word document, and then preview and print your work.

1. **Click the** Word program button W **on the taskbar**
   Word becomes the active program, and the document fills the screen.

2. **Click the** View tab **on the Ribbon**
   In most Office programs, the View tab on the Ribbon includes groups and commands for changing your view of the current document. You can also change views using the View buttons on the status bar.

3. **Click the** Web Layout button **in the Document Views group on the View tab**
   The view changes to Web Layout view, as shown in Figure A-13. This view shows how the document will look if you save it as a Web page.

4. **Click the** Print Layout button **on the View tab**
   You return to Print Layout view, the default view in Word.

5. **Click the** File tab, **then click** Print **on the navigation bar**
   The Print tab opens in Backstage view. The preview pane on the right side of the window automatically displays a preview of how your document will look when printed, showing the entire page on screen at once. Compare your screen to Figure A-14. Options in the Settings section enable you to change settings such as margins, orientation, and paper size before printing. To change a setting, click it, and then click the new setting you want. For instance, to change from Letter paper size to Legal, click Letter in the Settings section, then click Legal on the menu that opens. The document preview is updated as you change the settings. You also can use the Settings section to change which pages to print and even the number of pages you print on each sheet of printed paper. If you have multiple printers from which to choose, you can change from one installed printer to another by clicking the current printer in the Printer section, then clicking the name of the installed printer you want to use. The Print section contains the Print button and also enables you to select the number of copies of the document to print.

6. **Click the** Print button **in the Print section**
   A copy of the document prints, and Backstage view closes.

QUICK TIP
You can add the Quick Print button 🖨 to the Quick Access toolbar by clicking the Customize Quick Access Toolbar button, then clicking Quick Print. The Quick Print button prints one copy of your document using the default settings.

Customizing the Quick Access toolbar

You can customize the Quick Access toolbar to display your favorite commands. To do so, click the Customize Quick Access Toolbar button ▾ in the title bar, then click the command you want to add. If you don't see the command in the list, click More Commands to open the Quick Access Toolbar tab of the current program's Options dialog box. In the Options dialog box, use the Choose commands from list to choose a category, click the desired command in the list on the left, click Add to add it to the Quick Access toolbar, then click OK. To remove a button from the toolbar, click the name in the list on the right in the Options dialog box, then click Remove. To add a command to the Quick Access toolbar on the fly, simply right-click the button on the Ribbon, then click Add to Quick Access Toolbar on the shortcut menu. To move the Quick Access toolbar below the Ribbon, click the Customize Quick Access Toolbar button, and then click Show Below the Ribbon.

FIGURE A-13: **Web Layout view**

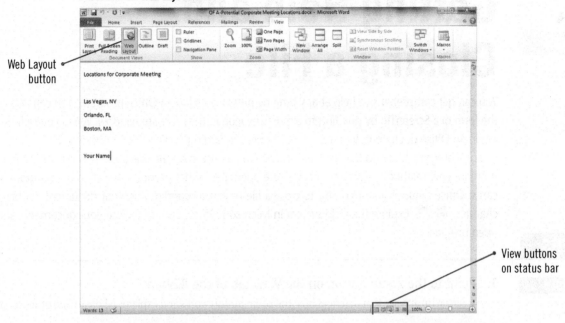

Web Layout button

View buttons on status bar

FIGURE A-14: **Print tab in Backstage view**

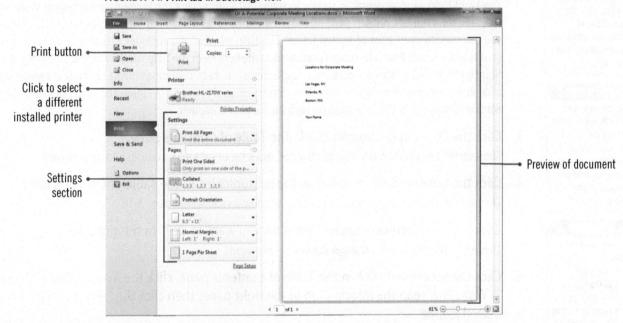

Print button

Click to select a different installed printer

Settings section

Preview of document

Creating a screen capture

A **screen capture** is a digital image of your screen, as if you took a picture of it with a camera. For instance, you might want to take a screen capture if an error message occurs and you want Technical Support to see exactly what's on the screen. You can create a screen capture using features found in Windows 7 or Office 2010. Windows 7 comes with the Snipping Tool, a separate program designed to capture whole screens or portions of screens. To open the Snipping Tool, click it on the Start menu or click All Programs, click Accessories, then click Snipping Tool. After opening the Snipping Tool, drag the pointer on the screen to select the area of the screen you want to capture. When you release the mouse button, the screen capture opens in the Snipping Tool window, and

you can save, copy, or send it in an e-mail. In Word, Excel, and PowerPoint 2010, you can capture screens or portions of screens and insert them in the current document using the Screenshot button on the Insert tab. And finally, you can create a screen capture by pressing [PrtScn]. (Keyboards differ, but you may find the [PrtScn] button in or near your keyboard's function keys.) Pressing this key places a digital image of your screen in the Windows temporary storage area known as the **Clipboard**. Open the document where you want the screen capture to appear, click the Home tab on the Ribbon (if necessary), then click the Paste button on the Home tab. The screen capture is pasted into the document.

Getting Help and Closing a File

You can get comprehensive help at any time by pressing [F1] in an Office program. You can also get help in the form of a ScreenTip by pointing to almost any icon in the program window. When you're finished working in an Office document, you have a few choices regarding ending your work session. You can close a file or exit a program by using the File tab or by clicking a button on the title bar. Closing a file leaves a program running, while exiting a program closes all the open files in that program as well as the program itself. In all cases, Office reminds you if you try to close a file or exit a program and your document contains unsaved changes. ▓▓▓▓▓ Explore the Help system in Microsoft Office, and then close your documents and exit any open programs.

STEPS

TROUBLE

If the Table of Contents pane doesn't appear on the left in the Help window, click the Show Table of Contents button 🌣 on the Help toolbar to show it.

1. **Point to the Zoom button on the View tab of the Ribbon**
   A ScreenTip appears that describes how the Zoom button works and explains where to find other zoom controls.

2. **Press [F1]**
   The Word Help window opens, as shown in Figure A-15, displaying the home page for help in Word on the right and the Table of Contents pane on the left. In both panes of the Help window, each entry is a hyperlink you can click to open a list of related topics. The Help window also includes a toolbar of useful Help commands and a Search field. The connection status at the bottom of the Help window indicates that the connection to Office.com is active. Office.com supplements the help content available on your computer with a wide variety of up-to-date topics, templates, and training. If you are not connected to the Internet, the Help window displays only the help content available on your computer.

QUICK TIP

You can also open the Help window by clicking the Microsoft Office Word Help button ❓ to the right of the tabs on the Ribbon.

3. **Click the Creating documents link in the Table of Contents pane**
   The icon next to Creating documents changes, and a list of subtopics expands beneath the topic.

4. **Click the Create a document link in the subtopics list in the Table of Contents pane**
   The topic opens in the right pane of the Help window, as shown in Figure A-16.

QUICK TIP

You can print the entire current topic by clicking the Print button 🖶 on the Help toolbar, then clicking Print in the Print dialog box.

5. **Click Delete a document under "What do you want to do?" in the right pane**
   The link leads to information about deleting a document.

6. **Click the Accessibility link in the Table of Contents pane, click the Accessibility features in Word link, read the information in the right pane, then click the Help window Close button ▬X▬**

7. **Click the File tab, then click Close on the navigation bar; if a dialog box opens asking whether you want to save your changes, click Save**
   The Potential Corporate Meeting Locations document closes, leaving the Word program open.

8. **Click the File tab, then click Exit on the navigation bar**
   Word closes, and the Excel program window is active.

9. **Click the File tab, click Exit on the navigation bar to exit Excel, click the PowerPoint program button 🅿 on the taskbar if necessary, click the File tab, then click Exit on the navigation bar to exit PowerPoint**
   Excel and PowerPoint both close.

FIGURE A-15: Word Help window

Help toolbar

Search field

The colors of your links may differ if the links have been visited previously

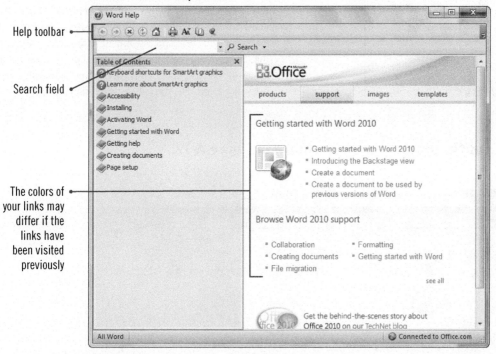

FIGURE A-16: Create a document Help topic

Print button

Icon indicates expanded topic

Create a document link

Create a document topic

Click to read how to perform the action described

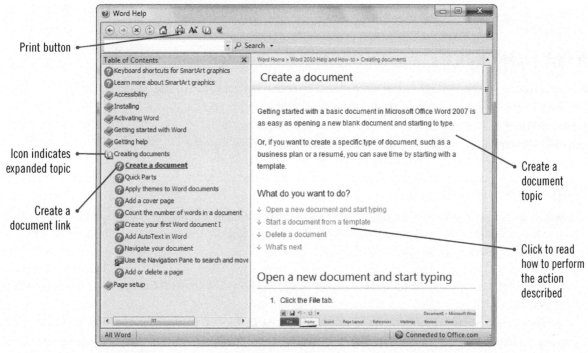

Recovering a document

Each Office program has a built-in recovery feature that allows you to open and save files that were open at the time of an interruption such as a power failure. When you restart the program(s) after an interruption, the Document Recovery task pane opens on the left side of your screen displaying both original and recovered versions of the files that were open. If you're not sure which file to open (original or recovered), it's usually better to open the recovered file because it will contain the latest information. You can, however, open and review all versions of the file that were recovered and save the best one. Each file listed in the Document Recovery task pane displays a list arrow with options that allow you to open the file, save it as is, delete it, or show repairs made to it during recovery.

Practice

For current SAM information, including versions and content details, visit SAM Central (http://www.cengage.com/samcentral). If you have a SAM user profile, you may have access to hands-on instruction, practice, and assessment of the skills covered in this unit. Since various versions of SAM are supported throughout the life of this text, check with your instructor for the correct instructions and URL/Web site for accessing assignments.

Concepts Review

Label the elements of the program window shown in Figure A-17.

FIGURE A-17

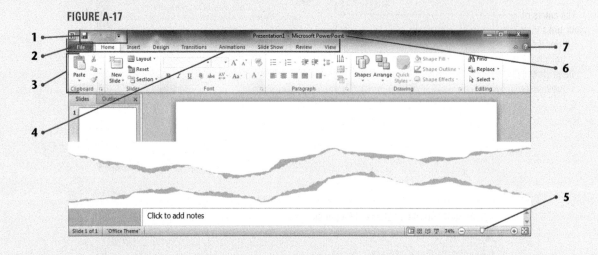

Match each project with the program for which it is best suited.

8. **Microsoft Access**
9. **Microsoft Excel**
10. **Microsoft Word**
11. **Microsoft PowerPoint**

a. Corporate convention budget with expense projections
b. Business cover letter for a job application
c. Department store inventory
d. Presentation for city council meeting

Independent Challenge 1

You just accepted an administrative position with a local independently owned produce vendor that has recently invested in computers and is now considering purchasing Microsoft Office for the company. You are asked to propose ways Office might help the business. You produce your document in Word.

a. Start Word, then save the document as **OF A-Microsoft Office Document** in the drive and folder where you store your Data Files.
b. Type **Microsoft Word**, press [Enter] twice, type **Microsoft Excel**, press [Enter] twice, type **Microsoft PowerPoint**, press [Enter] twice, type **Microsoft Access**, press [Enter] twice, then type your name.
c. Click the line beneath each program name, type at least two tasks suited to that program (each separated by a comma), then press [Enter].

Advanced Challenge Exercise

■ Press the [PrtScn] button to create a screen capture.
■ Click after your name, press [Enter] to move to a blank line below your name, then click the Paste button in the Clipboard group on the Home tab.

d. Save the document, then submit your work to your instructor as directed.
e. Exit Word.

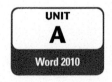

UNIT A Word 2010

Creating Documents with Word 2010

Files You Will Need:

WMP A-1.docx

Microsoft Word 2010 is a word processing program that makes it easy to create a variety of professional-looking documents, from simple letters and memos to newsletters, research papers, blog posts, business cards, résumés, financial reports, and other documents that include multiple pages of text and sophisticated formatting. In this unit, you will explore the editing and formatting features available in Word and create two documents.  You have been hired to work at the Riverwalk Medical Clinic, a large outpatient medical facility staffed by family physicians, specialists, nurses, and other allied health professionals. Shortly after reporting to your new position, the office manager, Tony Sanchez, R.N., asks you to use Word to create a memo to the clinic staff and a fax to the director of the clinic.

OBJECTIVES

Understand word processing software

Explore the Word program window

Start a document

Save a document

Select text

Format text using the Mini toolbar

Create a document using a template

View and navigate a document

Understanding Word Processing Software

A **word processing program** is a software program that includes tools for entering, editing, and formatting text and graphics. Microsoft Word is a powerful word processing program that allows you to create and enhance a wide range of documents quickly and easily. Figure A-1 shows the first page of a report created using Word and illustrates some of the Word features you can use to enhance your documents. The electronic files you create using Word are called **documents**. One of the benefits of using Word is that document files can be stored on a hard disk, CD, flash drive, or other storage device, making them easy to transport, exchange, and revise.  Before beginning your memo to the clinic staff, you explore the editing and formatting features available in Word.

You can use Word to accomplish the following tasks:

- **Type and edit text**

  The Word editing tools make it simple to insert and delete text in a document. You can add text to the middle of an existing paragraph, replace text with other text, undo an editing change, and correct typing, spelling, and grammatical errors with ease.

- **Copy and move text from one location to another**

  Using the more advanced editing features of Word, you can copy or move text from one location and insert it in a different location in a document. You can also copy and move text between documents. This means you don't have to retype text that is already entered in a document.

- **Format text and paragraphs with fonts, colors, and other elements**

  The sophisticated formatting tools in Word allow you to make the text in your documents come alive. You can change the size, style, and color of text, add lines and shading to paragraphs, and enhance lists with bullets and numbers. Creatively formatting text helps to highlight important ideas in your documents.

- **Format and design pages**

  The page-formatting features in Word give you power to design attractive newsletters, create powerful résumés, and produce documents such as research papers, business cards, CD labels, and books. You can change the paper size and orientation of your documents, organize text in columns, and control the layout of text and graphics on each page of a document. For quick results, Word includes preformatted cover pages, pull quotes, and headers and footers, as well as galleries of coordinated text, table, and graphic styles that you can rely on to give documents a polished look. If you are writing a research paper, Word makes it easy to manage reference sources and create footnotes, endnotes, and bibliographies.

- **Enhance documents with tables, charts, diagrams, and graphics**

  Using the powerful graphics tools in Word, you can spice up your documents with pictures, photographs, lines, shapes, and diagrams. You can also illustrate your documents with tables and charts to help convey your message in a visually interesting way.

- **Use Mail Merge to create form letters and mailing labels**

  The Word Mail Merge feature allows you to send personalized form letters to many different people. You can also use Mail Merge to create mailing labels, directories, e-mail messages, and other types of documents.

- **Share documents securely**

  The security features in Word make it quick and easy to remove comments, tracked changes, and unwanted personal information from your files before you share them with others. You can also add a password or a digital signature to a document and convert a file to a format suitable for publishing on the Web.

FIGURE A-1: A report created using Word

Add headers to every page

Insert graphics

Format the size and appearance of text

Create columns of text

Create tables

Add lines

Add bullets to lists

Create charts

Align text in paragraphs evenly

Add page numbers in footers

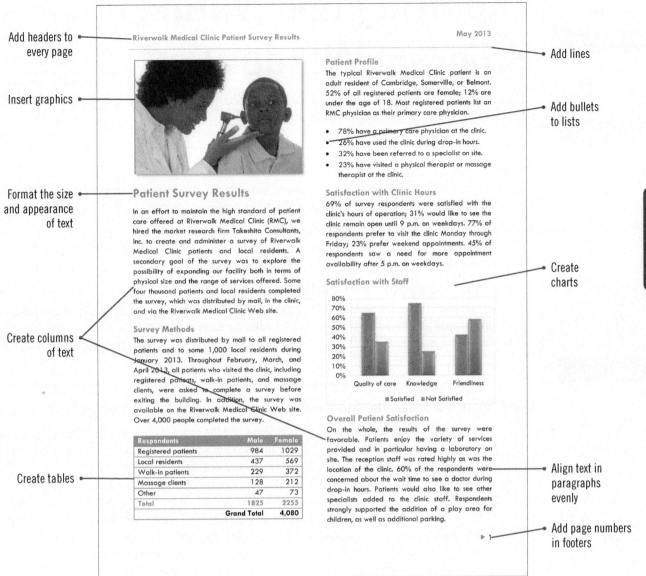

Planning a document

Before you create a new document, it's a good idea to spend time planning it. Identify the message you want to convey, the audience for your document, and the elements, such as tables or charts, you want to include. You should also think about the tone and look of your document—are you writing a business letter, which should be written in a pleasant, but serious tone and have a formal appearance, or are you creating a flyer that must be colorful, eye-catching, and fun to read? The purpose and audience for your document determine the appropriate design. Planning the layout and design of a document involves deciding how to organize the text, selecting the fonts to use, identifying the graphics to include, and selecting the formatting elements that will enhance the message and appeal of the document. For longer documents, such as newsletters, it can be useful to sketch the layout and design of each page before you begin.

Exploring the Word Program Window

When you start Word, a blank document appears in the document window in Print Layout view. ![icon] You examine the elements of the Word program window.

1. **Start** Word

    The **Word program window** opens, as shown in Figure A-2. The blinking vertical line in the document window is the **insertion point**. It indicates where text appears as you type.

2. **Move the mouse pointer around the Word program window**

    The mouse pointer changes shape depending on where it is in the Word program window. You use pointers to move the insertion point or to select text to edit. Table A-1 describes common pointers in Word.

3. **Place the mouse pointer over a button on the Ribbon**

    When you place the mouse pointer over a button or some other elements of the Word program window, a ScreenTip appears. A **ScreenTip** is a label that identifies the name of the button or feature, briefly describes its function, conveys any keyboard shortcut for the command, and includes a link to associated help topics, if any.

Using Figure A-2 as a guide, find the elements described below in your program window:

*   The **title bar** displays the name of the document and the name of the program. Until you give a new document a different name, its temporary name is Document1. The title bar also contains resizing buttons and the program Close button. These buttons are common to all Windows programs.

*   The **Quick Access toolbar** contains buttons for saving a document and for undoing, redoing, and repeating a change. You can modify the Quick Access toolbar to include the commands you use frequently.

*   The **File tab** provides access to **Backstage view**, where you manage files and the information about them. Backstage view includes commands related to working with documents, such as opening, printing, and saving a document. The File tab also provides access to resources for help using Word and to the Word Options dialog box, which is used to customize the way you use Word.

*   The **Ribbon** contains the Word tabs. Each **tab** on the Ribbon includes buttons for commands related to editing and formatting documents. The commands are organized in **groups**. For example, the Home tab includes the Clipboard, Font, Paragraph, Styles, and Editing groups. The Ribbon also includes the **Microsoft Word Help button**, which you use to access the Word Help system.

*   The **document window** displays the current document. You enter text and format your document in the document window.

*   The rulers appear in the document window in Print Layout view. The **horizontal ruler** displays left and right document margins as well as the tab settings and paragraph indents, if any, for the paragraph in which the insertion point is located. The **vertical ruler** displays the top and bottom document margins.

*   The **vertical scroll bar** and the **horizontal scroll bar** are used to display different parts of the document in the document window. The scroll bars include **scroll boxes** and **scroll arrows**, which you can use to scroll through a document.

*   The **status bar** displays the page number of the current page, the total number of pages and words in the document, and the status of spelling and grammar checking. It also includes the view buttons, the Zoom level button, and the Zoom slider. You can customize the status bar to display other information.

*   The **view buttons** on the status bar allow you to display the document in Print Layout, Full Screen Reading, Web Layout, Outline, or Draft view.

*   The **Zoom level** button and the **Zoom slider** provide quick ways to enlarge and decrease the size of the document in the document window, making it easy to zoom in on a detail of a document or to view the layout of the document as a whole.

Creating Documents with Word 2010

FIGURE A-2: Elements of the Word program window

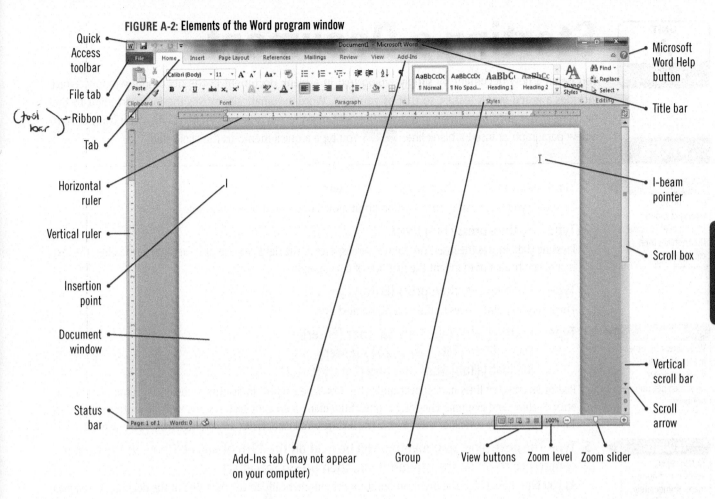

name	pointer	use to
I-beam pointer	I	Move the insertion point in a document or to select text
Click and Type pointers, including left-align and center-align	I≡ or I̲≡	Move the insertion point to a blank area of a document in Print Layout or Web Layout view; double-clicking with a Click and Type pointer automatically applies the paragraph formatting (alignment and indentation) required to position text or a graphic at that location in the document
Selection pointer	↖	Click a button or other element of the Word program window; appears when you point to elements of the Word program window
Right-pointing arrow pointer	↗	Select a line or lines of text; appears when you point to the left edge of a line of text in the document window
Hand pointer	🖑	Open a hyperlink; appears when you point to a hyperlink in a task pane or when you press [Ctrl] and point to a hyperlink in a document
Hide white space pointer	⊣⊢	Hide the white space in the top and bottom margins of a document in Print Layout view
Show white space pointer	⊢⊣	Show the white space in the top and bottom margins of a document in Print Layout view

TABLE A-1: Common mouse pointers in Word

Starting a Document

You begin a new document by simply typing text in a blank document in the document window. Word includes a **word-wrap** feature so that as you type, Word automatically moves the insertion point to the next line of the document when you reach the right margin. You only press [Enter] when you want to start a new paragraph or insert a blank line. You type a quick memo to the clinic staff.

TROUBLE

If you press the wrong key, press [Backspace] to erase the mistake, then try again.

1. **Type** Memorandum, **then press** [Enter] **twice**

   Each time you press [Enter] the insertion point moves to the start of the next line.

2. **Type** TO:, **then press** [Tab] **twice**

   Pressing [Tab] moves the insertion point several spaces to the right. You can use the [Tab] key to align the text in a memo header or to indent the first line of a paragraph.

3. **Type** All Employees, **then press** [Enter]

   The insertion point moves to the start of the next line.

QUICK TIP

Wavy lines and other automatic feature markers appear on screen but do not print.

4. **Type:** FROM: [Tab] [Tab] Tony Sanchez [Enter]
            DATE: [Tab] [Tab] July 7, 2013 [Enter]
            RE: [Tab] [Tab] Staff Meeting [Enter] [Enter]

   Red or green wavy lines may appear under the words you typed, indicating a possible spelling or grammar error. Spelling and grammar checking is one of the many automatic features you will encounter as you type. Table A-2 describes several of these automatic features. You can correct any typing errors you make later.

TROUBLE

To reverse an AutoCorrect adjustment, immediately click the Undo button on the Quick Access toolbar.

5. **Type** The next clinic staff meeting will be held on the 11th of July at 1 p.m. in the Kogan conference room on the ground floor., **then press** [Spacebar]

   As you type, notice that the insertion point moves automatically to the next line of the document. You also might notice that Word automatically changed "11th" to "11th" in the memo. This feature is called **AutoCorrect**. AutoCorrect automatically makes typographical adjustments and detects and adjusts typing errors, certain misspelled words (such as "taht" for "that"), and incorrect capitalization as you type.

6. **Type** Heading the agenda will be a discussion of our new community health fair, scheduled for September.

   When you type the first few characters of "September," the Word AutoComplete feature displays the complete word in a ScreenTip. **AutoComplete** suggests text to insert quickly into your documents. You can ignore AutoComplete for now. Your memo should resemble Figure A-3.

QUICK TIP

If you want uniform spacing between lines and paragraphs, apply the No Spacing style to the document by clicking the No Spacing button in the Styles group on the Home tab before you begin to type. Alternatively, select the text and then click the No Spacing button.

7. **Press** [Enter], **then type** The event will include free screenings and adult immunizations. A preliminary draft of the program for the health fair is attached. Bring your creative ideas for promoting and planning this exciting new event to the meeting.

   When you press [Enter] and type the new paragraph, notice that Word adds more space between the paragraphs than it does between the lines in each paragraph. This is part of the default style for paragraphs in Word, called the **Normal style**.

8. **Position the** I **pointer after** new **(but before the space) in the last sentence of the first paragraph, then click**

   Clicking moves the insertion point after "new."

9. **Press** [Backspace] **three times, then type** upcoming

   Pressing [Backspace] removes the character before the insertion point.

10. **Move the insertion point before** clinic **in the first sentence, then press** [Delete] **seven times to remove the word "clinic" and the space after it**

    Pressing [Delete] removes the character after the insertion point. Figure A-4 shows the revised memo.

Creating Documents with Word 2010

FIGURE A-3: Memo text in the document window

Memo title

Blank lines between paragraphs

Memo header

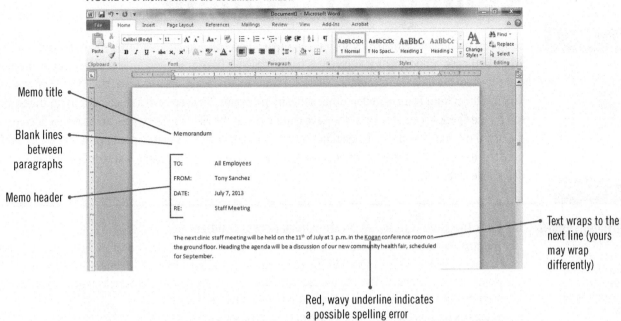

Text wraps to the next line (yours may wrap differently)

Red, wavy underline indicates a possible spelling error

FIGURE A-4: Edited memo text

Text inserted in the memo

No Spacing style

Normal style leaves more space between paragraphs than between lines

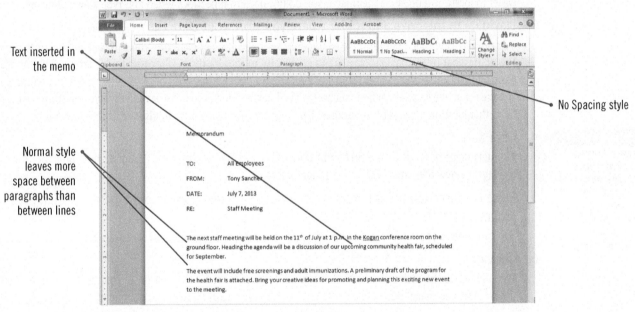

TABLE A-2: Automatic features that appear as you type in Word

feature	what appears	to use
AutoComplete	A ScreenTip suggesting text to insert appears as you type	Press [Enter] to insert the text suggested by the ScreenTip; continue typing to reject the suggestion
AutoCorrect	A small blue box appears when you place the pointer over text corrected by AutoCorrect; an AutoCorrect Options button 🗗 ▾ appears when you point to the blue box	Word automatically corrects typos, minor spelling errors, and capitalization, and adds typographical symbols (such as © and ™) as you type; to reverse an AutoCorrect adjustment, click the AutoCorrect Options list arrow, then click the option that will undo the action
Spelling and Grammar	A red wavy line under a word indicates a possible misspelling; a green wavy line under text indicates a possible grammar error	Right-click red- or green-underlined text to display a shortcut menu of correction options; click a correction option to accept it and remove the wavy underline

Saving a Document

To store a document permanently so you can open it and edit it at another time, you must save it as a **file**. When you **save** a document you give it a name, called a **filename**, and indicate the location where you want to store the file. Files created in Word 2010 are automatically assigned the .docx file extension to distinguish them from files created in other software programs. You can save a document using the Save button on the Quick Access toolbar or the Save command on the File tab. Once you have saved a document for the first time, you should save it again every few minutes and always before printing so that the saved file is updated to reflect your latest changes. ░░░░░ You save your memo using a descriptive filename and the default file extension.

STEPS

1. **Click the** Save button 🖫 **on the Quick Access toolbar**

   The first time you save a document, the Save As dialog box opens, as shown in Figure A-5. The default filename, Memorandum, appears in the File name text box. The default filename is based on the first few words of the document. The default file extension, .docx, appears in the Save as type list box. Table A-3 describes the functions of some of the buttons in the Save As dialog box.

2. **Type** WMP A-Staff Memo **in the File name text box**

   The new filename replaces the default filename. Giving your documents brief descriptive filenames makes it easier to locate and organize them later. You do not need to type .docx when you type a new filename.

3. **Navigate to the drive and folder where you store your Data Files**

   You can navigate to a different drive or folder in several ways. For example, you can click a drive or folder in the Address bar or the navigation pane to go directly to that location. Click the double arrow in the Address bar to display a list of drives and folders. You can also double-click a drive or folder in the folder window to change the active location. When you are finished navigating to the drive or folder where you store your Data Files, that location appears in the Address bar. Your Save As dialog box should resemble Figure A-6.

4. **Click** Save

   The document is saved to the drive and folder you specified in the Save As dialog box, and the title bar displays the new filename, WMP A-Staff Memo.docx.

5. **Place the insertion point before** September **in the first paragraph, type** early, **then press [Spacebar]**

   You can continue to work on a document after you have saved it with a new filename.

6. **Click** 🖫

   Your change to the memo is saved. After you save a document for the first time, you must continue to save the changes you make to the document. You can also press [Ctrl][S] to save a document.

Windows Live and Microsoft Office Web Apps

All Office programs include the capability to incorporate feedback—called online collaboration—across the Internet or a company network. Using **cloud computing** (work done in a virtual environment), you can take advantage of Web programs called Microsoft Office Web Apps, which are simplified versions of the programs found in the Microsoft Office 2010 suite. Because these programs are online, they take up no computer disk space and are accessed using Windows Live SkyDrive, a free service from Microsoft. Using Windows Live SkyDrive, you and your colleagues can create and store documents in a "cloud" and make the documents available to whomever you grant access. To use Windows Live SkyDrive, you need a free Windows Live ID, which you obtain at the Windows Live Web site. You can find more information in the "Working with Windows Live and Office Web Apps" appendix.

FIGURE A-5: Save As dialog box

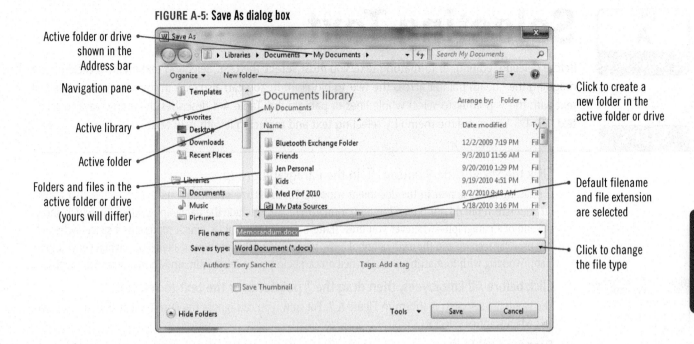

Active folder or drive shown in the Address bar

Navigation pane

Active library

Active folder

Folders and files in the active folder or drive (yours will differ)

Click to create a new folder in the active folder or drive

Default filename and file extension are selected

Click to change the file type

FIGURE A-6: File to be saved to the Unit A folder

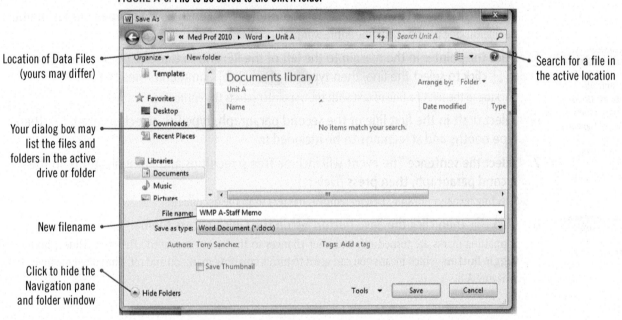

Location of Data Files (yours may differ)

Your dialog box may list the files and folders in the active drive or folder

New filename

Click to hide the Navigation pane and folder window

Search for a file in the active location

TABLE A-3: Save As dialog box buttons

button	use to
🔙 Back	Navigate back to the last location shown in the Address bar
🔜 Forward	Navigate to the location that was previously shown in the Address bar
Organize ▼	Open a menu of commands related to organizing the selected file or folder, including Cut, Copy, Delete, Rename, and Properties
New folder	Create a new folder in the current folder or drive
▤ ▼ Change your view	Change the way folder and file information is shown in the folder window in the Save As dialog box; click the Change your view button to toggle between views, or click the list arrow to open a menu of view options

Selecting Text

Before deleting, editing, or formatting text, you must **select** the text. Selecting text involves clicking and dragging the I-beam pointer across the text to highlight it. You can also click in the margin to the left of text with the 𝒜 pointer to select whole lines or paragraphs. Table A-4 describes the many ways to select text. ⬛⬛⬛ You revise the memo by selecting text and replacing it with new text.

1. **Click the** Show/Hide ¶ **button** ¶ **in the Paragraph group**

   Formatting marks appear in the document window. **Formatting marks** are special characters that appear on your screen but do not print. Common formatting marks include the paragraph symbol (¶), which shows the end of a paragraph—wherever you press [Enter]; the dot symbol (·), which represents a space—wherever you press [Spacebar]; and the arrow symbol (→), which shows the location of a tab stop—wherever you press [Tab]. Working with formatting marks turned on can help you to select, edit, and format text with precision.

   > **QUICK TIP**
   > You deselect text by clicking anywhere in the document window.

2. **Click before** All Employees, **then drag the** I **pointer over the text to select it**

   The words are selected, as shown in Figure A-7. For now, you can ignore the faint toolbar that appears over text when you first select it.

3. **Type** Medical Staff

   The text you type replaces the selected text.

4. **Double-click** Tony, **type your first name, double-click** Sanchez, **then type your last name**

   Double-clicking a word selects the entire word.

   > **TROUBLE**
   > If you delete text by mistake, immediately click the Undo button ↺ on the Quick Access toolbar to restore the deleted text to the document.

5. **Place the pointer in the margin to the left of the** RE: **line so that the pointer changes to** 𝒜, **click to select the line, then type** RE: [Tab] [Tab] Community Health Fair

   Clicking to the left of a line of text with the 𝒜 pointer selects the entire line.

6. **Select** draft **in the first line of the second paragraph, type** list, **select** program for, **then type** booths and screenings to be included in

7. **Select the sentence** The event will include free screenings and immunizations. **in the second paragraph, then press** [Delete]

   Selecting text and pressing [Delete] removes the text from the document.

   > **QUICK TIP**
   > Always save before and after editing text.

8. **Click** ¶, **then click the** Save button 🖫 **on the Quick Access toolbar**

   Formatting marks are turned off, and your changes to the memo are saved. The Show/Hide ¶ button is a **toggle button**, which means you can use it to turn formatting marks on and off. The edited memo is shown in Figure A-8.

FIGURE A-7: Text selected in the memo

Selected text

Left document margin

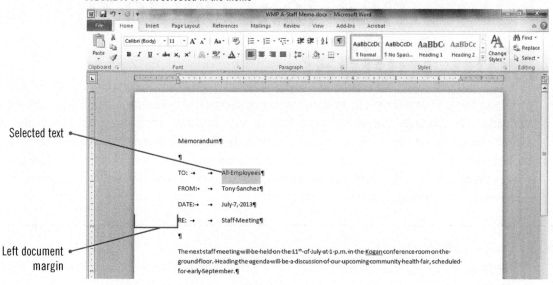

FIGURE A-8: Edited memo with replacement text

Replacement text

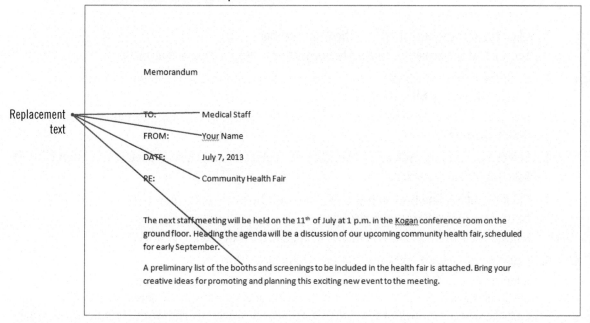

TABLE A-4: Methods for selecting text

to select	use the pointer to
Any amount of text	Drag over the text
A word	Double-click the word
A line of text	Click with the ⇗ pointer to the left of the line
A sentence	Press and hold [Ctrl], then click the sentence
A paragraph	Triple-click the paragraph or double-click with the ⇗ pointer to the left of the paragraph
A large block of text	Click at the beginning of the selection, press and hold [Shift], then click at the end of the selection
Multiple nonconsecutive selections	Select the first selection, then press and hold [Ctrl] as you select each additional selection
An entire document	Triple-click with the ⇗ pointer to the left of any text; press [Ctrl][A]; or click the Select button in the Editing group on the Home tab, and then click Select All

Formatting Text Using the Mini Toolbar

Formatting text is a fast and fun way to spruce up the appearance of a document and highlight important information. You can easily change the font, color, size, style, and other attributes of text by selecting the text and clicking a command on the Home tab. The **Mini toolbar**, which appears faintly above text when you first select it, also includes commonly used text and paragraph formatting commands. You enhance the appearance of the memo by formatting the text using the Mini toolbar. When you are finished, you preview the memo for errors and then print it.

STEPS

1. **Double-click Memorandum**

   The Mini toolbar appears in ghosted fashion over the selected text. When you point to the Mini toolbar, it becomes solid, as shown in Figure A-9. You click a formatting option on the Mini toolbar to apply it to the selected text. Table A-5 describes the function of the buttons on the Mini toolbar. The buttons on the Mini toolbar are also available on the Ribbon.

2. **Click the Center button ≣ on the Mini toolbar**

   The word "Memorandum" is centered between the left and right document margins.

3. **Click the Grow Font button A˄ on the Mini toolbar eight times, then click the Bold button B on the Mini toolbar**

   Each time you click the Grow Font button the selected text is enlarged. Applying **bold** to the text makes it thicker and darker.

4. **Select TO:, click B, select FROM:, click B, select DATE:, click B, select RE:, then click B**

   Bold is applied to the heading text.

5. **Click the blank line between the RE: line and the body text, then click the Bottom Border button ⊞ in the Paragraph group**

   A single-line border is added between the heading and the body text in the memo.

6. **Save the document, click the File tab, then click Print**

   Information related to printing the document appears on the Print tab in Backstage view. Options for printing the document appear on the left side of the Print tab and a preview of the document as it will look when printed appears on the right side, as shown in Figure A-10. Before you print a document, it's a good habit to examine it closely so you can identify and correct any problems.

7. **Click the Zoom In button ⊕ five times, then proofread your document carefully for errors**

   The document is enlarged in print preview. If you notice errors in your document, you need to correct them before you print. To do this, press [Esc] or click the Home tab to close Backstage view, correct any mistakes, save your changes, click the File tab, and then click the Print command again to be ready to print the document.

8. **Click the Print button on the Print tab**

   A copy of the memo prints using the default print settings. To change the current printer, change the number of copies to print, select what pages of a document to print, or modify another print setting, you simply change the appropriate setting on the Print tab before clicking the Print button.

9. **Click the File tab, then click Close**

   The document closes, but the Word program window remains open.

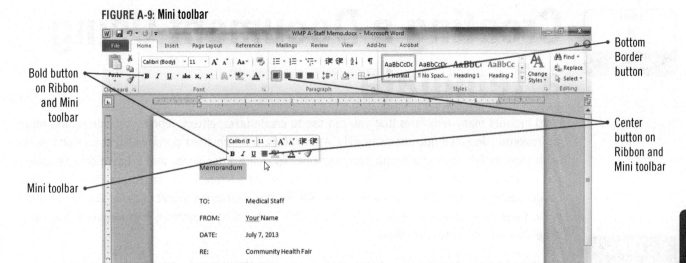

Bold button on Ribbon and Mini toolbar

Bottom Border button

Center button on Ribbon and Mini toolbar

Mini toolbar

Memorandum

TO: Medical Staff

FROM: Your Name

DATE: July 7, 2013

RE: Community Health Fair

FIGURE A-10: Preview of the completed memo

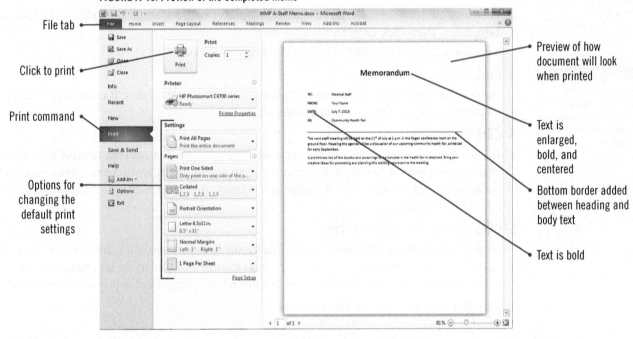

File tab

Click to print

Print command

Options for changing the default print settings

Preview of how document will look when printed

Text is enlarged, bold, and centered

Bottom border added between heading and body text

Text is bold

TABLE A-5: Buttons on the Mini toolbar

button	use to	button	use to
Calibri (E ▾	Change the font of text	I	Italicize text
11 ▾	Change the font size of text	U	Underline text
A˄	Make text larger	≡	Center text between the margins
A˅	Make text smaller	aby ▾	Apply colored highlighting to text
🔻	Decrease the indent level of a paragraph	A ▾	Change the color of text
🔺	Increase the indent level of a paragraph	🖌	Copy the formats applied to text to other text
B	Apply bold to text		

Word 2010

Creating a Document Using a Template

Word includes many templates that you can use to create faxes, letters, reports, brochures, and other professionally designed documents quickly. A **template** is a formatted document that contains place-holder text, which you replace with your own text. To create a document that is based on a template, you use the New command on the File tab, and then select a template to use. You can then customize the document and save it with a new filename. 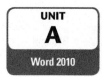 You want to fax a draft of the health fair program to Dr. Carla Zimmerman, director of the clinic, who is attending a conference in Morocco. You use a template to create a fax cover sheet.

STEPS

QUICK TIP
To create a new blank document, click Create.

1. **Click the File tab, then click New**

   The New tab opens in Backstage view, as shown in Figure A-11.

2. **Click Sample templates in the Available Templates section, scroll down the list of Available Templates, then click Oriel Fax**

   A preview of the Oriel Fax template appears in the preview section.

QUICK TIP
Double-clicking a template icon also opens a new document based on the template.

3. **Click Create**

   The Oriel Fax template opens as a new document in the document window. It contains placeholder text, which you can replace with your own information.

4. **Click [Pick the date]**

   The placeholder text is selected and appears inside a content control. A **content control** is an interactive object that you use to customize a document with your own information. A content control might include placeholder text, a drop-down list of choices, or a calendar. To deselect a content control, you click a blank area of the document.

5. **Click the Pick the date list arrow**

   A calendar opens below the content control. You use the calendar to select the date you want to appear on your document—simply click a date on the calendar to enter that date in the document. You can use the arrows to the left and right of the month and year to scroll the calendar and display a different month.

6. **Click the Today button on the calendar**

   The current date replaces the placeholder text.

7. **Click [TYPE THE RECIPIENT NAME], type Dr. Carla Zimmerman, Guest, click [Type the recipient fax number], then type 1-212-44-555-1510**

   You do not need to drag to select the placeholder text in a content control, you can simply click it. The text you type replaces the placeholder text.

QUICK TIP
You can delete a content control by right-clicking it, and then clicking Remove Content Control on the menu that opens.

8. **Click [Type the recipient phone number], press [Delete] twice, press [Backspace] seven times, then type HOTEL MARRAKECH, ROOM 1275**

   The recipient phone number content control is removed from the document.

9. **If the text in the From line is not your name, drag to select the text, then type your name**

   When the document is created, Word automatically enters the user name identified in the Word Options dialog box in the From line. This text is not placeholder text, so you have to drag to select it.

10. **Replace the remaining heading placeholder text with the text shown in Figure A-12, delete the CC: content control, click the File tab, click Save As, then save the document as WMP A-Zimmerman Fax to the drive and folder where you store your Data Files**

    The document is saved with the filename WMP A-Zimmerman Fax.

FIGURE A-11: New tab in Backstage view

Click to open an existing document

Types of templates available with an active Internet connection (yours may differ)

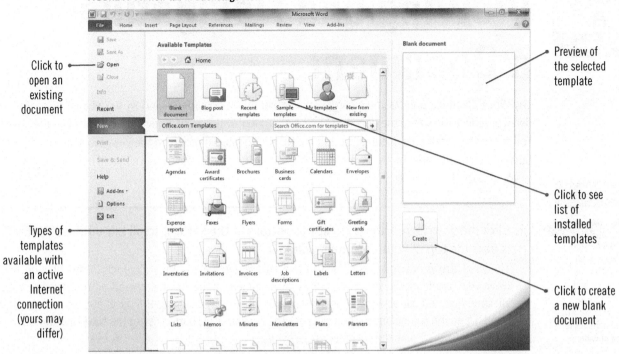

Preview of the selected template

Click to see list of installed templates

Click to create a new blank document

FIGURE A-12: Document created using the Oriel fax template

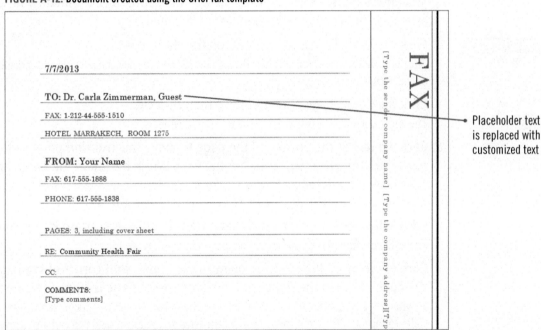

Placeholder text is replaced with customized text

Using the Undo, Redo, and Repeat commands

Word remembers the editing and formatting changes you make so that you can easily reverse or repeat them. You can reverse the last action you took by clicking the Undo button on the Quick Access toolbar, or you can undo a series of actions by clicking the Undo list arrow and selecting the action you want to reverse. When you undo an action using the Undo list arrow, you also undo all the actions above it in the list—that is, all actions that were performed after the action you selected. Similarly, you can keep the change you just reversed by using the Redo button

on the Quick Access toolbar. The Redo button appears only immediately after clicking the Undo button to undo a change.

If you want to repeat an action you just completed, you can use the Repeat button on the Quick Access toolbar. For example, if you just typed "thank you," clicking inserts "thank you" at the location of the insertion point. If you just applied bold, clicking applies bold to the currently selected text. You can also repeat the last action you took by pressing [F4].

Viewing and Navigating a Document

The Word Zoom feature lets you enlarge a document in the document window to get a close-up view of a detail or reduce the size of the document in the document window for an overview of the layout as a whole. You zoom in and out on a document using the tools in the Zoom group on the View tab and the Zoom level buttons and Zoom slider on the status bar. You find it is helpful to zoom in and out on the document as you finalize the fax cover sheet.

STEPS

QUICK TIP
When the horizontal scroll bar is available, you can use the scroll bar and the scroll box to move the document left and right in the document window.

1. **Click the** down scroll arrow ▼ **at the bottom of the vertical scroll bar until COMMENTS: is near the top of your document window**

   The scroll arrows or scroll bars allow you to **scroll** through a document. You scroll through a document when you want to display different parts of the document in the document window. You can also scroll by clicking the scroll bar above and below the scroll box, or by dragging the scroll box up or down in the scroll bar. In longer documents, you can click the Previous Page button ⬆ or the Next Page button ⬇ on the scroll bar to display the document page by page.

2. **Click** [Type comments], **then type** A draft list of the free screenings, adult immunizations, and information booths to be included in the September community health fair is attached. Please edit the list and return it to me.

QUICK TIP
You can also click the Zoom button in the Zoom group on the View tab to open the Zoom dialog box.

3. **Click the** Zoom level button 100% **on the status bar**

   The Zoom dialog box opens. You use the Zoom dialog box to select a zoom level for displaying the document in the document window.

4. **Click the** Whole page option button, **then click** OK

   The entire document is displayed in the document window.

5. **Click the text at the bottom of the page to move the insertion point to the bottom of the page, click the** View tab, **then click the** Page Width button **in the Zoom group**

   The document is enlarged to the width of the document window. When you enlarge a document, the area where the insertion point is located appears in the document window.

6. **Click in the** Urgent box, **type** x, **then click the** One Page button **in the Zoom group**

   The entire document is displayed in the document window.

7. **Click** Fax **to move the insertion point to the upper-right corner of the page, then move the** Zoom slider **to the right until the Zoom percentage is 100%, as shown in Figure A-13**

   Moving the Zoom slider to the right enlarges the document in the document window. Moving the zoom slider to the left allows you to see more of the page at a reduced size. You can also move the Zoom slider by clicking a point on the Zoom slide, or by clicking the Zoom Out and Zoom In buttons.

TROUBLE
Your company name content control might include the name of a company, such as Microsoft. Right-click it, click Remove Content Control, then select the text and press [Delete].

8. **Click the** Zoom In button ⊕ **three times, right-click the vertical placeholder** [Type the sender company name], **click** Remove Content Control, **right-click** [Type the company address], **click** Remove Content Control, **click** [Type the company phone number], **then type** Riverwalk Medical Clinic, Cambridge, MA

   The text you type replaces the vertical placeholder text. You do not always need to replace the placeholder text with the type of information suggested in the content control.

9. **Click** 130%, **click the** 100% option button, **click** OK, **then save the document**

   The completed fax cover sheet is shown in Figure A-14.

10. **Submit the document to your instructor, close the file, then exit Word**

Creating Documents with Word 2010

FIGURE A-13: Zoom slider

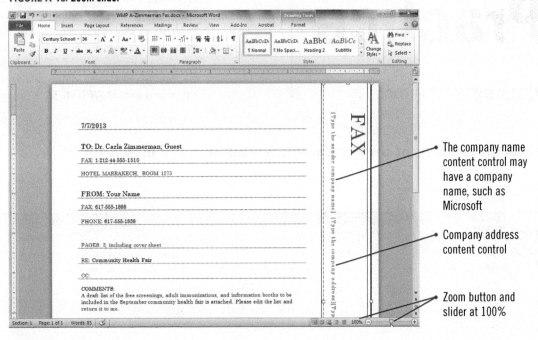

The company name content control may have a company name, such as Microsoft

Company address content control

Zoom button and slider at 100%

FIGURE A-14: Completed fax cover sheet

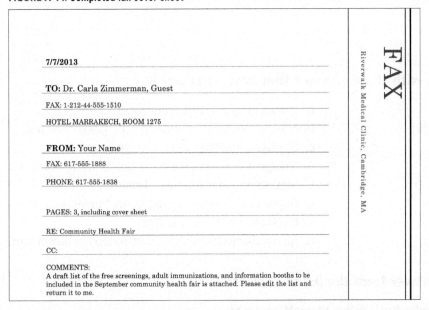

Using Word document views

Document **views** are different ways of displaying a document in the document window. Each Word view provides features that are useful for working on different types of documents. The default view, **Print Layout view**, displays a document as it will look on a printed page. Print Layout view is helpful for formatting text and pages, including adjusting document margins, creating columns of text, inserting graphics, and formatting headers and footers. Also useful is **Draft view**, which shows a simplified layout of a document, without margins, headers and footers, or graphics. When you want to quickly type, edit, and format text, it's often easiest to work in Draft view. Other Word views are helpful for performing specialized tasks. **Full Screen Reading view** displays document text so that it is easy to read and annotate. You can easily highlight content, add comments, and track and review changes in Full Screen Reading view. **Web Layout view** allows you to format Web pages or documents that will be viewed on a computer screen. In Web Layout view, a document appears just as it will when viewed with a Web browser. Finally, **Outline view** is useful for editing and formatting longer documents that include multiple headings. Outline view allows you to reorganize text by moving the headings. You switch between views by clicking the view buttons on the status bar or by using the commands on the View tab. Changing views does not affect how the printed document will appear. It simply changes the way you view the document in the document window.

Practice

For current SAM information, including versions and content details, visit SAM Central (http://www.cengage.com/samcentral). If you have a SAM user profile, you may have access to hands-on instruction, practice, and assessment of the skills covered in this unit. Since various versions of SAM are supported throughout the life of this text, check with your instructor for the correct instructions and URL/Web site for accessing assignments.

Concepts Review

Label the elements of the Word program window shown in Figure A-15.

FIGURE A-15

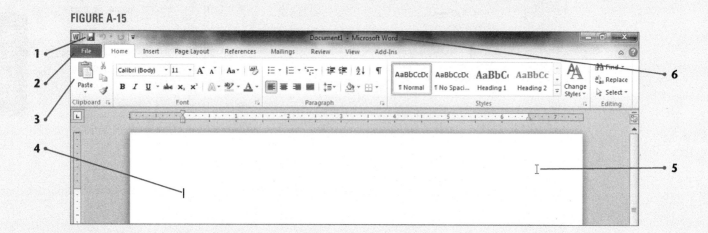

Match each term with the statement that best describes it.

7. **Template**
8. **Formatting marks**
9. **Status bar**
10. **Ribbon**
11. **AutoComplete**
12. **Horizontal ruler**
13. **AutoCorrect**
14. **Zoom slider**

a. Provides access to Word commands
b. A formatted document that contains placeholder text
c. Displays tab settings and paragraph indents
d. Enlarges and reduces the document in the document window
e. Suggests text to insert into a document
f. Displays the number of pages in the current document
g. Fixes certain errors as you type
h. Special characters that appear on screen but do not print

Select the best answer from the list of choices.

15. **Which tab includes buttons for formatting text?**
    a. View
    b. Page Layout
    c. Insert
    d. Home
16. **Which of the following shows the number of words in the document?**
    a. The status bar
    b. The Mini toolbar
    c. The title bar
    d. The Ribbon
17. **Which element of the Word program window shows the settings for the top and bottom document margins?**
    a. Vertical scroll bar
    b. View tab
    c. Vertical ruler
    d. Status bar
18. **Which of the following is not included in a ScreenTip for a command?**
    a. Description of the function of the command
    b. Link to a help topic on the command
    c. Keyboard shortcut for the command
    d. Alternative location of the command

Creating Documents with Word 2010

19. Which view is best for annotating text with comments and highlighting?

    a. Full Screen Reading view   **c.** Print Layout view

    b. Draft view   **d.** Outline view

20. What is the default file extension for a document created in Word 2010?

    a. .dot   **c.** .dotx

    b. .doc   **d.** .docx

Skills Review

1. Explore the Word program window.

    a. Start Word.

    b. Identify as many elements of the Word program window as you can without referring to the unit material.

    c. Click the File tab, then click the Info, Recent, New, Print, Save & Send, and Help commands.

    d. Click each tab on the Ribbon, review the groups and buttons on each tab, then return to the Home tab.

    e. Point to each button on the Home tab and read the ScreenTips.

    f. Click the view buttons to view the blank document in each view, then return to Print Layout view.

    g. Use the Zoom slider to zoom all the way in and all the way out on the document, then return to 100%.

2. Start a document.

    a. In a new blank document, type **FAX** at the top of the page, then press [Enter] two times.

    b. Type the following, pressing [Tab] as indicated and pressing [Enter] at the end of each line:

        To: [Tab] [Tab] **Valley OB/GYN**

        From: [Tab] [Tab] **Your Name**

        Date: [Tab] [Tab] **Today's date**

        Re: [Tab] [Tab] **Changes at PMC Labs**

        Pages: [Tab] [Tab] **2**

        Fax: [Tab] [Tab] **(802) 555-5478**

    c. Press [Enter] again, then type **Effective June 1st, PMC Labs will pick up laboratory specimens at 10:00 a.m. and 4:15 p.m. daily. We trust the addition of the afternoon pick up time will improve the efficiency of our service. All abnormal results will continue to be reported to your office by telephone.**

    d. Press [Enter], then type **As always, we welcome your comments and suggestions on how we can better serve you. Our clients are important to us.**

    e. Insert this sentence at the beginning of the second paragraph: **The lab will continue to be open until 7:00 p.m. for drop-in service.**

    f. Use the [Backspace] key to delete **2** in the Pages: line, then type **1**.

    g. Use the [Delete] key to delete **4:15** in the first paragraph, then type **3:30**.

3. Save a document.

    a. Click the Save button on the Quick Access toolbar.

    b. Save the document as **WMP A-Valley Fax** with the default file extension to the drive and folder where you store your Data Files.

    c. After your name, type a comma, press [Spacebar], then type **PMC Labs**.

    d. Save the document.

4. Select text.

    a. Turn on the display of formatting marks.

    b. Select the **Re:** line, then type **Re:** [Tab] [Tab] **New morning pick-up time**.

    c. Select **June 1st,** (including the comma) in the first sentence, then type **May 15th,** (including the comma).

    d. Select **afternoon** in the second sentence of the first paragraph, then type **morning**.

    e. Delete the sentence **Our clients are important to us.**

    f. Turn off the display of formatting marks, then save the document.

5. Format text using the Mini toolbar.

  a. Select FAX, then click the Grow Font button on the Mini toolbar 11 times.

  b. Apply bold to the word FAX, then center it on the page.

  c. Apply a bottom border under the word FAX.

  d. Apply bold to the following words in the fax heading: To:, From:, Date:, Re:, Pages:, and Fax:.

  e. Preview the document using the Print command.

  f. Zoom in on the document, then proofread the fax.

  g. Correct any typing errors in your document, then save the document. Compare your document to Figure A-16.

  h. Submit the fax to your instructor, then close the document.

6. Create a document using a template.

  a. Click the File tab, click New, then click Sample templates.

  b. Create a new document using the Origin Fax template.

  c. Insert today's date using the date content control.

  d. If your name is not on the From line, select the text in the From content control, then type your name.

  e. Click the "Type the sender phone number" placeholder text, press [Delete]; click the "Type the sender fax number" placeholder text, type 555-5748; click the "Type the sender company name" placeholder text, then type PMC Labs.

FIGURE A-16

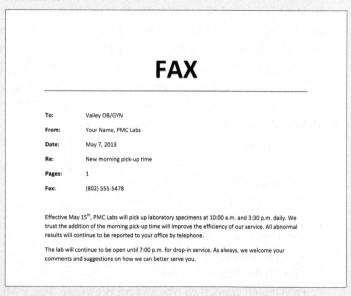

  f. Type Staff to replace the "To:" placeholder text; select "Phone:", type Re:; type New PMC Labs pick-up time to replace the "Type the recipient phone number" placeholder text; type 555-1176 to replace the "Type the recipient fax number" placeholder text; then type North Mountain Family Health to replace the "Type the recipient company name" placeholder text.

  g. Save the document with the filename WMP A-Lab Fax to the drive and folder where you store your Data Files.

7. View and navigate a document.

  a. Scroll down until Comments is near the top of your document window.

  b. Replace the Comments placeholder text with the following text: PMC Labs has added a morning pick-up time for laboratory specimens. Effective May 15th, PMC Labs will pick up specimens at 10:00 a.m. and 3:30 p.m.

  c. Use the Zoom dialog box to view the Whole Page.

  d. Click Comments to move the insertion point to the middle of the page, then use the Zoom slider to set the Zoom percentage at approximately 100%.

  e. Scroll to the bottom of the page, click in the Please Recycle box, type x if one is not added automatically when you click the box, then save your changes.

  f. Preview the document, then correct any errors, saving changes if necessary. Compare your document to Figure A-17. Submit the document to your instructor, close the file, then exit Word.

FIGURE A-17

Independent Challenge 1

Yesterday you interviewed for a job as marketing director at Oakland Medical Associates. You spoke with several people at the office, including Sharon Price, director of human resources, whose business card is shown in Figure A-18. You need to write a follow-up letter to Ms. Price, thanking her for the interview and expressing your interest in the practice and the position. She also asked you to send her some documents you have created, which you will enclose with the letter.

a. Start Word and save a new blank document as **WMP A-Price Letter** to the drive and folder where you store your Data Files.

b. Begin the letter by clicking the No Spacing button in the Styles group. You use this button to apply the No Spacing style to the document so that your document does not include extra space between paragraphs.

c. Type a personal letterhead for the letter that includes your name, address, telephone number, and e-mail address. If Word formats your e-mail address as a hyperlink, right-click your e-mail address, then click Remove Hyperlink. (*Note:* Format the letterhead after you finish typing the letter.)

d. Three lines below the bottom of the letterhead, type today's date.

e. Four lines below the date, type the inside address, referring to Figure A-18 for the address information. Be sure to include the recipient's title, company name, and full mailing address in the inside address.

f. Two lines below the inside address, type **Dear Ms. Price:** for the salutation.

g. Two lines below the salutation, type the body of the letter according to the following guidelines:

- In the first paragraph, thank her for the interview. Then restate your interest in the position and express your desire to work for the practice. Add any specific details you think will enhance the power of your letter.

- In the second paragraph, note that you are enclosing three samples of your work, and explain something about the samples you are enclosing.

- Type a short final paragraph.

FIGURE A-18

h. Two lines below the last body paragraph, type a closing, then four lines below the closing, type the signature block. Be sure to include your name in the signature block.

i. Two lines below the signature block, type an enclosure notation. (*Hint:* An enclosure notation usually includes the word "Enclosures" or the abbreviation "Enc." followed by the number of enclosures in parentheses.)

j. Format the letterhead with bold, centering, and a bottom border.

k. Save your changes.

l. Preview the letter, submit it to your instructor, then close the document and exit Word.

Independent Challenge 2

Your company has recently installed Word 2010 on its company network. As the training manager, it's your responsibility to teach employees how to use the new software productively. Now that they have begun working with Word 2010, several employees have asked you about sharing documents with colleagues using Windows Live SkyDrive. In response, you wrote a memo to all employees explaining Windows Live SkyDrive, some of its features, and how to register for a Windows Live ID. You now need to format the memo before distributing it.

a. Start Word, open the file **WMP A-1.docx** from the drive and folder where you store your Data Files, then read the memo to get a feel for its contents.

b. Save the file as **WMP A-SkyDrive Memo** to the drive and folder where you store your Data Files.

Independent Challenge 2 (continued)

c. Replace the information in the memo header with the information shown in Figure A-19. Make sure to include your name in the From line and the current date in the Date line.

d. Apply bold to **To:**, **From:**, **Date:**, and **Re:**.

e. Increase the size of **WORD TRAINING MEMORANDUM** to match Figure A-19, center the text on the page, add a border below it, then save your changes.

FIGURE A-19

> ## WORD TRAINING MEMORANDUM
>
> To: All employees
> From: Your Name, Training Manager
> Date: Today's Date
> Re: Windows Live SkyDrive

Advanced Challenge Exercise

■ Using the Font list on the Mini toolbar, apply a different font to **WORD TRAINING MEMORANDUM**. Make sure to select a font that is appropriate for a business memo.

■ Using the Font Color button on the Mini toolbar, change the color of **WORD TRAINING MEMORANDUM** to an appropriate color.

■ Save a copy of the memo in Word 97-2003 Document (*.doc) format as **WMP A-SkyDrive Memo ACE** to the drive or folder where you store your Data Files. (*Hint:* Use the Save as type list arrow in the Save As dialog box.)

f. Preview the memo, submit it to your instructor, then close the document and exit Word.

Independent Challenge 3

You are a cardiologist and research investigator for numerous trials pertaining to the study of heart disease. The president of the Allied Cardiology Association, Dr. Nathan Cummings, has asked you to be the keynote speaker at an upcoming conference on heart disease, to be held in Glacier National Park. You use one of the Word letter templates to write a letter to Dr. Cummings accepting the invitation and confirming the details. Your letter to Dr. Cummings should reference the following information:

- The conference will be held August 4–6, 2013, at the Many Glacier Hotel in the park.
- You have been asked to speak for an hour on Saturday, August 5, followed by one half hour for questions.
- Dr. Cummings suggested the lecture topic "Hope for the Heart: Advancements in Diagnosis and Treatment."
- Your talk will include a 45-minute slide presentation.
- The Allied Cardiology Association will make your travel arrangements.
- Your preference is to arrive at Glacier Park International Airport in Kalispell on the morning of Friday, August 4, and to depart on Monday, August 7. You would like to rent a car at the airport for the drive to the Many Glacier Hotel.
- You want to fly in and out of the airport closest to your home.

a. Start Word, click the File tab, click New, click Sample templates, and then select an appropriate letter template. Save the document as **WMP A-Cummings Letter** to the drive and folder where you store your Data Files.

b. Replace the placeholders in the letterhead with your personal information. Include your name, address, phone number, and e-mail address. Delete any placeholders that do not apply. (*Hints:* Depending on the template you choose, the letterhead might be located at the top or on the side of the document. You can press [Enter] when typing in a horizontal placeholder to add an additional line of text. You can also change the format of text typed in a placeholder. If your e-mail address appears as a hyperlink, right-click the e-mail address and click Remove Hyperlink.)

c. Use the Pick the date content control to select the current date.

d. Replace the placeholders in the inside address. Be sure to include Dr. Cumming's title and the name of the organization. Make up a street address and zip code.

e. Type **Dear Dr. Cummings:** for the salutation.

f. Use the information listed previously to type the body of the letter:
   - In the first paragraph, accept the invitation to speak.
   - In the second paragraph, confirm the important conference details, confirm your lecture topic, and provide any relevant details.

Creating Documents with Word 2010

Independent Challenge 3 (continued)

- In the third paragraph, state your travel preferences.
- Type a short final paragraph.

g. Type **Sincerely,** for the closing, then include your name in the signature block.

h. Adjust the formatting of the letter as necessary. For example, remove bold formatting or change the font color of text to a more appropriate color.

Advanced Challenge Exercise

- Zoom in on the title "Hope for the Heart: Advancements in Diagnosis and Treatment", delete any quotation marks, then apply italics to the title.
- Select one word in the letter, such as an adjective, and replace it with another similar word to improve the meaning of the sentence.
- Correct your spelling and grammar errors, if any, by right-clicking any red- or green-underlined text and then choosing from the options on the shortcut menu.
- View the letter in Full Screen Reading view, then click the Close button to return to Print Layout view.

i. Proofread your letter, make corrections as needed, then save your changes.

j. Submit the letter to your instructor, close the document, then exit Word.

Real Life Independent Challenge

This Independent Challenge requires an Internet connection.

The computer keyboard has become as essential an office tool as the pencil. The more adept you become at touch typing—the fastest and most accurate way to type—the more comfortable you will be working with computers and the more saleable your office skills to a potential employer. The Internet is one source of information on touch typing, and many Web sites include free typing tests and online tutorials to help you practice and improve your typing skills. In this independent challenge, you will take an online typing test to check your typing skills. You will then research the fundamentals of touch typing and investigate some of the ergonomic factors important to becoming a productive keyboard typist.

a. Use your favorite search engine to search the Internet for information on typing. Use the keywords **typing** and **typing ergonomics** to conduct your search.

b. Review the Web sites you find. Choose a site that offers a free online typing test, take the test, then print the Web page showing the results of your typing test if requested to do so by your instructor.

c. Start Word and save a new blank document as **WMP A-Touch Typing** to the drive and folder where you store your Data Files.

d. Type your name at the top of the document.

e. Type a brief report on the results of your research. Your report should answer the following questions:

- What are the URLs of the Web sites you visited to research touch typing and keyboard ergonomics? (*Hint*: A URL is a Web page's address. An example of a URL is www.course.com.)
- What are some benefits of using the touch typing method?
- On which keys should the fingers of the left and right hands rest when using the touch typing method?
- What ergonomic factors are important to keep in mind while typing?

f. Save your changes to the document, preview and submit it to your instructor, then close the document and exit Word.

Visual Workshop

Create the letter shown in Figure A-20. Before beginning to type, click the No Spacing button in the Styles group on the Home tab. Add the bottom border to the letterhead after typing the letter. Save the document as **WMP A-Insurance Letter** to the drive and folder where you store your Data Files, submit the letter to your instructor, then close the document and exit Word.

FIGURE A-20

Seattle Memorial Health Care

345 Madison Street, Seattle, WA 98111
Tel: 206-555-7283; www.seattlememorialhealth.com

April 27, 2013

Ms. Jessica Frank
827 Cherry Street
Seattle, WA 98102

Dear Ms. Frank:

Thank you for choosing Seattle Memorial Health Care as your health care provider.

As a result of your recent visit to our emergency facility, our records show your primary care insurance as Northwest Indemnity (#80053 0331), policy #446 38 9876, and group #732556-22-994. At this time, our records show you do not have a secondary care insurance provider.

If the insurance information in this letter is correct, no action is required on your part.

If the insurance information is incomplete or incorrect, please contact us with more accurate billing information by calling a Financial Counselor at (206) 993-5600.

Once we have billed your insurance, we will send you a statement identifying any patient responsibility.

Sincerely,

Your Name
Patient Business Services
Seattle Memorial Health Care

Creating Documents with Word 2010

Editing Documents

Files You Will Need:

WMP B-1.docx

WMP B-2.docx

WMP B-3.docx

WMP B-4.docx

WMP B-5.docx

WMP B-6.docx

WMP B-7.docx

The sophisticated editing features in Word make it easy to revise and polish your documents. In this unit, you learn how to revise an existing file by opening it, copying and moving text, and then saving the document as a new file. You also learn how to perfect your documents using proofing tools and how to quickly prepare a document for distribution to the public. You have been asked to edit and finalize a press release for a new lecture series sponsored by the Riverwalk Medical Clinic. The press release should provide information about the series so that newspapers, radio stations, and other media outlets can announce it to the public. Press releases from the Riverwalk Medical Clinic are disseminated by fax and by e-mail. Before distributing the file electronically to your lists of press contacts, you add several hyperlinks and then strip the file of private information.

OBJECTIVES

Cut and paste text

Copy and paste text

Use the Office Clipboard

Find and replace text

Check spelling and grammar

Research information

Add hyperlinks

Work with document properties

Cutting and Pasting Text

The editing features in Word allow you to move text from one location to another in a document. Moving text is often called **cut and paste**. When you **cut** text, it is removed from the document and placed on the **Clipboard**, a temporary storage area for text and graphics that you cut or copy from a document. You can then **paste**, or insert, text that is stored on the Clipboard in the document at the location of the insertion point. You cut and paste text using the Cut and Paste buttons in the Clipboard group on the Home tab. You can also move selected text by dragging it to a new location using the mouse. This operation is called **drag and drop**. ▓▓▓▓ You open the press release that was drafted by a colleague, save it with a new filename, and then reorganize the information in the press release using the cut-and-paste and drag-and-drop methods.

STEPS

1. **Start** Word, **click the** File tab, **click** Open, **navigate to the drive and folder where you store your Data Files, click** WMP B-1.docx, **then click** Open

   The document opens. Once you have opened a file, you can edit it and use the Save or the Save As command to save your changes. You use the **Save** command when you want to save the changes you make to a file, overwriting the file that is stored on a disk. You use the **Save As** command when you want to leave the original file intact and create a duplicate file with a different filename, file extension, or location.

2. **Click the** File tab, **click** Save As, **type** WMP B-Lecture PR **in the File name text box, then click** Save

   You can now make changes to the press release file without affecting the original file.

3. **Replace** Owen Spade **with your name, scroll down until the headline "Dr. Timothy Yalobush to Speak..." is at the top of your document window, then click the** Show/Hide ¶ **button** ¶ **in the Paragraph group on the Home tab to display formatting marks**

4. **Select** lead and other heavy metals, **(including the comma and the space after it) in the fourth body paragraph, then click the** Cut button ✂ **in the Clipboard group**

   The text is removed from the document and placed on the Clipboard. Word uses two different clipboards: the **system Clipboard** (the Clipboard), which holds just one item, and the **Office Clipboard**, which holds up to 24 items. The last item you cut or copy is always added to both clipboards. You'll learn more about the Office Clipboard in a later lesson.

5. **Place the insertion point before** pesticides **(but after the space) in the second line of the fourth paragraph, then click the** Paste button **in the Clipboard group**

   The text is pasted at the location of the insertion point, as shown in Figure B-1. The Paste Options button appears below text when you first paste it in a document. You'll learn more about the Paste Options button in the next lesson. For now, you can ignore it.

6. **Press and hold** [Ctrl], **click the sentence** Ticket prices include lunch. **in the third paragraph, then release** [Ctrl]

   The entire sentence is selected.

7. **Press and hold the mouse button over the selected text until the pointer changes to** ▯▨

   The pointer's vertical line is the insertion point. You drag the pointer to position the insertion point where you want the text to be inserted when you release the mouse button.

8. **Drag the pointer's vertical line to the end of the fifth paragraph (between the period and the paragraph mark) as shown in Figure B-2, then release the mouse button**

   The selected text is moved to the location of the insertion point. It is convenient to move text using the drag-and-drop method when the locations of origin and destination are both visible on the screen. Text is not placed on the Clipboard when you drag and drop it.

   > **TROUBLE**
   > If you make a mistake, click the Undo button ↶ on the Quick Access toolbar, then try again.

9. **Deselect the text, then click the** Save button 💾 **on the Quick Access toolbar**

Editing Documents

FIGURE B-1: Moved text with Paste Options button

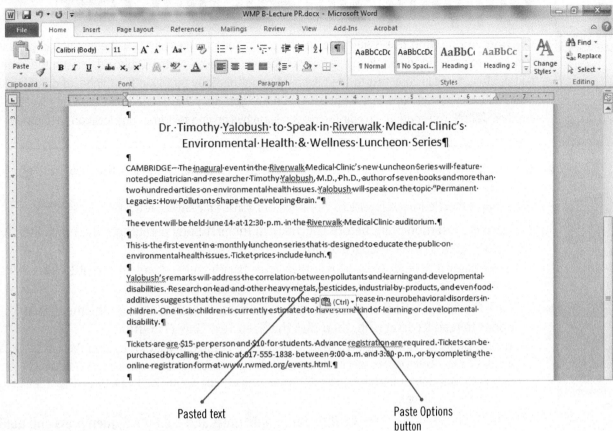

Pasted text

Paste Options button

FIGURE B-2: Dragging and dropping text in a new location

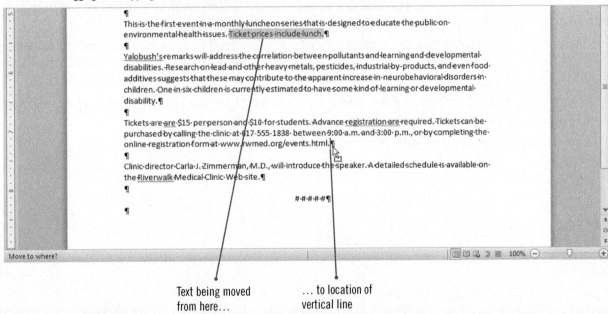

Text being moved from here…

… to location of vertical line

Using keyboard shortcuts

A **shortcut key** is a function key, such as [F1], or a combination of keys, such as [Ctrl][S], that you press to perform a command. For example, instead of using the Cut, Copy, and Paste commands on the Ribbon or the Mini toolbar, you can use the **keyboard shortcuts** [Ctrl][X] to cut text, [Ctrl][C] to copy text, and [Ctrl][V] to paste text. You can also press [Ctrl][S] to save changes to a document instead of clicking the Save button on the Quick Access toolbar or clicking Save on the File tab. Becoming skilled at using keyboard shortcuts can help you quickly accomplish many of the tasks you perform in Word. If a keyboard shortcut is available for a command, then it is listed in the ScreenTip for that command.

Copying and Pasting Text

Copying and pasting text is similar to cutting and pasting text, except that the text you **copy** is not removed from the document. Rather, a copy of the text is placed on the Clipboard, leaving the original text in place. You can copy text to the Clipboard using the Copy button in the Clipboard group on the Home tab, or you can copy text by pressing [Ctrl] as you drag the selected text from one location to another. ▦▦▦▦ You continue to edit the press release by copying text from one location to another.

1. **Select** Environmental Health & Wellness **in the headline, then click the** Copy button ▥ **in the Clipboard group**

   A copy of the selected text is placed on the Clipboard, leaving the original text you copied in place.

2. **Place the insertion point before** Luncheon **in the first body paragraph, then click the** Paste button **in the Clipboard group**

   "Environmental Health & Wellness" is inserted before "Luncheon," as shown in Figure B-3. Notice that the pasted text is formatted differently than the paragraph in which it was inserted.

3. **Click the** Paste Options button, **move the mouse over each button on the menu that opens to read its ScreenTip, then click the** Keep Text Only (T) button

   The formatting of "Environmental Health & Wellness" is changed to match the rest of the paragraph. The buttons on the Paste Options menu allow you to change the formatting of pasted text. You can choose to keep the original formatting (Keep Source Formatting), match the destination formatting (Merge Formatting), or paste the text unformatted (Keep Text Only).

4. **Select** www.rwmed.org **in the fifth paragraph, press and hold [Ctrl], then press and hold the mouse button until the pointer changes to** ▤

5. **Drag the pointer's vertical line to the end of the last paragraph, placing it between** site **and the period, release the mouse button, then release** [Ctrl]

   The text is copied to the last paragraph. Since the formatting of the text you copied is the same as the formatting of the destination paragraph, you can ignore the Paste Options button. Text is not copied to the Clipboard when you copy it using the drag-and-drop method.

6. **Place the insertion point before** www.rwmed.org **in the last paragraph, type** at followed by a space, **then save the document**

   Compare your document with Figure B-4.

Splitting the document window to copy and move items in a long document

If you want to copy or move items between parts of a long document, it can be useful to split the document window into two panes. This allows you to display the item you want to copy or move in one pane and the destination for the item in the other pane. To split a window, click the Split button in the Window group on the View tab, drag the horizontal split bar that appears to the location you want to split the window, and then click. Once the document window is split into two panes, you can drag the split bar to resize the panes and use the scroll bars in each pane to display different parts of the document. To copy or move an item from one pane to another, you can use the Cut, Copy, and Paste commands, or you can drag the item between the panes. When you are finished editing the document, double-click the split bar to restore the window to a single pane, or click the Remove Split button in the Window group on the View tab.

FIGURE B-3: Text pasted in document

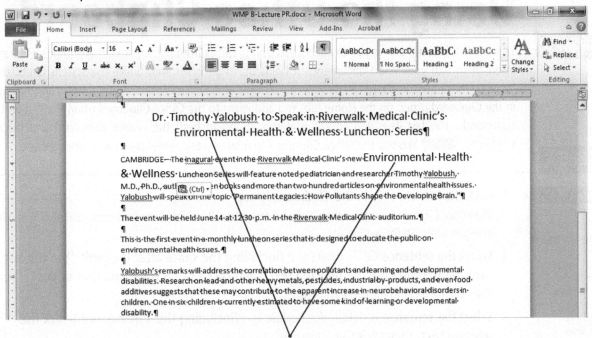

Formatting of the pasted text
matches the headline text

FIGURE B-4: Copied text in document

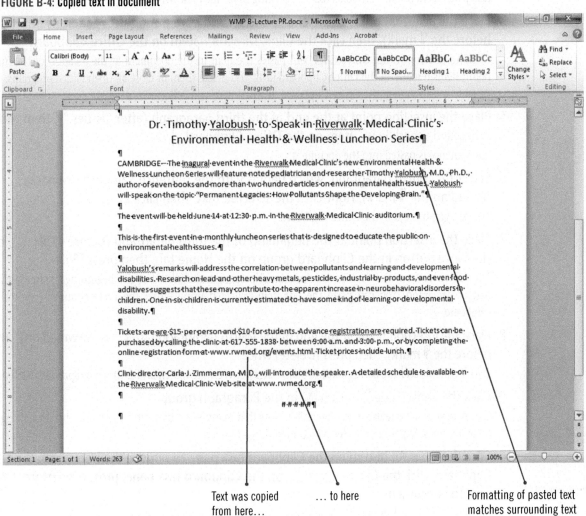

Text was copied   ... to here   Formatting of pasted text
from here...   matches surrounding text

Using the Office Clipboard

The Office Clipboard allows you to collect text and graphics from files created in any Office program and insert them into your Word documents. It holds up to 24 items and, unlike the system Clipboard, the items on the Office Clipboard can be viewed. To display the Office Clipboard, you simply click the launcher in the Clipboard group on the Home tab. You add items to the Office Clipboard using the Cut and Copy commands. The last item you collect is always added to both the system Clipboard and the Office Clipboard. **[icon]** You use the Office Clipboard to move several sentences in your press release.

STEPS

QUICK TIP

You can set the Office Clipboard to open automatically when you cut or copy two items consecutively by clicking Options in the Clipboard task pane, and then selecting Show Office Clipboard Automatically.

1. **Click the launcher [icon] in the Clipboard group**

   The Office Clipboard opens in the Clipboard task pane. It contains the Environmental Health & Wellness item you copied in the last lesson.

2. **Select the sentence Clinic director... (including the space after the period) in the last paragraph, right-click the selected text, then click Cut on the menu that opens**

   The sentence is cut to the Office Clipboard.

3. **Select the sentence A detailed schedule is... (including the ¶ mark), right-click the selected text, then click Cut**

   The Office Clipboard displays the items you cut or copied, as shown in Figure B-5. The icon next to each item indicates the items are from a Word document. The last item collected is displayed at the top of the Clipboard task pane. As new items are collected, the existing items move down the task pane.

4. **Place the insertion point at the end of the second paragraph (after "auditorium." but before the ¶ mark), then click the Clinic Director... item on the Office Clipboard**

   Clicking an item on the Office Clipboard pastes the item in the document at the location of the insertion point. Items remain on the Office Clipboard until you delete them or close all open Office programs. Also, if you add a 25th item to the Office Clipboard, the first item you collected is deleted.

5. **Place the insertion point at the end of the third paragraph (after "issues."), then click the A detailed schedule is... item on the Office Clipboard**

   The sentence is pasted into the document.

6. **Select the fourth paragraph, which begins with the sentence Yalobush's remarks... (including the ¶ mark), right-click the selected text, then click Cut**

   The paragraph is cut to the Office Clipboard.

7. **Place the insertion point at the beginning of the third paragraph (before "This..."), click the Paste button in the Clipboard group on the Home tab, then press [Enter]**

   The sentences from the "Yalobush's remarks..." paragraph are pasted at the beginning of the "This is the first..." paragraph. You can paste the last item collected using either the Paste command or the Office Clipboard.

8. **Place the insertion point at the end of the fourth paragraph (after "www.rwmed.org" and before the ¶ mark), then press [Delete] twice**

   Two ¶ symbols and the corresponding blank lines between the fourth and fifth paragraphs are deleted.

9. **Click the Show/Hide ¶ button [¶] in the Paragraph group**

   Compare your press release with Figure B-6. Note that many Word users prefer to work with formatting marks on at all times. Experiment to see which method you prefer.

QUICK TIP

To delete an individual item from the Office Clipboard, click the list arrow next to the item, then click Delete.

10. **Click the Clear All button on the Clipboard task pane to remove the items from the Office Clipboard, click the Close button [X] on the Clipboard task pane, press [Ctrl][Home], then save the document**

    Pressing [Ctrl][Home] moves the insertion point to the top of the document.

FIGURE B-5: Office Clipboard in Clipboard task pane

Clipboard task pane

Items stored on the Office Clipboard (yours may include additional items)

Click to change display options for the Office Clipboard

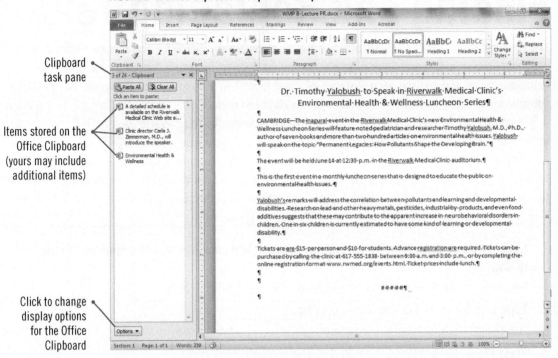

FIGURE B-6: Revised press release

Click to paste all the items on the Office Clipboard

Last item collected

First item moves down as more items are collected

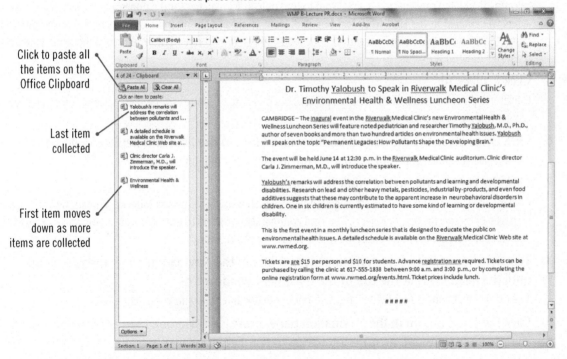

Copying and moving items between documents

You can also use the system and Office Clipboards to copy and move items between documents. To do this, open both documents and the Clipboard task pane in the program window. With multiple documents open, copy or cut an item from one document and then switch to the other document and paste the item. To switch between open documents, point to the Word icon on the taskbar, and then click the document you want to appear in the document window. You can also display more than one document at the same time by clicking the Arrange All button or the View Side by Side button in the Window group on the View tab.

Finding and Replacing Text

The Find and Replace feature in Word allows you to automatically search for and replace all instances of a word or phrase in a document. For example, you might need to substitute "wellness" for "well-being." To manually locate and replace each instance of "well-being" in a long document would be very time-consuming. By using the Replace command you can find and replace all occurrences of specific text at once, or you can choose to find and review each occurrence individually. You can also use the Find command to locate and highlight every occurrence of a specific word or phrase in a document. 🔷🔷🔷 The clinic director has decided to change the name of the lecture series from "Environmental Health & Wellness Luncheon Series" to "Environmental Health & Wellness Lecture Series." You use the Replace command to search the document for all instances of "Luncheon" and replace them with "Lecture."

STEPS

1. **Click the** Replace button **in the Editing group, then click** More **in the Find and Replace dialog box**

   The Find and Replace dialog box opens and expands, as shown in Figure B-7.

2. **Type** Luncheon **in the Find what text box**

   "Luncheon" is the text that will be replaced.

3. **Press [Tab], then type** Lecture **in the Replace with text box**

   "Lecture" is the text that will replace "Luncheon."

4. **Click the** Match case check box **in the Search Options section to select it**

   Selecting the Match case check box tells Word to find only exact matches for the uppercase and lowercase characters you entered in the Find what text box. You want to replace all instances of "Luncheon" in the proper name "Environmental Health & Wellness Luncheon Series." You do not want to replace "luncheon" when it refers to a lunchtime event.

5. **Click** Replace All

   Clicking Replace All changes all occurrences of "Luncheon" to "Lecture" in the press release. A message box reports two replacements were made.

6. **Click** OK **to close the message box, then click** Close **in the Find and Replace dialog box**

   Word replaced "Luncheon" with "Lecture" in two locations, but did not replace "luncheon."

7. **Click the** Find button **in the Editing group**

   Clicking the Find button opens the Navigation pane, which is used to browse a longer document by headings, by pages, or by specific text or objects. The Find command allows you to quickly locate all instances of text in a document. You use it to verify that Word did not replace "luncheon."

8. **Type** luncheon **in the Search document text box in the Navigation pane, then scroll up until the headline is at the top of the document window**

   The word "luncheon" is highlighted and selected in the document, as shown in Figure B-8.

9. **Click the** Close button **in the Navigation pane, press [Ctrl][Home], then save the document**

   The highlighting is removed from the text when you close the Navigation pane.

Editing Documents

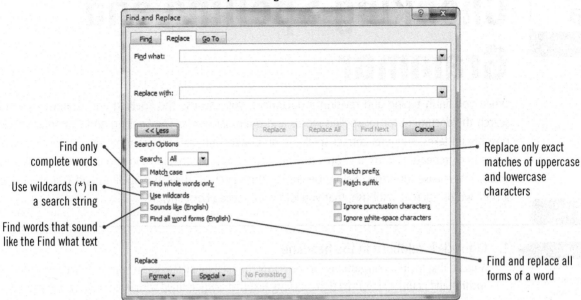

Find only complete words

Use wildcards (*) in a search string

Find words that sound like the Find what text

Replace only exact matches of uppercase and lowercase characters

Find and replace all forms of a word

FIGURE B-8: Found text highlighted in document

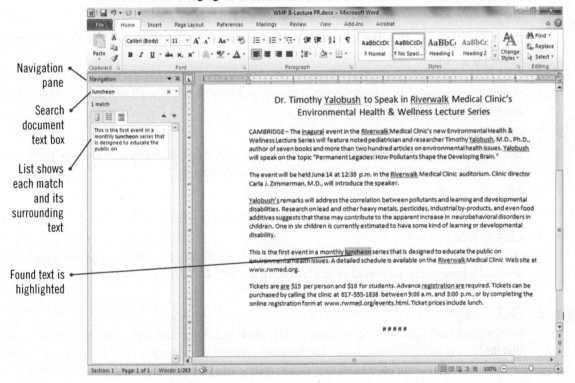

Navigation pane

Search document text box

List shows each match and its surrounding text

Found text is highlighted

Navigating a document using the Go To command

Rather than scrolling to move to a different place in a longer document, you can use the Go To command to quickly move the insertion point to a specific location. To move to a specific page, section, line, table, graphic, or other item in a document, you use the Go To tab in the Find and Replace dialog box. To open the Find and Replace dialog box with the Go To tab active, click the Page number button on the status bar. On the Go To tab in the Find and Replace dialog box, select the type of item you want to find in the Go to what list box, enter the relevant information about that item, and then click Go To or Next to move the insertion point to the item.

Checking Spelling and Grammar

When you finish typing and revising a document, you can use the Spelling and Grammar command to search the document for misspelled words and grammar errors. The Spelling and Grammar checker flags possible mistakes, suggests correct spellings, and offers remedies for grammar errors such as subject–verb agreement, repeated words, and punctuation. ▓▓▓▓ You use the Spelling and Grammar checker to search your press release for errors. Before beginning the search, you set the Spelling and Grammar checker to ignore words, such as Yalobush, that you know are spelled correctly.

TROUBLE

If Word flags your name as misspelled, right-click it, then click Ignore All. If "Yalobush" or "Riverwalk" are not flagged as misspelled, skip to Step 4.

1. **Right-click Yalobush in the headline**

   A menu that includes suggestions for correcting the spelling of "Yalobush" opens. You can correct individual spelling and grammar errors by right-clicking text that is underlined with a red or green wavy line and selecting a correction. Although "Yalobush" is not in the Word dictionary, it is spelled correctly in the document.

2. **Click Ignore All**

   Clicking Ignore All tells Word not to flag "Yalobush" as misspelled.

3. **Right-click Riverwalk at the top of the document, then click Ignore All**

   The red, wavy underline is removed from all instances of "Riverwalk."

QUICK TIP

To change the language used by the Word proofing tools, click the Language button in the Language group on the Review tab, click Set Proofing Language, then click the language you prefer on the menu that opens.

4. **Press [Ctrl][Home], click the Review tab, then click the Spelling & Grammar button in the Proofing group**

   The Spelling and Grammar: English (U.S.) dialog box opens, as shown in Figure B-9. The dialog box identifies "inagural" as misspelled and suggests possible corrections for the error. The word selected in the Suggestions box is the correct spelling.

5. **Click Change**

   Word replaces the misspelled word with the correctly spelled word. Next, the dialog box identifies "Yalobush's" as a misspelled word. "Yalobush's" is spelled correctly in the document.

6. **Click Ignore All**

   Word ignores the spelling. Next, the dialog box indicates that "are" is repeated in a sentence.

TROUBLE

You might need to correct other spelling and grammar errors.

7. **Click Delete**

   Word deletes the second occurrence of the repeated word. Next, the dialog box flags a subject–verb agreement error and suggests using "is" instead of "are," as shown in Figure B-10. The phrase selected in the Suggestions box is correct.

QUICK TIP

If Word does not offer a valid correction, correct the error yourself.

8. **Click Change**

   Word replaces "are" with "is" in the sentence, and the Spelling and Grammar dialog box closes. Keep in mind that the Spelling and Grammar checker identifies many common errors, but you cannot rely on it to find and correct all spelling and grammar errors in your documents. Always proofread your documents carefully.

9. **Click OK to complete the spelling and grammar check, press [Ctrl][Home], then save the document**

FIGURE B-9: Spelling and Grammar: English (U.S.) dialog box

Word identified as misspelled

Suggested correction

Adds the misspelled word and the correction to the AutoCorrect list

Ignores this occurrence of the word

Ignores all occurrences of the word

Adds the word to the Word dictionary

Changes the word to the selected correction

Changes all occurrences of the word to the selected correction

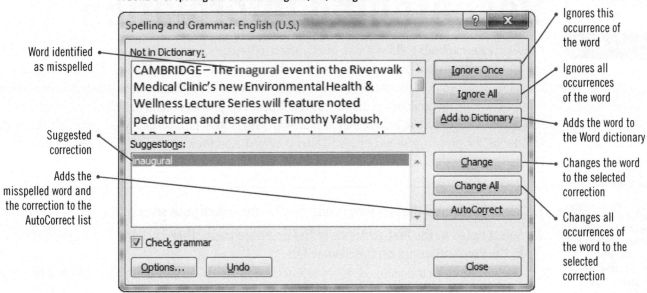

FIGURE B-10: Grammar error identified in Spelling and Grammar dialog box

Grammar error identified

Possible corrections

Check mark indicates grammar is being checked too

Displays an explanation of the grammar rule used to identify the error

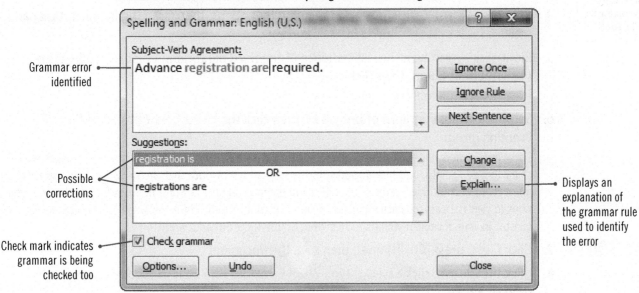

Inserting text with AutoCorrect

As you type, AutoCorrect automatically corrects many commonly misspelled words. By creating your own AutoCorrect entries, you can set Word to insert text that you type often, such as your name or contact information, or to correct words you misspell frequently. For example, you could create an AutoCorrect entry so that the name "Ronald T. Dawson" is automatically inserted whenever you type "rtd" followed by a space. You create AutoCorrect entries and customize other AutoCorrect and AutoFormat options using the AutoCorrect dialog box. To open the AutoCorrect dialog box, click the File tab, click Options, click Proofing in the Word Options dialog box that opens, and then click AutoCorrect Options. On the AutoCorrect tab in the AutoCorrect dialog box, type the text you want to be corrected automatically in the Replace text box (such as

"rtd"), type the text you want to be inserted in its place automatically in the With text box (such as "Ronald T. Dawson"), and then click Add. The AutoCorrect entry is added to the list. Click OK to close the AutoCorrect dialog box, and then click OK to close the Word Options dialog box. Word inserts an AutoCorrect entry in a document when you press [Spacebar] or a punctuation mark after typing the text you want Word to correct. For example, Word inserts "Ronald T. Dawson" when you type "rtd" followed by a space.

If you want to remove an AutoCorrect entry you created, simply open the AutoCorrect dialog box, select the AutoCorrect entry you want to remove in the list, click Delete, click OK, and then click OK to close the Word Options dialog box.

Researching Information

The Word Research feature allows you to quickly search reference sources and the World Wide Web for information related to a word or phrase. Among the reference sources available in the Research task pane is a Thesaurus, which you can use to look up synonyms for awkward or repetitive words. When you are working with an active Internet connection, the Research task pane also provides access to dictionary and translation sources, as well as to Web search engines such as Bing. ▓▓▓▓ After proofreading your document for errors, you decide the press release would read better if several adjectives were more descriptive. You use the Thesaurus to find synonyms.

STEPS

QUICK TIP

You can also click the Research button in the Proofing group to open the Research task pane.

QUICK TIP

To look up synonyms for a different word, type the word in the Search for text box, then click the green Start searching button.

QUICK TIP

To add or remove available reference sources, click Research options in the Research task pane.

1. **Scroll down until the headline is displayed at the top of your screen**

2. **Select noted in the first sentence of the first paragraph, then click the Thesaurus button in the Proofing group on the Review tab**

   The Research task pane opens, as shown in Figure B-11. "Noted" appears in the Search for text box, and possible synonyms for "noted" are listed under the Thesaurus: English (U.S.) heading in the task pane.

3. **Point to distinguished in the list of synonyms**

   A box containing a list arrow appears around the word.

4. **Click the list arrow, click Insert on the menu that opens, then close the Research task pane**

   "Distinguished" replaces "noted" in the press release.

5. **Right-click currently in the last sentence of the third paragraph, point to Synonyms on the menu that opens, then click now**

   "Now" replaces "currently" in the press release.

6. **Select the five paragraphs of body text, then click the Word Count button in the Proofing group**

   The Word Count dialog box opens, as shown in Figure B-12. The dialog box lists the number of pages, words, characters, paragraphs, and lines included in the selected text. Notice that the status bar also displays the number of words included in the selected text and the total number of words in the entire document. If you want to view the page, character, paragraph, and line count for the entire document, make sure nothing is selected in your document, and then click Word Count in the Proofing group.

7. **Click Close, press [Ctrl][Home], then save the document**

8. **Click the File tab, click Save As, type WMP B-Lecture PR Public in the File name text box, then click Save**

   The WMP B-Lecture PR file closes, and the WMP B-Lecture PR Public file is displayed in the document window. You will modify this file to prepare it for electronic release to the public.

Publishing a blog directly from Word

A **blog**, which is short for weblog, is an informal journal that is created by an individual or a group and available to the public on the Internet. A blog usually conveys the ideas, comments, and opinions of the blogger and is written using a strong personal voice. The person who creates and maintains a blog, the **blogger**, typically updates the blog daily. If you have or want to start a blog, you can configure Word to link to your blog site so that you can write, format, and publish blog entries directly from Word.

To create a new blog post, click the File tab, click New, then double-click Blog post to open a predesigned blog post document that you can customize with your own text, formatting, and images. You can also publish an existing document as a blog post by opening the document, clicking the File tab, clicking Save & Send, clicking Publish as Blog Post, and then clicking the Publish as Blog Post button. In either case, Word prompts you to log onto your personal blog account. To blog directly from Word, you must first obtain a blog account with a blog service provider. Resources, such as the Word Help system and online forums, provide detailed information on obtaining and registering your personal blog account with Word.

FIGURE B-11: Research task pane

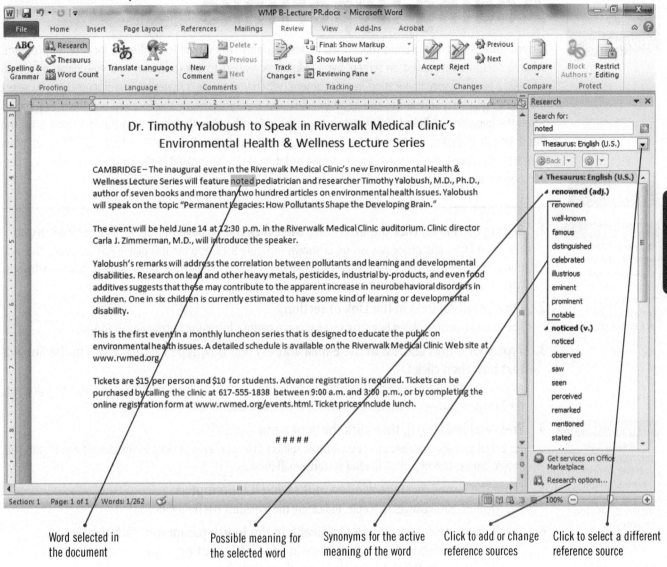

Word selected in the document

Possible meaning for the selected word

Synonyms for the active meaning of the word

Click to add or change reference sources

Click to select a different reference source

FIGURE B-12: Word Count dialog box

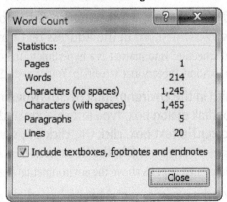

Adding Hyperlinks

A **hyperlink** is text or a graphic that, when clicked, "jumps" the viewer to a different location or program. When a document is viewed on screen, hyperlinks allow readers to link (or jump) to a Web page, an e-mail address, a file, or a specific location in a document. When you create a hyperlink in a document, you select the text or graphic you want to use as a hyperlink and then you specify the location you want to jump to when the hyperlink is clicked. You create a hyperlink using the Hyperlink button in the Links group on the Insert tab. Text that is formatted as a hyperlink appears as colored, underlined text. ▟▟▟ Your press contacts will receive the press release by e-mail or Internet fax. To make it easier for these people to access additional information about the series, you add several hyperlinks to the press release.

1. **Select your name, click the Insert tab, then click the Hyperlink button in the Links group**
   The Insert Hyperlink dialog box opens, as shown in Figure B-13. You use this dialog box to specify the location of the Web page, file, e-mail address, or position in the current document you want to jump to when the hyperlink—in this case, your name—is clicked.

2. **Click E-mail Address in the Link to section**
   The Insert Hyperlink dialog box changes so you can create a hyperlink to your e-mail address.

3. **Type your e-mail address in the E-mail address text box, type Lecture Series in the Subject text box, then click OK**
   As you type, Word automatically adds mailto: in front of your e-mail address. After you close the dialog box, the hyperlink text—your name—is formatted in blue and underlined.

4. **Press and hold [Ctrl], then click the your name hyperlink**
   An e-mail message addressed to you with the subject "Lecture Series" opens in the default e-mail program. People can use this hyperlink to send you an e-mail message.

5. **Close the e-mail message window, not saving it if prompted**
   The hyperlink text changes to purple, indicating the hyperlink has been followed.

6. **Scroll down, select environmental health in the fourth paragraph, click the Hyperlink button, click Existing File or Web Page in the Link to section, type www.cdc.gov/environmental in the Address text box, then click OK**
   As you type the Web address, Word automatically adds "http://" in front of "www." The text "environmental health" is formatted as a hyperlink to the Centers for Disease Control and Prevention's Environmental Health home page at www.cdc.gov/environmental. When clicked, the hyperlink will open the Web page in the default browser window.

7. **Select detailed schedule in the last sentence of the fourth paragraph, click the Hyperlink button, type www.rwmed.org in the Address text box, then click OK**
   The text "detailed schedule" is formatted as a hyperlink to the clinic Web site. If you point to a hyperlink in Word, the link to location appears in a ScreenTip. You can edit ScreenTip text to make it more descriptive.

8. **Right-click health in the environmental health hyperlink, click Edit Hyperlink, click ScreenTip in the Edit Hyperlink dialog box, type Information and links related to environmental health issues in the ScreenTip text box, click OK, click OK, save your changes, then point to the environmental health hyperlink in the document**
   The ScreenTip you created appears above the environmental health hyperlink, as shown in Figure B-14.

9. **Press [Ctrl], click the environmental health hyperlink, click the Word icon ⓦ on the taskbar, press [Ctrl], click the detailed schedule hyperlink, verify that the links opened in separate tabs in your browser, close the tabs, then click the Word icon ⓦ on the taskbar to return to the press release document in Word**
   Before distributing a document, it's important to test each hyperlink to verify it works as you intended.

FIGURE B-13: Insert Hyperlink dialog box

Create a hyperlink to a Web page or file

Create a hyperlink to a location in the current file

Create a hyperlink to a new blank document

Create a hyperlink to an e-mail address

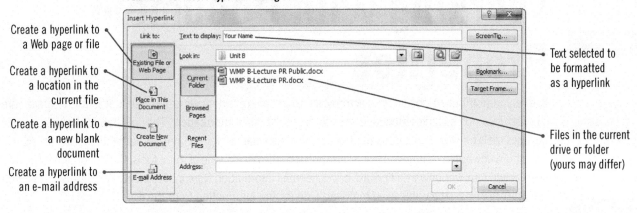

Text selected to be formatted as a hyperlink

Files in the current drive or folder (yours may differ)

FIGURE B-14: Hyperlinks in the document

Purple text indicates the hyperlink has been followed

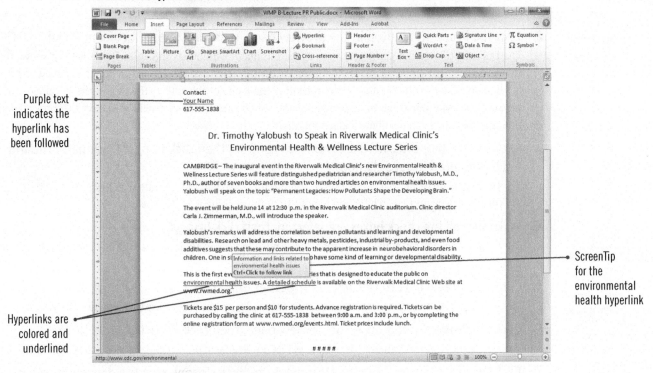

ScreenTip for the environmental health hyperlink

Hyperlinks are colored and underlined

E-mailing and faxing documents directly from Word

Word includes several options for distributing and sharing documents over the Internet directly from within Word, including e-mailing and faxing documents. When you e-mail a document from within Word, the document is sent as an attachment to an e-mail message using your default e-mail program. To e-mail a file, open the file in Word, click the File tab, click Save & Send, and then select one of the options under Send Using E-mail on the Save & Send tab. You can choose to attach the document as a Word file, a .pdf file, or an .xps file, or to send it as an Internet fax. When you click an option, a message window opens that includes the filename of the current file as the message subject and the file as an attachment. Type the e-mail address(es) of the recipient(s) in the To and Cc text boxes, any message you want in the message window, and then click Send on the message window toolbar to send the message. The default e-mail program sends a copy of the document to each recipient. Note that faxing a document directly from Word requires registration with a third-party Internet fax service. Fax services generally charge a monthly or per page fee for sending and receiving faxes.

Working with Document Properties

Before you distribute a document electronically to people outside your organization, it's wise to make sure the file does not include embedded private or confidential information. The Info tab in Backstage view includes tools for stripping a document of sensitive information, for securing its authenticity, and for guarding it from unwanted changes once it is distributed to the public. One of these tools, the Document Inspector, detects and removes unwanted private or confidential information from a document. ▓▓▓ Before sending the press release to the public, you remove all identifying information from the file.

To create or modify document properties for a file, type in the Document Properties panel text boxes.

1. **Press [Ctrl][Home], then click the File tab**

   Backstage view opens with the Info tab displayed. The Information pane, in the middle of the tab, includes options related to stripping the file of private information. See Table B-1. The preview pane, on the right side of the tab, displays basic information about the document. Notice that the file contains document properties. You might want to remove these before you distribute the press release to the public.

2. **Click the Properties button in the preview pane, then click Show Document Panel**

   The Document Properties panel opens above the document window, as shown in Figure B-15. It shows the standard document properties for the press release. **Document properties** are user-defined details about a file that describe its contents and origin, including the name of the author, the title of the document, and keywords that you can assign to help organize and search your files. You decide to remove this information from the file before you distribute it electronically.

3. **Click the File tab, click the Check for Issues button, then click Inspect Document, clicking Yes if prompted to save changes**

   The Document Inspector dialog box opens. You use this dialog box to indicate which private or identifying information you want to search for and remove from the document.

4. **Make sure all the check boxes are selected, then click Inspect**

   After a moment, the Document Inspector dialog box changes to indicate that the file contains document properties.

A document property, such as author name, might appear automatically in a content control in a document. Stripping a file of document properties does not remove this information from a content control.

5. **Click Remove All next to Document Properties, then click Close**

   The standard document property information is removed from the press release document.

6. **Click the Properties button in the preview pane, then click Show Document Panel**

   The Document Properties panel opens and shows that the document properties have been removed from the file.

7. **Click the Close button [X] in the Document Properties panel, save the document, submit it to your instructor, close the file, then exit Word**

   The completed press release is shown in Figure B-16.

TABLE B-1: Options on the Info tab

option	use to
Protect Document	Mark a document as final so that it is read-only and cannot be edited; encrypt a document so that a password is required to open it; restrict what kinds of changes can be made to a document and by whom; and add a digital signature to a document to verify its integrity
Check for Issues	Detect and remove unwanted information from a document, including document properties and comments; check for content that people with disabilities might find difficult to read; and check the document for features that are not supported by previous versions of Microsoft Word
Manage versions	Browse through and delete draft versions of unsaved files

Editing Documents

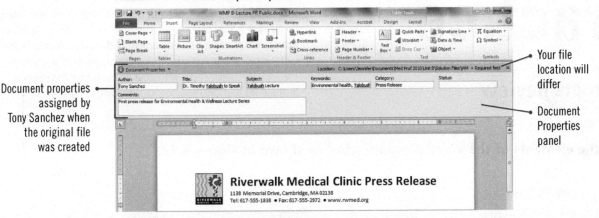

Document properties assigned by Tony Sanchez when the original file was created

Your file location will differ

Document Properties panel

FIGURE B-16: Completed press release for electronic distribution

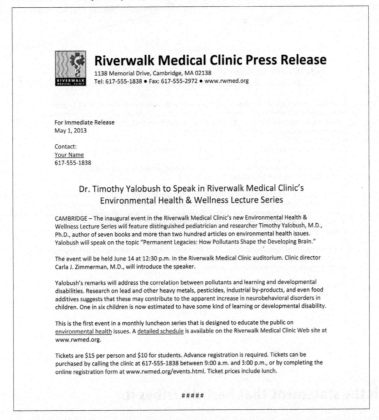

Viewing and modifying advanced document properties

The Document Properties panel includes summary information about the document that you enter to suit your needs. To view more detailed document properties, including those entered automatically by Word when the document is created, click the Document Properties button in the Document Properties panel, and then click Advanced Properties to open the Properties dialog box. You can also click the Properties button on the Info tab and then click Advanced Properties to open the Properties dialog box. The General, Statistics, and Contents tabs of the Properties dialog box display information about the file that is automatically created and updated by Word. The General tab shows the file type, location, size, and date and time the file was created and last modified; the Statistics tab displays information about revisions to the document along with the number of pages, words, lines, paragraphs, and characters in the file; and the Contents tab shows the title of the document.

You can define other document properties using the Properties dialog box Summary and Custom tabs. The Summary tab shows information similar to the information shown in the Document Properties panel. The Custom tab allows you to create new document properties, such as client, project, or date completed. To create a custom property, select a property name in the Name list box on the Custom tab, use the Type list arrow to select the type of data you want for the property, type the identifying detail (such as a project name) in the Value text box, and then click Add. When you are finished viewing or modifying the document properties, click OK to close the Properties dialog box, then click the Close button on the Document Properties panel.

Practice

Concepts Review

For current SAM information, including versions and content details, visit SAM Central (http://www.cengage.com/samcentral). If you have a SAM user profile, you may have access to hands-on instruction, practice, and assessment of the skills covered in this unit. Since various versions of SAM are supported throughout the life of this text, check with your instructor for the correct instructions and URL/Web site for accessing assignments.

Label the elements of the Word program window shown in Figure B-17.

FIGURE B-17

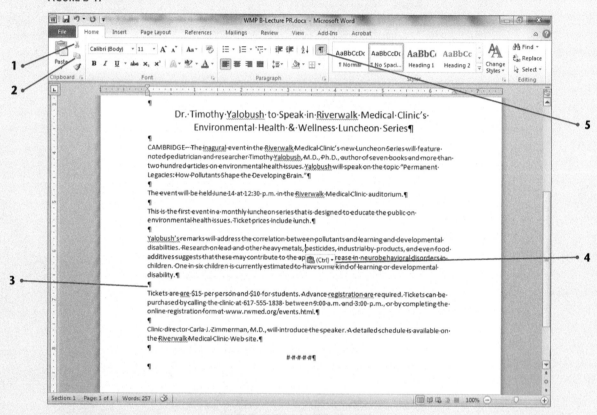

Match each term with the statement that best describes it.

6. Paste
7. Shortcut key
8. System Clipboard
9. Document properties
10. Office Clipboard
11. Cut
12. Thesaurus
13. Hyperlink
14. Blog

a. Command used to insert text stored on the Clipboard into a document
b. Temporary storage area for up to 24 items collected from Office files
c. Temporary storage area for only the last item cut or copied from a document
d. A function key or a combination of keys that perform a command when pressed
e. Text or a graphic that jumps the reader to a different location or program when clicked
f. An informal journal that is available to the public on the Internet
g. User-defined details about a file that describe its contents and origin
h. Feature used to suggest synonyms for words
i. Command used to remove text from a document and place it on the Clipboard

Select the best answer from the list of choices.

15. Which of the following statements is *not* true?

a. You can view the contents of the Office Clipboard.

b. The Office Clipboard can hold more than one item.

c. The last item cut or copied from a document is stored on the system Clipboard.

d. When you move text by dragging it, a copy of the text you move is stored on the system Clipboard.

16. What is the keyboard shortcut for the Paste command?

a. [Ctrl][P]

b. [Ctrl][X]

c. [Ctrl][V]

d. [Ctrl][C]

17. Which command is used to display a document in two panes in the document window?

a. Split

b. New Window

c. Arrange All

d. Two Pages

18. To locate and highlight all instances of a word in a document, which command do you use?

a. Find

b. Search

c. Select

d. Replace

19. A hyperlink *cannot* be linked to which of the following?

a. ScreenTip

b. Document

c. Web page

d. E-mail address

20. Which of the following is an example of a document property?

a. Permission

b. URL

c. Language

d. Keyword

Skills Review

1. Cut and paste text.

a. Start Word, click the File tab, then open the file WMP B-2.docx from the drive and folder where you store your Data Files.

b. Save the document with the filename **WMP B-PHF 2013 PR**.

c. Select **Your Name** and replace it with your name.

d. Display paragraph and other formatting marks in your document if they are not already displayed.

e. Use the Cut and Paste buttons to switch the order of the two sentences in the fourth paragraph (which begins The famous children's entertainer...).

f. Use the drag-and-drop method to switch the order of the second and third paragraphs.

g. Adjust the spacing if necessary so that there is one blank line between paragraphs, then save your changes.

2. Copy and paste text.

a. Use the Copy and Paste buttons to copy **PHF 2011** from the headline and paste it before the word **map** in the third paragraph.

b. Change the formatting of the pasted text to match the formatting of the third paragraph, then insert a space between **2011** and **map** if necessary.

c. Use the drag-and-drop method to copy **PHF** from the third paragraph and paste it before the word **stage** in the second sentence of the fourth paragraph, then save your changes.

3. Use the Office Clipboard.

a. Use the launcher in the Clipboard group to open the Clipboard task pane.

b. Scroll so that the first body paragraph is displayed at the top of the document window.

c. Select the fifth paragraph (which begins Health fair maps...) and cut it to the Office Clipboard.

d. Select the third paragraph (which begins Portsmouth is easily accessible...) and cut it to the Office Clipboard.

e. Use the Office Clipboard to paste the Health fair maps... item as the new fourth paragraph.

f. Use the Office Clipboard to paste the Portsmouth is easily accessible... item as the new fifth paragraph.

g. Adjust the spacing if necessary so there is one blank line between each of the six body paragraphs.

h. Turn off the display of formatting marks, clear and close the Office Clipboard, then save your changes.

Skills Review (continued)

4. Find and replace text.

  a. Using the Replace command, replace all instances of **2011** with **2013**.

  b. Replace all instances of **eighth** with **tenth**.

  c. Replace all instances of the abbreviation **st** with **street**, taking care to replace whole words only when you perform the replace. (*Hint*: Deselect Match case if it is selected.)

  d. Use the Find tab in the Find and Replace dialog box to find all instances of **st** in the document and to make sure no errors occurred when you replaced st with street. (*Hint*: Deselect the Find whole words only check box.)

  e. Save your changes to the press release.

5. Check spelling and grammar and research information.

  a. Switch to the Review tab.

  b. Move the insertion point to the top of the document, then use the Spelling and Grammar command to search for and correct any spelling and grammar errors in the press release.

  c. Use the Thesaurus to replace **famous** in the third paragraph with a different suitable word.

  d. Check the word count of the press release body text.

  e. Proofread your press release, correct any errors, then save your changes.

6. Add hyperlinks.

  a. Save the document as **WMP B-PHF 2013 PR Public**, then switch to the Insert tab.

  b. Select your name, then open the Insert Hyperlink dialog box.

  c. Create a hyperlink to your e-mail address with the subject **PHF 2013**.

  d. Test the your name hyperlink, then close the message window that opens. (*Hint*: Press [Ctrl], then click the hyperlink.)

  e. Select **NIH** in the last paragraph of the press release, then create a hyperlink to the Web page with the URL **www.nih.gov**.

  f. Right-click the NIH hyperlink, then edit the hyperlink ScreenTip to become **Information on the National Institutes of Health**.

  g. Point to the NIH hyperlink to view the new ScreenTip, then save your changes.

  h. If you are working with an active Internet connection, press [Ctrl], click the NIH hyperlink, view the NIH home page in the browser window, then close the browser window.

7. Work with document properties.

  a. Click the File tab, click the Properties button in the preview pane, then open the Document Properties panel to view the document properties for the press release.

  b. Click the File tab to return to Backstage view with the Info tab displayed, then use the Check for Issues command to run the Document Inspector.

  c. Remove the document property data, click the Home tab, close the Document Properties panel, then save your changes. The finished press release is shown in Figure B-18.

  d. Save the document, submit it to your instructor, close the file, then exit Word.

FIGURE B-18

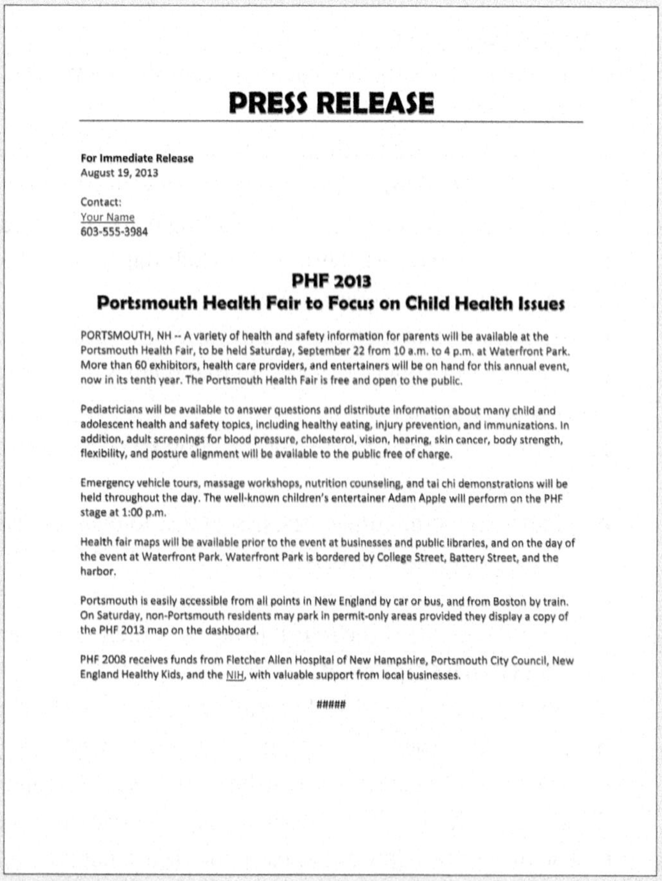

PRESS RELEASE

For Immediate Release
August 19, 2013

Contact:
Your Name
603-555-3984

PHF 2013
Portsmouth Health Fair to Focus on Child Health Issues

PORTSMOUTH, NH -- A variety of health and safety information for parents will be available at the Portsmouth Health Fair, to be held Saturday, September 22 from 10 a.m. to 4 p.m. at Waterfront Park. More than 60 exhibitors, health care providers, and entertainers will be on hand for this annual event, now in its tenth year. The Portsmouth Health Fair is free and open to the public.

Pediatricians will be available to answer questions and distribute information about many child and adolescent health and safety topics, including healthy eating, injury prevention, and immunizations. In addition, adult screenings for blood pressure, cholesterol, vision, hearing, skin cancer, body strength, flexibility, and posture alignment will be available to the public free of charge.

Emergency vehicle tours, massage workshops, nutrition counseling, and tai chi demonstrations will be held throughout the day. The well-known children's entertainer Adam Apple will perform on the PHF stage at 1:00 p.m.

Health fair maps will be available prior to the event at businesses and public libraries, and on the day of the event at Waterfront Park. Waterfront Park is bordered by College Street, Battery Street, and the harbor.

Portsmouth is easily accessible from all points in New England by car or bus, and from Boston by train. On Saturday, non-Portsmouth residents may park in permit-only areas provided they display a copy of the PHF 2013 map on the dashboard.

PHF 2008 receives funds from Fletcher Allen Hospital of New Hampshire, Portsmouth City Council, New England Healthy Kids, and the NIH, with valuable support from local businesses.

#####

Independent Challenge 1

Dr. Callahan, a physician in your office, is leaving her practice at Buffalo General Hospital for a practice at another hospital in Buffalo. She asks you to draft a letter to her patients informing them of the move. You'll create a change of address letter for Dr. Callahan by modifying a letter you wrote for another doctor.

a. Start Word, open the file WMP B-3.docx from the drive and folder where you store your Data Files, then save it as **WMP B-Change of Address Letter**. 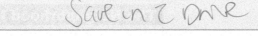 Save as

b. Replace the doctor's name and address, the date, the inside address, and the salutation with the text shown in Figure B-19.

FIGURE B-19   Save in Z Drive

Word 2010

Beatrice Callahan, M.D.
878 Elmwood Avenue, Buffalo, NY 14642; Tel: 585-555-8374

April 14, 2013

Mr. Merrill Frank
263 Montgomery Street
Buffalo, NY 14632

Dear Mr. Frank:

c. Use the Replace command to replace all instances of **Saint Mary's** with **Buffalo General**.

d. In the second body paragraph, replace the text **1478 Portland Street** with **878 Elmwood Avenue**.

e. Use the Find command to locate the word **superb**, then use the Thesaurus to replace the word with a synonym.

f. Create an AutoCorrect entry that inserts **Lake Memorial Hospital of the University of Buffalo** whenever you type **lmh**.

g. Select each instance of Highland Hospital, type **lmh** followed by a space, then delete the extra space before the period.

h. Move the last sentence of the first body paragraph so that it becomes the first sentence of the third body paragraph, adjusting the space as needed.

i. Replace Kate Champlain with **Beatrice Callahan** in the signature block, then replace the typists initials yi with your initials.

j. Use the Spelling and Grammar command to check for and correct spelling and grammar errors.

k. Delete the AutoCorrect entry you created for lmh. (*Hint*: Open the AutoCorrect dialog box, select the AutoCorrect entry you created, then click [Delete].)

Advanced Challenge Exercise

- Open the Document Properties panel, add your name as the author, change the title to **Beatrice Callahan, M.D.**, add the keywords **address change**, then add the comment **Change of address letter**.
- Open the Properties dialog box, review the properties on the Summary tab, then review the paragraph, line, word, and character count on the Statistics tab.
- On the Custom tab, add a property named **Office** with the value **Address Change**, then close the dialog box and the Document Properties panel.

l. Proofread the letter, correct any errors, save your changes, submit a copy to your instructor, close the document, then exit Word.

Independent Challenge 2

An advertisement for job openings in San Francisco caught your eye and you have decided to apply. The ad, shown in Figure B-20, was printed in last weekend's edition of your local newspaper. Instead of writing a cover letter from scratch, you revise a draft of a cover letter you wrote several years ago for a summer internship position.

a. Read the ad shown in Figure B-20 and decide for which position to apply. Choose the position that most closely matches your qualifications.

b. Start Word, open WMP B-4.docx from the drive and folder where you store your Data Files, then save it as **WMP B-Cover Letter**.

c. Replace the name, address, telephone number, and e-mail address in the letterhead with your own information.

d. Remove the hyperlink from the e-mail address.

e. Replace the date with today's date, then replace the inside address and the salutation with the information shown in Figure B-20.

f. Read the draft cover letter to get a feel for its contents.

g. Rework the text in the body of the letter to address your qualifications for the job you have chosen to apply for in the following ways:
- Delete the third paragraph.
- Adjust the first sentence of the first paragraph as follows: specify the job you are applying for, including the position code, and indicate where you saw the position advertised.
- Move the first sentence in the last paragraph, which briefly states your qualifications and interest in the position, to the end of the first paragraph, then rework the sentence to describe your current qualifications.
- Adjust the second paragraph as follows: describe your work experience and skills. Be sure to relate your experience and qualifications to the position requirements listed in the advertisement. Add a third paragraph if your qualifications are extensive.
- Adjust the final paragraph as follows: politely request an interview for the position and provide your phone number and e-mail address.

h. Include your name in the signature block.

i. When you are finished revising the letter, check it for spelling and grammar errors, and correct any mistakes. Make sure to remove any hyperlinks.

j. Save your changes to the letter, submit the file to your instructor, close the document, then exit Word.

FIGURE B-20

Bay Area Health
The Neighborhood Health Center

Bay Area Comprehensive Community Health Center (BACCHC), offering quality health care to the San Francisco community for over thirty years, is seeking candidates for the following positions:

Registered Nurses
Openings in Adult Medicine and Pediatrics. Must have two years of nursing experience. Current RN license and CPR required. **Position B12C6**

Laboratory Technician
Perform a variety of routine laboratory tests and procedures. Certification as MLT (ASCP) required, plus two years work experience. **Position C14B5**

Correspondence Coordinator
Process all correspondence mail in our medical records department. Must have knowledge of HIPAA regulations. Fluency with Microsoft Word required. **Position C13D4**

Medical Assistant
Maintain patient flow, assist physicians using sterile techniques, and educate patients on health issues. Must enjoy interacting with patients and be proficient with Microsoft Word. MA certification preferred. CPR required. **Position B16F5**

Positions offer competitive compensation, outstanding benefits, and career growth opportunities.

Send resume and cover letter referencing position code to:

Katherine Winn
Director of Human Resources
Bay Area Comprehensive Community Health Center
3826 Sacramento Street
San Francisco, CA 94118
Fax to 415-555-2939 or Email to hr@lcchc.com

Independent Challenge 3

As director of public education at Haven Community Hospital, you drafted a memo to the nursing staff asking them to help you finalize the schedule for the Healthy Living seminar series, which is presented by the nursing staff. Today, you'll examine the draft and make revisions before distributing it as an e-mail attachment.

a. Start Word, open the file WMP B-5.docx from the drive and folder where you store your Data Files, then save it as **WMP B-Healthy Living Memo**.

b. Replace Your Name with your name in the From line, then scroll down until the first body paragraph is at the top of the screen.

Advanced Challenge Exercise

- Use the Split command on the View tab to split the window under the first body paragraph, then scroll until the last paragraph of the memo is displayed in the bottom pane.
- Use the Cut and Paste buttons to move the sentence **If you are planning to lead...** from the first body paragraph to become the first sentence in the last paragraph of the memo.
- Double-click the split bar to restore the window to a single pane.

c. Use the [Delete] key to merge the first two paragraphs into one paragraph.

d. Use the Office Clipboard to reorganize the list of brown bag lunch topics so that the topics are listed in alphabetical order, then clear and close the Office Clipboard.

e. Use the drag-and-drop method to reorganize the list of Saturday morning lectures so that the lectures are listed in alphabetical order.

f. Select the phrase "Web site" in the first paragraph, then create a hyperlink to the URL **www.course.com** with the ScreenTip **2014 Healthy Living Series Schedule**.

g. Select "e-mail me" in the last paragraph, then create a hyperlink to your e-mail address with the subject **Final Healthy Living Series Schedule**.

h. Use the Spelling and Grammar command to check for and correct spelling and grammar errors. Be sure to read each choice and to make decisions based on the content of the memo.

i. Use the Document Inspector to strip the document of document property information, ignore any other content that is flagged by the Document Inspector, then close the Document Inspector.

j. Proofread the memo, correct any errors, save your changes, submit a copy to your instructor, close the document, then exit Word.

Real Life Independent Challenge

This Independent Challenge requires an Internet connection.

Reference sources—dictionaries, thesauri, style and grammar guides, and guides to business etiquette and procedure—are essential for day-to-day use in the workplace. Much of this reference information is available on the World Wide Web. In this independent challenge, you will locate general and medical reference sources on the Web and use some of them to look up medical terms. Your goal is to familiarize yourself with online reference sources so you can use them later in your work.

a. Start Word, open the file WMP B-6.docx from the drive and folder where you store your Data Files, then save it as **WMP B-Web Reference Sources**. This document contains the questions you will answer about the Web reference sources you find. You will type your answers to the questions in the document.

b. Replace the placeholder text at the top of the Web Reference Sources document with your name and the date.

c. Use your favorite search engine to search the Web for grammar and style guides, dictionaries, and thesauri. Use the keywords **grammar**, **usage**, **medical dictionary**, **glossary**, and **thesaurus** to conduct your search.

d. Complete the Web Reference Sources document, then proofread it and correct any mistakes.

e. Save the document, submit a copy to your instructor, close the document, then exit Word.

Visual Workshop

Open WMP B-7.docx from the drive and folder where you store your Data Files, then save the document as **WMP B-Termination Letter**. Replace the placeholders for the date, letterhead, inside address, salutation, and closing with the information shown in Figure B-21, then use the Office Clipboard to reorganize the sentences to match Figure B-21. Correct spelling and grammar errors, remove the document property information from the file, then submit a copy to your instructor.

FIGURE B-21

Your Name, M.D.
682 East 8th Avenue, Portland, ME 04105; Tel: 207-555-1728

12/9/2013

Mr. James Bush
44 Harbor Street
Portland, ME 04123

Dear Mr. Bush:

As a result of a change in our insurance affiliations, I am no longer able to provide medical care to you as your dermatologist. Consequently, you should identify another physician to assume your care.

If you have not received a referral to another provider or if you wish to contact a provider who has not previously cared for you, contact your primary care physician. You may also contact the Cumberland County Medical Society at 207-555-2983.

I will remain available to treat you for a limited time, not to exceed thirty (30) days from the date of this letter. Please try to transfer your care as soon as possible within this period. In the event you have an emergency prior to your transfer of care to another provider, you may contact me through my office.

Copies of your medical record will be sent to the new provider you have selected, upon receipt of your written authorization. A copy of a release form is enclosed for you to complete and return to this office, allowing the record to be transferred.

Sincerely,

Your Name, M.D.

Enc.
Certified Mail, Return Receipt Request
Mailed on December 9, 2013

Formatting Text and Paragraphs

Files You Will Need:

WMP C-1.docx
WMP C-2.docx
WMP C-3.docx
WMP C-4.docx
WMP C-5.docx
WMP C-6.docx

Formatting can enhance the appearance of a document, create visual impact, and help illustrate a document's structure. The formatting of a document can also set a tone, allowing readers to know at a glance if the document is business-like, informal, or fun. In this unit you learn how to format text using fonts and a variety of paragraph-formatting effects, such as borders, shading, and bullets. You also learn how to illustrate a document with clip art.  You have finished drafting the text for an information sheet on the flu to distribute to patients. Now, you need to format the information sheet so it is attractive and highlights the significant information.

OBJECTIVES

Format with fonts

Copy formats using the Format Painter

Change line and paragraph spacing

Align paragraphs

Work with tabs

Work with indents

Add bullets and numbering

Add borders and shading

Insert clip art

Formatting with Fonts

Formatting text with fonts is a quick and powerful way to enhance the appearance of a document. A **font** is a complete set of characters with the same typeface or design. Arial, Times New Roman, Courier, Tahoma, and Calibri are some of the more common fonts, but there are hundreds of others, each with a specific design and feel. Another way to change the appearance of text is to increase or decrease its **font size**. Font size is measured in points. A **point** is ¹/₇₂ of an inch. You change the font and font size of the body text, title, and headings in the information sheet. You select fonts and font sizes that enhance the tone of the document and help to structure the information visually for readers.

STEPS

1. **Start Word, open the file** WMP C-1.docx **from the drive and folder where you store your Data Files, then save it as** WMP C-Flu Info Sheet

   Notice that the name of the font used in the document, Calibri, is displayed in the Font list box in the Font group. The word "(Body)" in the Font list box indicates Calibri is the font used for body text in the current theme, the default theme. A **theme** is a related set of fonts, colors, styles, and effects that is applied to an entire document to give it a cohesive appearance. The font size, 11, appears in the Font Size list box in the Font group.

2. **Scroll the document to get a feel for its contents, press** [Ctrl][Home], **press** [Ctrl][A] **to select the entire document, then click the** Font list arrow **in the Font group**

   The Font list, which shows the fonts available on your computer, opens as shown in Figure C-1. The font names are formatted in the font. Font names can appear in more than one location on the font list.

3. **Drag the pointer slowly down the font names in the Font list, drag the scroll box to scroll down the Font list, then click** Garamond

   Dragging the pointer down the font list allows you to preview how the selected text will look in the highlighted font. Clicking a font name applies the font. The font of the flyer changes to Garamond.

4. **Click the** Font Size list arrow **in the Font group, drag the pointer slowly up and down the Font Size list, then click** 12

   Dragging the pointer over the font sizes allows you to preview how the selected text will look in the highlighted font size. Clicking 12 increases the font size of the selected text to 12 points.

5. **Select the title** Riverwalk Medical Clinic Influenza Information Sheet, **click the** Font list arrow, **scroll to and click** Trebuchet MS, **click the** Font Size list arrow, **click** 22, **then click the** Bold button B **in the Font group**

   The title is formatted in 22-point Trebuchet MS bold.

6. **Click the** Font Color list arrow A **in the Font group**

   A gallery of colors opens. It includes the set of theme colors in a range of tints and shades as well as a set of standard colors. You can point to a color in the gallery to preview it applied to the selected text.

7. **Click** Purple, Accent 4, Darker 25% **as shown in Figure C-2, then deselect the text**

   The color of the title text changes to purple. The active color on the Font Color button also changes to purple.

8. **Select the heading** Flu Vaccine, **then, using the Mini toolbar, click the** Font list arrow, **click** Trebuchet MS, **click the** Font Size list arrow, **click** 14, **click** A, **click** B, **then deselect the text**

   The heading is formatted in 14-point Trebuchet MS bold with a purple color. Notice that when you use the buttons on the Mini toolbar to format text, you cannot preview the formatting options in the document.

9. **Press** [Ctrl][Home], **then click the** Save button 📁 **on the Quick Access toolbar**

   Compare your document to Figure C-3.

Formatting Text and Paragraphs

FIGURE C-1: Font list

Fonts used in the default theme

List of recently used fonts (your list may differ)

Alphabetical list of all fonts on your computer (your list may differ)

Font list arrow

Font Size list arrow

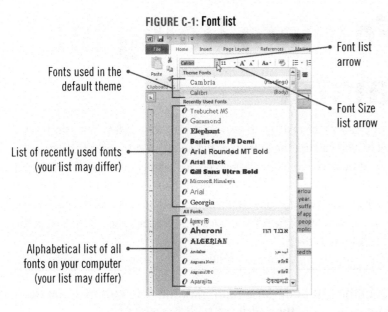

FIGURE C-2: Font Color Palette

Font Color list arrow

Name of color appears as a ScreenTip

Click to create a custom color

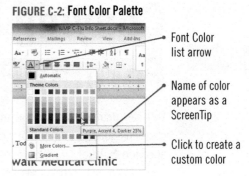

FIGURE C-3: Document formatted with fonts

Title formatted in 22-point Trebuchet MS, bold, purple

Body text formatted in 12-point Garamond

Heading formatted in 14-point Trebuchet MS, bold, purple

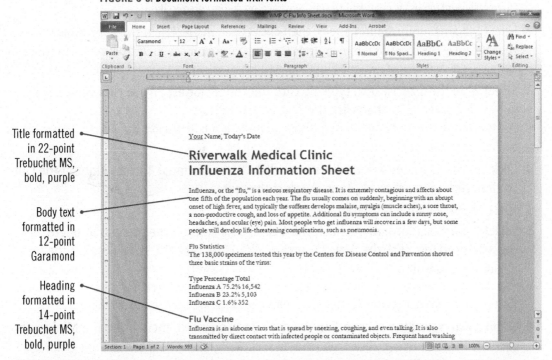

Adding a drop cap

A fun way to illustrate a document with fonts is to add a drop cap to a paragraph. A **drop cap** is a large initial capital letter, often used to set off the first paragraph of an article. To create a drop cap, place the insertion point in the paragraph you want to format, click the Insert tab, and then click the Drop Cap button in the Text group to open a menu of Drop cap options. Preview and select one of the options on the menu, or click Drop Cap Options to open the Drop Cap dialog box, shown in Figure C-4. In the Drop Cap dialog box, select the position, font, number of lines to drop, and the distance you want the drop cap to be from the paragraph text, and then click OK. The drop cap is added to the paragraph as a graphic object.

Once a drop cap is inserted in a paragraph, you can modify it by selecting it and then changing the settings in the Drop Cap dialog box. For even more interesting effects, you can enhance a drop cap with font color, font styles, or font effects. You can also fill the graphic object with shading or add a border around it. To enhance a drop cap, first select it, and then experiment with the formatting options available in the Font dialog box and in the Borders and Shading dialog box.

FIGURE C-4: Drop Cap dialog box

Drop Cap

Position

None   Dropped   In margin

Options

Font:
Garamond

Lines to drop: 3

Distance from text: 0"

OK   Cancel

Copying Formats Using the Format Painter

You can dramatically change the appearance of text by applying different font styles, font effects, and character-spacing effects. For example, you can use the buttons in the Font group to make text darker by applying **bold** or to make text slanted by applying **italic**. When you are satisfied with the formatting of certain text, you can quickly apply the same formats to other text using the Format Painter. The **Format Painter** is a powerful Word feature that allows you to copy all the format settings applied to selected text to other text that you want to format the same way. You spice up the appearance of the text in the document by applying different font styles and effects.

STEPS

1. **Select extremely contagious in the first body paragraph, click the Bold button B on the Mini toolbar, select the entire paragraph, then click the Italic button I**

   "Extremely contagious" is bold, and the entire paragraph is formatted in italic.

QUICK TIP

To change the case of selected text from lowercase to uppercase—and visa versa—click the Change Case button in the Font group, and then select the case style you want to use.

2. **Select Influenza Information Sheet, then click the launcher in the Font group**

   The Font dialog box opens, as shown in Figure C-5. You can use options on the Font tab to change the font, font style, size, and color of text, and to add an underline and apply font effects to text.

3. **Select 22 in the Size list box, type 42, click the Font color list arrow, click Olive Green, Accent 3, Darker 25%, then click the Text Effects button**

   The Format Text Effects dialog box opens. You use this dialog box to apply text effects, such as shadows, outlines, and reflections, to text.

4. **Click Shadow, click the Presets list arrow, click Offset Diagonal Bottom Right in the Outer section, click Close, click OK, then deselect the text**

   The text is larger, green, and has a shadow effect.

5. **Select Influenza Information Sheet, right-click, click Font on the menu that opens, click the Advanced tab, click the Scale list arrow, click 80%, click OK, then deselect the text**

   You use the Advanced tab in the Font dialog box to change the scale, or width, of the selected characters, to alter the spacing between characters, or to raise or lower the characters. Decreasing the scale of the characters makes them narrower and gives the text a tall, thin appearance, as shown in Figure C-6.

6. **Scroll down, select the subheading When to Be Vaccinated, then, using the Mini toolbar, click the Font list arrow, click Trebuchet MS, click B, click I, click the Font Color list arrow A ▾, click Olive Green, Accent 3, Darker 25%, then deselect the text**

   The subheading is formatted in Trebuchet MS, bold, italic, and green.

TROUBLE

Move the pointer over the document text to see the pointer.

7. **Select When to Be Vaccinated, then click the Format Painter button in the Clipboard group**

   The pointer changes to ▨I.

8. **Scroll down, select Who Should Be Vaccinated with the ▨I pointer, then deselect the text**

   The subheading is formatted in Trebuchet MS, bold, italic, and green, as shown in Figure C-7.

9. **Scroll up as needed, select Flu Vaccine, then double-click**

   Double-clicking the Format Painter button allows the Format Painter to remain active until you turn it off. By keeping the Format Painter active, you can apply formatting to multiple items.

QUICK TIP

You can also press [Esc] to turn off the Format Painter.

10. **Scroll down, select the headings Prevention, Treatment, and Medications with the ▨I pointer, click to turn off the Format Painter, then save your changes**

    The headings are formatted in 14-point Trebuchet MS bold with a purple font color.

Formatting Text and Paragraphs

FIGURE C-5: Font tab in Font dialog box

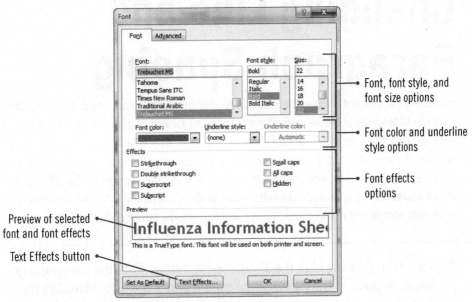

Font, font style, and font size options

Font color and underline style options

Font effects options

Preview of selected font and font effects

Text Effects button

FIGURE C-6: Font and character spacing effects applied to text

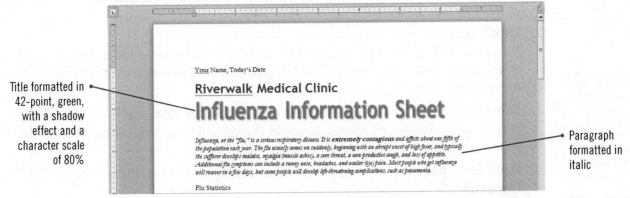

Title formatted in 42-point, green, with a shadow effect and a character scale of 80%

Paragraph formatted in italic

FIGURE C-7: Formats copied and applied using the Format Painter

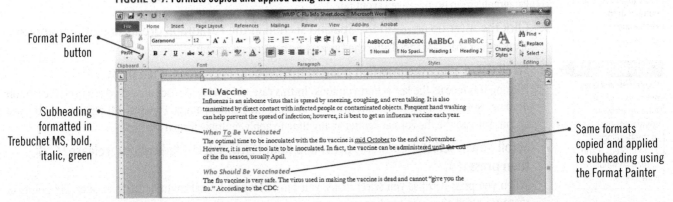

Format Painter button

Subheading formatted in Trebuchet MS, bold, italic, green

Same formats copied and applied to subheading using the Format Painter

Underlining text

Another creative way to call attention to text and to jazz up the appearance of a document is to apply an underline style to words you want to highlight. The Underline list arrow in the Font group displays straight, dotted, wavy, dashed, and mixed underline styles, along with a gallery of colors from which to choose. To apply an underline to text, simply select it, click the Underline list arrow, and then select an underline style from the list. For a wider variety of underline styles, click More Underlines in the list, and then select an underline style in the Font dialog box. You can change the color of an underline at any time by selecting the underlined text, clicking the Underline list arrow, pointing to Underline Color, and then choosing from the options in the color gallery. If you want to remove an underline from text, select the underlined text, and then click the Underline button.

Changing Line and Paragraph Spacing

Increasing the amount of space between lines adds more white space to a document and can make it easier to read. Adding space before and after paragraphs can also open up a document and improve its appearance. You use the Line and Paragraph Spacing list arrow in the Paragraph group on the Home tab to quickly change line spacing. To change paragraph spacing, you use the Spacing options in the Paragraph group on the Page Layout tab. Line and paragraph spacing are measured in points. ▓▓▓▓ You increase the line spacing of several paragraphs and add extra space under each heading to give the flyer a more open feel. You work with formatting marks turned on, so you can see the paragraph marks (¶).

STEPS

1. **Press [Ctrl][Home], click the** Show/Hide ¶ button **¶ in the Paragraph group, place the insertion point in the italicized paragraph under the title, then click the** Line and Paragraph Spacing list arrow **‡≡▾ in the Paragraph group on the Home tab**

   The Line Spacing list opens. This list includes options for increasing the space between lines. The check mark on the Line Spacing list indicates the current line spacing.

2. **Click** 1.15

   The space between the lines in the paragraph increases to 1.15 lines. Notice that you do not need to select an entire paragraph to change its paragraph formatting; simply place the insertion point in the paragraph you want to format.

QUICK TIP
Word recognizes any string of text that ends with a paragraph mark as a paragraph, including titles, headings, and single lines in a list.

3. **Select the** four-line list **that begins with "Type Percentage Total", click** ‡≡▾**, then click** 1.5

   The line spacing between the selected paragraphs changes to 1.5. To change the paragraph-formatting features of more than one paragraph, you must select the paragraphs.

4. **Scroll down, place the insertion point in the heading** Flu Vaccine**, then click the** Page Layout tab

   The paragraph spacing settings for the active paragraph are shown in the Before and After text boxes in the Paragraph group on the Page Layout tab.

QUICK TIP
You can also type a number in the Before and After text boxes.

5. **Click the** After up arrow **in the Spacing section in the Paragraph group so that 6 pt appears**

   Six points of space are added after the Flu Vaccine heading paragraph.

TROUBLE
If your [F4] key does not work, use the After up arrow to apply 6 pts of space to the headings listed in Steps 6 and 7, then continue with Step 8.

6. **Scroll down, place the insertion point in the heading** Prevention**, then press [F4]**

   Pressing [F4] repeats the last action you took. In this case, six points of space are added after the Prevention heading. Note that using [F4] is not the same as using the Format painter. Pressing [F4] repeats only the last action. You can use the Format Painter at any time to apply multiple format settings.

7. **Scroll down, select** Treatment**, press and hold [Ctrl], select** Medications**, release [Ctrl], then press [F4]**

   When you press [Ctrl] as you select items, you can select and format multiple items at once. Six points of space are added after each heading.

QUICK TIP
Adjusting the space between paragraphs is a more precise way to add white space to a document than inserting blank lines.

8. **Press [Ctrl][Home], place the insertion point in** Influenza Information Sheet**, click the** Before up arrow **in the Spacing section in the Paragraph group twice so that 12 pt appears**

   The second line of the title has 12 points of space before it. Compare your document with Figure C-8.

9. **Click the** Home tab**, click** ¶**, then save your changes**

Formatting Text and Paragraphs

FIGURE C-8: Line and paragraph spacing applied to document

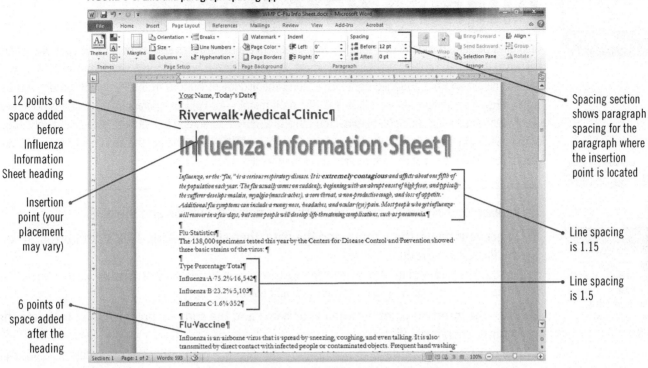

12 points of space added before Influenza Information Sheet heading

Insertion point (your placement may vary)

6 points of space added after the heading

Spacing section shows paragraph spacing for the paragraph where the insertion point is located

Line spacing is 1.15

Line spacing is 1.5

Formatting with Quick Styles

You can also apply multiple format settings to text in one step by applying a style. A **style** is a set of formats, such as font, font size, and paragraph alignment, that are named and stored together. Formatting a document with styles is a quick and easy way to give it a professional appearance. To make it even easier, Word includes sets of styles, called **Quick Styles**, that are designed to be used together in a document to make it attractive and readable. A Quick Style set includes styles for a title, several heading levels, body text, quotes, and lists. The styles in a Quick Style set use common fonts, colors, and formats so that using the styles together in a document gives the document a cohesive look.

To view the active set of Quick Styles, click the More button ⬇ in the Styles group on the Home tab to expand the Quick Styles gallery, shown in Figure C-9. As you move the pointer over each style in the gallery, a preview of the style is applied to the selected text. To apply a style to the selected text, you simply click the style in the Quick Styles gallery. To remove a style from selected text, you click the Clear Formatting button 🔲 in the Font group or in the Quick Styles gallery.

If you want to change the active set of Quick Styles to a Quick Style set with a different design, click the Change Styles button in the Styles group, point to Style Set, and then select the Quick Style set that best suits your document's content, tone, and audience.

When you change the Quick Style set, a complete set of new fonts and colors is applied to the entire document. You can also change the color scheme or font used in the active Quick Style set by clicking the Change Styles button, pointing to Colors or to Fonts, and then selecting from the available color schemes or font options.

FIGURE C-9: Quick Styles gallery

Aligning Paragraphs

Changing paragraph alignment is another way to enhance a document's appearance. Paragraphs are aligned relative to the left and right margins in a document. By default, text is **left-aligned**, which means it is flush with the left margin and has a ragged right edge. Using the alignment buttons in the Paragraph group, you can **right-align** a paragraph—make it flush with the right margin—or **center** a paragraph so that it is positioned evenly between the left and right margins. You can also **justify** a paragraph so that both the left and right edges of the paragraph are flush with the left and right margins. ▓▓▓▓ You change the alignment of several paragraphs at the beginning of the information sheet to make it more visually interesting.

STEPS

1. **Replace Your Name, Today's Date with your name, a comma, and the date**

2. **Select your name, the comma, and the date, then click the Align Text Right button ▤ in the Paragraph group**

    The text is aligned with the right margin. In Page Layout view, the place where the white and shaded sections of the horizontal ruler meet shows the left and right margins.

3. **Place the insertion point between your name and the comma, press [Delete] to delete the comma, then press [Enter]**

    The new paragraph containing the date is also right-aligned. Pressing [Enter] in the middle of a paragraph creates a new paragraph with the same text and paragraph formatting as the original paragraph.

4. **Select the two-line title, then click the Center button ▤ in the Paragraph group**

    The two paragraphs that make up the title are centered between the left and right margins.

5. **Scroll down as needed, place the insertion point in the Flu Vaccine heading, then click ▤**

    The Flu Vaccine heading is centered.

6. **Place the insertion point in the italicized paragraph under the title, then click the Justify button ▤ in the Paragraph group**

    The paragraph is aligned with both the left and right margins, as shown in Figure C-10. When you justify a paragraph, Word adjusts the spacing between words so that each line in the paragraph is flush with the left and the right margins.

7. **Place the insertion point in Flu Vaccine, then click the launcher ▣ in the Paragraph group**

    The Paragraph dialog box opens, as shown in Figure C-11. The Indents and Spacing tab shows the paragraph format settings for the paragraph where the insertion point is located. You can check or change paragraph format settings using this dialog box.

8. **Click the Alignment list arrow, click Left, click OK, then save your changes**

    The Flu Vaccine heading is left-aligned.

Formatting Text and Paragraphs

FIGURE C-10: Modified paragraph alignment

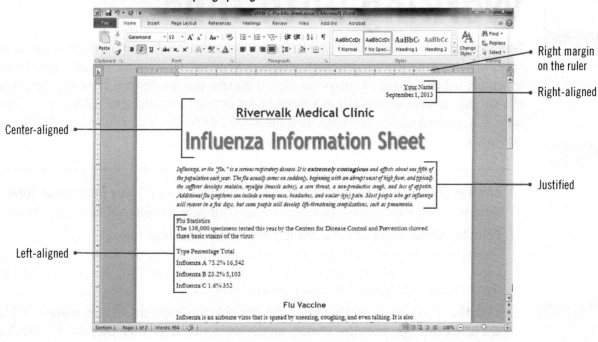

Center-aligned

Left-aligned

Right margin on the ruler

Right-aligned

Justified

FIGURE C-11: Indents and Spacing tab in Paragraph dialog box

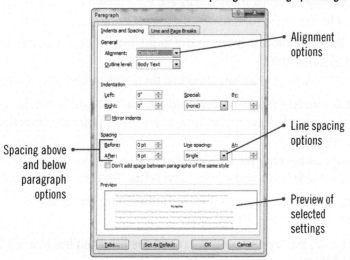

Spacing above and below paragraph options

Alignment options

Line spacing options

Preview of selected settings

Formatting a document using themes

Changing the theme applied to a document is another powerful and efficient way to tailor a document's look and feel, particularly when a document is formatted with a Quick Style set. By default, all documents created in Word are formatted with the default Office theme—which uses Calibri as the font for the body text—but you can change the theme at any time to fit the content, tone, and purpose of a document. When you change the theme for a document, a complete set of new theme colors, fonts, and effects is applied to the whole document.

To preview how various themes look when applied to the current document, click the Themes button in the Themes group on the Page Layout tab, and then move the pointer over each theme in the gallery and notice how the document changes. When you click the theme you like, all document content that uses theme colors, all text

that is formatted with a style, including default body text, and all table styles and graphic effects change to the colors, fonts, and effects used by the theme. In addition, the gallery of colors changes to display the set of theme colors, and the active Quick Style set changes to employ the theme colors and fonts. Note that changing the theme does not affect the formatting of text to which font formatting has already been applied, nor does it change any standard or custom colors used in the document.

If you want to tweak the document design further, you can modify it by applying a different set of theme colors, heading and body text fonts, or graphic effects. To do this, simply click the Theme Colors, Theme Fonts, or Theme Effects button in the Themes group, move the pointer over each option in the gallery to preview it in the document, and then click the option you like best.

Working with Tabs

Tabs allow you to align text at a specific location in a document. A **tab stop** is a point on the horizontal ruler that indicates the location at which to align text. By default, tab stops are located every ½" from the left margin, but you can also set custom tab stops. Using tabs, you can align text to the left, right, or center of a tab stop, or you can align text at a decimal point or insert a bar character. Table C-1 describes the different types of tab stops. You set tabs using the horizontal ruler or the Tabs dialog box. 🔲🔲🔲🔲🔲 You use tabs to format the statistical information on the flu so it is easy to read.

STEPS

1. Scroll as needed, then select the four-line list beginning with "Type Percentage Total"

Before you set tab stops for existing text, you must select the paragraphs for which you want to set tabs.

2. Point to the tab indicator 🔲 at the left end of the horizontal ruler

The icon that appears in the tab indicator indicates the active type of tab; pointing to the tab indicator displays a ScreenTip with the name of the active tab type. By default, left tab is the active tab type. Clicking the tab indicator scrolls through the types of tabs and indents.

3. Click the tab indicator to see each of the available tab and indent types, make Left Tab the active tab type, click the 1" mark on the horizontal ruler, then click the 3½" mark on the horizontal ruler

A left tab stop is inserted at the 1" mark and the 3½" on the horizontal ruler. Clicking the horizontal ruler inserts a tab stop of the active type for the selected paragraph or paragraphs.

4. Click the tab indicator twice so the Right Tab icon 🔲 is active, then click the 5" mark on the horizontal ruler

A right tab stop is inserted at the 5" mark on the horizontal ruler, as shown in Figure C-12.

5. Place the insertion point before Type in the first line in the list, press [Tab], place the insertion point before Percentage, press [Tab], place the insertion point before Total, then press [Tab]

Inserting a tab before "Type" left-aligns the text at the 1" mark, inserting a tab before "Percentage" left-aligns the text at the 3½" mark, and inserting a tab before "Total" right-aligns "Total" at the 5" mark.

6. Insert a tab at the beginning of each remaining line in the list

The paragraphs left-align at the 1" mark.

7. Insert a tab before each percentage in the list, then insert a tab before each total number in the list

The percentages left-align at the 3½" mark. The total numbers right-align at the 5" mark.

8. Select the four lines of tabbed text, drag the right tab stop to the 5½" mark on the horizontal ruler, then deselect the text

Dragging the tab stop moves it to a new location. The total numbers right-align at the 5½" mark.

9. Select the last three lines of tabbed text, click the launcher 🔲 in the Paragraph group, then click the Tabs button at the bottom of the Paragraph dialog box

The Tabs dialog box opens, as shown in Figure C-13. You can use the Tabs dialog box to set tab stops, change the position or alignment of existing tab stops, clear tab stops, and apply tab leaders to tabs. **Tab leaders** are lines that appear in front of tabbed text.

10. Click 3.5" in the Tab stop position list box, click the 2 option button in the Leader section, click Set, click 5.5" in the Tab stop position list box, click the 2 option button in the Leader section, click Set, click OK, deselect the text, then save your changes

A dotted tab leader is added before each 3.5" and 5.5" tab stop in the last three lines of tabbed text, as shown in Figure C-14.

Formatting Text and Paragraphs

FIGURE C-12: Left and right tab stops on the horizontal ruler

Left tab stops

Right Tab icon in tab indicator

Right tab stop

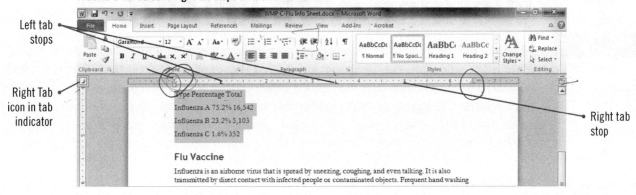

FIGURE C-13: Tabs dialog box

Select the tab stop you want to modify

Select Leader options

Apply the selected settings to the selected tab stop

Clears the selected tab stop

Clears all tab stops

Line Spacur Para

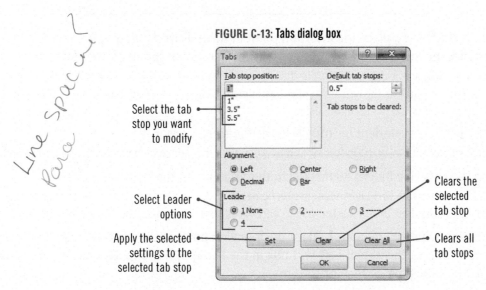

FIGURE C-14: Tab leaders

Tab leader

Tabbed text left-aligned with left tab stop

Tabbed text right-aligned with right tab stop

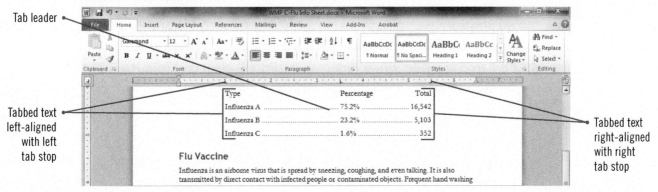

TABLE C-1: Types of tabs

tab	use to
Left tab	Set the start position of text so that text runs to the right of the tab stop as you type
Center tab	Set the center align position of text so that text stays centered on the tab stop as you type
Right tab	Set the right or end position of text so that text moves to the left of the tab stop as you type
Decimal tab	Set the position of the decimal point so that numbers align around the decimal point as you type
Bar tab	Insert a vertical bar at the tab position

Formatting Text and Paragraphs

Working with Indents

When you **indent** a paragraph, you move its edge in from the left or right margin. You can indent the entire left or right edge of a paragraph, just the first line, or all lines except the first line. The **indent markers** on the horizontal ruler indicate the indent settings for the paragraph in which the insertion point is located. Dragging an indent marker to a new location on the ruler is one way to change the indentation of a paragraph; changing the indent settings in the Paragraph group on the Page Layout tab is another; and using the indent buttons in the Paragraph group on the Home tab is a third. Table C-2 describes different types of indents and some of the methods for creating each. ▰▰▰ You indent several paragraphs in the information sheet.

STEPS

QUICK TIP
Press [Tab] at the beginning of a paragraph to indent the first line ½".

1. **Press [Ctrl][Home], place the insertion point in the italicized paragraph under the title, then click the Increase Indent button ▤ in the Paragraph group on the Home tab**
   The entire paragraph is indented ½" from the left margin, as shown in Figure C-15. The indent marker also moves to the ½" mark on the horizontal ruler. Each time you click the Increase Indent button, the left edge of a paragraph moves another ½" to the right.

2. **Click the Decrease Indent button ▤ in the Paragraph group**
   The left edge of the paragraph moves ½" to the left, and the indent marker moves back to the left margin.

TROUBLE
Take care to drag only the First Line Indent marker. If you make a mistake, click the Undo button ↺ on the Quick Access toolbar, then try again.

3. **Drag the First Line Indent marker ▽ to the ¼" mark on the horizontal ruler**
   Figure C-16 shows the First Line Indent marker being dragged. The first line of the paragraph is indented ¼". Dragging the First Line Indent marker indents only the first line of a paragraph.

4. **Scroll to the bottom of page 1, place the insertion point in the quotation, click the Page Layout tab, click the Indent Left text box in the Paragraph group, type .5, click the Indent Right text box, type .5, then press [Enter]**
   The left and right edges of the paragraph are indented ½" from the margins, as shown in Figure C-17.

5. **Press [Ctrl][Home], place the insertion point in the italicized paragraph, then click the launcher ▣ in the Paragraph group**
   The Paragraph dialog box opens. You can use the Indents and Spacing tab to check or change the alignment, indentation, and paragraph and line spacing settings applied to a paragraph.

6. **Click the Special list arrow, click (none), click OK, then save your changes**
   The first line indent is removed from the paragraph.

Clearing formatting

If you are unhappy with the way text is formatted, you can use the Clear Formatting command to return the text to the default format settings. The default format includes font and paragraph formatting: text is formatted in 11-point Calibri, and paragraphs are left-aligned with 1.15 point line spacing, 10 points of space below, and no indents. To clear formatting from text and return it to the default format, select the text you want to clear, and then click the Clear Formatting button in the Font group on the Home tab. If you prefer to return the text to the default font and remove all paragraph formatting, making the text 11-point Calibri, left-aligned, single spaced, with no paragraph spacing or indents, select the text and then simply click the No Spacing button in the Styles group on the Home tab.

Formatting Text and Paragraphs

FIGURE C-15: Indented paragraph

First Line Indent marker

Hanging Indent marker

Left Indent marker

Increase Indent button

Decrease Indent button

Right Indent marker

Indented paragraph

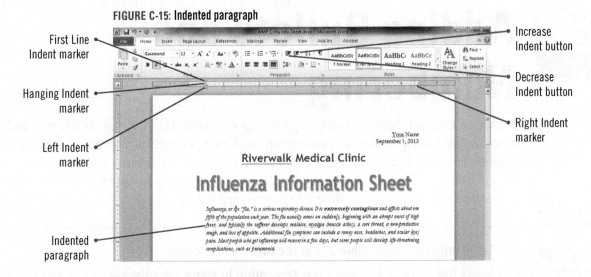

FIGURE C-16: Dragging the First Line Indent marker

First Line Indent marker being dragged to the ¼" mark

Dotted line shows position of First Line Indent marker

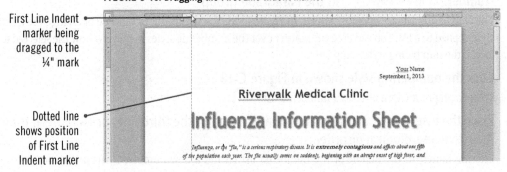

FIGURE C-17: Paragraph indented from the left and right

Paragraph indented ½" from left margin

Paragraph indented ½" from right margin

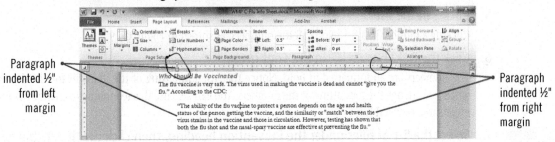

TABLE C-2: Types of indents

indent type: description	to create
Left indent: The left edge of a paragraph is moved in from the left margin	Drag the Left Indent marker ⬚ on the ruler to the right to the position where you want the left edge of the paragraph to align
Right indent: The right edge of a paragraph is moved in from the right margin	Drag the Right Indent marker △ on the ruler to the left to the position where you want the right edge of the paragraph to align
First line indent: The first line of a paragraph is indented more than the subsequent lines	Drag the First Line Indent marker ▽ on the ruler to the right to the position where you want the first line of the paragraph to begin; or activate the First Line Indent marker ▽ in the tab indicator, and then click the ruler at the position where you want the first line of the paragraph to begin
Hanging indent: The subsequent lines of a paragraph are indented more than the first line	Drag the Hanging Indent marker △ on the ruler to the right to the position where you want the hanging indent to begin; or activate the Hanging Indent marker ▭ in the tab indicator, and then click the ruler at the position where you want the second and remaining lines of the paragraph to begin
Negative indent (or Outdent): The left edge of a paragraph is moved to the left of the left margin	Drag the Left Indent marker ⬚ on the ruler to the left to the position where you want the negative indent to begin

Formatting Text and Paragraphs

Adding Bullets and Numbering

Formatting a list with bullets or numbering can help to organize the ideas in a document. A **bullet** is a character, often a small circle, that appears before the items in a list to add emphasis. Formatting a list as a numbered list helps illustrate sequences and priorities. You can quickly format a list with bullets or numbering by using the Bullets and Numbering buttons in the Paragraph group on the Home tab. ▰▰▰▰▰ You format the lists in the information sheet with numbers and bullets.

STEPS

QUICK TIP

To change the style, font, number format, and alignment of the numbers in a list, right-click the list, point to Numbering, then click Define New Number Format.

1. **Scroll until the top of page 2 is at the top of your screen**

2. **Select the four-line list above the Prevention heading, click the Home tab, then click the Numbering list arrow 📋▾ in the Paragraph group**

   The Numbering Library opens, as shown in Figure C-18. You use this list to choose or change the numbering style applied to a list. You can drag the pointer over the numbering styles to preview how the selected text will look if the numbering style is applied.

3. **Click the numbering style shown in Figure C-18**

   The paragraphs are formatted as a numbered list.

QUICK TIP

To remove a bullet or number, select the paragraph(s), then click 📋 or 📋.

4. **Place the insertion point after vaccine at the end of the third line, press [Enter], then type An active neurological disorder**

   Pressing [Enter] in the middle of the numbered list creates a new numbered paragraph and automatically renumbers the remainder of the list. Similarly, if you delete a paragraph from a numbered list, Word automatically renumbers the remaining paragraphs.

5. **Click 1 in the list**

   Clicking a number in a list selects all the numbers, as shown in Figure C-19.

6. **Click the Bold button B in the Font group**

   The numbers are all formatted in bold. Notice that the formatting of the items in the list does not change when you change the formatting of the numbers. You can also use this technique to change the formatting of bullets in a bulleted list.

QUICK TIP

To use a symbol or a picture for a bullet character, click Define New Bullet in the Bullet list, and then select from the options in the Define New Bullet dialog box.

7. **Select the list of rules under the Prevention heading, then click the Bullets button 📋 in the Paragraph group**

   The five paragraphs are formatted as a bulleted list using the most recently used bullet style.

8. **Click a bullet in the list to select all the bullets, click the Bullets list arrow 📋▾ in the Paragraph group, click the check mark bullet style, click the document to deselect the text, then save your changes**

   The bullet character changes to a check mark, as shown in Figure C-20.

Creating multilevel lists

You can create lists with hierarchical structures by applying a multilevel list style to a list. To create a **multilevel list**, also called an outline, begin by applying a multilevel list style using the Multilevel List list arrow 📋▾ in the Paragraph group on the Home tab, then type your outline, pressing [Enter] after each item. To demote items to a lower level of importance in the outline, place the insertion point in the item, then click the Increase Indent button 📋 in the Paragraph group on the Home tab. Each time you indent a paragraph, the item is demoted to a lower level in the outline. Similarly, you can use the Decrease Indent button 📋 to promote an item to a higher level in the outline. You can also create a hierarchical structure in any bulleted or numbered list by using 📋 and 📋 to demote and promote items in the list. To change the multilevel list style applied to a list, select the list, click 📋, and then select a new style.

Formatting Text and Paragraphs

FIGURE C-18: Numbering list

Numbering list arrow

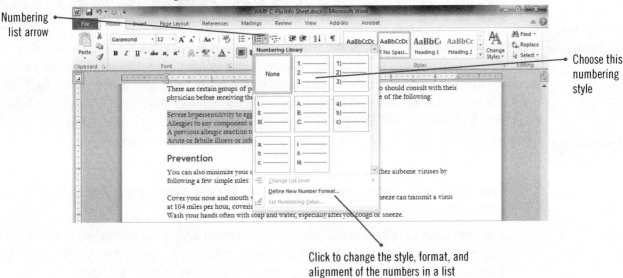

Choose this numbering style

Click to change the style, format, and alignment of the numbers in a list

FIGURE C-19: Numbered list

Bullets button

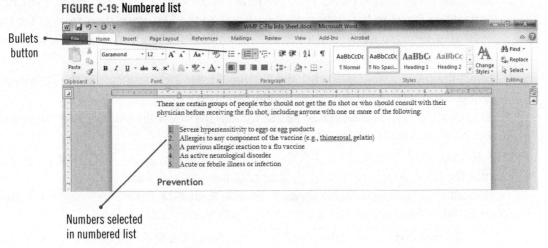

Numbers selected in numbered list

FIGURE C-20: Check mark bullets applied to the list

Numbers are bold

Check mark bullets applied to list

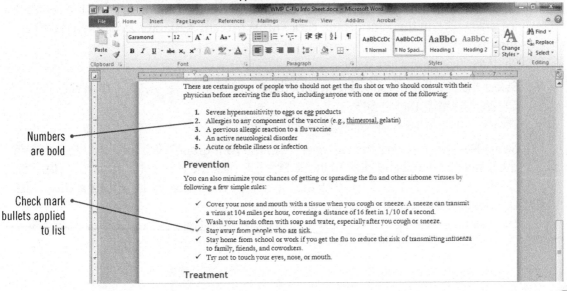

Formatting Text and Paragraphs

Adding Borders and Shading

Borders and shading can add color and splash to a document. **Borders** are lines you add above, below, to the side, or around words or paragraphs. You can format borders using different line styles, colors, and widths. **Shading** is a color or pattern you apply behind words or paragraphs to make them stand out on a page. You apply borders and shading using the Borders button and the Shading button in the Paragraph group on the Home tab. ▓▓▓▓ You enhance the Flu Statistics information by adding shading to it. You also apply a border around the tabbed text to set it off from the rest of the document.

STEPS

1. **Press [Ctrl][Home], then scroll down until the Flu Statistics heading is at the top of your screen**

2. **Click and drag to select** Flu Statistics, **the paragraph and blank line below it, and the four paragraphs of tabbed text; click the Shading list arrow** ▒▾ **in the Paragraph group on the Home tab, click** Purple, Accent 4, Lighter 60%, **then deselect the text**
   Light purple shading is applied to the seven paragraphs. Notice that the shading is applied to the entire width of the paragraphs, despite the tab settings.

3. **Select the** seven shaded paragraphs, **drag the** Left Indent marker ▢ **to the ¾" mark on the horizontal ruler, drag the** Right Indent marker △ **to the 5¾" mark, then deselect the text**
   The shading for the paragraphs is indented from the left and right, which makes it look more attractive, as shown in Figure C-21.

4. **Select the** seven paragraphs, **click the** Bottom Border list arrow ▦ ▾ **in the Paragraph group, click** Outside Borders, **then deselect the text**
   A black outside border is added around the selected text. The style of the border added is the most recently used border style, in this case the default, a thin black line.

5. **Select the** seven paragraphs, **click the** Outside Borders list arrow ▦▾, **click** No Border, **click the** No Border list arrow ▦ ▾, **then click** Borders and Shading
   The Borders and Shading dialog box opens, as shown in Figure C-22. You use the Borders tab to change the border style, color, and width, and to add boxes and lines to words or paragraphs.

6. **Click the** Box box **in the Setting section, scroll down the Style list, click the** double-line style, **click the** Color list arrow, **click** Purple, Accent 4, Darker 25%, **click the** Width list arrow, **click** 1½ pt, **click** OK, **then deselect the text**
   A 1½-point dark purple double-line border is added around the tabbed text.

7. **Select the** seven paragraphs, **click the** Bold button **B** **in the Font group, click the** Font Color list arrow ▲▾ **in the Font group, click** Purple, Accent 4, Darker 25%, **then deselect the text**
   The text changes to bold dark purple.

8. **Select the** first line **of tabbed text, click the** Font Color list arrow ▲▾, **then click** Olive Green, Accent 3, Darker 50%
   The text in the first line of tabbed text changes to green.

9. **Select** Flu Statistics, **click the** launcher ▣ **in the Font group, click the** Font tab **if it is not the active tab, scroll and click** 14 **in the Size list, click the** Font color list arrow, **click** Olive Green, Accent 3, Darker 50%, **click the** Small caps check box **in the Effects section, click** OK, **deselect the text, then save your changes**
   The Flu Statistics heading is enlarged and changed to green, small caps, as shown in Figure C-23. When you change text to small caps, the lowercase letters are changed to uppercase letters in a smaller font size.

FIGURE C-21: Shading applied to the tabbed text

Indent markers show width of the shaded paragraphs

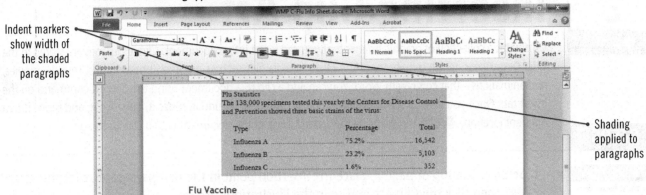

Shading applied to paragraphs

FIGURE C-22: Borders tab in Borders and Shading dialog box

Select border formats before applying them in the Preview area

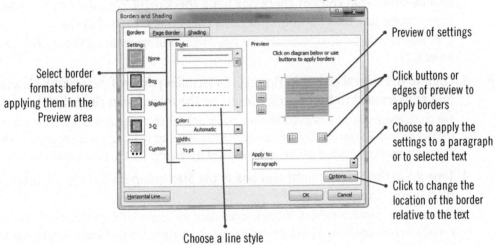

Preview of settings

Click buttons or edges of preview to apply borders

Choose to apply the settings to a paragraph or to selected text

Click to change the location of the border relative to the text

Choose a line style

FIGURE C-23: Borders and shading applied to the document

Text formatted in green, small caps

Double-line, 1½-point, purple, box border

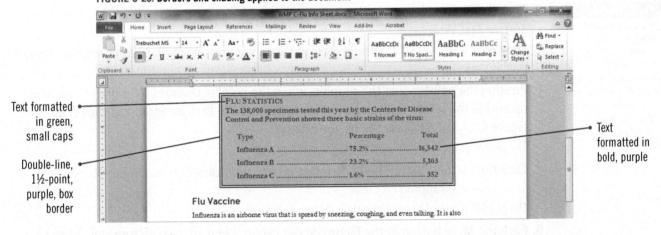

Text formatted in bold, purple

Highlighting text in a document

The Highlight tool allows you to mark and find important text in a document. **Highlighting** is transparent color that is applied to text using the Highlight pointer. To highlight text, click the Text Highlight Color list arrow in the Font group on the Home tab, select a color, then use the I-beam part of the pointer to select the text you want to highlight. Click to turn off the Highlight pointer. To remove highlighting, select the highlighted text, click, then click No Color. Highlighting prints, but it is used most effectively when a document is viewed on screen.

Inserting Clip Art

Clip art is a collection of graphic images that you can insert into a document. Clip art images are stored in the **Clip Organizer**, which is a library of the **clips**—media files such as graphics, photographs, sounds, movies, and animations—that come with Word. You can add a clip to a document using the Clip Art command on the Insert tab. Once you insert a clip art image, you can wrap text around it, resize it, enhance it, and move it to a different location. ▓▓▓ You illustrate the second page of the document with a clip art image.

STEPS

QUICK TIP
You must be working with an active Internet connection to complete this lesson.

1. **Scroll to the top of page 2, place the insertion point in the first paragraph, click the Insert tab, then click the Clip Art button in the Illustrations group**

   The Clip Art task pane opens. You can use this task pane to search for clips related to a keyword.

2. **Select the text in the Search for text box if necessary, type sneezing, make sure the Include Office.com content check box has a check mark, click the Results should be list arrow, make sure only Photographs has a check mark, then click Go**

   Clips that have the keyword "sneezing" associated with them appear in the Clip Art task pane, as shown in Figure C-24.

TROUBLE
Select a different clip if the clip shown in Figure C-24 is not available to you.

3. **Point to the clip called out in Figure C-24 (scrolling down if necessary), click the list arrow that appears next to the clip, click Insert on the menu, then close the Clip Art task pane**

   The clip is inserted at the location of the insertion point. When a graphic is selected, the active tab changes to the Picture Tools Format tab. This tab contains commands used to adjust, enhance, arrange, and size graphics. The white circles that appear on the square edges of the graphic are the **sizing handles**.

4. **Type 2.5 in the Shape Height text box in the Size group on the Picture Tools Format tab, then press [Enter]**

   The size of the graphic is reduced. When you decreased the height of the graphic, the width decreased proportionally. You can also resize a graphic proportionally by dragging a corner sizing handle. Now that the graphic is smaller, you can see that it was inserted at the location of the insertion point. Until you apply text wrapping to a graphic, it is part of the line of text in which it was inserted (an **inline graphic**). To move a graphic independently of text, you must make it a **floating graphic**.

QUICK TIP
To position a graphic using precise measurements, click the Position button, click More Layout Options, then adjust the settings on the Position tab in the Layout dialog box.

5. **Click the Position button in the Arrange group, then click Position in Middle Center with Square Text Wrapping**

   The graphic is moved to the middle of the page and the text wraps around it. Applying text wrapping to the graphic made it a floating graphic. A floating graphic can be moved anywhere on a page.

6. **Position the pointer over the graphic, when the pointer changes to ⁺↔ drag the graphic up and to the left so its top aligns with the top of the first paragraph as shown in Figure C-25, then release the mouse button**

   The graphic is moved to the upper-left corner of the page.

7. **Click the Position button in the Arrange group, then click Position in Top Right with Square Text Wrapping**

   The graphic is moved to the upper-right corner of the page.

8. **Click the More button in the Picture Styles group, point to each picture style to see a preview of the style applied to the graphic, then click Drop Shadow Rectangle**

   A drop shadow effect is applied to the graphic.

9. **Click the View tab, then click the Two Pages button**

   The completed document is shown in Figure C-26.

TROUBLE
If your document is longer than two pages, reduce the size of the clip art graphic by dragging the lower-left corner sizing handle up and to the right.

10. **Save your changes, submit the document to your instructor, then close the document and exit Word**

Formatting Text and Paragraphs

FIGURE C-24: Clip Art task pane

Type search keyword here

Select to include content from Office.com

Select this clip

Select type of clips

Clips with the keyword "sneezing"

Search for clips online

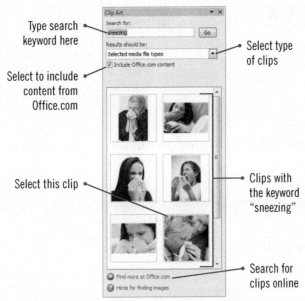

FIGURE C-25: Graphic being moved to a new location

Faded image shows graphic as it is being dragged; position the graphic as shown here

Move pointer

Sizing handles

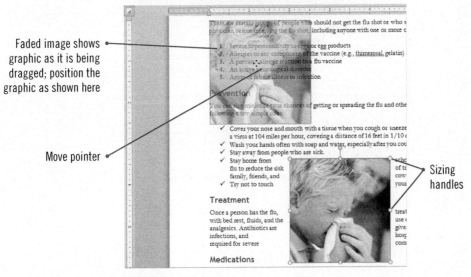

FIGURE C-26: Completed document

Text wrapped around graphic

Shadow effect

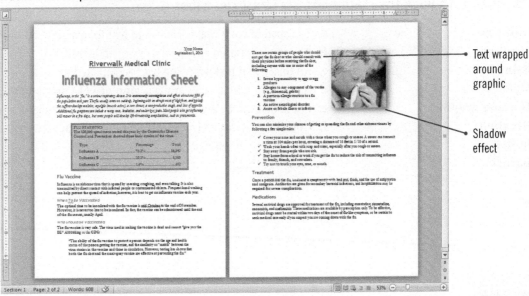

Practice

Concepts Review

For current SAM information, including versions and content details, visit SAM Central (http://www.cengage.com/samcentral). If you have a SAM user profile, you may have access to hands-on instruction, practice, and assessment of the skills covered in this unit. Since various versions of SAM are supported throughout the life of this text, check with your instructor for the correct instructions and URL/Web site for accessing assignments.

Label each element of the Word program window shown in Figure C-27.

FIGURE C-27

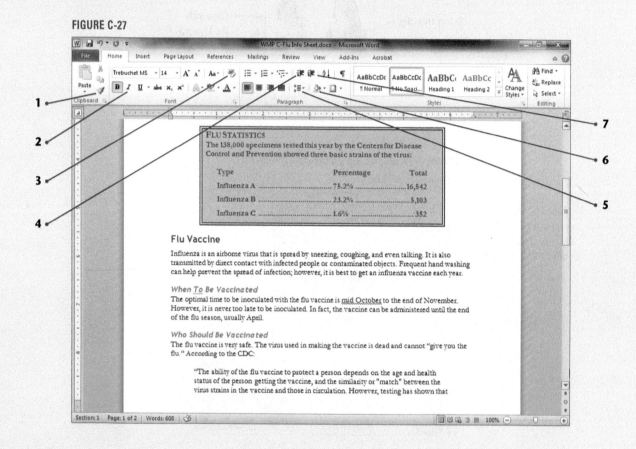

Match each term with the statement that best describes it.

8. Inline graphic   a. Transparent color that is applied to text to mark it in a document

9. Shading   b. A unit of measurement equal to $1/72$ of an inch

10. Point   c. An image that text wrapping has been applied to

11. Style   d. A character that appears at the beginning of a paragraph to add emphasis

12. Floating graphic   e. A line that can be applied above, below, or to the sides of a paragraph

13. Highlight   f. Color or pattern that is applied behind text to make it look attractive

14. Bullet   g. A set of format settings

15. Border   h. An image that is inserted as part of a line of text

Select the best answer from the list of choices.

16. **What is Calibri?**
    a. A character format
    b. A style
    c. A font
    d. A text effect

17. **Which type of indent results in subsequent lines of a paragraph being indented more than the first line?**
    a. Right indent
    b. First line indent
    c. Negative indent
    d. Hanging indent

18. **What is the most precise way to increase the amount of white space between two paragraphs?**
    a. Indent the paragraphs
    b. Change the font size
    c. Change the before paragraph spacing for the second paragraph
    d. Change the line spacing of the paragraphs

19. **Which button is used to align a paragraph with both the left and right margins?**
    a.
    b.
    c.
    d.

20. **Which dialog box is used to change the scale of characters?**
    a. Tabs
    b. Font
    c. Paragraph
    d. Borders and Shading

Skills Review

1. **Format with fonts.**
    a. Start Word, open the file WMP C-2.docx from the drive and folder where you store your Data Files, save it as **WMP C-Scheduling Guidelines**, then scroll through the document to get a feel for its contents.
    b. Press [Ctrl][A], then format the text in 12-point Californian FB. Choose a different serif font if Californian FB is not available to you.
    c. Press [Ctrl][Home], format the report title **Saint Joan Family Health** in 36-point Berlin Sans FB Demi. Choose a different sans serif font if Berlin Sans FB Demi is not available to you.
    d. Change the font color of the report title to Red, Accent 2.
    e. Format the subtitle **Guidelines for Scheduling and Processing Patients** in 18-point Berlin Sans FB Demi, then press [Enter] before Processing in the subtitle.
    f. Format the heading **Our policy** in 14-point Berlin Sans FB Demi with the Red, Accent 2 font color.
    g. Press [Ctrl][Home], then save your changes to the report.

2. **Copy formats using the Format Painter.**
    a. Use the Format Painter to copy the format of the Our policy heading to the following headings: **Five-step approach...**, **Determining the time...**, **Processing new patients**.
    b. Show formatting marks, then format the paragraph under the Our policy heading in italic.
    c. Format **Appointment Time**, the first line in the six-line list under the Determining the time... heading, in bold, small caps, with Red, Accent 2, Darker 50% font color.
    d. Change the font color of the five lines under Appointment Time to Red, Accent 2, Darker 50%.
    e. Scroll to the top of the report, change the character scale of Saint Joan Family Health to 80%, then save your changes.

3. **Change line and paragraph spacing.**
    a. Change the line spacing of the three-line list under the first body paragraph to 1.5 lines.
    b. Add 12 points of space after the title Saint Joan Family Health.
    c. Add 12 points of space after the Our policy heading, then add 12 points of space after each additional heading in the report (Five-step approach..., Determining the time..., Processing new patients).

Skills Review (continued)

   d. Add 6 points of space after each paragraph in the list under the Five-step approach... heading, except the last paragraph.

   e. Change the line spacing of the six-line list under the Determining the time... heading that begins with Appointment Time to 1.15.

   f. Add 6 points of space after each paragraph under the Processing new patients... heading.

   g. Press [Ctrl][Home], then save your changes to the report.

4. Align paragraphs.

   a. Press [Ctrl][A] to select the entire document, then justify all the paragraphs.

   b. Center the report title and its subtitle.

   c. Press [Ctrl][End], type your name, press [Enter], type the current date, then right-align your name and the date.

   d. Save your changes to the report.

5. Work with tabs.

   a. Scroll up and select the six-line list of appointment time information under the Determining the time... heading.

   b. Set left tab stops at the 1¾" mark and the 3¾" mark.

   c. Insert a tab at the beginning of each line in the list.

   d. In the first line, insert a tab before Time. In the second line, insert a tab before 45 minutes. In the remaining lines, insert a tab before each number.

   e. Select all the lines, then drag the first tab stop to the 2" mark on the horizontal ruler.

   f. Select the last five lines, then insert dotted line tab leaders before the 3¾" tab stop.

   g. Press [Ctrl][Home], then save your changes to the report.

6. Work with indents.

   a. Indent the paragraph under the Our policy heading ½" from the left and ½" from the right.

   b. Indent the first line of each of the three body paragraphs under the Determining the time... heading ½".

   c. Press [Ctrl][Home], then save your changes to the report.

7. Add bullets and numbering.

   a. Apply bullets to the three-line list under the first body paragraph. Change the bullet style to small black circles if that is not the current bullet symbol.

   b. Change the font color of the bullets to Red, Accent 2.

   c. Scroll down until the Five-step approach... heading is at the top of your screen.

   d. Format the five-paragraph list under the Five-step approach... heading as a numbered list.

   e. Format the numbers in 12-point Berlin Sans FB Demi, then change the font color to Red, Accent 2.

   f. Scroll down until the Processing new patients... heading is at the top of your screen, then format the paragraphs under the heading as a bulleted list using check marks as the bullet style.

   g. Change the font color of the bullets to Red, Accent 2, press [Ctrl][Home], then save your changes to the report.

8. Add borders and shading.

   a. Add a 1-point Orange, Accent 6, Darker 25% border below the Our policy heading.

   b. Use the Format Painter or the F4 key to add the same border to the other headings in the report (Five-step approach..., Determining the time..., Processing new patients).

   c. Under the Determining the time... heading, select the six lines of tabbed text, which are formatted in red, then apply Orange, Accent 6, Lighter 40% shading to the paragraphs.

   d. Select the six lines of tabbed text again if necessary, then add a 1½-point Orange, Accent 6, Darker 25% single line box border around the paragraphs.

   e. Indent the shading and border around the paragraphs 1¾" from the left and 1¾" from the right.

   f. Turn off the display of formatting marks, then save your changes.

9. Insert clip art.

   a. Press [Ctrl][Home], then open the Clip Art task pane.

   b. Click the Results should be in list arrow, make sure All media types has a check mark, then search for clips related to the keyword **appointment**.

Skills Review (continued)

c. Insert the clip shown in Figure C-28, then close the Clip Art task pane. (*Note*: An active Internet connection is needed to select the clip shown in the figure. Select a different clip if this one is not available to you. It is best to select a clip that is similar in shape to the clip shown in Figure C-28.)

d. Select the graphic if necessary, then drag the upper-right sizing handle down and to the left so that the graphic is about 1" wide.

e. Use the Position command to position the clip art in the top left with square text wrapping.

f. Use the Shape Width text box in the Size group on the Format tab to change the width of the graphic to 1.3".

g. Apply Simple Frame, Black picture style to the graphic.

h. Save your changes to the document, submit it to your instructor, close the file, and then exit Word.

FIGURE C-28

Saint Joan Family Health

Guidelines for Scheduling and Processing Patients

A well-managed schedule of appointments is an important factor in delivering quality health care to patients, and is critical to the smooth and efficient running of Saint Joan Family Health. With that in mind, there are several factors to consider when scheduling patients for appointments:

- The specialty and personal preferences of each physician.
- The type of appointment required by the patient's condition.
- The urgency with which the patient needs to see a physician.

Our policy

Our patients have entrusted us with their health care. Many physicians charge patients who fail to keep appointments. At Saint Joan Family Health, we extend equal consideration to patients who take time out of their busy work day to allow us to participate in their health care. We respect that patients make every effort to arrive on time for appointments, and we endeavor to be available to them when they arrive.

Five-step approach to scheduling appointments

1. When a patient calls to schedule an appointment, assess the reason for the appointment and determine the urgency and how much time will be needed.
2. Ask the patient when he or she is not available for the appointment. This demonstrates a willingness to accommodate the patient's needs.
3. Offer the patient at least two choices of available times, if possible. Always state the day of the week, the date, and the time. This enables the patient to choose between alternatives and demonstrates the importance of the patient's input.
4. Repeat the agreed upon time to the patient. If the patient is present at the time of the booking, write down the day, date, and time of the appointment on an appointment reminder card and give it to the patient.
5. Close with an expression of anticipation of the next visit, such as "We'll see you at 10:00 a.m. on March 1st." This provides further verification of the date.

Determining the time required for an appointment

The time allotted for an appointment is particular to each physician's specialty and the patient's condition. Physicians are as frustrated as patients if appointments do not run smoothly, or if not enough time has been allowed to adequately address the patient's needs. The following table offers general guidelines for determining the amount of time to book for each type of appointment:

Appointment	Time
New patient	45 minutes
Complete physical	30 minutes
Counseling	30 minutes
Sick visit	15 minutes
Other	15 minutes

In addition, it is important to schedule into each day several "emergency" booking slots that can be used to accommodate patients who need same day appointments. This is particularly critical during flu season. Be sure to analyze the appointment schedule regularly to ensure that it is meeting the needs of patients and physicians.

When a patient telephones to book an appointment, it is important to obtain his/her full name (ask for correct spelling), current home and work phone numbers (for contact purposes), and the reason for the visit. Patients sometimes object to providing this personal information. When this happens, you can explain to the patient that you require this information to schedule an adequate amount of time for the appointment, and so that any paperwork or special equipment that might be required will be ready when he/she arrives. Also, reassure the patient that all information he/she provides to Saint Joan Family Health remains confidential.

Processing new patients

- ✓ Gather as much information as you can from the new patient over the telephone when he/she calls to book an appointment.
- ✓ Ask the patient to complete a patient information form as soon as he/she arrives at the office, and check the form for completeness.
- ✓ Photocopy the patient's insurance card(s).
- ✓ Ask the patient to read and sign a copy of our privacy notice.
- ✓ Enter the information from the patient information form into our database.

Your Name
Today's Date

Independent Challenge 1

You work for Prairie Orthopedic Associates. Your boss has given you the text for a Notice of Patient Rights and Responsibilities and has asked you to format it on letterhead. It's important that the Notice has a clean, striking design, and reflects the practice's professionalism.

a. Start Word, open the file WMP C-3.docx from the drive and folder where you store your Data Files, save it as **WMP C-Notice of Rights**, then read the document to get a feel for its contents. Figure C-29 shows how you will format the letterhead.

FIGURE C-29

Prairie Orthopedic Associates

1900 East Prairie SE, Suite 108, Grand Rapids, MI 49503; Tel: 616-555-2921; Fax: 616-555-2231

Karl Rattan, M.D.   Margaret Canton, M.D.   Elise McDonald, M.D.   Edward Kaplan, M.D.   Mary Shipman, M.D.

b. Select the entire document, change the style to No Spacing, then change the font to 11-point Californian FB.

c. In the first paragraph, format **Prairie Orthopedic Associates** in 36-point Californian FB, then change the character spacing to 80%.

d. Change the font size of the next two paragraphs—the address and the physician information—to 9 point, then bold the paragraph that lists the physicians.

e. Center the three-line letterhead.

f. Add 6 points of space after the address line paragraph, then add a ½-point black border below the address line paragraph.

g. With the insertion point in the address line, open the Borders and Shading dialog box, click Options to open the Border and Shading Options dialog box, change the Bottom setting to 5 pt, then click OK twice to adjust the location of the border relative to the line of text.

h. Format the title **Patient Rights and Responsibilities** in 16-point Trebuchet MS, bold, then center the title.

i. Format the following headings (including the colons) in 12-point Trebuchet MS, bold: **Your Rights as a Patient**, **Your Responsibilities as a Patient**, **Advance Directives**, **Financial Concerns**, **Income Guidelines**, and **Acknowledgement of Receipt.....**

j. Format the lists under Your Rights as a Patient and Your Responsibilities as a Patient as bulleted lists, using a bullet style of your choice.

k. Apply bold italic to **Living Wills and Durable Powers of Attorney for Healthcare** under the Advance Directives heading.

l. Center the Income Guidelines heading, select the 9-line list under the heading, then set a left tab stop at the 1¾" mark and right tab stops at the 3½" and 4¾" marks. Insert tabs before every line in the list, then insert tabs before every $.

m. Select the text in the first line of tabbed text, then apply an underline. Select the remaining eight lines of tabbed text, then add dotted line tab leaders to the 3½" and 4¾" tab stops.

n. Type your name as the patient name, then type the current date.

o. Examine the document carefully for formatting errors, and make any necessary adjustments.

p. Save the document, submit it to your instructor, then close the file and exit Word.

Formatting Text and Paragraphs

Independent Challenge 2

Your employer, Learn and Be Healthy, is a nonprofit organization devoted to educating the public on health issues. Your boss has written the text for a flyer about Peripheral Artery Disease, and asks you to format it so that it is eye catching and attractive.

a. Open the file WMP C-4.docx from the drive and folder where you store your Data Files, save it as **WMP C-PAD Flyer**, then read the document. Figure C-30 shows how you will format the first several paragraphs of the flyer.

FIGURE C-30

LEARN AND BE HEALTHY
Peripheral Artery Disease

What is peripheral artery disease?
Peripheral artery disease (PAD) is a circulation disorder that is caused by fatty buildups (atherosclerosis) in the inner walls of arteries. These fatty buildups block normal blood flow. PAD is a type of peripheral vascular disease (PVD), which refers to diseases of blood vessels outside the heart and brain.

b. Select the entire document, change the style to No Spacing, then change the font to 10.5-point Arial Narrow. (*Hint*: Select the font size, they type 10.5.)

c. Center the first line, **Learn and Be Healthy**, and apply shading to the paragraph. Choose a dark custom shading color of your choice for the shading color. (*Hint*: Click More Colors, then select a color from the Standard or Custom tab.) Format the text in 26-point Arial Narrow, bold, with a white font color. Expand the character spacing by 8 points. (*Hint*: Use the Advanced tab in the Font dialog box, set the Spacing to Expanded, and then type 8 in the By text box.)

d. Format the second line, **Peripheral Artery Disease**, in 36-point Arial Black. Change the character scale to 90%, then center the line.

e. Format each question heading in 12-point Arial, bold. Change the font color to the same custom color used for shading the title. (*Note*: The color now appears in the Recent Colors section of the Font Color gallery.) Add a single-line ½-point black border under each heading.

f. Format each subheading (**PAD may require...** and **Lifestyle changes...**) in 10.5-point Arial, bold. Add 3 points of spacing before each subheading. (*Hint*: Select 0 in the Before text box, type 3, then press Enter.)

g. Indent each body paragraph and subheading ¼", except for the last two lines in the document.

h. Format the three lines under the **PAD may require...** subheading as a bulleted list. Use a bullet symbol of your choice, and format the bullets in the custom font color.

i. Format the six lines under the **Lifestyle changes...** subheading as a bulleted list. If necessary, use the Format Painter to copy the bullet style you just applied to the six-line list.

j. Format the **For more information** heading in 14-point Arial, bold, with the custom font color, then center the heading.

k. Format the last line in 11-point Arial Narrow, and center the line. In the contact information, replace Your Name with your name, then apply bold to your name.

Advanced Challenge Exercise

- Change the font color of the Peripheral Artery Disease heading to a dark gray, and add a shadow effect.
- Add a shadow effect to each question heading.
- Add a 2¼-point dotted black border above the For more information heading.

l. Examine the document carefully for formatting errors, and make any necessary adjustments.

m. Save the flyer, submit it to your instructor, then close the file and exit Word.

Independent Challenge 3

One of your responsibilities as patient care coordinator at Metropolitan Healthcare is to facilitate patient-staff interactions to achieve excellent care for patients at the facility. You have drafted a memo to Metropolitan Healthcare staff to outline several ways they can encourage patients to be involved in their own healthcare. You need to format the memo so it is professional looking and easy to read.

a. Start Word, open the file WMP C-5.docx from the drive and folder where you store your Data Files, then save it as **WMP C-Metropolitan Healthcare Memo**.

b. Select the heading **Metropolitan Healthcare Memorandum**, apply the Quick Style Title to it, then center the heading. (*Hint*: Open the Quick Style gallery, then click the Title style.)

c. In the memo header, replace Today's Date and Your Name with the current date and your name.

d. Select the four-line memo header, set a left tab stop at the ¾" mark, then insert tabs before the date, the recipient's name, your name, and the subject of the memo.

e. Apply the Quick Style Strong to **Date:**, **To:**, **From:**, and **Re:**.

f. Apply the Quick Style Heading 2 to the headings **Encourage questions**, **Offer an interpreter**, **Identify yourself**, and **Ensure medication safety**.

g. Under the Offer an interpreter heading, apply the Quick Style Intense Emphasis to the words **Interpreters' hours:** and **Languages:**.

h. On the second page of the document, format the list under the Ensure medication safety heading as a multi-level list. Figure C-31 shows the hierarchical structure of the outline. (*Hint*: Apply a multilevel list style, then use the Increase Indent and Decrease Indent buttons to change the level of importance of each item.)

i. Change the outline numbering style to the bullet numbering style shown in Figure C-31 if a different style is used in your outline.

FIGURE C-31

- ❖ Information patients need to share with healthcare providers
  - ➢ Details about everything they take
    - ▪ Prescription medications
    - ▪ Non-prescription medications
      - • Aspirin
      - • Antacids
      - • Laxatives
      - • Etc.
    - ▪ Vitamins
    - ▪ Herbs or other supplements
      - • St. John's Wort
      - • Ginko biloba
      - • Etc.
  - ➢ Information about allergic reactions to medications
    - ▪ Rashes
    - ▪ Difficulty breathing
    - ▪ Etc.
  - ➢ Details of illnesses or medical conditions
    - ▪ High blood pressure
    - ▪ Glaucoma
    - ▪ Diabetes
    - ▪ Thyroid disease
    - ▪ Etc.
- ❖ Information healthcare providers need to share with patients
  - ➢ What each prescribed medication is and what it is used for
    - ▪ Name of medication
    - ▪ Purpose of medication
    - ▪ Dosage
    - ▪ Side effects
    - ▪ Drug interactions
  - ➢ Written directions for the dosage and purpose
    - ▪ "Take once a day for high blood pressure"

Advanced Challenge Exercise

- ■ Zoom out on the memo so that two pages are displayed in the document window, then, using the Change Styles button, change the style set to Modern.

- ■ Using the Change Case button, change the title Metropolitan Healthcare Memorandum so that only the initial letter of each word is capitalized.

- ■ Using the Themes button on the Page Layout tab, change the theme applied to the document to a different appropriate theme.

- ■ Using the Theme Fonts button, change the fonts to a font set of your choice. Choose fonts that allow the document to fit on two pages.

- ■ Using the Theme Colors button, change the colors to a color palette of your choice.

- ■ Apply different styles and adjust other formatting elements as necessary to make the memo attractive, eye catching, and readable. The finished memo should fit on two pages.

j. Save the document, submit it to your instructor, then close the file and exit Word.

Formatting Text and Paragraphs

Real Life Independent Challenge

The fonts you choose for a document can have a major effect on the document's tone. Not all fonts are appropriate for use in a business or medical document, and some fonts, especially those with a definite theme, are appropriate only for specific purposes. In this Independent Challenge, you will use font formatting and other formatting features to design a letterhead and a fax coversheet for yourself or your place of work. The letterhead and coversheet should not only look professional and attract interest, but also say something about the character of your place of work or your personality. Figure C-32 shows an example of a letterhead for a chiropractor.

a. Start Word, and save a new blank document as **WMP C-Personal Letterhead** to the drive and folder where you store your Data Files.

b. Type your name or the name of your place of work, your address, your phone number, your fax number, and your Web site or e-mail address.

c. Format your name or the name of your place of work in a font that expresses your personality or says something about the nature of your place of work. Use fonts, font colors, font effects, borders, shading, paragraph formatting, and other formatting features to design a letterhead that is appealing and professional.

d. Save your changes, submit the document to your instructor, then close the file.

e. Open a new blank document, and save it as **WMP C-Personal Fax Coversheet**. Type FAX, your name or the name of your place of work, your address, your phone number, your fax number, and your Web site or e-mail address at the top of the document.

f. Type a fax header that includes the following: Date; To; From; Re; Number of pages, including cover sheet; and Comments.

g. Format the information in the fax coversheet using fonts, font effects, borders, shading, paragraph formatting, and other formatting features. Since a fax coversheet is designed to be faxed, all fonts and other formatting elements should be black.

h. Save your changes, submit the document to your instructor, close the file, then exit Word.

FIGURE C-32

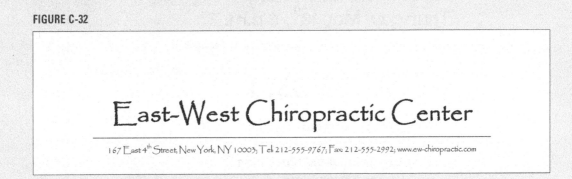

East-West Chiropractic Center

167 East 4th Street, New York, NY 10003; Tel 212-555-9767; Fax 212-555-2992; www.ew-chiropractic.com

Visual Workshop

Open the file WMP C-6.docx from the drive and folder where you store your Data Files. Create the flyer shown in Figure C-33. (*Hints*: Use Berlin Sans FB or a similar font, and a font color of your choice. Align the text in the box using a right and then a left tab stop. Use paragraph spacing to adjust the spacing between paragraphs, if necessary, so that all the text fits on one page.) Save the flyer as **WMP C-Simple Steps**, then submit a copy to your instructor.

FIGURE C-33

Simple Steps

12 Week Adult Weight Management and Exercise Program

This series will help you find a balanced approach to healthy eating and consistent activity. The program includes group exercise, behavioral nutrition classes, and individual counseling.

Free information session
Thursday, May 18th, 6 p.m.

The Wellness Center at Valley Community Hospital

Call: 555-3374

Program participants receive:
- A free fitness assessment
- An individualized fitness plan
- A pedometer

Register by:	**May 27th**
Classes begin:	**June 4th**
Space is limited:	**Call today!**

Fee for the program is $259. The cost may be reimbursed by insurance.
For more information, contact Your Name.

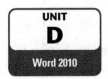

UNIT D
Word 2010

Creating and Formatting Tables

Tables are commonly used to display information for quick reference and analysis. In this unit, you learn how to create and modify a table in Word, how to sort table data and perform calculations, and how to format a table with borders and shading. You also learn how to use a table to structure the layout of a page. You are preparing a summary budget for an advertising campaign aimed at the greater Cambridge market. The goals of the ad campaign are to educate the community about the services provided by the Riverwalk Medical Clinic and to attract new patients. You decide to format the budget information as a table so that it is easy to read and analyze.

OBJECTIVES

Insert a table

Insert and delete rows and columns

Modify rows and columns

Sort table data

Split and merge cells

Perform calculations in tables

Apply a table style

Create a custom format for a table

©Jeffrey Coolidge/Photodisc/Getty Images

Inserting a Table

A **table** is a grid made up of rows and columns of cells that you can fill with text and graphics. A **cell** is the box formed by the intersection of a column and a row. The lines that divide the columns and rows and help you see the grid-like structure of a table are called **borders**. You can create a table in a document by using the Table command in the Tables group on the Insert tab. Once you have created a table, you can add text and graphics to it. ⬛⬛⬛ You begin by inserting a blank table and adding text to it.

STEPS

QUICK TIP

Click the View Ruler button 🔲 at the top of the vertical scroll bar to display the rulers if they are not already displayed.

1. **Start Word, click the View tab, then click the Page Width button in the Zoom group**

2. **Click the Insert tab, then click the Table button in the Tables group**

   The Table menu opens. It includes a grid for selecting the number of columns and rows you want the table to contain, as well as several commands for inserting a table. Table D-1 describes these commands. As you move the pointer across the grid, a preview of the table with the specified number of columns and rows appears in the document at the location of the insertion point.

3. **Point to the second box in the fourth row to select 2×4 Table, then click**

   A table with two columns and four rows is inserted in the document, as shown in Figure D-1. Black borders surround the table cells. The insertion point is in the first cell in the first row.

TROUBLE

Don't be concerned if the paragraph spacing under the text in your table is different from that shown in the figures.

4. **Type Location, then press [Tab]**

   Pressing [Tab] moves the insertion point to the next cell in the row.

5. **Type Cost, press [Tab], then type The Boston Globe**

   Pressing [Tab] at the end of a row moves the insertion point to the first cell in the next row.

6. **Press [Tab], type 5,075, press [Tab], then type the following text in the table, pressing [Tab] to move from cell to cell**

   WickedLocal.com   1,080
   Cambridge River Festival   600

7. **Press [Tab]**

   Pressing [Tab] at the end of the last cell of a table creates a new row at the bottom of the table, as shown in Figure D-2. The insertion point is located in the first cell in the new row.

TROUBLE

If you pressed [Tab] after the last row, click the Undo button ↻ on the Quick Access toolbar to remove the new blank row.

8. **Type the following, pressing [Tab] to move from cell to cell and to create new rows**

   Boston Herald   1,760
   Boston.com   1,250
   Mass mailing   1,440
   Cambridge Chronicle   1,860

9. **Click the Save button 🔲 on the Quick Access toolbar, then save the document as WMP D-Clinic Ad Budget to the drive and folder where you store your Data Files**

   The table is shown in Figure D-3.

TABLE D-1: Table menu commands

command	use to
Insert Table	Create a table with any number of columns and rows and select an AutoFit behavior
Draw Table	Create a complex table by drawing the table columns and rows
Convert Text to Table	Convert text that is separated by tabs, commas, or another separator character into a table
Excel Spreadsheet	Insert a blank Excel worksheet into the document as an embedded object
Quick Tables	Insert a preformatted table template and replace the placeholder data with your own data

FIGURE D-1: Blank table

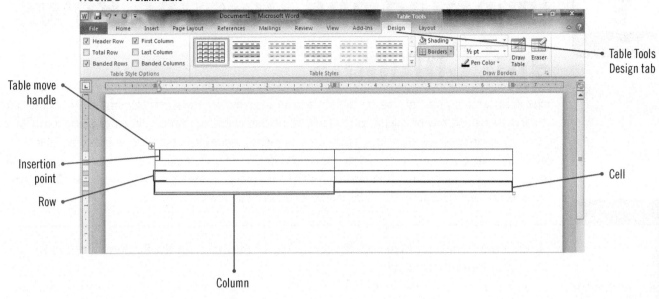

Table move handle

Insertion point

Row

Table Tools Design tab

Cell

Column

FIGURE D-2: New row in table

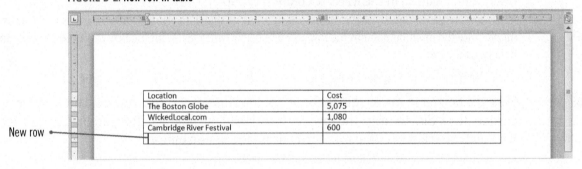

New row

Location	Cost
The Boston Globe	5,075
WickedLocal.com	1,080
Cambridge River Festival	600

FIGURE D-3: Text in the table

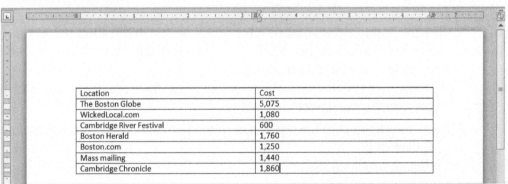

Location	Cost
The Boston Globe	5,075
WickedLocal.com	1,080
Cambridge River Festival	600
Boston Herald	1,760
Boston.com	1,250
Mass mailing	1,440
Cambridge Chronicle	1,860

Converting text to a table and a table to text

Another way to create a table is to convert text that is separated by a tab, a comma, or another separator character into a table. For example, to create a two-column table of last and first names, you could type the names as a list with a comma separating the last and first name in each line, and then convert the text to a table. The separator character—a comma in this example—indicates where you want to divide the table into columns, and a paragraph mark indicates where you want to begin a new row. To convert text to a table, select the text, click the Table button in the Tables group on the Insert tab, and then click Convert Text to Table. In the Convert Text to Table dialog box, select from the options for structuring and formatting the table, and then click OK to create the table.

Conversely, you can convert a table to text that is separated by tabs, commas, or some other character by selecting the table, clicking the Table Tools Layout tab, and then clicking the Convert to Text button in the Data group.

Word 2010

Inserting and Deleting Rows and Columns

You can easily modify the structure of a table by adding and removing rows and columns. First, you must click or select an existing row or column in the table to indicate where you want to insert or delete a row or a column. You can select any element of a table using the Select command in the Table group on the Table Tools Layout tab, but it is often easier to select rows and columns using the mouse. To insert or delete rows and columns, you use the commands in the Rows & Columns group on the Table Tools Layout tab. ▰▰▰▰▰ You add new rows and columns to the table, and delete unnecessary rows.

STEPS

1. **Click the Home tab, then click the Show/Hide ¶ button ¶ in the Paragraph group to display formatting marks**

   An end of cell mark appears at the end of each cell and an end of row mark appears at the end of each row.

2. **Click the Table Tools Layout tab, click the first cell of the Boston.com row, then click the Insert Above button in the Rows & Columns group**

   A new row is inserted directly above the Boston.com row, as shown in Figure D-4. To insert a single row, you simply place the insertion point in the row above or below where you want the new row to be inserted, and then insert the row.

3. **Click the first cell of the new row, type Boston Phoenix, press [Tab], then type 2,850**

4. **Place the pointer in the margin to the left of the WickedLocal.com row until the pointer changes to ⌐, click to select the row, press and hold the mouse button, drag down to select the Cambridge River Festival row, then release the mouse button**

   The two rows are selected, including the end of row marks.

5. **Click the Insert Below button in the Rows & Columns group**

   Two new rows are added below the selected rows. To insert multiple rows, you select the number of rows you want to insert before inserting the rows.

6. **Click the Boston Herald row, click the Delete button in the Rows & Columns group, click Delete Rows, select the two blank rows, right-click the selected rows, then click Delete Rows on the menu that opens**

   The Boston Herald row and the two blank rows are deleted. If you select a row and press [Delete], you delete only the contents of the row, not the row itself.

7. **Place the pointer over the top border of the Location column until the pointer changes to ↓, then click**

   The entire column is selected.

8. **Click the Insert Left button in the Rows & Columns group, then type Type**

   A new column is inserted to the left of the Location column, as shown in Figure D-5.

9. **Click in the Location column, click the Insert Right button in the Rows & Columns group, then type Details in the first cell of the new column**

   A new column is added to the right of the Location column.

10. **Press [↓] to move the insertion point to the next cell in the Details column, click the Home tab, click ¶ to turn off the display of formatting marks, enter the text shown in Figure D-6 in each cell in the Details and Type columns, then save your changes**

    You can use the arrow keys to move the insertion point from cell to cell. Notice that text wraps to the next line in the cell as you type. Compare your table to Figure D-6.

Creating and Formatting Tables

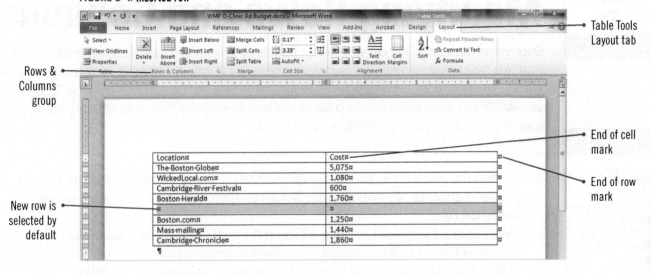

Table Tools
Layout tab

Rows & Columns group

End of cell mark

End of row mark

New row is selected by default

FIGURE D-5: Inserted column

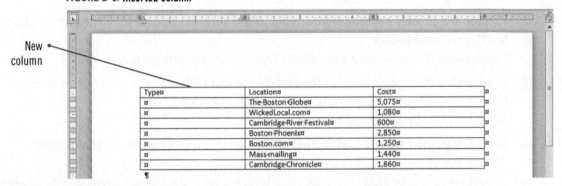

New column

FIGURE D-6: Text in Type and Details columns

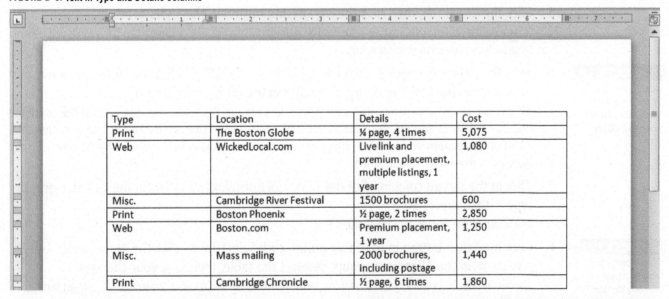

Type	Location	Details	Cost
Print	The Boston Globe	¼ page, 4 times	5,075
Web	WickedLocal.com	Live link and premium placement, multiple listings, 1 year	1,080
Misc.	Cambridge River Festival	1500 brochures	600
Print	Boston Phoenix	½ page, 2 times	2,850
Web	Boston.com	Premium placement, 1 year	1,250
Misc.	Mass mailing	2000 brochures, including postage	1,440
Print	Cambridge Chronicle	½ page, 6 times	1,860

Copying and moving rows and columns

You can copy and move rows and columns within a table in the same manner you copy and move text. Select the row or column you want to move, then use the Copy or Cut button to place the selection on the Clipboard. Place the insertion point in the location where you want to insert the row or column, then click the Paste button to paste the selection. Rows are inserted above the row containing the insertion point; columns are inserted to the left of the column containing the insertion point. You can also copy or move columns and rows by selecting them and using the pointer to drag them to a new location in the table.

Modifying Rows and Columns

Once you create a table, you can easily adjust the size of columns and rows to make the table easier to read. You can change the width of columns and the height of rows by dragging a border, by using the AutoFit command, or by setting precise measurements in the Cell Size group on the Table Tools Layout tab. ░░░░░ You adjust the size of the columns and rows to make the table more attractive and easier to read. You also center the text vertically in each table cell.

STEPS

1. **Position the pointer over the border between the first and second columns until the pointer changes to ⁺‖⁺, then drag the border to approximately the ½" mark on the horizontal ruler**

   The dotted line that appears as you drag represents the border. Dragging the column border changes the width of the first and second columns: the first column is narrower and the second column is wider. When dragging a border to change the width of an entire column, make sure no cells are selected in the column. You can also drag a row border to change the height of the row above it.

2. **Position the pointer over the right border of the Location column until the pointer changes to ⁺‖⁺, then double-click**

   Double-clicking a column border automatically resizes the column to fit the text.

3. **Double-click the right border of the Details column with the ⁺‖⁺ pointer, then double-click the right border of the Cost column with the ⁺‖⁺ pointer**

   The widths of the Details and Cost columns are adjusted.

4. **Move the pointer over the table, then click the table move handle ⊞ that appears outside the upper-left corner of the table**

   Clicking the table move handle selects the entire table. You can also use the Select button in the Table group on the Table Tools Layout tab to select an entire table.

5. **Click the Home tab, then click the No Spacing button in the Styles group**

   Changing the style to No Spacing removes the paragraph spacing below the text in each table cell, if your table includes extra paragraph spacing.

6. **With the table still selected, click the Table Tools Layout tab, click the Distribute Rows button ⊞ in the Cell Size group, then click in the table to deselect it**

   All the rows in the table become the same height, as shown in Figure D-7. You can also use the Distribute Columns button to make all the columns the same width, or you can use the AutoFit button to make the width of the columns fit the text, to adjust the width of the columns so the table is justified between the margins, or to set fixed column widths.

7. **Click in the Details column, click the Table Column Width text box in the Cell Size group, type 4, then press [Enter]**

   The width of the Details column changes to 4".

8. **Click the Select button in the Table group, click Select Table, click the Align Center Left button ▤ in the Alignment group, deselect the table, then save your changes**

   The text is centered vertically in each table cell, as shown in Figure D-8. You can use the alignment buttons in the Alignment group to change the vertical and horizontal alignment of the text in selected cells or in the entire table.

FIGURE D-7: Resized columns and rows

Table move handle: click to select the table; drag to move the table

Rows are all the same height

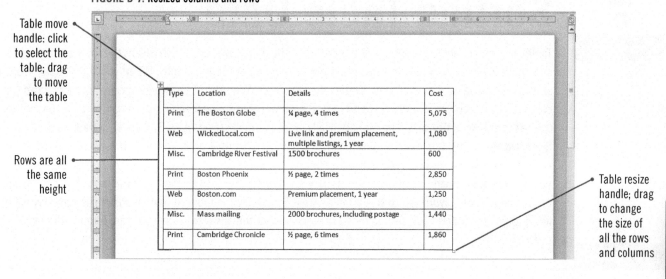

Table resize handle; drag to change the size of all the rows and columns

Type	Location	Details	Cost
Print	The Boston Globe	¼ page, 4 times	5,075
Web	WickedLocal.com	Live link and premium placement, multiple listings, 1 year	1,080
Misc.	Cambridge River Festival	1500 brochures	600
Print	Boston Phoenix	½ page, 2 times	2,850
Web	Boston.com	Premium placement, 1 year	1,250
Misc.	Mass mailing	2000 brochures, including postage	1,440
Print	Cambridge Chronicle	½ page, 6 times	1,860

FIGURE D-8: Text centered vertically in cells

Column is widened

Text is centered vertically in the cell

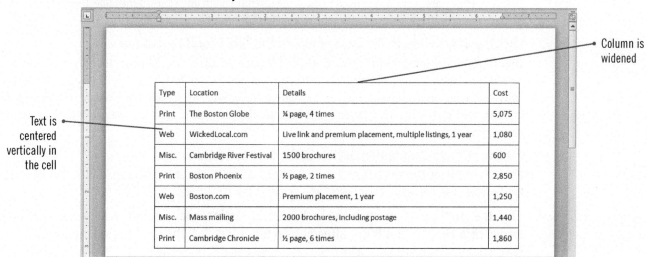

Type	Location	Details	Cost
Print	The Boston Globe	¼ page, 4 times	5,075
Web	WickedLocal.com	Live link and premium placement, multiple listings, 1 year	1,080
Misc.	Cambridge River Festival	1500 brochures	600
Print	Boston Phoenix	½ page, 2 times	2,850
Web	Boston.com	Premium placement, 1 year	1,250
Misc.	Mass mailing	2000 brochures, including postage	1,440
Print	Cambridge Chronicle	½ page, 6 times	1,860

Setting advanced table properties

When you want to wrap text around a table, indent a table, or set other advanced table properties, you click the Properties command in the Table group on the Table Tools Layout tab to open the Table Properties dialog box, shown in Figure D-9. By using the Table tab in this dialog box, you can set a precise width for the table, change the horizontal alignment of the table between the margins, indent the table, and set text wrapping options for the table. You can also click Options on the Table tab to open the Table Options dialog box, which you use to customize the table's default cell margins and the spacing between table cells. Alternatively, click Borders and Shading on the Table tab to open the Borders and Shading dialog box, which you can use to create a custom format for the table.

The Column, Row, and Cell tabs in the Table Properties dialog box allow you to set an exact width for columns, to specify an exact height for rows, and to indicate an exact size for individual cells. The Alt Text tab is used to add alternative text for a table that will appear on a Web page.

FIGURE D-9: Table Properties dialog box

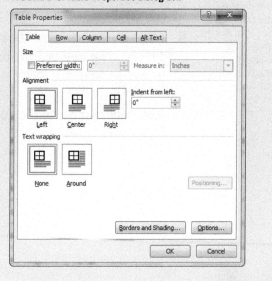

Word 2010

Word 83

Sorting Table Data

Tables are often easier to interpret and analyze when the data is **sorted**, which means the rows are organized in alphabetical or sequential order based on the data in one or more columns. When you sort a table, Word arranges all the table data according to the criteria you set. You set sort criteria by specifying the column (or columns) by which you want to sort and indicating the sort order—ascending or descending—you want to use. **Ascending order** lists data alphabetically or sequentially (from A to Z, 0 to 9, or earliest to latest). **Descending order** lists data in reverse alphabetical or sequential order (from Z to A, 9 to 0, or latest to earliest). You can sort using the data in one column or multiple columns. When you sort by multiple columns you must select primary, secondary, and tertiary sort criteria. You use the Sort command in the Data group on the Table Tools Layout tab to sort a table. You sort the table so that all ads of the same type are listed together. You also add secondary sort criteria so that the ads within each type are listed in descending order by cost.

1. **Place the insertion point anywhere in the table**

   To sort an entire table, you simply need to place the insertion point anywhere in the table. If you want to sort specific rows only, then you must select the rows you want to sort.

2. **Click the Sort button in the Data group on the Table Tools Layout tab**

   The Sort dialog box opens, as shown in Figure D-10. You use this dialog box to specify the column or columns by which you want to sort, the type of information you are sorting (text, numbers, or dates), and the sort order (ascending or descending). Column 1 is selected by default in the Sort by list box. Since you want to sort your table first by the information in the first column—the type of ad (Print, Web, or Misc.)—you don't change the Sort by criteria.

3. **Click the Descending option button in the Sort by section**

   The ad type information will be sorted in descending—or reverse alphabetical—order, so that the "Web" ads will be listed first, followed by the "Print" ads, and then the "Misc." ads.

4. **Click the Then by list arrow in the first Then by section, click Column 4, click the Type list arrow, click Number if it is not already selected, then click the Descending option button**

   Within the Web, Print, and Misc. groups, the rows will be sorted by the cost of the ad, which is the information contained in the fourth column. The rows will appear in descending order within each group, with the most expensive ad listed first.

5. **Click the Header row option button in the My list has section to select it**

   The table includes a **header row**, which is the first row of a table that contains the column headings. You select the Header row option button when you do not want the header row included in the sort.

6. **Click OK, then deselect the table**

   The rows in the table are sorted first by the information in the Type column and second by the information in the Cost column, as shown in Figure D-11. The first row of the table, which is the header row, is not included in the sort.

7. **Save your changes to the document**

Creating and Formatting Tables

FIGURE D-10: Sort dialog box

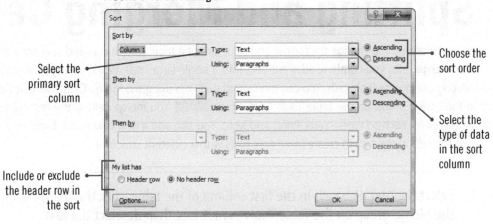

Select the primary sort column

Include or exclude the header row in the sort

Choose the sort order

Select the type of data in the sort column

FIGURE D-11: Sorted table

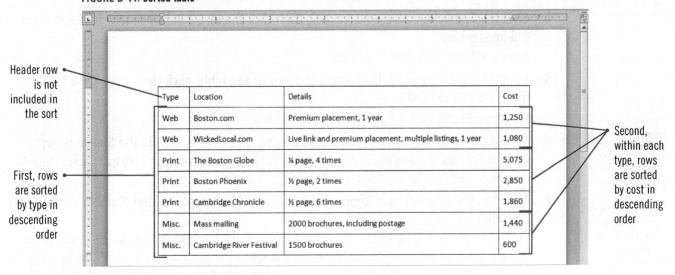

Header row is not included in the sort

First, rows are sorted by type in descending order

Second, within each type, rows are sorted by cost in descending order

Type	Location	Details	Cost
Web	Boston.com	Premium placement, 1 year	1,250
Web	WickedLocal.com	Live link and premium placement, multiple listings, 1 year	1,080
Print	The Boston Globe	¼ page, 4 times	5,075
Print	Boston Phoenix	½ page, 2 times	2,850
Print	Cambridge Chronicle	½ page, 6 times	1,860
Misc.	Mass mailing	2000 brochures, including postage	1,440
Misc.	Cambridge River Festival	1500 brochures	600

Sorting lists and paragraphs

In addition to sorting table data, you can use the Sort command to alphabetize text or sort numerical data. When you want to sort data that is not formatted as a table, such as lists and paragraphs, you use the Sort command in the Paragraph group on the Home tab. To sort lists and paragraphs, select the items you want included in the sort, then click the Sort button. In the Sort Text dialog box, use the Sort by list arrow to select the sort by criteria (paragraphs or fields), use the Type list arrow to select the type of data (text, numbers, or dates), and then click the Ascending or Descending option button to choose a sort order.

When sorting text information in a document, the term "fields" refers to text or numbers that are separated by a character, such as a tab or a comma. For example, you might want to sort a list of names alphabetically. If the names you want to sort are listed in "Last name, First name" order, then last name and first name are each considered a field. You can choose to sort the list in alphabetical order by last name or by first name. Use the Options button in the Sort Text dialog box to specify the character that separates the fields in your lists or paragraphs, along with other sort options.

Splitting and Merging Cells

A convenient way to change the format and structure of a table is to merge and split the table cells. When you **merge** cells, you combine adjacent cells into a single larger cell. When you **split** a cell, you divide an existing cell into multiple cells. You can merge and split cells using the Merge Cells and Split Cells commands in the Merge group on the Table Tools Layout tab. ████████ You merge cells in the first column to create a single cell for each ad type—Web, Print, and Misc. You also add a new row to the bottom of the table, and split the cells in the row to create three new rows with a different structure.

STEPS

1. **Select the two Web cells in the first column of the table, click the Merge Cells button in the Merge group on the Table Tools Layout tab, then deselect the text**

   The two Web cells merge to become a single cell. When you merge cells, Word converts the text in each cell into a separate paragraph in the merged cell.

2. **Select the first Web in the cell, then press [Delete]**

3. **Select the three Print cells in the first column, click the Merge Cells button, type Print, select the two Misc. cells, click the Merge Cells button, then type Misc.**

   The three Print cells merge to become one cell and the two Misc. cells merge to become one cell.

4. **Click the Cambridge River Festival cell, then click the Insert Below button in the Rows & Columns group**

   A row is added to the bottom of the table.

5. **Select the first three cells in the new last row of the table, click the Merge Cells button, then deselect the cell**

   The three cells in the row merge to become a single cell.

6. **Click the first cell in the last row, then click the Split Cells button in the Merge group**

   The Split Cells dialog box opens, as shown in Figure D-12. You use this dialog box to split the selected cell or cells into a specific number of columns and rows.

7. **Type 1 in the Number of columns text box, press [Tab], type 3 in the Number of rows text box, click OK, then deselect the cells**

   The single cell is divided into three rows of equal height. When you split a cell into multiple rows, the width of the original column does not change. When you split a cell into multiple columns, the height of the original row does not change. If the cell you split contains text, all the text appears in the upper-left cell.

8. **Click the last cell in the Cost column, click the Split Cells button, repeat Step 7, then save your changes**

   The cell is split into three rows, as shown in Figure D-13. The last three rows of the table now have only two columns.

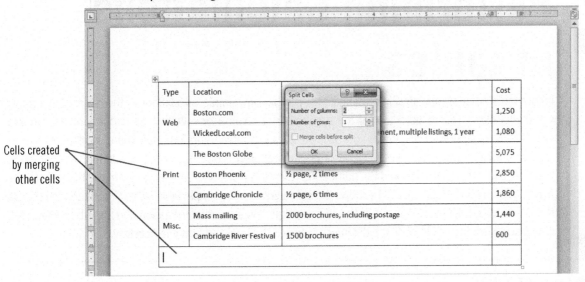

Cells created by merging other cells

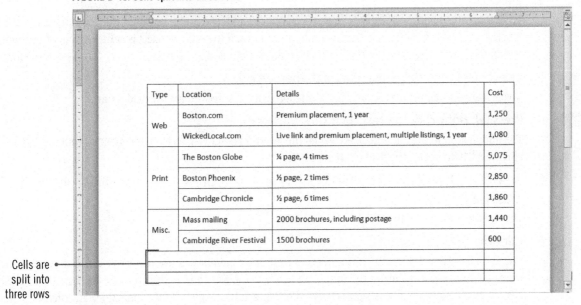

Cells are split into three rows

Changing cell margins

By default, table cells have .08" left and right cell margins with no spacing between the cells, but you can adjust these settings for a table using the Cell Margins button in the Alignment group on the Table Tools Layout tab. First, place the insertion point in the table, and then click the Cell Margins button to open the Table Options dialog box. Enter new settings for the top, bottom, left, and right cell margins in the text boxes in the Default cell margins section of the dialog box, or select the Allow spacing between cells check box and then enter a setting in the Cell spacing section to increase the spacing between table cells. You can also deselect the Automatically resize to fit contents check box in the Options section of the dialog box to turn off the setting that causes table cells to widen to fit the text as you type. Any settings you change in the Table Options dialog box are applied to the entire table.

Word 2010

Performing Calculations in Tables

If your table includes numerical information, you can perform simple calculations in the table. The Formula command allows you to quickly total the numbers in a column or row, and to perform other standard calculations, such as averages. When you calculate data in a table using formulas, you use cell references to refer to the cells in the table. Each cell has a unique **cell reference** composed of a letter and a number; the letter represents its column and the number represents its row. For example, the cell in the third row of the fourth column is cell D3. Figure D-14 shows the cell references in a simple table. 🖾🖾🖾 You use the Formula command to calculate the total cost of the ad campaign. You also add information about the budgeted cost, and create a formula to calculate the difference between the total and budgeted costs.

STEPS

QUICK TIP
If a column or row contains blank cells, you must type a zero in any blank cell before using the SUM function.

1. **Click the first blank cell in column 1, type Total Cost, press [Tab], then click the Formula button in the Data group on the Table Tools Layout tab**

   The Formula dialog box opens, as shown in Figure D-15. The SUM function appears in the Formula text box followed by the reference for the cells to include in the calculation, (ABOVE). The formula =SUM(ABOVE) indicates that Word will sum the numbers in the cells above the active cell.

2. **Click OK**

   Word totals the numbers in the cells above the active cell and inserts the sum as a field. You can use the SUM function to quickly total the numbers in a column or a row. If the cell you select is at the bottom of a column of numbers, Word totals the column. If the cell is at the right end of a row of numbers, Word totals the row.

3. **Select 600 in the cell above the total, then type 750**

   If you change a number that is part of a calculation, you must recalculate the field result.

QUICK TIP
To change a field result to regular text, click the field to select it, then press [Ctrl][Shift][F9].

4. **Press [↓], right-click the cell, then click Update Field**

   The information in the cell is updated. When the insertion point is in a cell that contains a formula, you can also press [F9] to update the field result.

5. **Press [Tab], type Budgeted, press [Tab], type 13,850, press [Tab], type Difference, then press [Tab]**

   The insertion point is in the last cell of the table.

6. **Click the Formula button**

   The Formula dialog box opens. Word proposes to sum the numbers above the active cell, but you want to insert a formula that calculates the difference between the total and budgeted costs. You can type simple custom formulas using a plus sign (+) for addition, a minus sign (–) for subtraction, an asterisk (*) for multiplication, and a slash (/) for division.

QUICK TIP
Cell references are determined by the number of columns in each row, not by the number of columns in the table. Therefore, rows 9 and 10 have only two columns.

7. **Select =SUM(ABOVE) in the Formula text box, then type =B9–B10**

   You must type an equal sign (=) to indicate that the text following it is a formula. You want to subtract the budgeted cost in the second column of row 10 from the total cost in the second column of row 9; therefore, you type a formula to subtract the value in cell B10 from the value in cell B9.

8. **Click OK, then save your changes**

   The difference appears in the cell, as shown in Figure D-16.

Creating and Formatting Tables

FIGURE D-14: Cell references in a table

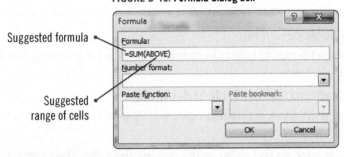

	A	B	C	D
1	A1	B1	C1	D1
2	A2	B2	C2	D2
3	A3	B3	C3	D3

Column D (fourth column)

Row 3

Cell reference indicates the cell's column and row

FIGURE D-15: Formula dialog box

Suggested formula

Suggested range of cells

Formula

Formula:
=SUM(ABOVE)
Number format:

Paste function: Paste bookmark:

OK   Cancel

FIGURE D-16: Difference calculated in table

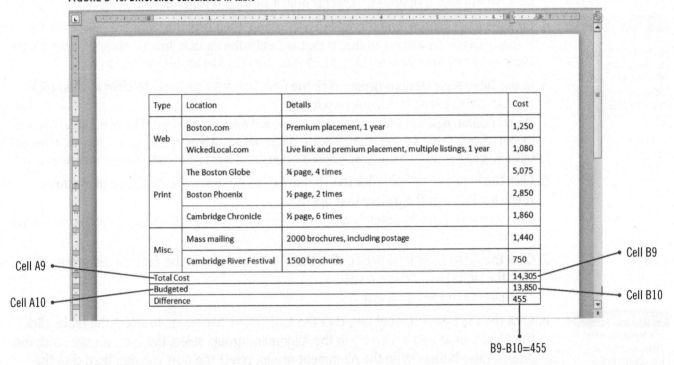

Type	Location	Details	Cost
Web	Boston.com	Premium placement, 1 year	1,250
	WickedLocal.com	Live link and premium placement, multiple listings, 1 year	1,080
Print	The Boston Globe	¼ page, 4 times	5,075
	Boston Phoenix	½ page, 2 times	2,850
	Cambridge Chronicle	½ page, 6 times	1,860
Misc.	Mass mailing	2000 brochures, including postage	1,440
	Cambridge River Festival	1500 brochures	750
Total Cost			14,305
Budgeted			13,850
Difference			455

Cell A9

Cell A10

Cell B9

Cell B10

B9-B10=455

Working with formulas

In addition to the SUM function, Word includes formulas for averaging, counting, and rounding data, to name a few. To use a Word formula, delete any text in the Formula text box, type =, click the Paste function list arrow in the Formula dialog box, select a function, and then insert the cell references of the cells you want to include in the calculation in parentheses after the name of the function. When entering formulas, you must separate cell references by a comma. For example, if you want to average the values in cells A1, B3, and C4, enter the formula =AVERAGE(A1,B3,C4). You must separate cell ranges by a colon. For example, to total the values in cells A1 through A9, enter the formula =SUM(A1:A9). To display the result of a calculation in a particular number format, such as a decimal percentage (0.00%), click the Number format list arrow in the Formula dialog box and select a number format. Word inserts the result of a calculation as a field in the selected cell.

Applying a Table Style

Adding shading and other design elements to a table can help give it a polished appearance and make the data easier to read. Word includes predefined, built-in table styles that you can apply to a table to format it quickly. Table styles include borders, shading, fonts, alignment, colors, and other formatting effects. You can apply a table style to a table using the buttons in the Table Styles group on the Table Tools Design tab. You want to enhance the appearance of the table with shading, borders, and other formats, so you apply a table style to the table. After applying a style, you change the theme colors to a more pleasing palette.

1. **Click the Table Tools Design tab**

   The Table Tools Design tab includes buttons for applying table styles and for adding, removing, and customizing borders and shading in a table.

2. **Click the More button ▼ in the Table Styles group**

   The gallery of table styles opens, as shown in Figure D-17. You point to a table style in the gallery to preview the style applied to the table.

3. **Move the pointer over several styles in the gallery, then click the Light Grid – Accent 4 style**

   The Light Grid – Accent 4 style is applied to the table, as shown in Figure D-18. Because of the structure of the table, this style neither enhances the table nor helps make the data more readable.

4. **Click the More button ▼ in the Table Styles group, then click the Light List – Accent 4 style**

   This style works better with the structure of the table, and makes the table data easier to read. Notice that the alignment of the text in the table changed back to top left when you applied a table style.

5. **In the Table Style Options group, click the First Column check box to clear it, then click the Banded Columns check box to select it**

   The bold formatting is removed from the first column, and column borders are added to the table. When the banded columns or banded rows setting is active, borders are added between the columns or rows, or the odd columns or rows are formatted differently from the even columns or rows to make the table data easier to read.

6. **Click the Page Layout tab, click the Theme Colors list arrow ▣▼ in the Themes group, then click Paper in the gallery that opens**

   The color palette for the document changes to the colors used in the Paper theme, and the table color changes to lavender.

7. **Click the Table Tools Design tab, click the More button ▼ in the Table Styles group, then click the Light List – Accent 6 style**

   The table color changes to blue-gray.

8. **Click the Table Tools Layout tab, click the table move handle ⊕ to select the table, click the Align Center Left button ▤ in the Alignment group, select the Type column, click the Align Center button ▤ in the Alignment group, select the Cost column, then click the Align Center Right button ▤ in the Alignment group**

   First, the data in the table is left-aligned and centered vertically, then the data in the Type column is centered, and finally the data in the Cost column is right-aligned.

9. **Select the last three rows of the table, click the Bold button B on the Mini toolbar, then click the Align Center Right button ▤ in the Alignment group on the Table Tools Layout tab**

   The text in the last three rows is right-aligned and bold is applied.

10. **Select the first row of the table, click the Center button ▤ on the Mini toolbar, click the Font Size list arrow on the Mini toolbar, click 14, deselect the row, then save your changes**

    The text in the header row is centered and enlarged, as shown in Figure D-19. You can also use the alignment buttons in the Paragraph group on the Home tab to change the alignment of text in a table.

Creating and Formatting Tables

FIGURE D-17: Gallery of table styles

Options for customizing table style settings

Modify an existing table style

Remove a table style from a table

Create a new table style

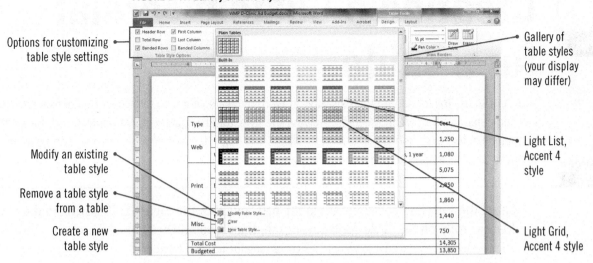

Gallery of table styles (your display may differ)

Light List, Accent 4 style

Light Grid, Accent 4 style

FIGURE D-18: Light Grid, Accent 4 style applied to table

The shading applied to the merged cells is confusing

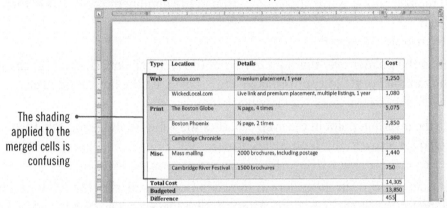

Type	Location	Details	Cost
Web	Boston.com	Premium placement, 1 year	1,250
	WickedLocal.com	Live link and premium placement, multiple listings, 1 year	1,080
Print	The Boston Globe	¾ page, 4 times	5,075
	Boston Phoenix	½ page, 2 times	2,850
	Cambridge Chronicle	½ page, 6 times	1,860
Misc.	Mass mailing	2000 brochures, including postage	1,440
	Cambridge River Festival	1500 brochures	750
Total Cost			14,305
Budgeted			13,850
Difference			455

FIGURE D-19: Light List, Accent 6 style (Paper theme) applied to table

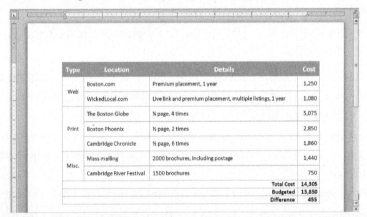

Type	Location	Details	Cost
Web	Boston.com	Premium placement, 1 year	1,250
	WickedLocal.com	Live link and premium placement, multiple listings, 1 year	1,080
Print	The Boston Globe	¾ page, 4 times	5,075
	Boston Phoenix	½ page, 2 times	2,850
	Cambridge Chronicle	½ page, 6 times	1,860
Misc.	Mass mailing	2000 brochures, including postage	1,440
	Cambridge River Festival	1500 brochures	750
		Total Cost	14,305
		Budgeted	13,850
		Difference	455

Using tables to lay out a page

Tables are often used to display information for quick reference and analysis, but you can also use tables to structure the layout of a page. You can insert any kind of information in the cell of a table—including graphics, bulleted lists, charts, and other tables (called **nested tables**). For example, you might use a table to lay out a résumé, a newsletter, or a Web page. When you use a table to lay out a page, you generally remove the table borders to hide the table structure from the reader. After you remove borders, it can be helpful to display the table gridlines onscreen while you work. **Gridlines** are blue dotted lines that show the boundaries of cells, but do not print. If your document will be viewed online—for example, if you are planning to e-mail your résumé to potential employers—you should turn off the display of gridlines before you distribute the document so that it looks the same online as it looks when printed. To turn gridlines off or on, click the View Gridlines button in the Table group on the Table Tools Layout tab.

Creating a Custom Format for a Table

You can also use the formatting tools available in Word to create your own table designs. For example, you can add or remove borders and shading; vary the line style, thickness, and color of borders; and change the orientation of text from horizontal to vertical. ⬛⬛⬛ You adjust the text direction, shading, and borders in the table to make it easier to understand at a glance.

STEPS

1. **Select the Type and Location cells in the first row, click the Merge Cells button in the Merge group on the Table Tools Layout tab, then type Ad Location**
   The two cells are combined into a single cell containing the text "Ad Location."

2. **Select the Web, Print, and Misc. cells in the first column, click the Bold button B on the Mini toolbar, click the Text Direction button in the Alignment group twice, then deselect the cells**
   The text is rotated 270 degrees.

3. **Position the pointer over the right border of the Web cell until the pointer changes to ┼‖┼, then drag the border to approximately the ¼" mark on the horizontal ruler**
   The width of the column containing the vertical text narrows.

4. **Place the insertion point in the Web cell, click the Table Tools Design tab, then click the Shading list arrow in the Table Styles group**
   The gallery of shading colors for the Paper theme opens.

5. **Click Gold, Accent 3 in the gallery as shown in Figure D-20, click the Print cell, click the Shading list arrow, click Lavender, Accent 4, click the Misc. cell, click the Shading list arrow, then click Blue-Gray, Accent 6**
   Shading is applied to each cell.

6. **Drag to select the six white cells in the Web rows (rows 2 and 3), click the Shading list arrow, then click Gold, Accent 3, Lighter 60%**

7. **Repeat Step 6 to apply Lavender, Accent 4, Lighter 60% shading to the Print rows and Blue-Gray, Accent 6, Lighter 60% shading to the Misc. rows**
   Shading is applied to all the cells in rows 1–8.

8. **Select the last three rows of the table, click the Borders list arrow in the Table Styles group, click No Border on the menu that opens, then click in the table to deselect the rows**
   The top, bottom, left, and right borders are removed from each cell in the selected rows.

9. **Click the Pen Color list arrow in the Draw Borders group, click Blue-Gray, Accent 6, select the Total Cost row, click the Borders list arrow, click Top Border, click the 13,850 cell, click the Borders list arrow, then click Bottom Border**
   The active pen color for borders is Blue-Gray, Accent 6. You use the buttons in the Draw Borders group to change the active pen color, line weight, and line style settings before adding a border to a table. A top border is added to each cell in the Total Cost row, and a bottom border is added below 13,850. The completed table is shown in Figure D-21.

10. **Press [Ctrl][Home], press [Enter], type your name, save your changes, submit the document to your instructor, close the document, then exit Word**
    Press [Enter] at the beginning of a table to move the table down one line in a document.

Creating and Formatting Tables

FIGURE D-20: Gallery of shading colors from the Origin theme

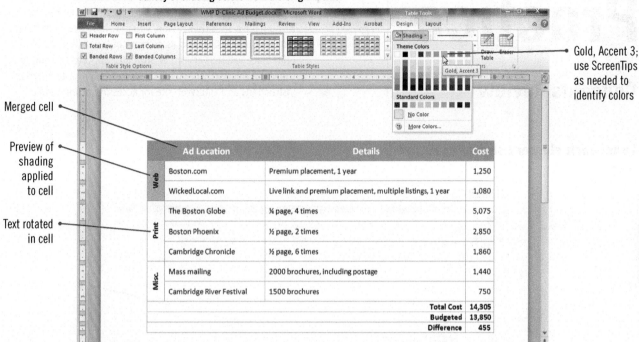

Merged cell

Preview of shading applied to cell

Text rotated in cell

Gold, Accent 3; use ScreenTips as needed to identify colors

FIGURE D-21: Completed table

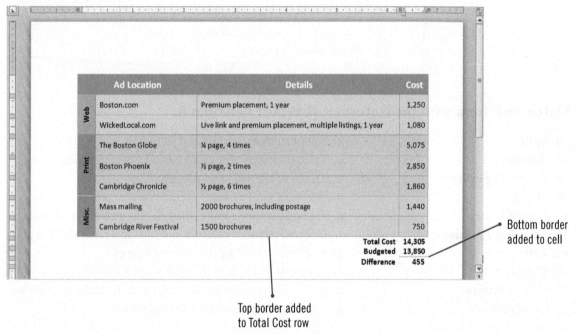

Bottom border added to cell

Top border added to Total Cost row

Drawing a table

The Word Draw Table feature allows you to draw table cells exactly where you want them. To draw a table, click the Table button on the Insert tab, and then click Draw Table. If a table is already started, you can click the Draw Table button in the Draw Borders group on the Table Tools Design tab to turn on the Draw pointer , and then click and drag to draw a cell. Using the same method, you can draw borders within the cell to create columns and rows, or draw additional cells attached to the first cell. Click the Draw Table button to turn off

the draw feature. The borders you draw are added using the active line style, line weight, and pen color settings.

If you want to remove a border from a table, click the Eraser button in the Draw Borders group to activate the Eraser pointer , and then click the border you want to remove. Click the Eraser button to turn off the erase feature. You can use the Draw pointer and the Eraser pointer to change the structure of any table, not just the tables you draw from scratch.

Word 2010

Practice

Concepts Review

For current SAM information, including versions and content details, visit SAM Central (http://www.cengage.com/samcentral). If you have a SAM user profile, you may have access to hands-on instruction, practice, and assessment of the skills covered in this unit. Since various versions of SAM are supported throughout the life of this text, check with your instructor for the correct instructions and URL/Web site for accessing assignments.

Label each element shown in Figure D-22.

FIGURE D-22

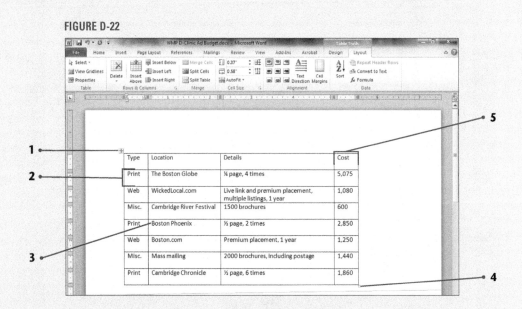

Match each term with the statement that best describes it.

6. Split
7. Borders
8. Ascending order
9. Merge
10. Nested table
11. Descending order
12. Cell
13. Header row
14. Cell reference
15. Gridlines

a. Sort order that organizes text from A to Z
b. The box formed by the intersection of a column and a row
c. An object inserted in a table cell
d. The first row of a table that contains the column headings
e. To combine two or more adjacent cells into one larger cell
f. Lines that separate columns and rows in a table and that print
g. To divide an existing cell into multiple cells
h. Lines that show columns and rows in a table but that do not print
i. A cell address composed of a column letter and a row number
j. Sort order that organizes text from Z to A

Select the best answer from the list of choices.

16. Which button do you use to change the alignment of text in a cell?
    a. [image]
    b. [image]
    c. [image]
    d. [image]

17. Which of the following is the cell reference for the third cell in the second column?
    a. 3B
    b. B3
    c. C2
    d. 2C

18. What happens when you double-click a column border?
    a. The column width is adjusted to fit the text.
    b. The columns in the table are distributed evenly.
    c. A new column is added to the left.
    d. A new column is added to the right.

19. **Which of the following is _not_ a valid way to add a new row to the bottom of a table?**
   a. Click in the bottom row, open the Properties dialog box, then insert a row using the options on the Row tab.
   b. Place the insertion point in the last cell of the last row, then press [Tab].
   c. Right-click the bottom row, point to Insert, then click Insert Rows Below.
   d. Click in the bottom row, then click the Insert Below button in the Rows & Columns group on the Table Tools Layout tab.

20. **Which of the following is _not_ a correct formula for adding the values in cells A1, A2, and A3?**
   a. =A1+A2+A3
   b. =SUM(A1~A3)
   c. =SUM(A1,A2,A3)
   d. =SUM(A1:A3)

Skills Review

1. **Insert a table.**
   a. Start Word, then save the new blank document as **WMP D-Flu Mortality** to the drive and folder where you store your Data Files.
   b. Type your name, press [Enter] twice, type **Influenza Mortality in Selected Major Cities**, then press [Enter].
   c. Insert a table that contains four columns and four rows.
   d. Type the text shown in Figure D-23, pressing [Tab] to add rows as necessary. (*Note*: Do not format text or the table at this time.)
   e. Save your changes.

2. **Insert and delete rows and columns.**
   a. Insert a row above the Philadelphia row, then type the following text in the new row:
      Houston   315   112   13
   b. Delete the Boston row.

FIGURE D-23

City	>=65	25-64	<25
Boston	272	115	8
San Diego	129	68	3
Philadelphia	523	198	27
Detroit	217	143	17
Miami	186	98	9
Phoenix	138	57	6

   c. Insert a column to the right of the <25 column, type **Date Reported** in the header row, then enter a June 2013 date in each cell in the column using the format MM/DD/YY (for example, 06/27/13).
   d. Move the Date Reported column to the right of the City column, then save your changes.

3. **Modify rows and columns.**
   a. Double-click the border between the first and second columns to resize the columns.
   b. Drag the border between the second and third columns to the $1^3/_4$" mark on the horizontal ruler.
   c. Double-click the right border of the >=65, 25-64, and <25 columns.
   d. Select the >=65, 25-64, and <25 columns, then distribute the columns evenly.
   e. Select the table, apply the No Spacing style, select rows 2–7, set the row height to exactly .3", then save your changes.

4. **Sort table data.**
   Perform three separate sorts as follows:
   a. Sort the table data, excluding the header row, in descending order by the information in the >=65 column, then click OK.
   b. Sort the table data, excluding the header row, in ascending order by date reported, then click OK.
   c. Sort the table data, excluding the header row, by city name in alphabetical order, click OK, then save your changes.

5. **Split and merge cells.**
   a. Insert a row above the header row, then merge the first cell in the new row with the City cell.
   b. Merge the second cell in the new row with the Date Reported cell.
   c. Merge the three remaining blank cells in the first row into a single cell, then type **Mortality by Age** in the merged cell.
   d. Add a new row to the bottom of the table.
   e. Merge the first two cells in the new row, then type **Average Mortality by Age** in the merged cell.
   f. Select the first seven cells in the first column (from City to San Diego), open the Split Cells dialog box, clear the Merge cells before split check box, then split the cells into two columns.
   g. Type **State** as the heading for the new column, then enter the following text in the remaining cells in the column:
      MI, TX, FL, PA, AZ, CA.
   h. Double-click the right border of the first column to resize the column, then save your changes.

Word 95

Word 2010

Skills Review (continued)

6. **Perform calculations in tables.**

   a. Place the insertion point in the last cell in the >=65 column.

   b. Open the Formula dialog box, delete the text in the Formula text box, type **=average(above)**, then click OK.

   c. Repeat Step b to insert the average number of cases in each age category in the last cell in the 25-64 and <25 columns.

   d. Change the value of the >=65 mortality rate for Phoenix to **182**.

   e. Recalculate the average for the number of cases reported for the >=65 category. (*Hint:* Right-click the cell and select Update Field, or use [F9].)

   f. Double-click the right border of the first column to resize the column, then double-click the right border of the >=65, 25-64, and <25 columns to resize the columns.

   g. Select the last three columns in the table, distribute the columns evenly, then save your changes.

7. **Apply a table style.**

   a. Click the Table Tools Design tab, preview table styles applied to the table, and then apply an appropriate style. Was the style you chose effective?

   b. Apply the Light Shading style to the table, then remove the style from First Column and Banded Rows.

   c. Apply bold to the >=65, 25-64, and <25 column headings, and to the bottom row of the table.

   d. Center the table between the margins, center the table title **Influenza Mortality in Selected Major Cities**, increase the font size of the title to 14 points, apply bold, then save your changes.

8. **Create a custom format for a table.**

   a. Select the entire table, then use the Align Center button in the Alignment group on the Table Tools Layout tab to center the text in every cell vertically and horizontally.

   b. Center right-align the dates in column 3 and the numbers in columns 4–6.

   c. Center left-align the city names and state abbreviations in columns 1 and 2, but not the column headings.

   d. Center right-align the text in the bottom row. Make sure the text in the header row is still centered.

   e. Change the theme colors to Executive.

   f. Select all the cells in the header row, including the >=65, 25-64, and <25 column headings, change the shading color to Dark Green, Accent 5, then change the font color to white.

   g. Apply Dark Green, Accent 5, Lighter 60% shading to the cells containing the city names and state abbreviations, and Dark Green Accent 5, Lighter 80% shading to the cells containing the dates.

   h. To the cells containing the >=65, 25-64, and <25 data (excluding the Average Mortality data), apply Indigo, Accent 1, Lighter 60% shading; Orange, Accent 3, Lighter 60% shading; and Red, Accent 2, Lighter 60% shading, respectively.

   i. Apply Dark Green Accent 5, Lighter 80% shading to the last row of the table.

   j. Add a ½-point white bottom border to the Mortality by Age cell in the header row. (*Hint:* Change the Line Weight to ½ pt, change the Pen Color to White, then add the bottom border.)

   k. Add a 1½-point black border around the outside of the table. (*Hint:* Select the table, open the Borders and Shading dialog box, then add the outside border.)

   l. Add a ½-point black top border to the Detroit row and to the last row of the table. (*Hint:* Do not remove any borders.)

   m. Compare your table to Figure D-24, make any necessary adjustments, save your changes, submit a copy to your instructor, close the file, then exit Word.

FIGURE D-24

Influenza Mortality in Selected Major Cities

| City | State | Date Reported | Mortality by Age | | |
			>=65	25-64	<25
Detroit	MI	06/14/13	217	143	17
Houston	TX	06/07/13	315	112	13
Miami	FL	06/22/13	186	98	9
Philadelphia	PA	06/25/13	523	198	27
Phoenix	AZ	06/28/13	182	57	6
San Diego	CA	06/11/13	129	68	3
Average Mortality by Age			258.67	112.67	12.5

Creating and Formatting Tables

Independent Challenge 1

You are the office manager for a dental office. In preparation for a meeting about next year's budget, you create a table showing quarterly expenditures for the fiscal year 2013.

a. Start Word, then save the new blank document as **WMP D-2013 Expenditures** to the drive and folder where you store your Data Files.

b. Type the table heading **Quarterly Expenditures, Fiscal Year 2013** at the top of the document, then press [Enter] twice.

c. Insert a table with five columns and four rows, then enter the data shown in Figure D-25 into the table, adding rows as necessary. (*Note*: Do not format text or the table at this time.)

d. Resize the columns to fit the text.

e. Sort the table rows in alphabetical order by Item.

f. Add a new row to the bottom of the table, type **Total** in the first cell, then enter a formula in each remaining cell in the new row to calculate the sum of the cells above it.

FIGURE D-25

Item	Q1	Q2	Q3	Q4
Impression Products	1283	1627	1374	1723
Instruments	920	847	862	798
Anesthetics	1023	948	926	897
Cements and Liners	834	812	912	1029
Finishing and Polishing	463	394	472	289
Pins and Posts	730	695	463	586

g. Add a new column to the right side of the table, type **Total** in the first cell, then enter a formula in each remaining cell in the new column to calculate the sum of the cells to the left of it. (*Hint*: Make sure the formula you insert in each cell sums the cells to the left, not the cells above. In the last cell in the last column, you can sum the cells to the left or the cells above; either way the total should be the same.)

h. Apply a table style to the table. Select a style that enhances the information contained in the table, and adjust the Table Style Options to suit the content.

i. Center the text in the header row, left-align the remaining text in the first column, then right-align the numerical data in the table.

j. Enhance the table with fonts, font colors, shading, and borders to make the table attractive and easy to read at a glance.

k. Increase the font size of the table heading to 18 points, then center the table heading and the table on the page.

l. Press [Ctrl][End], press [Enter], type your name, save your changes, submit the file to your instructor, close the file, then exit Word.

Independent Challenge 2

You are a medical assistant in a busy family practice office. One of your responsibilities at the office is to create a list of scheduled appointments for the day. You find it easiest to format this information as a table.

a. Start Word, open the file WMP D-1.docx, then save it as **WMP D-April 14 Appointments** to the drive and folder where you store your Data Files.

b. Center the table heading, then increase the font size to 18 points.

c. Turn on formatting marks, select the tabbed text in the document, then convert the text to a table.

d. Add a row above the first row in the table, then enter the following column headings in the new header row: **Last Name, First Name, DOB, Phone, Physician, Time**.

e. Apply an appropriate table style to the table. Add or remove the style from various elements of the table using the options in the Table Style Options group, as necessary.

f. Adjust the column widths so that the table is attractive and readable.

g. Make the height of each row at least .25".

h. Center left-align the text in each cell in the first column, then Center Align the text in each cell in the DOB and Phone columns.

i. Center right-align the text in each cell in the Time column, including the column heads.

j. Center the column headings, then center the entire table on the page.

k. Sort the table by last name and then by first name in alphabetical order.

Independent Challenge 2 (continued)

Advanced Challenge Exercise

- Sort the entire table by physician in alphabetical order.
- Change the shading color of the Boxer, Dixon, and Wilson rows, each to a different color.
- Sort the table by Time and then by Physician, in ascending order. Move the Time column to become the first column in the table, then adjust the column width to fit the text. Move the rows for the appointments from 9:30 to 12:30 to the beginning of the table.

l. Enhance the table with borders, shading, fonts, and other formats, if necessary, to make it attractive and readable.

m. Type your name at the bottom of the document or in the footer, save your changes, submit a copy of the table to your instructor, close the document, then exit Word.

Independent Challenge 3

You work in a pediatrician's office. Your boss has given you data on appropriate Ibuprofen and Acetaminophen doses for children and has asked you to format the information for parents. You'll use tables to lay out the information so it is easily understandable.

a. Start Word, open the file WMP D-2.docx from the drive and folder where you store your Data Files, then save it as **WMP D-Dosages**. Read the document to get a feel for its contents.

b. Merge the cell in the first row of the table, then merge the cells in the Acetaminophen Doses row.

c. Insert a new row under the first row. Type **One dose lasts 6-8 hours** in the new cell.

d. Insert a new row under the Acetaminophen Doses row. Type **One dose lasts 4-6 hours** in the new row.

e. Change all the text in the table to 10-point Arial, then center all the text horizontally and vertically in the cells. (*Hint*: Use the Center Align button.)

f. Make the height of each row at least .25".

g. Select the third row of the table, copy it, then paste the row below the One dose lasts 4-6 hours row.

h. Split the table above the Acetaminophen Doses row, then press [Enter].

i. Refer to Figure D-26 and follow the steps below as you format the Ibuprofen and Acetaminophen tables. (*Hint*: Turn on gridlines to help you see the structure of the table as you format it.)

j. Format the header row in 14-point Arial, bold, then remove all the borders.

k. Format the second row in 12-point Arial, then remove all the borders.

l. In each column, merge the cells in rows 3 and 4. Remove the left border from the first cell in the new row 3. In the remaining cells in the row, apply bold to the text, then add a top border.

m. Apply bold to the text in the fourth row, then apply Orange, Accent 6 shading to the cells.

n. In the fifth row, merge the cells in columns 2-6, then apply bold to the text in the merged cell.

o. In columns 2-5, merge all adjoining blank cells, then remove the borders between the blank cells. (*Hint*: You might need to reapply borders to some adjacent cells after you remove the borders between the blank cells.)

FIGURE D-26

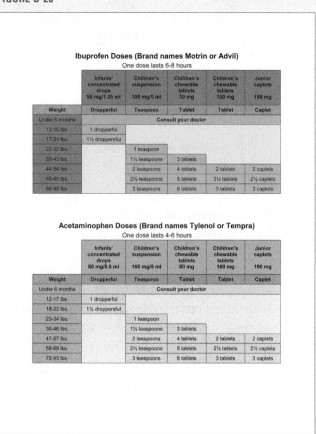

Independent Challenge 3 (continued)

p. Repeat Steps j-o to format the Acetaminophen table.

q. In the Ibuprofen table, apply Blue, Accent 1 shading to the cells in row 3, columns 2-6, and to the cells in column 1, rows 5-12.

r. Apply Blue, Accent 1, Lighter 80% shading to the blank cells in columns 2-5.

s. Apply Blue, Accent 1, Lighter 40% shading to the remaining table cells in columns 2-5.

t. Repeat Steps q-s to apply shading to the Acetaminophen table, using shades of Olive Green, Accent 3 shading.

Advanced Challenge Exercise

- In both tables, change the font color of the third row to white, then change the font color of the cells in column 1, rows 5-12 to white.
- Change the theme colors to a palette of your choice.
- Adjust the shading in each table so that the table is attractive and the dosage information is presented as clearly as possible.

u. Examine the document for errors, then make any necessary adjustments.

v. Press [Ctrl][End], press [Enter], type your name, save your changes to the document, preview it, submit the file to your instructor, close the file, then exit Word.

Real Life Independent Challenge

This Independent Challenge requires an Internet connection.

A well-written and well-formatted résumé gives you an advantage when it comes to getting a job interview. In a winning résumé, the content and format support your career objective and effectively present your background and qualifications. One simple way to create a résumé is to lay out the page using a table. In this exercise you research guidelines for writing and formatting résumés. You then create your own résumé using a table for its layout.

a. Use your favorite search engine to search the Web for information on writing and formatting résumés. Use the keywords **resume advice**.

b. Print helpful advice on writing and formatting résumés from at least two Web sites.

c. Think about the information you want to include in your résumé. The header should include your name, address, telephone number, and e-mail address. The body should include your career objective and information on your education, work experience, and skills. You may want to add additional information.

d. Sketch a layout for your résumé using a table as the underlying grid. Include the table rows and columns in your sketch.

e. Start Word, open a new blank document, then save it as **WMP D-My Resume** to the drive and folder where you store your Data Files.

f. Set appropriate margins, then insert a table to serve as the underlying grid for your résumé. Split and merge cells, and adjust the size of the table columns as necessary.

g. Type your résumé in the table cells. Take care to use a professional tone and keep your language to the point.

h. Format your résumé with fonts, bullets, and other formatting features. Adjust the spacing between sections by resizing the table columns and rows.

i. When you are satisfied with the content and format of your résumé, remove the borders from the table, then hide the gridlines if they are visible. You may want to add some borders back to the table to help structure the résumé for readers.

j. Check your résumé for spelling and grammar errors.

k. Save your changes, preview your résumé, submit a copy to your instructor, close the file, then exit Word.

Visual Workshop

Create the calendar shown in Figure D-27 using a table to lay out the entire page. (*Hint*: The font is Century Gothic.) Type your name in the last table cell, save the calendar with the file name **WMP D-October 2013** to the drive and folder where you store your Data Files, then print a copy.

FIGURE D-27

Atlantic Community Hospital
Community Education Calendar

October 2013

Sunday	Monday	Tuesday	Wednesday	Thursday	Friday	Saturday
		1 Diabetes Mgmt. Education 1:30 p.m.	**2**	**3**	**4** Yoga 9:00 a.m.	**5** Women's AA 9:00 a.m. AA 8:00 p.m.
6 OA 6:30 p.m.	**7**	**8** Diabetes Mgmt. Education 1:30 p.m.	**9**	**10** Nursing Mother's Support Group 10:00 a.m.	**11** Yoga 9:00 a.m.	**12** Women's AA 9:00 a.m. AA 8:00 p.m.
13 OA 6:30 p.m.	**14** Cancer Support Group 7:00 p.m.	**15** Diabetes Mgmt. Education 1:30 p.m.	**16**	**17**	**18** Yoga 9:00 a.m.	**19** Women's AA 9:00 a.m. AA 8:00 p.m.
20 OA 6:30 p.m.	**21**	**22** Diabetes Mgmt. Education 1:30 p.m.	**23** Stroke Support Group 1:30 p.m.	**24** Nursing Mother's Support Group 10:00 a.m.	**25** Yoga 9:00 a.m.	**26** Women's AA 9:00 a.m. AA 8:00 p.m.
27 OA 6:30 p.m.	**28** Cancer Support Group 7:00 p.m.	**29** Diabetes Mgmt. Education 1:30 p.m.	**30**	**31**		Your Name

All groups meet in Conference Room 1.
For more information, call 555-4745

Formatting Documents

Files You Will Need:

WMP E-1.docx

WMP E-2.docx

WMP E-3.docx

WMP E-4.docx

WMP E-5.docx

WMP E-6.docx

WMP E-7.docx

The page-formatting features of Word allow you to lay out and design documents of all types, including reports, brochures, newsletters, and research documents. In this unit, you learn how to change the document margins, add page numbers, insert headers and footers, and format text in columns. You also learn how to work with the Word reference features to add footnotes, insert citations, and create a bibliography. You have written and formatted the text for an informational report for Riverwalk Medical Clinic patients about staying healthy while traveling. You are now ready to format the pages. You plan to organize the text in columns, to illustrate the report with a table, and to add footnotes and a bibliography.

OBJECTIVES

Set document margins

Create sections and columns

Insert page breaks

Insert page numbers

Add headers and footers

Insert a table

Add footnotes and endnotes

Insert citations

Manage sources and create a bibliography

Setting Document Margins

Changing a document's margins is one way to change the appearance of a document and control the amount of text that fits on a page. The **margins** of a document are the blank areas between the edge of the text and the edge of the page. When you create a document in Word, the default margins are 1" at the top, bottom, left, and right sides of the page. You can adjust the size of a document's margins using the Margins command on the Page Layout tab or using the rulers. ⬛⬛⬛⬛ The report should be a four-page document when finished. You begin by reducing the size of the document margins so that more text fits on each page.

STEPS

TROUBLE
Click the View Ruler button 🔲 at the top of the vertical scroll bar to display the rulers if they are not already displayed.

1. **Start Word, open the file** WMP E-1.docx **from the drive and folder where you store your Data Files, then save it as** WMP E-Healthy Traveler
   The report opens in Print Layout view.

2. **Scroll through the report to get a feel for its contents, then press** [Ctrl][Home]
   The report is currently five pages long. Notice that the status bar indicates the page where the insertion point is located and the total number of pages in the document.

3. **Click the** Page Layout tab, **then click the** Margins button **in the Page Setup group**
   The Margins menu opens. You can select predefined margin settings from this menu, or you can click Custom Margins to create different margin settings.

QUICK TIP
You can also click the launcher 🔲 in the Page Setup group to open the Page Setup dialog box.

4. **Click** Custom Margins
   The Page Setup dialog box opens with the Margins tab displayed, as shown in Figure E-1. You can use the Margins tab to change the top, bottom, left, or right document margin, to change the orientation of the pages from portrait to landscape, and to alter other page layout settings. **Portrait orientation** means a page is taller than it is wide; **landscape orientation** means a page is wider than it is tall. This report uses portrait orientation. You can also use the Orientation button in the Page Setup group on the Page Layout tab to change the orientation of a document.

5. **Click the** Top down arrow **three times until 0.7" appears, then click the** Bottom down arrow **until 0.7" appears**
   The top and bottom margins of the report will be .7". Notice that the margins in the Preview section of the dialog box change as you adjust the margin settings.

QUICK TIP
The minimum allowable margin settings depend on your printer and the size of the paper you are using. Word displays a warning message if you set margins that are too narrow for your printer.

6. **Press** [Tab], **type** .7 **in the Left text box, press** [Tab], **then type** .7 **in the Right text box**
   The left and right margins of the report will also be .7". You can change the margin settings by using the arrows or by typing a value in the appropriate text box.

7. **Click** OK
   The document margins change to .7", as shown in Figure E-2. The location of each margin (right, left, top, and bottom) is shown on the horizontal and vertical rulers at the intersection of the white and shaded areas. You can also change a margin setting by using the pointer to drag the intersection to a new location on the ruler.

8. **Click the** View tab, **then click the** Two Pages button **in the Zoom group**
   The first two pages of the document appear in the document window.

9. **Scroll down to view all five pages of the report, press** [Ctrl][Home], **click the** Page Width button **in the Zoom group, then save your changes**

Formatting Documents

FIGURE E-1: Margins tab in Page Setup dialog box

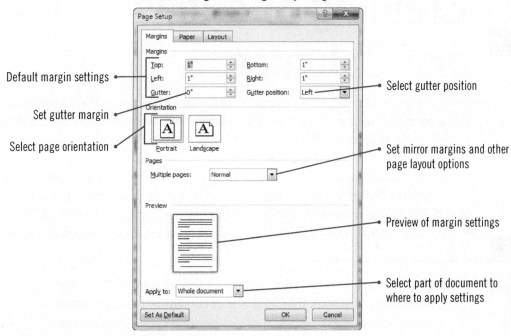

Default margin settings

Set gutter margin

Select page orientation

Select gutter position

Set mirror margins and other page layout options

Preview of margin settings

Select part of document to where to apply settings

FIGURE E-2: Report with smaller margins

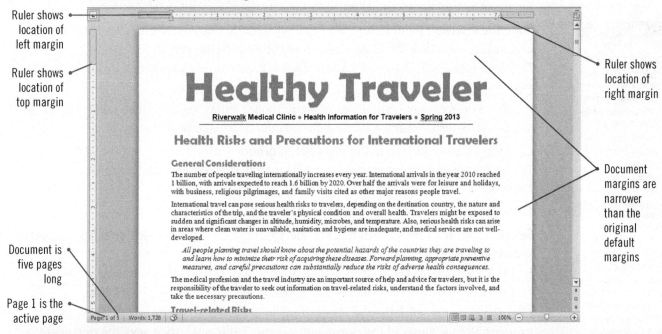

Ruler shows location of left margin

Ruler shows location of top margin

Document is five pages long

Page 1 is the active page

Ruler shows location of right margin

Document margins are narrower than the original default margins

Changing orientation, margin settings, and paper size

By default, the documents you create in Word use an 8½" × 11" paper size in portrait orientation with the default margin settings. You can change the orientation, margin settings, and paper size to common settings using the Orientation, Margins, and Size buttons in the Page Setup group on the Page Layout tab. You can also adjust these settings and others in the Page Setup dialog box. For example, to change the layout of multiple pages, use the Multiple pages list arrow on the Margins tab to create pages that use mirror margins, that include two pages per sheet of paper, or that are formatted using a book fold. **Mirror margins** are used in a document with facing pages, such as a magazine, where the margins on the left page

of the document are a mirror image of the margins on the right page. Documents with mirror margins have inside and outside margins, rather than right and left margins. Another type of margin is a gutter margin, which is used in documents that are bound, such as books. A **gutter** adds extra space to the left, top, or inside margin to allow for the binding. Add a gutter to a document by adjusting the setting in the Gutter position text box on the Margins tab. To change the size of the paper used, use the Paper size list arrow on the Paper tab to select a standard paper size, or enter custom measurements in the Width and Height text boxes.

Creating Sections and Columns

Dividing a document into sections allows you to format each section of the document with different page layout settings. A **section** is a portion of a document that is separated from the rest of the document by section breaks. **Section breaks** are formatting marks that you insert in a document to show the end of a section. Once you have divided a document into sections, you can format each section with different column, margin, page orientation, header and footer, and other page layout settings. By default, a document is formatted as a single section, but you can divide a document into as many sections as you like. ⬛⬛⬛ You insert a section break to divide the document into two sections, and then format the text in the second section in two columns. First, you customize the status bar to display section information.

STEPS

QUICK TIP

Use the Customize Status Bar menu to turn on and off the display of information in the status bar.

1. **Right-click the status bar, click Section on the Customize Status Bar menu that opens (if it is not already checked), then click the document to close the menu**
   The status bar indicates the insertion point is located in section 1 of the document.

2. **Click the Home tab, then click the Show/Hide ¶ button ¶ in the Paragraph group**
   Turning on formatting marks allows you to see the section breaks you insert in a document.

QUICK TIP

When you insert a section break at the beginning of a paragraph, Word inserts the break at the end of the previous paragraph. A section break stores the formatting information for the preceding section.

3. **Place the insertion point before the heading General Considerations, click the Page Layout tab, then click the Breaks button in the Page Setup group**
   The Breaks menu opens. You use this menu to insert different types of section breaks. See Table E-1.

4. **Click Continuous**
   Word inserts a continuous section break, shown as a dotted double line, above the heading. The document now has two sections. Notice that the status bar indicates the insertion point is in section 2.

5. **Click the Columns button in the Page Setup group**
   The columns menu opens. You use this menu to format text using preset column formats or to create custom columns.

QUICK TIP

When you delete a section break, you delete the section formatting of the text before the break. That text becomes part of the following section, and it assumes the formatting of that section.

6. **Click More Columns to open the Columns dialog box**

7. **Select Two in the Presets section, click the Spacing down arrow twice until 0.3" appears as shown in Figure E-3, then click OK**
   Section 2 is formatted in two columns of equal width with .3" of spacing between, as shown in Figure E-4. Formatting text in columns is another way to increase the amount of text that fits on a page.

8. **Click the View tab, click the Two Pages button in the Zoom group, scroll down to examine all four pages of the document, press [Ctrl][Home], then save the document**
   The text in section 2—all the text below the continuous section break—is formatted in two columns. Text in columns flows automatically from the bottom of one column to the top of the next column.

TABLE E-1: Types of section breaks

section	function
Next page	Begins a new section and moves the text following the break to the top of the next page
Continuous	Begins a new section on the same page
Even page	Begins a new section and moves the text following the break to the top of the next even-numbered page
Odd page	Begins a new section and moves the text following the break to the top of the next odd-numbered page

Formatting Documents

FIGURE E-3: Columns dialog box

Select a preset format for columns

Change the number of columns

Select to add a line between columns

Set space between columns

Set custom widths and spacing for columns

Preview of current settings

Select to create columns of equal width

Select part of document to where to apply format

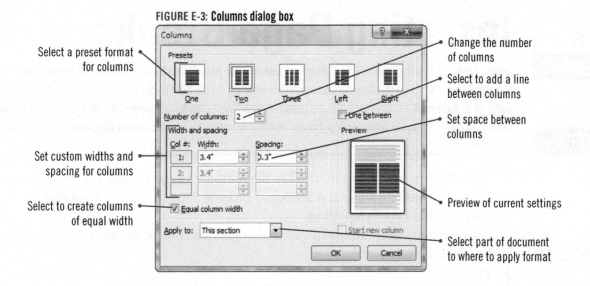

FIGURE E-4: Continuous section break and columns

Text in section 1 is formatted in one column

Insertion point in section 2

Text in section 2 is formatted in two columns

Continuous section break

Columns of text

Section 2 is the active section

Document is now four pages long

Changing page layout settings for a section

Dividing a document into sections allows you to vary the layout of a document. In addition to applying different column settings to sections, you can apply different margins, page orientation, paper size, vertical alignment, header and footer, page numbering, footnotes, endnotes, and other page layout settings. For example, if you are formatting a report that includes a table with many columns, you might want to change the table's page orientation to landscape so that it is easier to read. To do this, you would insert a section break before and after the table to create a section that contains only the table, and then you would change the page orientation of the section that contains the table to landscape. If the table does not fill the page, you could also change the vertical alignment of the table so that it is centered vertically on the page. To do this, use the Vertical alignment list arrow on the Layout tab of the Page Setup dialog box.

To check or change the page layout settings for an individual section, place the insertion point in the section, then open the Page Setup dialog box. Select any options you want to change, click the Apply to list arrow, click This section, then click OK. When you select This section in the Apply to list box, the settings are applied to the current section only. If you select Whole document in the Apply to list box, the settings are applied to all the sections in the document. Use the Apply to list arrow in the Columns dialog box or the Footnote and Endnote dialog box to change those settings for a section.

Inserting Page Breaks

As you type text in a document, Word inserts an **automatic page break** (also called a soft page break) when you reach the bottom of a page, allowing you to continue typing on the next page. You can also force text onto the next page of a document by using the Breaks command to insert a **manual page break** (also called a hard page break). ▰▰▰▰ You insert manual page breaks where you know you want to begin each new page of the report.

1. **Click the Page Width button, scroll to the bottom of page 1, place the insertion point before the heading Malaria: A Serious..., click the Page Layout tab, then click the Breaks button in the Page Setup group**

   The Breaks menu opens. You also use this menu to insert page, column, and text-wrapping breaks. Table E-2 describes these types of breaks.

2. **Click Page**

   Word inserts a manual page break before "Malaria: A Serious Health Risk for Travelers" and moves all the text following the page break to the beginning of the next page, as shown in Figure E-5. The page break appears as a dotted line in Print Layout view when formatting marks are displayed. Page break marks are visible on the screen but do not print.

3. **Scroll down, place the insertion point before the heading Preventive Options... on page 2, press and hold [Ctrl], then press [Enter]**

   Pressing [Ctrl][Enter] is a fast way to insert a manual page break. The heading is forced to the top of the third page.

4. **Scroll to the bottom of page 3, place the insertion point before the heading Insurance for Travelers on page 3, then press [Ctrl][Enter]**

   The heading is forced to the top of the fourth page.

5. **Scroll up, click to the left of the page break on page 2 with the selection pointer ⇗ to select the page break, then press [Delete]**

   The manual page break is deleted and the text from pages 2 and 3 flows together. You can also use the selection pointer to click to the left of a section or a column break to select it.

6. **Place the insertion point before the heading Medical Kit.... on page 2, then press [Ctrl][Enter]**

   The heading is forced to the top of the third page.

7. **Click the View tab, click the Two Pages button in the Zoom group, scroll to view all four pages of the document, then save your changes**

   Pages 3 and 4 are shown in Figure E-6.

Controlling automatic pagination

Another way to control the flow of text between pages (or between columns) is to apply pagination settings to specify where Word positions automatic page breaks. For example, you might want to make sure an article appears on the same page as its heading, or you might want to prevent a page from breaking in the middle of the last paragraph of a report. To manipulate automatic pagination, simply select the paragraphs(s) or line(s) you want to control, click the launcher in the Paragraph group on the Home or Page Layout tab, click the Line and Page Breaks tab in the Paragraph dialog box, select one or more of the following settings in the Pagination section, and then click OK. Pagination settings include the following:

- Keep with next setting—apply to any paragraph you want to appear together with the next paragraph on a single page in

  order to prevent the page from breaking between the paragraphs.

- Keep lines together setting—apply to selected paragraph or lines to prevent a page from breaking in the middle of a paragraph or between certain lines.
- Page break before setting—apply to specify that a selected paragraph follows an automatic page break.
- Widow/Orphan control setting—turned on by default in the Pagination section of the dialog box. This setting ensures that at least two lines of a paragraph appear at the top and bottom of every page. In other words, it prevents a page from beginning with just the last line of a paragraph (a **widow**), and prevents a page from ending with only the first line of a new paragraph (an **orphan**).

FIGURE E-5: Manual page break in document

Text that follows break is forced onto the next page

Insertion point on page 2 of document

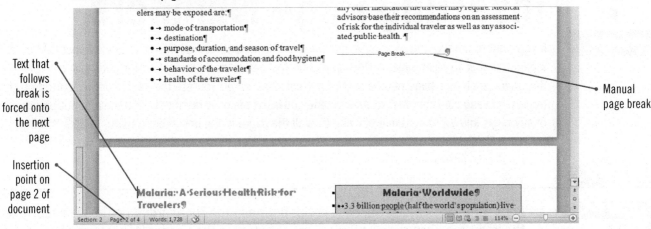

FIGURE E-6: Pages 3 and 4

Manual page break

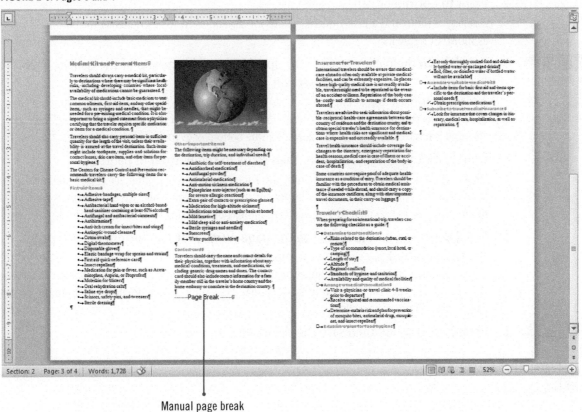

Manual page break

TABLE E-2: Types of breaks

break	function
Page	Forces the text following the break to begin at the top of the next page
Column	Forces the text following the break to begin at the top of the next column
Text Wrapping	Forces the text following the break to begin at the beginning of the next line

Inserting Page Numbers

If you want to number the pages of a multiple-page document, you can insert a page number field to add a page number to each page. A **field** is a code that serves as a placeholder for data that changes in a document, such as a page number or the current date. When you use the Page Number button on the Insert tab to add page numbers to a document, you insert the page number field at the top, bottom, or side of any page, and Word automatically numbers all the pages in the document for you. ▓▓▓▓▓▓ You insert a page number field so that page numbers will appear centered between the margins at the bottom of each page in the document.

STEPS

QUICK TIP

Point to Current Position to insert a page number field at the location of the insertion point.

1. **Press [Ctrl][Home], click the** Page Width button **in the Zoom group on the View tab, click the** Insert tab, **then click the** Page Number button **in the Header & Footer group**

   The Page Number menu opens. You use this menu to select the position for the page numbers. If you choose to add a page number field to the top, bottom, or side of a document, a page number will appear on every page in the document. If you choose to insert it in the document at the location of the insertion point, the field will appear on that page only.

2. **Point to** Bottom of Page

   A gallery of formatting and alignment options for page numbers to be inserted at the bottom of a page opens, as shown in Figure E-7.

QUICK TIP

To change the location or formatting of page numbers, click the Page Number button, point to a page number location, then select a format from the gallery.

3. **Scroll down the gallery to view the options, scroll to the top of the gallery, then click** Plain Number 2 **in the Simple section**

   A page number field containing the number 1 is centered in the Footer area at the bottom of page 1 of the document, as shown in Figure E-8. The document text is gray, or dimmed, because the Footer area is open. Text that is inserted in a Footer area appears at the bottom of every page in a document.

4. **Double-click the** document text, **then scroll to the bottom of page 1**

   Double-clicking the document text closes the Footer area. The page number is now dimmed because it is located in the Footer area, which is no longer the active area. When the document is printed, the page numbers appear as normal text. You will learn more about working with the Footer area in the next lesson.

5. **Scroll down the document to see the page number at the bottom of each page**

   Word numbered each page of the report automatically, and each page number is centered at the bottom of the page. If you want to change the numbering format or start page numbering with a different number, you can simply click the Page Number button, click Format Page Numbers, and then choose from the options in the Page Number Format dialog box.

QUICK TIP

To remove page numbers from a document, click the Page Number button, then click Remove Page Numbers.

6. **Press [Ctrl][Home], then save the document**

Moving around in a long document

Rather than scrolling to move to a different place in a long document, you can use the Browse by Object feature to move the insertion point to a specific location quickly. Browse by Object allows you to browse to the next or previous page, section, line, table, graphic, or other item of the same type in a document. To do this, first click the Select Browse Object button ⊚ below the vertical scroll bar to open a palette of object types. On this palette, click the button for the type of item you want to browse through, and then click the Next ⬇ or Previous ⬆ buttons to scroll through the items of that type in the document.

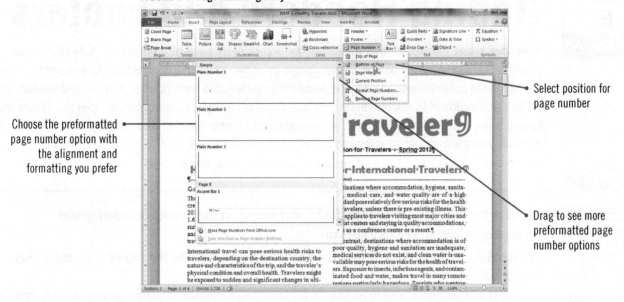

Choose the preformatted page number option with the alignment and formatting you prefer

Select position for page number

Drag to see more preformatted page number options

FIGURE E-8: Page number in document

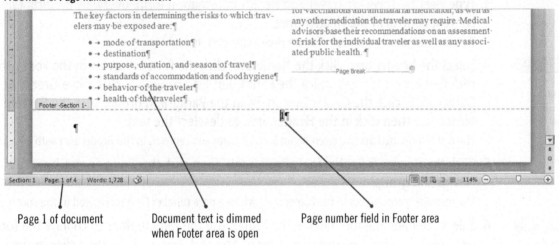

Page 1 of document

Document text is dimmed when Footer area is open

Page number field in Footer area

Inserting Quick Parts

The Word Quick Parts feature makes it easy to insert reusable pieces of content into a document quickly. The **Quick Parts** items you can insert include fields, such as for the current date or the total number of pages in a document; document property information, such as the author and title of a document; and building blocks, which are customized content that you create, format, and save for future use.

To insert a Quick Part into a document at the location of the insertion point, click the Quick Parts button in the Text group on the Insert tab (or, if headers and footers are open, click the Quick Parts button in the Insert group on the Header & Footer Tools Design tab), and then select the type of Quick Part you want to insert. To insert a field into a document, click Field on the Quick Parts menu that opens, click the name of the field you want to insert in the Field dialog box, and then click OK. Field information is updated automatically each time the document is opened or saved.

To insert a document property, point to Document Property on the Quick Parts menu, and then click the property you want to insert. The property is added to the document as a content control and contains the document property information you entered in the Document panel. If you did not assign a document property, the content control contains a placeholder, which you can replace with your own text. Once you replace the placeholder text—or edit the document property information that appears in the content control—this text replaces the document property information in the Document panel.

To insert a building block, click Building Blocks Organizer on the Quick Parts menu, select the building block you want, and then click Insert. You will learn more about working with building blocks in later lessons.

Adding Headers and Footers

A **header** is text or graphics that appears at the top of every page of a document. A **footer** is text or graphics that appears at the bottom of every page. In longer documents, headers and footers often contain the title of the publication or chapter, the name of the author, or a page number. You can add headers and footers to a document by double-clicking the top or bottom margin of a document to open the Header and Footer areas, and then inserting text and graphics into them. You can also use the Header or Footer command on the Insert tab to insert predesigned headers and footers that you can modify to include your information. You create a header that includes the name of the report.

STEPS

QUICK TIP
Unless you set different headers and footers for different sections, the information you insert in any Header or Footer area appears on every page in the document.

1. **Click the Insert tab, then click the Header button in the Header & Footer group**

   A gallery of built-in header designs opens.

2. **Scroll down the gallery to view the header designs, scroll to the top of the gallery, then click Blank**

   The Header and Footer areas open, and the document text is dimmed. When the document text is dimmed, it cannot be edited. The Header & Footer Tools Design tab also opens and is the active tab, as shown in Figure E-9. This tab is available whenever the Header and Footer areas are open.

3. **Type Healthy Traveler: Travel and Health Information from Riverwalk Medical Clinic in the content control in the Header area**

   This text will appear at the top of every page in the document.

QUICK TIP
You can also use the Insert Alignment Tab button in the Position group to left-, center-, and right-align text in the Header and Footer areas.

4. **Select the header text, click the Home tab, click the Font list arrow in the Font group, click Berlin Sans FB Demi, click the Font Color list arrow ▲▾, click Olive Green, Accent 3, Darker 25%, click the Center button ≡ in the Paragraph group, click the Bottom Border button ⊞, then click in the Header area to deselect the text**

   The text is formatted in olive green Berlin Sans FB Demi and centered in the Header area with a bottom border.

5. **Click the Header & Footer Tools Design tab, then click the Go to Footer button in the Navigation group**

   The insertion point moves to the Footer area, where a page number field is centered in the Footer area.

QUICK TIP
To change the distance between the header and footer and the edge of the page, change the Header from Top and Footer from Bottom settings in the Position group.

6. **Select the page number field in the footer, use the Mini toolbar to change the formatting to Berlin Sans FB Demi and Olive Green, Accent 3, Darker 25%, then click in the Footer area to deselect the text and field**

   The footer text is formatted in olive green Berlin Sans FB Demi.

7. **Click the Close Header and Footer button in the Close group, then scroll down until the bottom of page 1 and the top of page 2 appear in the document window**

   The Header and Footer areas close, and the header and footer text is dimmed, as shown in Figure E-10.

8. **Press [Ctrl][Home]**

   The report already includes the name of the document at the top of the first page, making the header information redundant. You can modify headers and footers so that the header and footer text does not appear on the first page of a document or a section.

9. **Position the pointer over the header text at the top of page 1, then double-click**

   The Header and Footer areas open. The Options group on the Header & Footer Tools Design tab includes options for creating a different header and footer for the first page of a document or a section, and for creating different headers and footers for odd- and even-numbered pages.

QUICK TIP
To remove headers or footers from a document, click the Header or Footer button, and then click Remove Header or Remove Footer.

10. **Click the Different First Page check box to select it, click the Close Header and Footer button, scroll to see the header and footer on pages 2, 3, and 4, then save the document**

    The header and footer text is removed from the Header and Footer areas on the first page.

Formatting Documents

FIGURE E-9: Header area

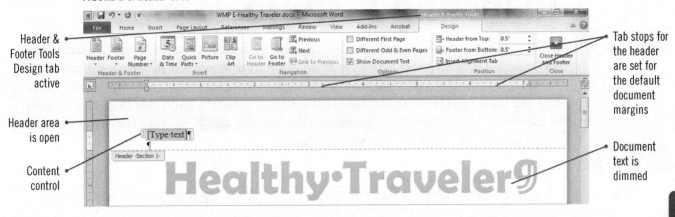

Header & Footer Tools Design tab active

Header area is open

Content control

Tab stops for the header are set for the default document margins

Document text is dimmed

[Type text]

Header -Section 1-

Healthy·Traveler

FIGURE E-10: Header and footer in document

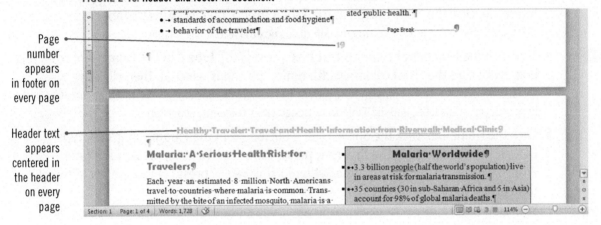

Page number appears in footer on every page

Header text appears centered in the header on every page

standards of accommodation and food hygiene¶
behavior of the traveler¶

ated public health.¶

Page Break

19

Healthy·Traveler:·Travel·and·Health·Information·from·Riverwalk·Medical·Clinic¶

Malaria:·A·Serious·Health·Risk·for·Travelers¶

Each·year·an·estimated·8·million·North·Americans· travel·to·countries·where·malaria·is·common.·Trans- mitted·by·the·bite·of·an·infected·mosquito, malaria·is·a·

Malaria·Worldwide¶
- 3.3·billion·people·(half·the·world's·population)·live· in·areas·at·risk·for·malaria·transmission.¶
- 35·countries·(30·in·sub-Saharan·Africa·and·5·in·Asia)· account·for·98%·of·global·malaria·deaths.¶

Section: 1   Page: 1 of 4   Words: 1,728

Adding a custom header or footer to the gallery

When you design a header that you want to use again in other documents, you can add it to the Header gallery by saving it as a building block. **Building blocks** are reusable pieces of formatted content or document parts, including headers and footers, page numbers, and text boxes, that are stored in galleries. Building blocks include predesigned content that comes with Word, as well as content that you create and save for future use. For example, you might create a custom header that contains your company name and logo and is formatted using the fonts, border, and colors you use in all company documents.

To add a custom header to the Header gallery, select all the text in the header, including the last paragraph mark, click the Header button, and then click Save Selection to Header Gallery. In the

Create New Building Block dialog box that opens, type a unique name for the header in the Name text box, click the Gallery list arrow and select the appropriate gallery, verify that the Category is General, and then type a brief description of the new header design in the Description text box. This description appears in a ScreenTip when you point to the custom header in the gallery. When you are finished, click OK. The new header appears in the Header gallery under the General category.

To remove a custom header from the Header gallery, right-click it, click Organize and Delete, make sure the appropriate building block is selected in the Building Blocks Organizer that opens, click Delete, click Yes, and then click Close. You can follow the same process to add or remove a custom footer to the Footer gallery.

Inserting a Table

Adding a table to a document is a useful way to illustrate information that is intended for quick reference and analysis. A table is a grid of columns and rows that you can fill with text and graphics. A cell is the box formed by the intersection of a column and a row. The lines that divide the columns and rows of a table and help you see the grid-like structure of the table are called borders. A simple way to insert a table into a document is to use the Insert Table command on the Insert tab. You add a table to page 2 showing the preventive options for serious travel health diseases.

STEPS

1. **Scroll until the heading Preventive Options... is at the top of your document window**

2. **Select the heading Preventive Options... and the two paragraph marks below it, click the Page Layout tab, click the Columns button in the Page Setup group, click One, click the heading to deselect the text, then scroll down to see the bottom half of page 2**

   A continuous section break is inserted before the heading and after the second paragraph mark, creating a new section, section 3, as shown in Figure E-11. The document now includes four sections, with the heading Preventive Options... in Section 3. Section 3 is formatted as a single column.

3. **Place the insertion point before the first paragraph mark below the heading, click the Insert tab, click the Table button in the Tables group, then click Insert Table**

   The Insert Table dialog box opens. You use this dialog box to create a blank table.

QUICK TIP
To delete a table, click in the table, click the Table Tools Layout tab, click the Delete button in the Rows & Columns group, then click Delete Table.

4. **Type 5 in the Number of columns text box, press [Tab], type 6 in the Number of rows text box, make sure the Fixed column width option button is selected, then click OK**

   A blank table with five columns and six rows is inserted in the document. The insertion point is in the upper-left cell of the table, and the Table Tools Design tab becomes the active tab.

5. **Click the Home tab, click the Show/Hide ¶ button ¶ in the Paragraph group, type Disease in the first cell in the first row, press [Tab], type Vaccine, press [Tab], type Prophylaxis Drug, press [Tab], type Eat and Drink Safely, press [Tab], type Avoid Insects, then press [Tab]**

   Pressing [Tab] moves the insertion point to the next cell in the row or to the first cell in the next row.

QUICK TIP
You can also click in a cell to move the insertion point to it.

6. **Type Malaria, press [Tab][Tab], click the Bullets list arrow ≣ ▾ in the Paragraph group, click the check mark style, press [Tab][Tab], then click the Bullets button ≣**

   The active bullet style changes to a check mark. A check mark is added to a cell when you click the Bullets button.

TROUBLE
If you pressed [Tab] after the last row, click the Undo button ↻ on the Quick Access toolbar to remove the blank row.

7. **Type the text shown in Figure E-12 in the table cells**

   Don't be concerned if the text wraps to the next line in a cell as you type because you will adjust the width of the columns later.

8. **Click the Table Tools Layout tab, click the AutoFit button in the Cell Size group, click AutoFit Contents, click the AutoFit button again, then click AutoFit Window**

   The width of the table columns is adjusted to fit the text and then the window.

QUICK TIP
You can also format table text using the buttons on the Mini toolbar or the Home tab.

9. **Click the Select button in the Table group, click Select Table, click the Align Center button ▤ in the Alignment group, click Disease in the table, click the Select button, click Select Column, click the Align Center Left button ▤, then click in the table to deselect the column**

   The text in the table is centered in each cell, and then the text in the first column is left-aligned.

10. **Click the Table Tools Design tab, click the More button ▾ in the Table Styles group to expand the Table Styles gallery, click the Light List – Accent 3 style, then save your changes**

    The Light List - Accent 3 table style is applied to the table, as shown in Figure E-13. A table style includes format settings for the text, borders, and shading in a table.

FIGURE E-11: New section

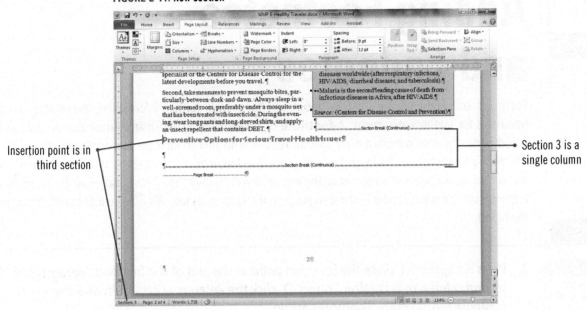

Insertion point is in third section

Section 3 is a single column

FIGURE E-12: Text in table

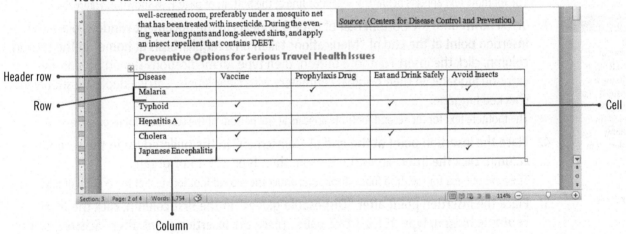

Header row

Row

Cell

Column

FIGURE E-13: Completed table

Preventive Options for Serious Travel Health Issues

Disease	Vaccine	Prophylaxis Drug	Eat and Drink Safely	Avoid Insects
Malaria		✓		✓
Typhoid	✓		✓	
Hepatitis A	✓			
Cholera	✓		✓	
Japanese Encephalitis	✓			✓

Formatting Documents

Adding Footnotes and Endnotes

Footnotes and endnotes are used in documents to provide further information, explanatory text, or references for text in a document. A **footnote** or **endnote** is an explanatory note that consists of two linked parts: the note reference mark that appears next to text to indicate that additional information is offered in a footnote or endnote, and the corresponding footnote or endnote text. Word places footnotes at the end of each page and endnotes at the end of the document. You insert and manage footnotes and endnotes using the tools in the Footnotes group on the References tab. ▰▰▰▰▰ You add several footnotes to the report.

STEPS

TROUBLE
Scroll up as needed to see the note reference mark; then scroll down to see the footnote.

1. **Press [Ctrl][Home], place the insertion point at the end of the first body paragraph in the second column of text (after "resort."), click the** References tab, **then click the** Insert Footnote button **in the Footnotes group**

   A note reference mark, in this case a superscript 1, appears after "resort.", and the insertion point moves below a separator line at the bottom of the page. A note reference mark can be a number, a symbol, a character, or a combination of characters.

2. **Type** Behavior is a critical factor, regardless of the quality of accommodations. For example, going outdoors in a malaria-endemic area could result in becoming infected with malaria.

   The footnote text appears below the separator line at the bottom of page 1, as shown in Figure E-14.

QUICK TIP
To change the number format of the note reference mark or to use a symbol instead of a character, click the launcher ⊡ in the Footnotes group, select from the options in the Footnote and Endnote dialog box, then click Apply.

3. **Scroll down until the bottom half of page 3 appears in the document window, place the insertion point at the end of "Medications taken on a regular basis at home" in the second column, click the** Insert Footnote button, **then type** All medications should be stored in carry-on luggage, in their original containers with clear labels. Carry a duplicate supply in checked luggage.

   The footnote text for the second footnote appears at the bottom of the second column on page 3.

4. **Place the insertion point at the end of "Sunscreen" in the bulleted list in the second column, click the** Insert Footnote button, **then type** SPF 15 or greater.

   The footnote text for the third footnote appears under the second footnote text at the bottom of page 3.

5. **Place the insertion point after "Disposable gloves" in the first column, click the** Insert Footnote button, **type** At least two pairs., **place the insertion point after "Scissors, safety pins, and tweezers" in the first column, click the** Insert Footnote button, **then type** Pack these items in checked luggage.

   Notice that when you inserted new footnotes between existing footnotes, Word automatically renumbered the footnotes. The new footnotes appear at the bottom of the first column on page 3, as shown in Figure E-15.

6. **Press [Ctrl][Home], then click the** Next Footnote button **in the Footnotes group**

   The insertion point moves to the first reference mark in the document.

QUICK TIP
To convert all footnotes to endnotes, click the launcher ⊡ in the Footnotes group, click Convert, click OK, then click Close.

7. **Click the** Next Footnote button, **press [Delete] to select the number 2 reference mark, then press [Delete] again**

   The second reference mark and associated footnote are deleted from the document and the footnotes are renumbered automatically. You must select a reference mark to delete a footnote; you can not simply delete the footnote text itself.

8. **Press [Ctrl][Home], then save your changes**

FIGURE E-14: Footnote in the document

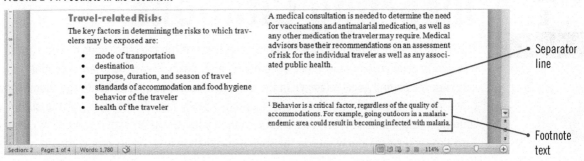

Separator line

Footnote text

FIGURE E-15: Renumbered footnotes in the document

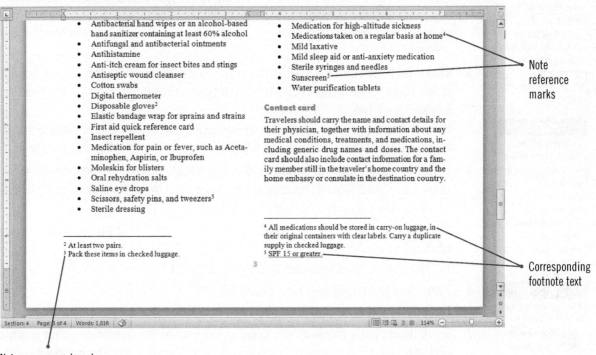

Note reference marks

Corresponding footnote text

Notes are renumbered when a new note is added

Inserting Citations

The Word References feature allows you to keep track of the reference sources you consult when writing research papers, reports, and other documents, and makes it easy to insert a citation in a document. A **citation** is a parenthetical reference in the document text that gives credit to the source for a quotation or other information used in a document. Citations usually include the name of the author and, for print sources, a page number. When you insert a citation you can use an existing source or create a new source. Each time you create a new source, the source information is saved on your computer so that it is available for use in any document. ▓▓▓▓▒ The report already includes two citations. You add several more citations to the report.

1. **Place the insertion point after "people travel" but before the period at the end of the first paragraph in the first column of text, click the Style list arrow in the Citations & Bibliography group, then click APA Fifth Edition**

   You will format the sources and citations in the report using the style recommended by the American Psychological Association (APA).

2. **Click the Insert Citation button in the Citations & Bibliography group**

   A list of the sources already used in the document opens. You can choose to cite one of these sources, create a new source, or add a placeholder for a source. When you add a new citation to a document, the source is added to the list of master sources that is stored on the computer. The new source is also associated with the document.

3. **Click Add New Source, click the Type of Source list arrow in the Create Source dialog box, scroll down to view the available source types, click Report, then click the Corporate Author check box**

   You select the type of source and enter the source information in the Create Source dialog box. The fields available in the dialog box change, depending on the type of source selected.

4. **Enter the data shown in Figure E-16 in the Create Source dialog box, then click OK**

   The citation (World Tourism Organization, 2012) appears at the end of the paragraph. Because the source is a print publication, it needs to include a page number.

5. **Click the citation to select it, click the Citation Options list arrow on the right side of the citation, then click Edit Citation**

   The Edit Citation dialog box opens, as shown in Figure E-17.

6. **Type 19 in the Pages text box, then click OK**

   The page number 19 is added to the citation.

7. **Scroll down, place the insertion point at the end of the quotation (after ...consequences.), click the Insert Citation button, click Add New Source, enter the information shown in Figure E-18, then click OK**

   A citation for the Web publication from where the quotation was taken is added to the report. No page number is used in this citation because the source is a Web site.

8. **Scroll to the bottom of page 2, click under the table, type Source:, italicize Source:, click after Source:, click the Insert Citation button, then click Johnson, Margaret in the list of sources**

   The citation (Johnson) appears under the table.

9. **Click the citation, click the Citation Options list arrow, click Edit Citation, type 55 in the Pages text box, click OK, then save your changes**

   The page number 55 is added to the citation.

FIGURE E-16: Adding a Report source

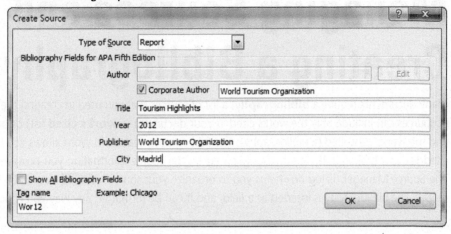

FIGURE E-17: Edit Citation dialog box

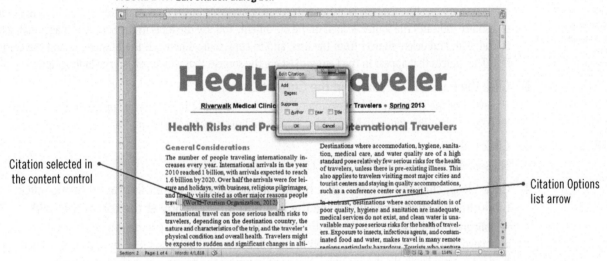

Citation selected in the content control

Citation Options list arrow

FIGURE E-18: Adding a Web publication source

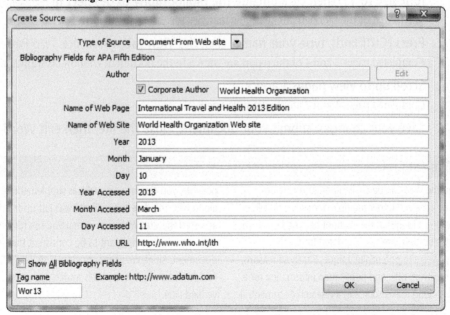

Managing Sources and Creating a Bibliography

Many documents require a **bibliography**, a list of sources that you used in creating the document. The list of sources can include only the works cited in your document (a **works cited** list) or both the works cited and the works consulted (a bibliography). The Bibliography feature in Word allows you to generate a works cited list or a bibliography automatically based on the source information you provide for the document. The Source Manager dialog box helps you to organize your sources. 🖥️ You add a bibliography to the report. The bibliography is inserted as a field, and it can be formatted any way you choose.

STEPS

QUICK TIP
You must copy sources from the Master List to the Current List for the sources to be available when you open the document on another computer.

1. **Press [Ctrl][End] to move the insertion point to the end of the document, then click the Manage Sources button in the Citations & Bibliography group**
   The Source Manager dialog box opens, as shown in Figure E-19. The Master List shows the sources available on your computer. The Current List shows the sources available in the current document. A check mark next to a source indicates the source is cited in the document. You use the tools in the Source Manager dialog box to add, edit, and delete sources from the lists, and to copy sources between the Master List and the Current List. The sources that appear in the Current List are the sources that will appear in the bibliography.

2. **Click the Baker, Mary source in the Current List**
   A preview of the citation and bibliographical entry for the source in MLA style appears in the Preview box. You do not want this source to be included in your bibliography for the report.

3. **Click Delete**
   The source is removed from the Current List.

4. **Click Close, click the Bibliography button in the Citations & Bibliography group, click Bibliography, then scroll up to see the heading Bibliography at the top of the field**
   A Bibliography field is added at the location of the insertion point. The bibliography includes all the sources associated with the document, formatted in the MLA style for bibliographies. The text in the Bibliography field is formatted with the default styles. You want to format the text to match the rest of the report.

TROUBLE
Don't be concerned if the list of sources becomes gray when you select the heading Bibliography. This simply indicates the Bibliography field is active. Text that is selected is highlighted in blue.

5. **Select Bibliography; apply the following formats: Berlin Sans FB Demi, bold, and the Blue, Accent 1 font color; drag down the list of sources to select the entire list and change the font size to 11; then click outside the bibliography to deselect it**
   The format of the bibliography text now matches the rest of the report.

6. **Press [Ctrl][End], type your name, click the View tab, then click Two Pages**
   Completed pages 3 and 4 of the report are shown in the document window, as shown in Figure E-20.

7. **Scroll up to view pages 1 and 2**
   Completed pages 1 and 2 are shown in Figure E-21.

8. **Save your changes, submit your document, close the file, then exit Word**

Working with Web sources

Publications found on the Web can be challenging to document. Many Web sites can be accessed under multiple domains, and URLs change frequently or are so long that they cannot be typed easily. In addition, electronic publications are often updated frequently, making each visit to a Web site potentially unique. For these reasons, it's best to rely on the author, title, and publication information for a Web publication when citing it as a source in a research document. If possible, you can include a URL as supplementary information only, along with the date the Web site was last updated and the date you accessed the site. Whatever format you use for citing Web publications, it's important to be consistent throughout your document. Since Web sites are often removed, it's also a good idea to download or print any Web source you use so that it can be verified later.

FIGURE E-19: Source Manager dialog box

Your Master List will contain the two sources you added and either no additional sources or different additional sources

Preview of the citation and bibliography entry for the selected source in APA style (as defined by Word)

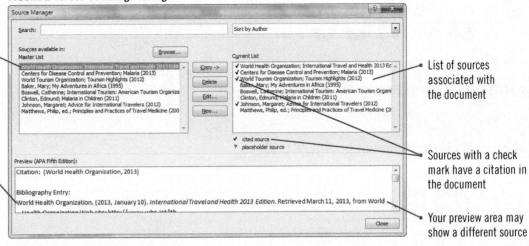

List of sources associated with the document

Sources with a check mark have a citation in the document

Your preview area may show a different source

FIGURE E-20: Completed pages 3 and 4

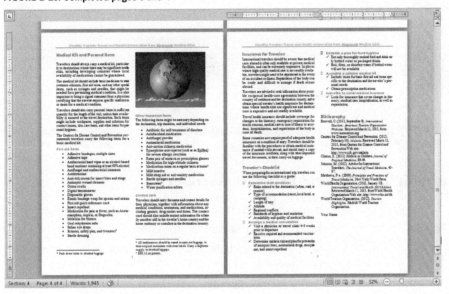

FIGURE E-21: Completed pages 1 and 2

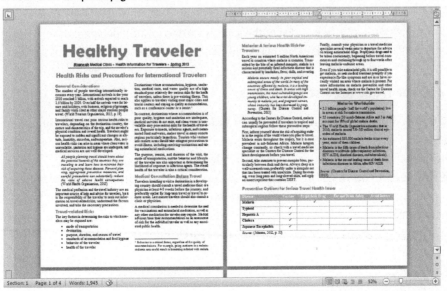

Practice

For current SAM information, including versions and content details, visit SAM Central (http://www.cengage.com/samcentral). If you have a SAM user profile, you may have access to hands-on instruction, practice, and assessment of the skills covered in this unit. Since various versions of SAM are supported throughout the life of this text, check with your instructor for the correct instructions and URL/Web site for accessing assignments.

Concepts Review

Label each element shown in Figure E-22.

FIGURE E-22

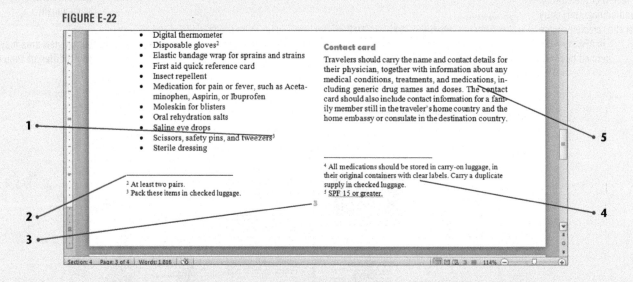

Match each term with the statement that best describes it.

6. Table
7. Manual page break
8. Section break
9. Footer
10. Header
11. Citation
12. Field
13. Margin
14. Bibliography

a. A parenthetical reference in the document text that gives credit to a source
b. The blank area between the edge of the text and the edge of the page
c. A formatting mark that divides a document into parts that can be formatted differently
d. Text or graphics that appear at the bottom of every page in a document
e. A placeholder for information that changes
f. A formatting mark that forces the text following the mark to begin at the top of the next page
g. Text or graphics that appear at the top of every page in a document
h. A list of the sources used to create a document
i. A grid of columns and rows that you can fill with text and graphics

Select the best answer from the list of choices.

15. **Which type of break do you insert if you want to balance the columns in a section?**
    a. Manual page break
    b. Text wrapping break
    c. Column break
    d. Continuous section break

16. **Which type of break can you insert if you want to force text to begin on the next page?**
    a. Text wrapping break
    b. Next page section break
    c. Automatic page break
    d. Continuous section break

17. **Which of the following cannot be inserted using the Quick Parts command?**
    a. Document property
    b. AutoText building block
    c. Page break
    d. Page number field

18. **Which of the following do documents with mirror margins always have?**
    - **a.** Inside and outside margins
    - **b.** Different first page headers and footers
    - **c.** Gutters
    - **d.** Landscape orientation

19. **What name describes formatted pieces of content that are stored in galleries?**
    - **a.** Field
    - **b.** Header
    - **c.** Property
    - **d.** Building Block

20. **Which appears at the end of a document?**
    - **a.** Citation
    - **b.** Endnote
    - **c.** Footnote
    - **d.** Page break

Skills Review

1. **Set document margins.**
    - **a.** Start Word, open the file WMP E-2.docx from the drive and folder where you store your Data Files, then save it as **WMP E-Elmwood Fitness**.
    - **b.** Change the top and bottom margin settings to Moderate: 1" top and bottom, and .75" left and right.
    - **c.** Save your changes to the document.
2. **Create sections and columns.**
    - **a.** Turn on the display of formatting marks, then customize the status bar to display sections if they are not displayed already.
    - **b.** Insert a continuous section break before the **Welcome to the Elmwood Fitness Center** heading.
    - **c.** Format the text in section 2 in two columns, then save your changes to the document.
3. **Insert page breaks.**
    - **a.** Scroll to page 3, then insert a manual page break before the heading **Facilities and Services**.
    - **b.** Scroll down and insert a manual page break before the heading **Membership**, then press [Ctrl][Home].
    - **c.** On page 1, select the heading **Welcome to the Elmwood Fitness Center** and the paragraph mark below it, use the Columns button to format the selected text as one column, then center the heading on the page.
    - **d.** Follow the direction in Step c to format the heading **Facilities and Services** and the paragraph mark below it on page 3, and the heading **Membership** and the paragraph mark below it on page 4, as one column, with centered text, then save your changes to the document.
4. **Insert page numbers.**
    - **a.** Insert page numbers in the document at the bottom of the page. Select the Plain Number 2 page number style from the gallery.
    - **b.** Close the Footer area, scroll through the document to view the page number on each page, then save your changes to the document.
5. **Add headers and footers.**
    - **a.** Double-click the margin at the top of a page to open the Header and Footer areas.
    - **b.** With the insertion point in the Header area, click the Quick Parts button in the Insert Group on the Header & Footer Tools Design tab, point to Document Property, then click Author.
    - **c.** Replace the text in the Author content control with your name, press [End] to move the insertion point out of the content control, then press [Spacebar]. (*Note:* If your name does not appear in the header, right-click the Author content control, click Remove Content Control, then type your name in the header.)
    - **d.** Click the Insert Alignment Tab button in the Position group, select the Right option button and keep the alignment relative to the margin, then click OK in the dialog box to move the insertion point to the right margin.
    - **e.** Use the Insert Date and Time command in the Insert group to insert the current date using a format of your choice as static text. (*Hint:* Be sure the Update automatically check box is not checked.)
    - **f.** Apply italic to the text in the header.
    - **g.** Move the insertion point to the Footer area.
    - **h.** Double-click the page number to select it, then format the page number in bold and italic.

Skills Review (continued)

    i. Move the insertion point to the header on page 1 if it is not already there, use the Header & Footer Tools Design tab to create a different header and footer for the first page of the document, type your name in the First Page Header area, then apply italic to your name.

    j. Close headers and footers, scroll to view the header and footer on each page, then save your changes to the document.

6. Insert a table.

    a. On page 4, double-click the word Table to select it at the end of the Membership Rates section, press [Delete], open the Insert Table dialog box, then create a table with two columns and five rows.

    b. Apply the purple Light List - Accent 4 table style to the table.

    c. Press [Tab] to leave the first cell in the header row blank, then type **Rate**.

    d. Press [Tab], then type the following text in the table, pressing [Tab] to move from cell to cell.

Enrollment/Individual	$100
Enrollment/Couple	$150
Monthly membership/Individual	$35
Monthly membership/Couple	$60

    e. With the insertion point in the table, right-click the table, use the AutoFit command to select the AutoFit to Contents option, and then select the AutoFit to Window option. (*Note*: In this case AutoFit to Window fits the table to the width of the column of text.)

    f. Save your changes to the document.

7. Add footnotes and endnotes.

    a. Press [Ctrl][Home], scroll down, place the insertion point at the end of the first body paragraph, insert a footnote, then type **People who are active live longer and feel better.**

    b. Place the insertion point at the end of the first paragraph under the Benefits of Exercise heading, insert a footnote, then type **There are 1,440 minutes in every day. Schedule 30 of them for physical activity.**

    c. Place the insertion point at the end of the first paragraph under the Tips for Staying Motivated heading, insert a footnote, type **Always consult your physician before beginning an exercise program.**, then save your changes.

8. Insert citations.

    a. Place the insertion point at the end of the second paragraph under the Benefits of Exercise heading (after "down from 52% in 2010" but before the period), then change the style for citations and bibliography to APA Fifth Edition.

    b. Insert a citation, add a new source, enter the source information shown in the Create Source dialog box in Figure E-23, then click OK.

FIGURE E-23

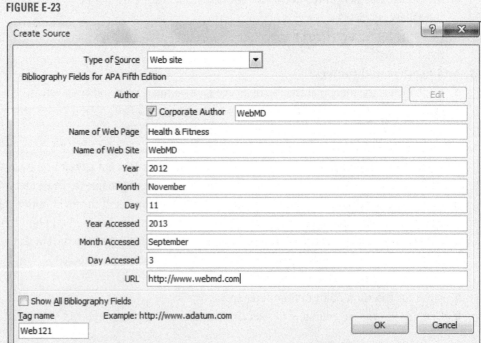

Skills Review (continued)

   c. Place the insertion point at the end of the italicized quotation in the second column of text, insert a citation, then select Jason, Laura from the list of sources.
   d. Edit the citation to include the page number **25**.
   e. Scroll to page 2, place the insertion point at the end of the "Be a morning exerciser" paragraph but before the ending period, insert a citation for WebMD, then save your changes.

9. Manage sources and create a bibliography.
   a. Press [Ctrl][End], then open the Source Manager dialog box.
   b. Select the source Health, National Institute of in the Current List, click Edit, click the Corporate Author check box, edit the entry so it reads **National Institutes of Health**, click OK, click Yes if prompted, then click Close.
   c. Insert a bibliography.
   d. Select Bibliography, then change the font to 14-point Tahoma with a black font color. Pages 1 and 4 of the formatted document are shown in Figure E-24.
   e. Save your changes to the document, submit it to your instructor, then close the document and exit Word.

FIGURE E-24

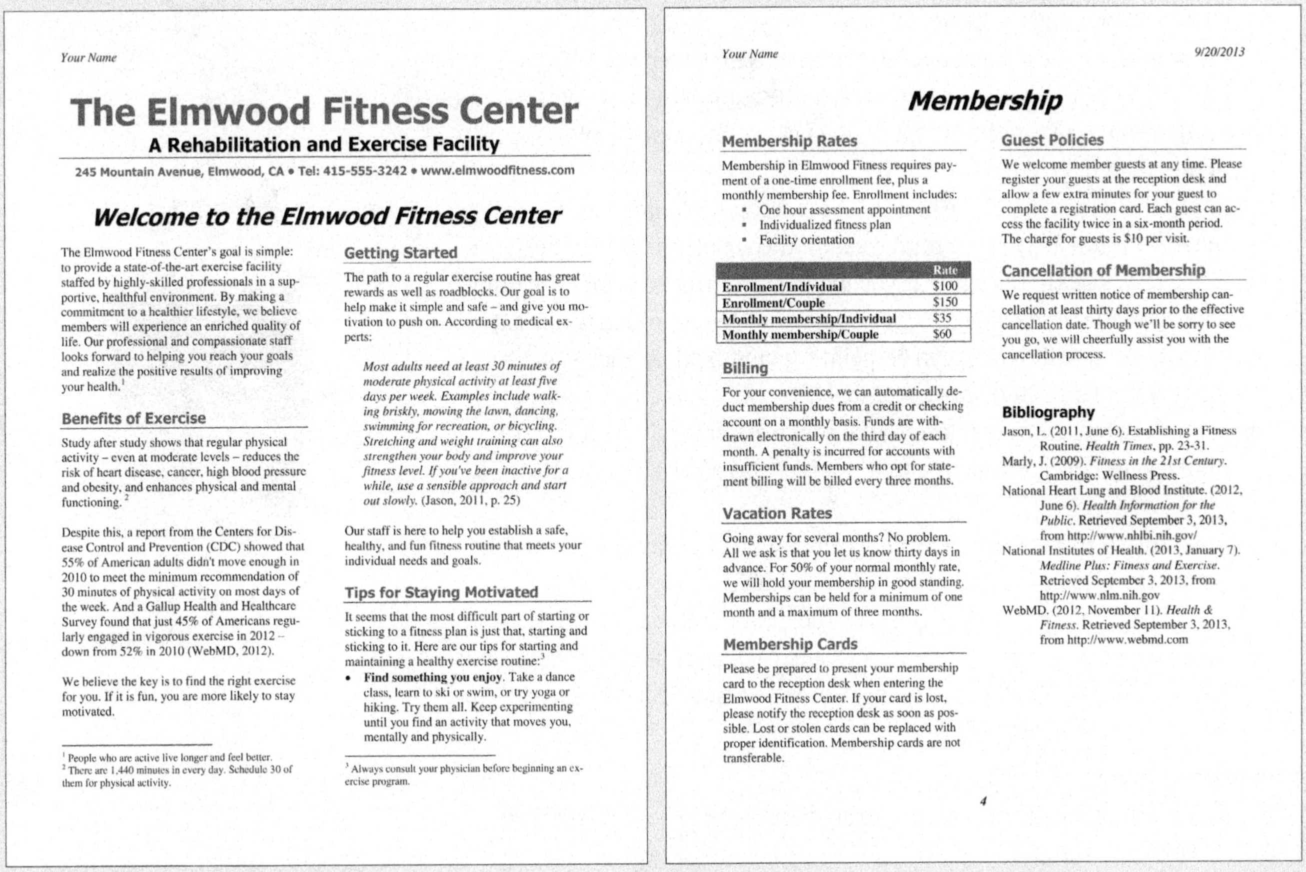

Your Name

The Elmwood Fitness Center

A Rehabilitation and Exercise Facility

245 Mountain Avenue, Elmwood, CA • Tel: 415-555-3242 • www.elmwoodfitness.com

Welcome to the Elmwood Fitness Center

The Elmwood Fitness Center's goal is simple: to provide a state-of-the-art exercise facility staffed by highly-skilled professionals in a supportive, healthful environment. By making a commitment to a healthier lifestyle, we believe members will experience an enriched quality of life. Our professional and compassionate staff looks forward to helping you reach your goals and realize the positive results of improving your health.[1]

Benefits of Exercise

Study after study shows that regular physical activity – even at moderate levels – reduces the risk of heart disease, cancer, high blood pressure and obesity, and enhances physical and mental functioning.[2]

Despite this, a report from the Centers for Disease Control and Prevention (CDC) showed that 55% of American adults didn't move enough in 2010 to meet the minimum recommendation of 30 minutes of physical activity on most days of the week. And a Gallup Health and Healthcare Survey found that just 45% of Americans regularly engaged in vigorous exercise in 2012 – down from 52% in 2010 (WebMD, 2012).

We believe the key is to find the right exercise for you. If it is fun, you are more likely to stay motivated.

Getting Started

The path to a regular exercise routine has great rewards as well as roadblocks. Our goal is to help make it simple and safe – and give you motivation to push on. According to medical experts:

> *Most adults need at least 30 minutes of moderate physical activity at least five days per week. Examples include walking briskly, mowing the lawn, dancing, swimming for recreation, or bicycling. Stretching and weight training can also strengthen your body and improve your fitness level. If you've been inactive for a while, use a sensible approach and start out slowly.* (Jason, 2011, p. 25)

Our staff is here to help you establish a safe, healthy, and fun fitness routine that meets your individual needs and goals.

Tips for Staying Motivated

It seems that the most difficult part of starting or sticking to a fitness plan is just that, starting and sticking to it. Here are our tips for starting and maintaining a healthy exercise routine:[3]

- **Find something you enjoy**. Take a dance class, learn to ski or swim, or try yoga or hiking. Try them all. Keep experimenting until you find an activity that moves you, mentally and physically.

[1] People who are active live longer and feel better.
[2] There are 1,440 minutes in every day. Schedule 30 of them for physical activity.
[3] Always consult your physician before beginning an exercise program.

Your Name *9/20/2013*

Membership

Membership Rates

Membership in Elmwood Fitness requires payment of a one-time enrollment fee, plus a monthly membership fee. Enrollment includes:

- One hour assessment appointment
- Individualized fitness plan
- Facility orientation

	Rate
Enrollment/Individual	$100
Enrollment/Couple	$150
Monthly membership/Individual	$35
Monthly membership/Couple	$60

Billing

For your convenience, we can automatically deduct membership dues from a credit or checking account on a monthly basis. Funds are withdrawn electronically on the third day of each month. A penalty is incurred for accounts with insufficient funds. Members who opt for statement billing will be billed every three months.

Vacation Rates

Going away for several months? No problem. All we ask is that you let us know thirty days in advance. For 50% of your normal monthly rate, we will hold your membership in good standing. Memberships can be held for a minimum of one month and a maximum of three months.

Membership Cards

Please be prepared to present your membership card to the reception desk when entering the Elmwood Fitness Center. If your card is lost, please notify the reception desk as soon as possible. Lost or stolen cards can be replaced with proper identification. Membership cards are not transferable.

Guest Policies

We welcome member guests at any time. Please register your guests at the reception desk and allow a few extra minutes for your guest to complete a registration card. Each guest can access the facility twice in a six-month period. The charge for guests is $10 per visit.

Cancellation of Membership

We request written notice of membership cancellation at least thirty days prior to the effective cancellation date. Though we'll be sorry to see you go, we will cheerfully assist you with the cancellation process.

Bibliography

Jason, L. (2011, June 6). Establishing a Fitness Routine. *Health Times*, pp. 23-31.
Marly, J. (2009). *Fitness in the 21st Century*. Cambridge: Wellness Press.
National Heart Lung and Blood Institute. (2012, June 6). *Health Information for the Public*. Retrieved September 3, 2013, from http://www.nhlbi.nih.gov/
National Institutes of Health. (2013, January 7). *Medline Plus: Fitness and Exercise*. Retrieved September 3, 2013, from http://www.nlm.nih.gov
WebMD. (2012, November 11). *Health & Fitness*. Retrieved September 3, 2013, from http://www.webmd.com

4

Independent Challenge 1

You are the owner of the Muscular Therapy Center, which offers a variety of massage services to clients. You have begun work on the text for a brochure advertising your business and are now ready to lay out the pages and prepare the final copy. The brochure will be printed on both sides of an 8½" × 11" sheet of paper, and folded in thirds.

a. Start Word, open the file WMP E-3.docx from the drive and folder where you store your Data Files, then save it as **WMP E-Massage Brochure**. Read the document to get a feel for its contents.

b. Change the page orientation to landscape, and change all four margins to .5".

c. Format the document in three columns of equal width.

d. On page 2, insert a next page section break before the heading **Welcome to the Muscular Therapy Center**.

e. On page 1, insert column breaks before the headings **Menu of Massage Services** and **Shiatsu Massage**.

f. Change the column spacing in section 1 (which is the first page) to .4", then add lines between the columns on the first page.

g. Double-click the bottom margin to open the footer area, create a different header and footer for the first page, then type **A variety of choices to meet your needs.** in the First Page Footer - Section 1- area.

h. Center the text in the footer area, format it in 14-point Papyrus, all caps, bold, with an Olive Green, Accent 3, Darker 50% font color, then close headers and footers.

FIGURE E-25

i. On page 2, insert a column break before Your Name, then press [Enter] 21 times to move the contact information to the bottom of the second column.

j. Replace Your Name with your name, then center the contact information in the column.

k. Insert a column break at the bottom of the second column. Type the text shown in Figure E-25 in the third column, then apply the No Spacing style to the text. Refer to the figure as you follow the instructions for formatting the text in the third column. (*Hint*: Remove any hyperlinks that appear.)

l. Format Therapeutic Massage in 28-point Papyrus, bold. Format Muscular Therapy Center in 20-point Papyrus bold.

m. Format the remaining text in 14-point Papyrus. Center all the text in the third column, then change the font color to Olive Green, Accent 3, Darker 50%.

n. Insert the clip art graphic shown in Figure E-25 or another appropriate clip art graphic. Do not wrap text around the graphic. Apply the Soft Edge Rectangle picture style to the graphic. (*Hint*: Use the search term massage.)

o. Resize the graphic and add or remove blank paragraphs in the third column of your brochure so that the spacing between elements roughly matches the spacing shown in Figure E-25.

Advanced Challenge Exercise

- Insert a different appropriate clip art graphic at the bottom of the first column on page 2.
- Apply text wrapping to the graphic, then resize the graphic and position it so it enhances the design of the brochure.
- Apply a suitable picture style or picture effect to the graphic.

p. Save your changes, then submit a copy to your instructor. If possible, you can print the brochure with the two pages back to back so that the brochure can be folded in thirds.

q. Close the document and exit Word.

Therapeutic
Massage

at the
Muscular Therapy
Center

The Skill of Massage
The Art of Healing

Independent Challenge 2

You work in the Campus Safety Department at Pacific State University Hospital. You have written the text for an informational flyer about parking regulations on the hospital campus, and now you need to format the flyer so it is attractive and readable.

- **a.** Start Word, open the file WMP E-4.docx from the drive and folder where you store your Data Files, then save it as **WMP E-Parking FAQ**. Read the document to get a feel for its contents.
- **b.** Change all four margins to .7".
- **c.** Insert a continuous section break before **1. May I drive a car to work at the hospital?** (*Hint*: Place the insertion point before May.)
- **d.** Scroll down and insert a next page section break before **Sample Parking Permit**.
- **e.** Format the text in section 2 in three columns of equal width with .3" of space between the columns.
- **f.** Hyphenate the document using the automatic hyphenation feature. (*Hint*: Use the Hyphenation button in the Page Setup group on the Page Layout tab.)
- **g.** Add a 3-point dotted-line bottom border to the blank paragraph under Pacific State University Hospital (PSUH). (*Hint*: Place the insertion point before the paragraph mark under Pacific State University Hospital…)
- **h.** Open the Header area, and insert your name in the header. Right-align your name, and format it in 10-point Arial.
- **i.** Add the following text to the footer, inserting symbols between words as indicated: **Parking and Shuttle Service Office • 54 Buckley Street • PSUH • 942-555-2227**. (*Hint*: Click the Symbol command in the Symbols group on the Insert tab to insert a symbol.)
- **j.** Format the footer text in 9-point Arial Black, and center it in the footer.
- **k.** Apply a 3-point dotted-line border above the footer text. Make sure to apply the border to the paragraph.
- **l.** Add a continuous section break at the end of section 2 to balance the columns in section 2.
- **m.** Add the clip art graphic shown in Figure E-26 (or another appropriate clip art graphic) to the upper-right corner of the document, above the border. Make sure the graphic does not obscure the border. (*Hint*: Apply text wrapping to the graphic before positioning it.)
- **n.** Place the insertion point on page 2 (which is section 4). Change the page orientation of section 4 to landscape.
- **o.** Change the vertical alignment of section 4 to center. (*Hint*: Use the Vertical Alignment list arrow on the Layout tab in the Page Setup dialog box.)
- **p.** Apply an appropriate table style to the table, such as the style shown in Figure E-27. (*Hint*: Check and uncheck the options in the Table Style Options group on the Table Tools Design tab to customize the style so it enhances the table data.)
- **q.** Save your changes, submit your work, close the document, then exit Word.

FIGURE E-26

Frequently Asked Questions

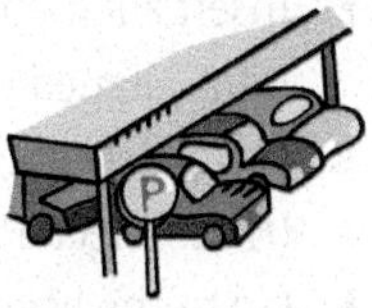

Parking & Shuttle Service Office

Pacific State University Hospital (PSUH)

FIGURE E-27

Sample Parking Permit

Pacific State University Hospital **Office of Parking and Shuttle Service** 2013-14 Parking Permit	
License number:	VA 498 359
Make:	Subaru
Model:	Forester
Year:	2011
Color:	Blue
Permit Issue Date:	September 8, 2013
Permit Expiration Date:	September 7, 2014
Restrictions: ***Parking is permitted in the Pacific State University Hospital Greene Street lot 24 hours a day, 7 days a week. Shuttle service is available from the Greene Street lot to the hospital and other campus locations from 6 a.m. to 11 p.m. Monday through Friday. Parking is also permitted in any on-campus lot from 4:30 p.m. Friday to midnight Sunday.***	

Independent Challenge 3

A book publisher would like to publish an article you wrote on stormwater pollution in Australia as a chapter in a forthcoming book called *Environmental Issues for the New Millennium*. The publisher has requested that you format your article like a book chapter before submitting it for publication, and has provided you with a style sheet. According to the style sheet, the citations and bibliography should be formatted in Chicago style. You have already created the sources for the chapter, but you need to insert the citations.

a. Start Word, open the file WMP E-5.docx from the drive and folder where you store your Data Files, then save it as **WMP E-Chapter 7**.

FIGURE E-28

b. Change the font of the entire document to 11-point High Tower Text. If this font is not available to you, select a different font suitable for the pages of a book. Change the alignment to justified.

c. Change the paper size to 6" × 9".

d. Create mirror margins. (*Hint*: Use the Multiple pages list arrow.) Change the top and bottom margins to .8", change the inside margin to .4", change the outside margin to .6", and create a .3" gutter to allow room for the book's binding.

e. Change the Zoom level to Page Width, open the Header and Footer areas, then apply the setting to create different headers and footers for odd- and even-numbered pages.

f. In the odd-page header, type **Chapter 7**, insert a small square symbol, then type **The Health Effects of Stormwater Pollution**.

g. Format the header text in 9-point High Tower Text italic, then right-align the text.

h. In the even-page header, type your name.

i. Format the header text in 9-point High Tower Text italic. The even-page header should be left-aligned.

j. Insert a left-aligned page number field in the even-page footer area, format it in 10-point High Tower Text, insert a right-aligned page number field in the odd-page footer area, then format it in 10-point High Tower Text.

k. Format the page numbers so that the first page of your chapter, which is Chapter 7 in the book, begins on page 101. (*Hint*: Select a page number field, click the Page Number button, then click Format Page Numbers.)

l. Go to the beginning of the document, press [Enter] 10 times, type **Chapter 7: The Health Effects of Stormwater Pollution**, press [Enter] twice, type your name, then press [Enter] twice.

m. Format the chapter title in 16-point Calibri bold, format your name in 14-point Calibri, then left-align the title text and your name.

n. Click the References tab, make sure the citations and bibliography style is set to Chicago Fifteenth Edition, place the insertion point at the end of the first body paragraph on page 1 but before the ending period, insert a citation for Alice Burke, et. al., then add the page number 40 to the citation, as shown in Figure E-28.

o. Add the citations listed in Table E-3 to the document using the sources already associated with the document.

TABLE E-3

page	location for citation	source	page number
2	End of the first complete paragraph (after ...WCSMP, but before the period)	City of Weston	3
3	End of the first complete paragraph (after ...pollution, but before the colon)	Jensen	135
4	End of second paragraph (after ...health effects, but before the period)	City of Weston	5
4	End of fourth bulleted list item (after 1 month.)	Seawatch	None
5	End of third paragraph (after ...problem arises, but before the period)	Burke, et. al.	55
6	End of first sentence (after ...stormwater system, but before the period)	City of Weston	7
6	End of first paragraph under Conclusion (after ...include, but before the colon)	Jensen	142

Independent Challenge 3 (continued)

p. Press [Ctrl][End], insert a Works Cited list, format the Works Cited heading in 11-point High Tower Text, black font color, bold, then format the list of works cited in High Tower Text.

Advanced Challenge Exercise

- Scroll to page 4 in the document, place the insertion point at the end of the paragraph above the Potential health effects... heading, press [Enter] twice, type **Table 1: Total annual pollutant loads per year in the Fairy Creek Catchment**, format the text as bold, then press [Enter] twice.

- Insert a table with four columns and four rows.

- Type the text shown in Figure E-29 in the table. Do not be concerned when the text wraps to the next line in a cell.

FIGURE E-29

Area	Nitrogen	Phosphorus	Suspended solids
Fairy Creek	9.3 tonnes	1.2 tonnes	756.4 tonnes
Durras Arm	6.2 tonnes	.9 tonnes	348.2 tonnes
Cabbage Tree Creek	9.8 tonnes	2.3 tonnes	485.7 tonnes

- Apply the Light List table style. Make sure the text in the header row is bold, then remove any bold formatting from the text in the remaining rows.

- Use AutoFit to make the table fit the contents, then use AutoFit to make the table fit the window.

q. Save your changes, submit your work, then close the document and exit Word.

Real Life Independent Challenge

One of the most common opportunities to use the page layout features of Word is when formatting a research paper. The format recommended by the *Publication Manual of the American Psychological Association*, a style guide that includes information on preparing, writing, and formatting research papers, is the standard format used by many programs for medical professionals. In this independent challenge, you will research the APA guidelines for formatting a research paper and use the guidelines you find to format the pages of a sample research report.

a. Use your favorite search engine to search the Web for information on the APA guidelines for formatting a research report. Use the keywords **APA Style** and **research paper format** to conduct your search.

b. Look for information on the proper formatting for the following aspects of a research paper: paper size, margins, line spacing, paragraph indentation, page numbers, short title, title page, abstract, and first page of the body of the report. Also find information on proper formatting for citations and a references page. Print the information you find.

c. Start Word, open the file WMP E-6.docx from the drive and folder where you store your Data Files, then save it as **WMP E-APA Research Paper**. Using the information you learned, format this document as a research report.

d. Adjust the margins, set the line spacing, and add a short title and page numbers to the document header in the format recommended by the APA. Use **Advances in the Treatment of Type 1 Diabetes** as the title for your sample report, use your name as the author name, and make up information about your affiliation (for example, your school or class), if necessary. You do not need to include a running head. Make sure to format the title page exactly as the APA style dictates.

e. Format the remaining text as the abstract and body of the research report.

f. Create three sources, insert three citations in the document—a book, a journal article, and a Web site—and create a references page, following APA style. If necessary, edit the format of the citations and references page to conform to APA format. (*Note*: For this practice document, you are allowed to make up sources. Never make up sources for real research papers.)

g. Save the document, submit a copy to your instructor, close the document, then exit Word.

Word 2010

Visual Workshop

Open the file WMP E-7.docx from the drive and folder where you store your Data Files, then modify it to create the article shown in Figure E-30. (*Hint*: Change all four margins to .6". Add the footnotes as shown in the figure. To locate the clip art image, search using the keyword **hiker**, and be sure only the Illustrations check box in the Results should be in list box in the Clip Art task pane has a check mark. Select a different clip if the clip shown in the figure is not available to you.) Save the document with the filename **WMP E-Lyme Disease**, then print a copy.

FIGURE E-30

TRAVELER'S HEALTH WATCH

On the Lookout for Lyme Disease

By Your Name

Lyme disease, an inflammatory disease transmitted by the bite of a deer tick, has become a serious public health risk in certain areas of the United States and Canada. Campers, hikers, fishermen, outdoor enthusiasts, and other travelers or residents in endemic areas who have frequent or prolonged exposure to tick habitats are at increased risk for Lyme disease.

How ticks spread the disease

The bacterium that causes Lyme disease is spread by the bite of infected *Ixodes* ticks, commonly known as deer ticks. Ticks can attach to any part of the human body, but are most often found in hairy areas such as the scalp, groin, and armpit. In most cases the tick must be attached for at least 48 hours before the bacteria can be transmitted. During the spring and summer months, when people dress lightly and spend more time outdoors, the young (nymphal) ticks are most often responsible for spreading the disease. These ticks are tiny (about the size of the head of a pin) and rarely noticed, making it difficult for people to find and remove an infected tick.

Tick habitat and geographic distribution

The risk of exposure to infected ticks in greatest in woods and in thick brush or long grass, but ticks can also be carried by animals into lawns and gardens and into houses by pets. In the United States, most infections occur in the:
- Northeast, from Maryland to Massachusetts.
- North central states, mostly in Wisconsin and Minnesota.
- West coast, particularly California.

Symptoms and signs

Early Lyme disease is characterized initially by *erythema migrans*, the bull's eye rash that often occurs on the skin around a tick bite. The rash usually appears within three days to one month after being bitten. Other flulike symptoms of early Lyme disease include fatigue, headache, chills and fever, muscle and joint pain, and swollen lymph nodes.[1]

Treatment and prognosis

Lyme disease can usually be cured by antibiotics if treatment begins in the early stages of infection. Most people who are treated in the later stages also respond well to antibiotics, although some may have persistent or recurring symptoms.

Protection from tick bites

Here are some precautions to decrease the chances of being bitten by a tick:
- Avoid tick-infested areas, particularly in May, June, and July.[2]
- Wear light-colored clothing, including long pants, socks, and long-sleeved shirts.
- Tuck pant legs into socks or boots and shirt into pants so ticks cannot crawl under clothing.
- Spray insect repellent containing a 20-30% concentration of DEET on clothes and exposed skin other than the face.
- Walk in the center of trails to avoid contact with overgrown brush and grass.
- Wash and dry clothing at a high temperature, inspect body surfaces carefully, and remove attached ticks with tweezers. ∎

---
[1] If left untreated, Lyme disease can result in chronic arthritis and nerve and heart dysfunction.
[2] Ticks are especially common near deer trails.

Merging Word Documents

A mail merge operation combines a standard document, such as a form letter, with customized data, such as a set of names and addresses, to create a set of personalized documents. You can perform a mail merge to create letters, labels, and other documents used in mass mailings, or to create standard documents that typically include customized information, such as business cards. In this unit, you learn how to use both the Mail Merge task pane and the commands on the Mailings tab to perform a mail merge. You need to send a letter to patients who recently had a routine mammogram screening, informing them that their mammogram showed no evidence of cancer. You also need to send a reminder card to patients who need to schedule an appointment for a routine mammogram. You use mail merge to create a personalized form letter about the mammogram, and mailing labels for the reminder cards.

OBJECTIVES

Understand mail merge

Create a main document

Design a data source

Enter and edit records

Add merge fields

Merge data

Create labels

Sort and filter records

©Jeffrey Coolidge/Photodisc/Getty Images

Understanding Mail Merge

When you perform a **mail merge**, you merge a standard Word document with a file that contains customized information for many individuals or items. The standard document is called the **main document**. The file with the unique data for individual people or items is called the **data source**. Merging the main document with a data source results in a **merged document** that contains customized versions of the main document, as shown in Figure F-1. The Mail Merge task pane steps you through the process of setting up and performing a mail merge. You can also perform a mail merge using the commands on the Mailings tab. ▓▓▓▓ You decide to use the Mail Merge task pane to create your form letters and the commands on the Mailings tab to create your mailing labels. Before beginning, you explore the steps involved in performing a mail merge.

- **Create the main document**

  The main document contains the text—often called **boilerplate text**—that appears in every version of the merged document. The main document also includes the merge fields, which indicate where the customized information is inserted when you perform the merge. You insert the merge fields in the main document after you have created or selected the data source. You can create a main document using either the current document, a template, or an existing document.

- **Create a data source or select an existing data source**

  The data source is a file that contains the unique information for each individual or item, such as a person's name. It provides the information that varies in every version of the merged document. A data source is composed of data fields and data records. A **data field** is a category of information, such as last name, first name, street address, city, or postal code. A **data record** is a complete set of related information for an individual or an item, such as one person's name and address. It is easiest to think of a data source file as a table: the header row contains the names of the data fields (the **field names**), and each row in the table is an individual data record. You can create a new data source, or you can use an existing data source, such as a data source created in Word, an Outlook contact list, an Access database, or an Excel worksheet.

- **Identify the fields to include in the data source and enter the records**

  When you create a new data source, you must first identify the fields to include, such as first name, last name, and street address if you are creating a data source that will include addresses. It is also important to think of and include all the fields you will need (not just the obvious ones) before you begin to enter data. For example, if you are creating a data source that includes names and addresses, you might need to include fields for a person's middle name, title, apartment number, department name, or country, even if some records in the data source will not include that information. Once you have identified the fields and set up your data source, you are ready to enter the data for each record.

- **Add merge fields to the main document**

  A **merge field** is a placeholder that you insert in the main document to indicate where the data from each record should be inserted when you perform the merge. For example, you insert a zip code merge field in the location where you want to insert a zip code. The merge fields in a main document must correspond with the field names in the associated data source. Merge fields must be inserted, not typed, in the main document. The Mail Merge task pane and the Mailings tab provide access to the dialog boxes you use to insert merge fields.

- **Merge the data from the data source into the main document**

  Once you have established your data source and inserted the merge fields in the main document, you are ready to perform the merge. You can merge to a new file, which contains a customized version of the main document for each record in the data source, or you can merge directly to a printer or e-mail message.

FIGURE F-1: Mail merge process

Exam Date	Title	First Name	Last Name	Address Line 1	City	State	Zip Code	Country
10/2/13	Ms.	Sarah	Bass	62 Cloud St.	Somerville	MA	02144	US
10/3/13	Ms.	Claudia	Beck	23 Plum St.	Boston	MA	02483	US
9/30/13	Ms.	Anne	Gans	456 Elm St.	Arlington	MA	02474	US
10/2/13	Ms.	Jane	Miller	48 East Ave.	Vancouver	BC	V6F 1AH	CANADA
10/1/13	Ms.	Laura	Bright	56 Pearl St.	Cambridge	MA	02139	US

Field name

Data record

Data source document

Main document

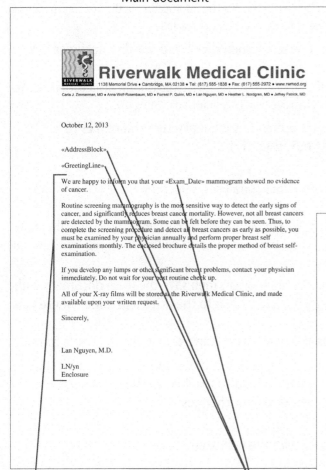

Merged document

Boilerplate text

Merge fields

Customized information

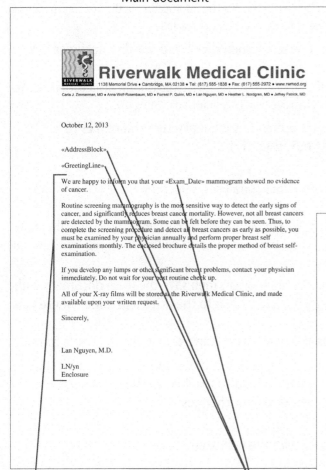
(Riverwalk Medical Clinic main document)

October 12, 2013

«AddressBlock»

«GreetingLine»

We are happy to inform you that your «Exam_Date» mammogram showed no evidence of cancer.

Routine screening mammography is the most sensitive way to detect the early signs of cancer, and significantly reduces breast cancer mortality. However, not all breast cancers are detected by the mammogram. Some can be felt before they can be seen. Thus, to complete the screening procedure and detect all breast cancers as early as possible, you must be examined by your physician annually and perform proper breast self examinations monthly. The enclosed brochure details the proper method of breast self-examination.

If you develop any lumps or other significant breast problems, contact your physician immediately. Do not wait for your next routine check up.

All of your X-ray films will be stored at the Riverwalk Medical Clinic, and made available upon your written request.

Sincerely,

Lan Nguyen, M.D.

LN/yn
Enclosure

(Merged document)

October 12, 2013

Ms. Sarah Bass
62 Cloud St.
Somerville, MA 02144

Dear Ms. Bass:

We are happy to inform you that your 10/2/13 mammogram showed no evidence of cancer.

Routine screening mammography is the most sensitive way to detect the early signs of cancer, and significantly reduces breast cancer mortality. However, not all breast cancers are detected by the mammogram. Some can be felt before they can be seen. Thus, to complete the screening procedure and detect all breast cancers as early as possible, you must be examined by your physician annually and perform proper breast self examinations monthly. The enclosed brochure details the proper method of breast self-examination.

If you develop any lumps or other significant breast problems, contact your physician immediately. Do not wait for your next routine check up.

All of your X-ray films will be stored at the Riverwalk Medical Clinic, and made available upon your written request.

Sincerely,

Lan Nguyen, M.D.

LN/yn
Enclosure

Creating a Main Document

The first step in performing a mail merge is to create the main document—the file that contains the boilerplate text. You can create a main document from scratch, save an existing document as a main document, or use a mail merge template to create a main document. The Mail Merge task pane walks you through the process of selecting the type of main document to create. ▓▓▓ You use an existing form letter for your main document. You begin by opening the Mail Merge task pane.

TROUBLE

A document, blank or otherwise, must be open in the program window for the commands on the Mailings tab to be available.

1. **Start** Word, **click the** Mailings tab, **click the** Start Mail Merge button **in the Start Mail Merge group, then click** Step by Step Mail Merge Wizard

   The Mail Merge task pane opens, as shown in Figure F-2, and displays information for the first step in the mail merge process: Select document type (the type of merge document to create).

2. **Make sure the Letters option button is selected, then click** Next: Starting document **to continue with the next step**

   The task pane displays the options for the second step: Select starting document (the main document). You can use the current document, start with a mail merge template, or use an existing file.

QUICK TIP

If you choose "Use the current document" and the current document is blank, you can create a main document from scratch. Either type the boilerplate text at this step, or wait until the task pane prompts you to do so.

3. **Select the** Start from existing document option button, **make sure (More files...) is selected in the Start from existing list box, then click** Open

   The Open dialog box opens.

4. **Navigate to the location where you store your Data Files, select the file** WMP F-1.docx, **then click** Open

   The letter that opens contains the boilerplate text for the main document. Notice the filename in the title bar is Document1. When you create a main document that is based on an existing document, Word gives the main document a default temporary filename.

5. **Click the** Save button 🖫 **on the Quick Access toolbar, then save the main document with the filename** WMP F-Mammogram Results Letter Main **to the drive and folder where you store your Data Files**

   It's a good idea to include "main" in the filename so that you can easily recognize the file as a main document.

6. **Click the** Zoom level button **on the status bar, click the** 100% option button, **click** OK, **select** October 9, 2013 **in the letter, type today's date, scroll down, select** Lan Nguyen, **type your name, press** [Ctrl][Home], **then save your changes**

   The edited main document is shown in Figure F-3.

7. **Click** Next: Select recipients **to continue with the next step**

   You continue with Step 3 of 6 in the next lesson.

Using mail merge template

If you are creating letters or faxes, you can use a mail merge template to start your main document. Each template includes boilerplate text (which you can customize), and merge fields (which you can match to the field names in your data source). To create a main document that is based on a mail merge template, click the Start from a template option button in the Step 2 of 6 Mail Merge task pane, and then click Select template. In the Select Template dialog box, select a template from the Letters or Faxes tab that includes the word "Merge" in its name, and then click OK to create the document. Once you have created the main document, you can customize it with your own information: edit the boilerplate text; change the document format; or add, remove, or modify the merge fields.

Before performing the merge, make sure to match the names of the merge fields used in the template with the field names used in your data source. To match the field names, click the Match Fields button in the Write & Insert Fields group on the Mailings tab, and then use the list arrows in the Match Fields dialog box to select the field name in your data source that corresponds to each address field component in the main document.

FIGURE F-2: Step 1 of 6 Mail Merge task pane

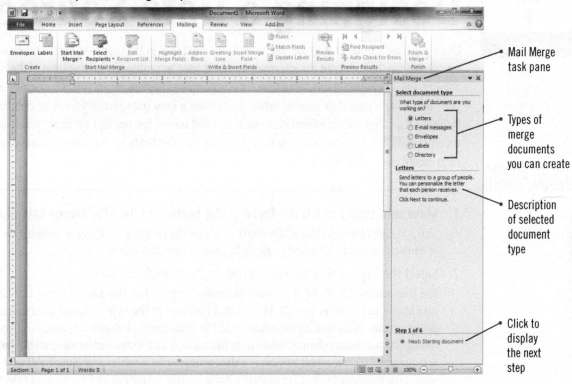

Mail Merge task pane

Types of merge documents you can create

Description of selected document type

Click to display the next step

FIGURE F-3: Main document with Step 2 of 6 Mail Merge task pane

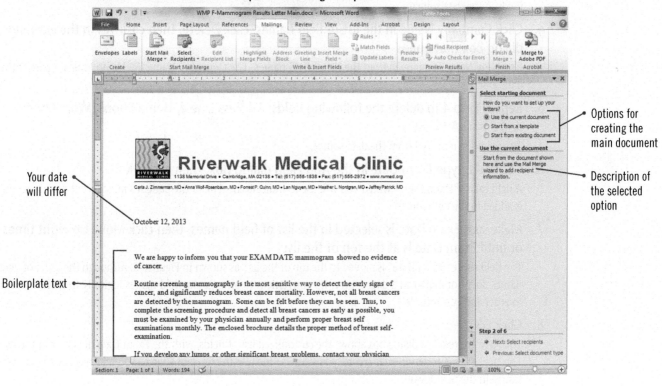

Your date will differ

Boilerplate text

Options for creating the main document

Description of the selected option

Designing a Data Source

Once you have identified the main document, the next step in the mail merge process is to identify the data source, the file that contains the information that is used to customize each version of the merge document. You can use an existing data source that already contains the records you want to include in your merge, or you can create a new data source. When you create a new data source you must determine the fields to include—the categories of information, such as a first name, last name, city, or zip code—and then add the records. You create a new data source that includes fields for the name, address, and exam date for each recent mammogram patient.

STEPS

1. **Make sure Step 3 of 6 is displayed at the bottom of the Mail Merge task pane**

   Step 3 of 6 involves selecting a data source to use for the merge. You can use an existing data source, use a list of contacts created in Microsoft Outlook, or create a new data source.

2. **Select the Type a new list option button, then click Create**

   The New Address List dialog box opens, as shown in Figure F-4. You use this dialog box both to design your data source and to enter records. The column headings in the Type recipient information... section of the dialog box are fields that are commonly used in form letters, but you can customize your data source by adding and removing columns (fields) from this table. A data source can be merged with more than one main document, so it's important to design a data source to be flexible. The more fields you include in a data source, the more flexible it is. For example, if you include separate fields for a person's title, first name, middle name, and last name, you can use the same data source to create an envelope addressed to "Mr. John Montgomery Smith" and a form letter with the greeting "Dear John."

3. **Click Customize Columns**

   The Customize Address List dialog box opens. You use this dialog box to add, delete, rename, and reorder the fields in the data source.

4. **Click Company Name in the list of field names, click Delete, then click Yes in the warning dialog box that opens**

   Company Name is removed from the list of field names. The Company Name field is no longer a part of the data source.

5. **Repeat Step 4 to delete the following fields: Address Line 2, Home Phone, Work Phone, and E-mail Address**

   The fields are removed from the data source.

6. **Click Add, type Exam Date in the Add Field dialog box, then click OK**

   A field called "Exam Date," which you will use to indicate the date of the patient's most recent mammogram, is added to the data source.

7. **Make sure Exam Date is selected in the list of field names, then click Move Up eight times or until Exam Date is at the top of the list**

   The field name "Exam Date" is moved to the top of the list, as shown in Figure F-5. Although the order of field names does not matter in a data source, it's convenient to arrange the field names logically to make it easier to enter and edit records.

8. **Click OK**

   The New Address List dialog box shows the customized list of fields, with the Exam Date field first in the list. The next step is to enter each record you want to include in the data source. You add records to the data source in the next lesson.

FIGURE F-4: **New Address List dialog box**

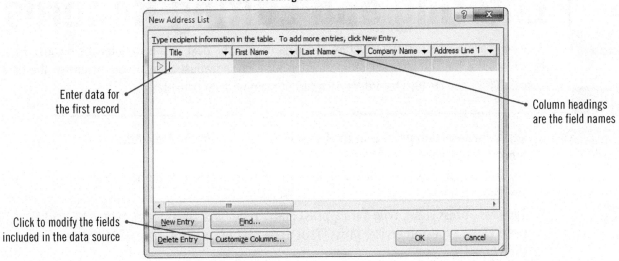

Enter data for the first record

Column headings are the field names

Click to modify the fields included in the data source

FIGURE F-5: **Customize Address List dialog box**

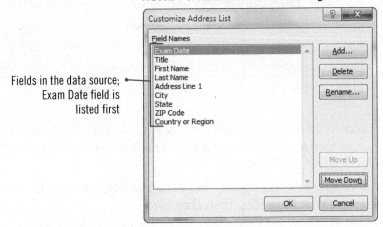

Fields in the data source; Exam Date field is listed first

Merging with an Outlook data source

If you maintain lists of contacts in Microsoft Outlook, you can use one of your Outlook contact lists as a data source for a merge. To merge with an Outlook data source, click the Select from Outlook contacts option button in the Step 3 of 6 Mail Merge task pane, then click Choose Contacts Folder to open the Choose Profile dialog box. In this dialog box, use the Profile Name list arrow to select the profile you want to use, then click OK to open the Select Contacts dialog box. In this dialog box, select the contact list you want to use as the data source, and then click OK. All the contacts included in the selected folder appear in the Mail Merge Recipients dialog box. Here you can refine the list of recipients to include in the merge by sorting and filtering the records. When you are satisfied, click OK in the Mail Merge Recipients dialog box.

Entering and Editing Records

Once you have established the structure of a data source, the next step is to enter the records. Each record includes the complete set of information for each individual or item you include in the data source. ⬛⬛⬛ You create a record for each recent mammogram patient.

STEPS

QUICK TIP

Be careful not to add spaces or extra punctuation after an entry in a field, or these will appear when the data is merged.

1. **Verify the insertion point is in the Exam Date text box in the New Address List dialog box, type 10/2/13, then press [Tab]**

   "10/2/13" appears in the Exam Date field, and the insertion point moves to the next column in the table, the Title field.

2. **Type Ms., press [Tab], type Sarah, press [Tab], type Bass, press [Tab], type 62 Cloud St., press [Tab], type Somerville, press [Tab], type MA, press [Tab], type 02144, press [Tab], then type US**

   Data is entered in all the fields for the first record. You used each field for this record, but it's okay to leave a field blank if you do not need it for a record.

3. **Click New Entry**

   The record for Sarah Bass is added to the data source, and the dialog box displays empty fields for the next record, as shown in Figure F-6.

QUICK TIP

You can also press [Tab] at the end of the last field to start a new record.

4. **Enter the following four records, pressing [Tab] to move from field to field, and clicking New Entry at the end of each record except the last:**

Exam Date	Title	First Name	Last Name	Address Line 1	City	State	ZIP Code	Country
10/3/13	Ms.	Claudia	Beck	23 Plum St.	Boston	MA	02483	US
9/30/13	Ms.	Anne	Gans	456 Elm St.	Arlington	MA	02474	US
10/2/13	Ms.	Jane	Miller	48 East Ave.	Vancouver	BC	V6F 1AH	CANADA
10/1/13	Ms.	Laura	Bright	56 Pearl St.	Cambridge	MA	02139	US

5. **Click OK**

   The Save Address List dialog box opens. Data sources are saved by default in the My Data Sources folder so that you can easily locate them to use in other merge operations. Data sources you create in Word are saved in Microsoft Office Address Lists (*.mdb) format.

TROUBLE

If a check mark appears in the blank record under Laura Bright, click the check mark to eliminate the record from the merge.

6. **Type WMP F-Mammogram Patients in the File name text box, navigate to the drive and folder where you store your Data Files, then click Save**

   The data source is saved, and the Mail Merge Recipients dialog box opens, as shown in Figure F-7. The dialog box shows the records in the data source in table format. You can use the dialog box to sort and filter records, and to select the recipients to include in the mail merge. You will learn more about sorting and filtering in a later lesson. The check marks in the second column indicate the records that will be included in the merge.

7. **Click WMP F-Mammogram Patients.mdb in the Data Source list box at the bottom of the dialog box, then click Edit**

   The Edit Data Source dialog box opens, as shown in Figure F-8. You use this dialog box to edit a data source, including adding and removing fields, editing field names, adding and removing records, and editing existing records.

8. **Click Ms. in the Title field of the Anne Gans record to select it, type Dr., click OK, then click Yes**

   The data in the Title field for Anne Gans changes from "Ms." to "Dr.", and the Edit Data Source dialog box closes.

QUICK TIP

If you want to add new records or modify existing records, click Edit recipient list in the task pane.

9. **Click OK in the Mail Merge Recipients dialog box**

   The dialog box closes. The file type and filename of the data source attached to the main document now appear under Use an existing list in the Mail Merge task pane.

Merging Word Documents

FIGURE F-6: Record in New Address List dialog box

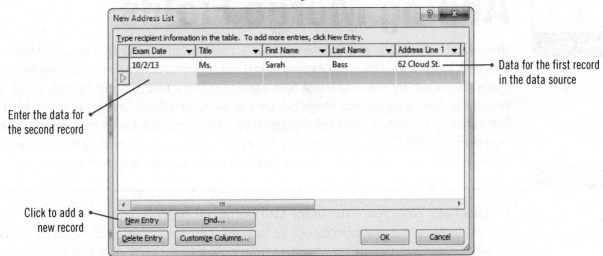

Enter the data for the second record

Data for the first record in the data source

Click to add a new record

FIGURE F-7: Mail Merge Recipients dialog box

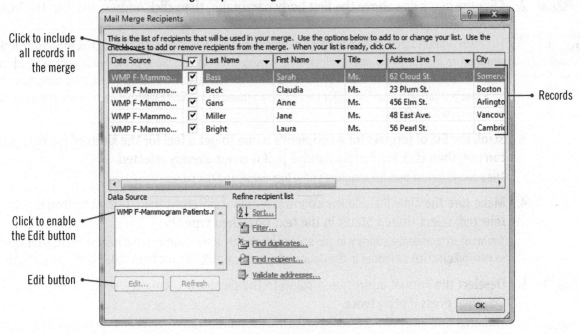

Click to include all records in the merge

Records

Click to enable the Edit button

Edit button

FIGURE F-8: Edit Data Source dialog box

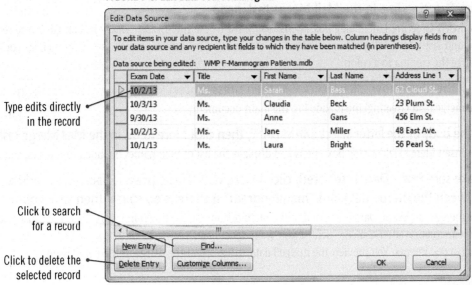

Type edits directly in the record

Click to search for a record

Click to delete the selected record

Adding Merge Fields

After you have created and identified the data source, the next step is to insert the merge fields in the main document. Merge fields serve as placeholders for text that is inserted when the main document and the data source are merged. The names of merge fields correspond to the field names in the data source. You can insert merge fields using the Mail Merge task pane or the Address Block, Greeting Line, and Insert Merge Field buttons in the Write & Insert Fields group on the Mailings tab. You cannot type merge fields into the main document. ████ You use the Mail Merge task pane to insert merge fields for the inside address and greeting of the letter. You also insert a merge field for the exam date in the body of the letter.

1. **Click Next: Write your letter in the Mail Merge task pane**

   The Mail Merge task pane shows the options for Step 4 of 6: Write your letter. During this step, you write or edit the boilerplate text and insert the merge fields in the main document. Since your form letter is already written, you are ready to add the merge fields to it.

2. **Click the blank line above the first body paragraph, then click Address block in the Mail Merge task pane**

   The Insert Address Block dialog box opens, as shown in Figure F-9. You use this dialog box to specify the fields you want to include in an address block. In this merge, the address block is the inside address of the form letter. An address block automatically includes fields for the recipient's name, street, city, state, and postal code, but you can select the format for the recipient's name and indicate whether to include a company name or country in the address.

3. **Scroll the list of formats for a recipient's name to get a feel for the kinds of formats you can use, then click Mr. Joshua Randall Jr. if it is not already selected**

   The selected format uses the recipient's title, first name, and last name.

4. **Make sure the Only include the country/region if different than: option button is selected, select United States in the text box, then type US**

   You want to include the country in the address block only if the country is different than the United States, so you indicate that all entries in the Country field, except "US," should be included in the printed address.

5. **Deselect the Format address according to the destination country/region check box, click OK, then press [Enter] twice**

   The merge field AddressBlock is added to the main document. Chevrons (<< and >>) surround a merge field to distinguish it from the boilerplate text.

6. **Click Greeting line in the Mail Merge task pane**

   The Insert Greeting Line dialog box opens. You want to use the format "Dear Mr. Randall:" (the recipient's title and last name, followed by a colon) for a greeting. The default format uses a comma, so you have to change the comma to a colon.

7. **Click the , list arrow, click :, click OK, then press [Enter]**

   The merge field GreetingLine is added to the main document.

8. **In the body of the letter select EXAM DATE, then click More items in the Mail Merge task pane**

   The Insert Merge Field dialog box opens and displays the list of field names included in the data source.

9. **Make sure Exam Date is selected, click Insert, click Close, press [Spacebar] to add a space between the merge field and "mammogram" if there is no space, then save your changes**

   The merge field Exam_Date is inserted in the main document, as shown in Figure F-10. You must type spaces and punctuation after a merge field if you want spaces and punctuation to appear in that location in the merged documents. You preview the merged data and perform the merge in the next lesson.

Merging Word Documents

FIGURE F-9: Insert Address Block dialog box

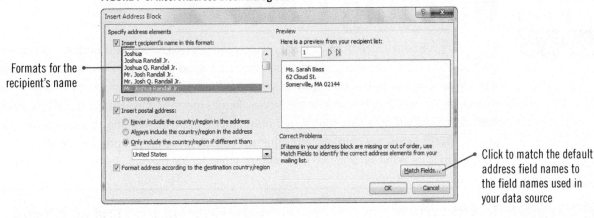

Formats for the recipient's name

Click to match the default address field names to the field names used in your data source

FIGURE F-10: Merge fields in the main document

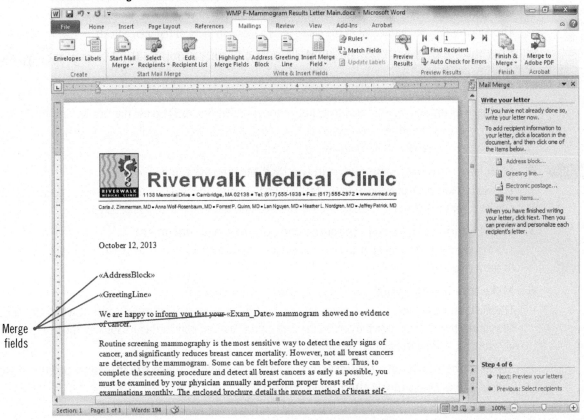

Merge fields

Matching fields

The merge fields you insert in a main document must correspond with the field names in the associated data source. If you are using the Address Block merge field, you must make sure that the default address field names correspond with the field names used in your data source. If the default address field names do not match the field names in your data source, click Match Fields in the Insert Address Block dialog box, then use the list arrows in the Match Fields dialog box to select the field name in the data source that corresponds to each default address field name. You can also click the Match Fields button in the Write & Insert Fields group on the Mailings tab to open the Match Fields dialog box.

Merging Data

Once you have added records to your data source and inserted merge fields in the main document, you are ready to perform the merge. Before merging, it's a good idea to preview the merged data to make sure the printed documents will appear as you want them to. You can preview the merge using the task pane or the Preview Results button in the Preview Results group on the Mailings tab. When you merge the main document with the data source, you must choose between merging to a new file or directly to a printer. 🖨️📋 Before merging the form letter with the data source, you preview the merge to make sure the data appears in the letter as you intended. You then merge the two files to a new document.

STEPS

QUICK TIP
To adjust the main document, click the Preview Results button in the Preview Results group on the Mailings tab, then make any necessary changes. Click the Preview Results button again to preview the merged data.

1. **Click** Next: Preview your letters **in the Mail Merge task pane, then scroll down as necessary to see the exam date in the document**

   The data from the first record in the data source appears in place of the merge fields in the main document, as shown in Figure F-11. Always preview a document to verify that the merge fields, punctuation, page breaks, and spacing all appear as you intend before you perform the merge.

2. **Click the** Next Recipient button >> **in the Mail Merge task pane**

   The data from the second record in the data source appears in place of the merge fields.

3. **Click the** Go to Record text box **in the Preview Results group on the Mailings tab, type** 4, **then press [Enter]**

   The data for the fourth record appears in the document window. The non-U.S. country name, in this case Canada, is included in the address block, just as you specified. You can also use the First Record ⏮️, Previous Record ◀, Next Record ▶, and Last Record buttons ⏭️ in the Preview Results group to preview the merged data. Table F-1 describes other commands on the Mailings tab.

QUICK TIP
If your data source contains many records, you can merge directly to a printer to avoid creating a large file.

4. **Click** Next: Complete the merge **in the Mail Merge task pane**

   The options for Step 6 of 6 appear in the Mail Merge task pane. Merging to a new file creates a document with one letter for each record in the data source. This allows you to edit the individual letters.

5. **Click** Edit individual letters **to merge the data to a new document**

   The Merge to New Document dialog box opens. You can use this dialog box to specify the records to include in the merge.

6. **Make sure the** All option button **is selected, then click** OK

   The main document and the data source are merged to a new document called Letters1, which contains a customized form letter for each record in the data source. You can now further personalize the letters without affecting the main document or the data source.

7. **Scroll to the fourth letter (addressed to Ms. Jane Miller), place the insertion point before V6F in the address block, then press [Enter]**

   The postal code is now consistent with the proper format for a Canadian address.

8. **Click the** Save button 💾 **on the Quick Access toolbar to open the Save As dialog box, then save the merged document as** WMP F-Mammogram Results Letter Merge **to the drive and folder where you store your Data Files**

   You may decide not to save a merged file if your data source is large. Once you have created the main document and the data source, you can create the letters by performing the merge again.

TROUBLE
Print only one letter if you are required to submit a printed document to your instructor.

9. **Submit the document to your instructor, then close all open Word files, saving changes if prompted**

FIGURE F-11: Preview of merged data

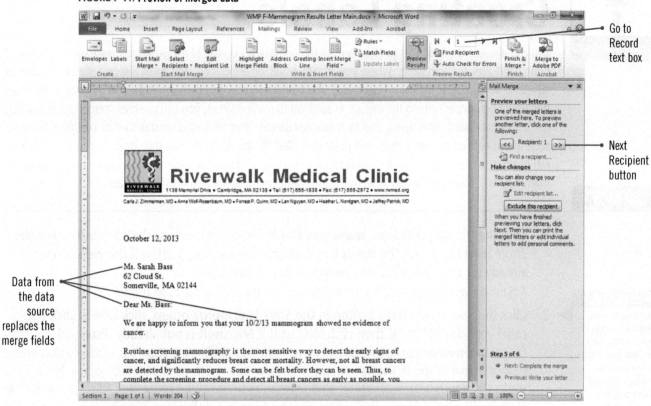

Go to Record text box

Next Recipient button

Data from the data source replaces the merge fields

TABLE F-1: Commands on the Mailings tab

command	use to
Envelopes	Create and print an individual envelope
Labels	Create and print an individual label
Start Mail Merge	Select the type of mail merge document to create and start the mail merge process
Select Recipients	Attach an existing data source to a main document or create a new data source
Edit Recipient List	Edit, sort, and filter the associated data source
Highlight Merge Fields	Highlight the merge fields in the main document
Address Block	Insert an Address Block merge field in the main document
Greeting Line	Insert a Greeting Line merge field in the main document
Insert Merge Field	Insert a merge field from the data source in the main document
Rules	Set rules to control how Word merges the data in the data source with the main document
Match Fields	Match the names of address or greeting fields used in a main document with the field names used in the data source
Update Labels	Update all the labels in a label main document to match the content and formatting of the first label
Preview Results	Switch between viewing the main document with merge fields or with merged data
Find Recipient	Search for a specific record in the merged document
Auto Check for Errors	Check for and report errors in the merge
Finish & Merge	Specify whether to merge to a new document or directly to a printer or e-mail, and then complete the merge

Creating Labels

You can also use the Mail Merge task pane or the commands on the Mailings tab to create mailing labels or print envelopes for a mailing. When you create labels or envelopes, you must select a standard label or envelope size to use as the main document, select a data source, and then insert the merge fields in the main document before performing the merge. In addition to mailing labels, you can use mail merge to create labels for CDs, videos, and other items, and to create documents that are based on standard or custom label sizes, such as business cards, name tags, and postcards. ▰▰▰ You decide to use the commands on the Mailings tab to create mailing labels for the reminder card you will send to all patients who need to schedule a routine mammogram. You create a new label main document and attach an existing data source.

STEPS

1. **Click the File tab, click New, make sure Blank document is selected, click Create, click the Zoom level button on the status bar, click the 100% option button if the view is not already set to 100%, click OK, then click the Mailings tab**

   A blank document must be open for the commands on the Mailings tab to be available.

QUICK TIP
To create an envelope mail merge, click Envelopes on the Start Mail Merge list to open the Envelope Options dialog box, and then select the envelope size and other options.

2. **Click the Start Mail Merge button in the Start Mail Merge group, click Labels, click the Label vendors list arrow, then click Microsoft if Microsoft is not already displayed**

   The Label Options dialog box opens, as shown in Figure F-12. You use this dialog box to select a label size for your labels and to specify the type of printer you plan to use. The name Microsoft appears in the Label vendors list box. You can use the Label vendors list arrow to select other brand name label vendors, such as Avery or Office Depot. Many standard-sized labels for mailings, CD/DVD faces, business cards, postcards, and other types of labels are listed in the Product number list box. The type, height, width, and page size for the selected product are displayed in the Label information section.

TROUBLE
If your labels do not match Figure F-13, click the Undo button on the Quick Access toolbar, then repeat Step 3, making sure to click the second instance of 30 Per Page.

3. **Click the second instance of 30 Per Page in the Product number list, click OK, click the Table Tools Layout tab, click View Gridlines in the Table group to turn on the display of gridlines if they are not displayed, then click the Mailings tab**

   A table with gridlines appears in the main document, as shown in Figure F-13. Each table cell is the size of a label for the label product you selected.

4. **Save the label main document with the filename WMP F-Mammogram Reminder Labels Main to the drive and folder where you store your Data Files**

   Next, you need to select a data source for the labels.

5. **Click the Select Recipients button in the Start Mail Merge group, then click Use Existing List**

   The Select Data Source dialog box opens.

QUICK TIP
To create or change the return address for an envelope mail merge, click the File tab, click Options, click Advanced in the left pane of the Word Options dialog box, then scroll down the right pane and enter the return address in the Mailing address text box in the General section.

6. **Navigate to the drive and folder where you store your Data Files, open the file WMP F-2.mdb, then save your changes**

   The data source file is attached to the label main document and <<Next Record>> appears in every cell in the table except the first cell, which is blank. In the next lesson you sort and filter the records before performing the mail merge.

FIGURE F-12: Label Options dialog box

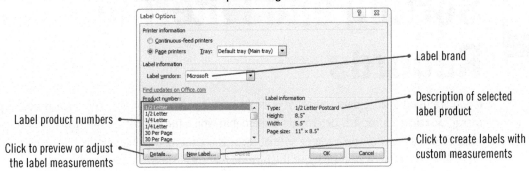

Label product numbers

Click to preview or adjust the label measurements

Label brand

Description of selected label product

Click to create labels with custom measurements

FIGURE F-13: Label main document

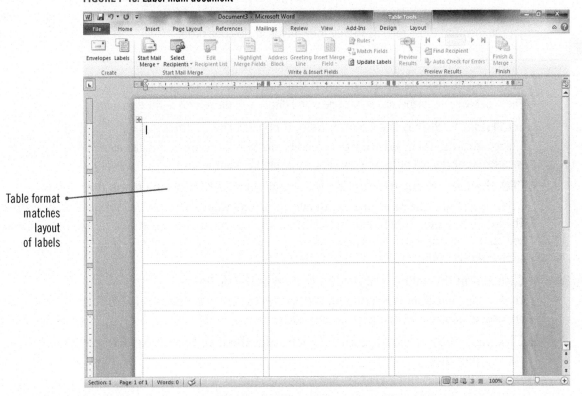

Table format matches layout of labels

Printing individual envelopes and labels

The Mail Merge feature enables you to easily print envelopes and labels for mass mailings, but you can also quickly format and print individual envelopes and labels using the Envelopes or Labels commands in the Create group on the Mailings tab. Simply click the Envelopes button or Labels button to open the Envelopes and Labels dialog box. On the Envelopes tab, shown in Figure F-14, type the recipient's address in the Delivery address box and the return address in the Return address box. Click Options to open the Envelope Options dialog box, which you can use to select the envelope size, change the font and font size of the delivery and return addresses, and change the printing options. When you are ready to print the envelope, click Print in the Envelopes and Labels dialog box. The procedure for printing an individual label is similar to printing an individual envelope: enter the recipient's address in the Address box on the Labels tab, click Options to select a label product number, click OK, and then click Print.

FIGURE F-14: Envelopes and Labels dialog box

Sorting and Filtering Records

If you are using a large data source, you might want to sort and/or filter the records before performing a merge. **Sorting** the records determines the order in which the records are merged. For example, you might want to sort an address data source so that records are merged alphabetically by last name or in zip code order. **Filtering** the records pulls out the records that meet specific criteria and includes only those records in the merge. For instance, you might want to filter a data source to send a mailing only to people who live in the state of New York. You can use the Mail Merge Recipients dialog box both to sort and to filter a data source. 🔧 You apply a filter to the data source so that only United States addresses are included in the merge. You then sort those records so that they merge in zip code order.

STEPS

1. **Click the** Edit Recipient List button **in the Start Mail Merge group**

   The Mail Merge Recipients dialog box opens and displays all the records in the data source.

2. **Scroll right to display the Country field, then click the** Country column heading

   The records are sorted in ascending alphabetical order by country, with Canadian records listed first. If you want to reverse the sort order, you can click the column heading again.

3. **Click the** Country column heading list arrow, **then click** US **on the menu that opens**

   A filter is applied to the data source so that only the records with "US" in the Country field will be merged. The grayish-blue arrow in the Country column heading indicates that a filter has been applied to the column. You can filter a data source by as many criteria as you like. To remove a filter, click a column heading list arrow, then click (All).

4. **Click** Sort **in the Refine recipient list section of the dialog box**

   The Filter and Sort dialog box opens with the Sort Records tab displayed. You can use this dialog box to apply more advanced sort and filter options to the data source.

5. **Click the** Sort by list arrow, **click** ZIP Code, **click the first** Then by list arrow, **click** Last Name, **then click** OK

   The Mail Merge Recipients dialog box (shown in Figure F-15) now displays only the records with a US address sorted first in zip code order, and then alphabetically by last name.

6. **Click** OK

   The sort and filter criteria you set are saved for the current merge.

7. **Click the** Address Block button **in the Write & Insert Fields group, then click** OK **in the Insert Address Block dialog box**

   The Address Block merge field is added to the first label.

8. **Click the** Update Labels button **in the Write & Insert Fields group**

   The merge field is copied from the first label to every label in the main document.

9. **Click the** Preview Results button **in the Preview Results group**

   A preview of the merged label data appears in the main document, as shown in Figure F-16. Only U.S. addresses are included, and the labels are organized in zip code order, with recipients with the same zip code listed in alphabetical order.

10. **Click the** Finish & Merge button **in the Finish group, click** Edit Individual Documents, **click** OK **in the Merge to New Document dialog box, replace** Ms. Julia Packer **with your name in the first label, save the document as** WMP F-Mammogram Reminder Labels US Only Zip Code Merge **to the drive and folder where you store your Data Files, submit the labels to your instructor, save and close all open files, then exit Word**

Merging Word Documents

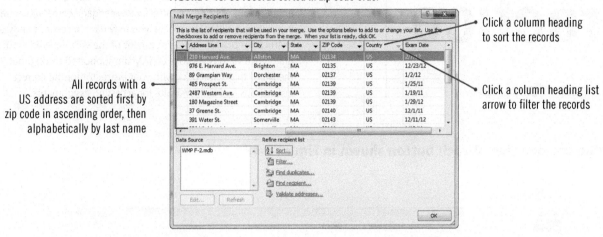

All records with a
US address are sorted first by
zip code in ascending order, then
alphabetically by last name

Click a column heading
to sort the records

Click a column heading list
arrow to filter the records

FIGURE F-16: Merged labels

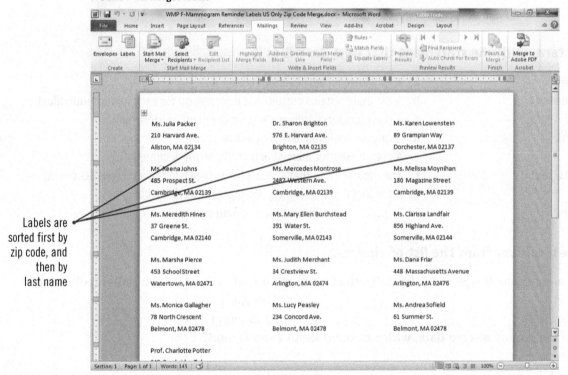

Labels are
sorted first by
zip code, and
then by
last name

Inserting individual merge fields

You must include proper punctuation, spacing, and blank lines between the merge fields in a main document if you want punctuation, spaces, and blank lines to appear between the data in the merge documents. For example, to create an address line with a city, state, and zip code, you insert the City merge field, type a comma and a space, insert the State merge field, type a space, and then insert the ZIP Code merge field: <<City>>, <<State>> <<ZIP Code>>.

You can insert an individual merge field by clicking the Insert Merge Field list arrow in the Write & Insert Fields group and then selecting the field name from the menu that opens. Alternatively, you can click the Insert Merge Field button to open the Insert Merge Field dialog box, which you can use to insert several merge fields at once by clicking a field name in the dialog box, clicking Insert, clicking another field name, clicking Insert, and so on. When you have finished inserting the merge fields, click Close to close the dialog box. You can then add spaces, punctuation, and lines between the merge fields you inserted in the main document.

Practice

Concepts Review

For current SAM information, including versions and content details, visit SAM Central (http://www.cengage.com/samcentral). If you have a SAM user profile, you may have access to hands-on instruction, practice, and assessment of the skills covered in this unit. Since various versions of SAM are supported throughout the life of this text, check with your instructor for the correct instructions and URL/Web site for accessing assignments.

Describe the function of each button shown in Figure F-17.

FIGURE F-17

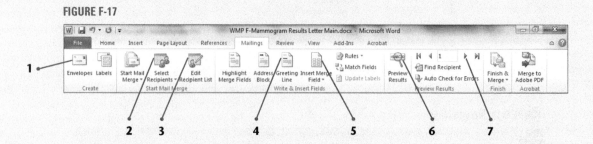

Match each term with the statement that best describes it.

8. **Data record**
9. **Main document**
10. **Data field**
11. **Data source**
12. **Sort**
13. **Boilerplate text**
14. **Filter**
15. **Merge field**

a. To organize records in a sequence
b. A file that contains customized information for each item or individual
c. A complete set of information for one item or individual
d. A category of information in a data source
e. A placeholder for merged data in the main document
f. The standard text that appears in every version of a merged document
g. A file that contains boilerplate text and merge fields
h. To pull out records that meet certain criteria

Select the best answer from the list of choices.

16. **In a mail merge, which type of file contains the information that varies for each individual or item?**
   a. Data source
   b. Main document
   c. Sorted document
   d. Filtered document

17. **To change the font of merged data, which element should you format?**
   a. Boilerplate text
   b. Field name
   c. Data record
   d. Merge field

18. **Which command is used to synchronize the field names in a data source with the merge fields in a document?**
   a. Rules
   b. Update Labels
   c. Match Fields
   d. Highlight Merge Fields

19. **Which action do you perform on a data source in order to merge only certain records?**
   a. Filter records
   b. Delete records
   c. Edit records
   d. Sort records

20. **Which action do you perform on a data source to reorganize the order of the records for a merge?**
   a. Edit records
   b. Sort records
   c. Filter records
   d. Delete records

Merging Word Documents

Skills Review

1. **Create a main document.**
   a. Start Word, change the style of the document to No Spacing, then open the Mail Merge task pane.
   b. Use the Mail Merge task pane to create a letter main document, click Next, then select the current (blank) document.
   c. At the top of the blank document, type **New England Health and Life**, press [Enter], then type **1375 Harbor Street, Portsmouth, NH 03828; Tel: 603-555-8457; www.nehealthandlife.net**.
   d. Press [Enter] five times, type today's date, press [Enter] five times, then type **We are writing to confirm your choice of a Primary Care Physician in STATE. According to our records, you selected PCP as your Primary Care Physician.**
   e. Press [Enter] twice, then type **It's important that you contact your Primary Care Physician to coordinate all your medical care. If you need to see a specialist, your Primary Care Physician will refer you to one who is affiliated with his or her hospital or medical group.**
   f. Press [Enter] twice, then type **If the physician listed above is not the one you selected, please call Member Services at 1-800-555-1328.**
   g. Press [Enter] twice, type **Sincerely,** press [Enter] four times, type your name, press [Enter], then type **Member Services.**
   h. Center the first two lines of text, change the font used for New England Health and Life to 20 point Gill Sans Ultra Bold, then remove the hyperlink in the second line of text. (*Hint*: Right-click the hyperlink.)
   i. Save the main document as **WMP F-Subscriber PCP Letter Main** to the drive and folder where you store your Data Files.

2. **Design a data source.**
   a. Click Next, select the Type a new list option button in the Step 3 of 6 Mail Merge task pane, then click Create.
   b. Click Customize Columns in the New Address List dialog box, then remove these fields from the data source: Company Name, Address Line 2, Country or Region, Home Phone, Work Phone, and E-mail Address.
   c. Add an **ID** field and a **PCP** field to the data source. Be sure these fields follow the ZIP Code field.
   d. Rename the Address Line 1 field **Street**, then click OK to close the Customize Address List dialog box.

3. **Enter and edit records.**
   a. Add the records shown in Table F-2 to the data source.

TABLE F-2

Title	First Name	Last Name	Street	City	State	ZIP Code	ID	PCP
Mr.	Rich	Sargent	34 Mill St.	Exeter	NH	03833	MT3948	Susan Trifilo, M.D.
Mr.	Eric	Jenkins	289 Sugar Hill Rd.	Franconia	NH	03632	CZ2846	Richard Pattavina, M.D.
Ms.	Mary	Curtis	742 Main St.	Derby	VT	04634	MT1928	Edwin Marsh, M.D.
Mr.	Alex	Field	987 Ocean Rd.	Portsmouth	NH	03828	CF8725	Rebecca Keller, M.D.
Ms.	Eva	Juarez	73 Bay Rd.	Durham	NH	03814	MK2991	Anna Doherty, M.D.
Ms.	Molly	Reed	67 Apple St.	Northfield	MA	01360	CG8231	Bruce Dewey, M.D.
Ms.	Jenna	Suzuki	287 Mountain Rd.	Dublin	NH	03436	MT1878	Lisa Giaimo, M.D.

   b. Save the data source as **WMP F-Subscriber Data** to the drive and folder where you store your Data Files.
   c. Change the PCP for record 2 (Eric Jenkins) from Richard Pattanvina, M.D. to **Diana Ray, M.D.**
   d. Click OK to close the Mail Merge Recipients dialog box.

4. **Add merge fields.**
   a. Click Next, then in the blank line above the first body paragraph, insert an Address Block merge field.
   b. In the Insert Address Block dialog box, click Match Fields.
   c. Click the list arrow next to Address 1 in the Match Fields dialog box, click Street, then click OK. (*Hint*: If a warning box opens, click Yes, then click OK to close the dialog box.)
   d. Press [Enter] twice, type **Member ID:**, insert a space, then insert the ID merge field.
   e. Press [Enter] twice, insert a Greeting Line merge field using the default greeting line format, then press [Enter].
   f. In the first body paragraph, replace STATE with the State merge field and PCP with the PCP merge field. (*Note*: Make sure to insert a space before or after each merge field as needed.) Save your changes to the main document.

Skills Review (continued)

5. Merge data.

  a. Click Next to preview the merged data, then use the Next Record button to scroll through each letter, examining it carefully for errors.

  b. Click the Preview Results button on the Mailings tab, make any necessary adjustments to the main document, save your changes, then click the Preview Results button to return to the preview of the document.

  c. Click Next, click Edit individual letters, then merge all the records to a new file.

  d. Save the merged document as **WMP F-Subscriber PCP Letter Merge** to the drive and folder where you store your Data Files. The last letter is shown in Figure F-18. Submit the file or a copy of the last letter per your instructor's directions, then save and close all open files.

6. Create labels.

  a. Open a new blank document, click the Start Mail Merge button on the Mailings tab, then create a Labels main document.

  b. In the Label Options dialog box, select Avery US Letter 5160 Easy Peel Address labels, then click OK.

  c. Click the Select Recipients button, then open the WMP F-Subscriber Data.mdb file you created.

  d. Save the label main document as **WMP F-Subscriber Labels Main** to the drive and folder where you store your Data Files.

7. Sort and filter records.

  a. Click the Edit Recipient List button, filter the records so that only the records with NH in the State field are included in the merge, sort the records in zip code order, then click OK.

  b. Insert an Address Block merge field using the default settings, click the Preview Results button, then notice that the street address is missing. (*Note*: When you preview results, you see only one record at a time.)

  c. Click the Preview Results button, then click the Match Fields button to open the Match Fields dialog box.

  d. Click the list arrow next to Address 1, click Street, then click OK. (*Hint*: If a warning box opens, click Yes, then click OK to close the dialog box.)

  e. Click the Preview Results button to preview the merged data, and notice that the address block now includes the street address.

  f. Click the Update Labels button, examine the merged data for errors, then correct any mistakes.

  g. Merge all the records to an individual document, shown in Figure F-19, then save the merged file as **WMP F-Subscriber Labels NH Only Merge** to the drive and folder where you store your Data Files.

  h. In the first label, change Ms. Jenna Suzuki to your name, submit the document to your instructor, save and close all open Word files, then exit Word.

FIGURE F-18

New England Health and Life

1375 Harbor Street, Portsmouth, NH 03828; Tel: 603-555-8457; www.nehealthandlife.net

September 1, 2013

Ms. Jenna Suzuki
287 Mountain Rd.
Dublin, NH 03436

Member ID: MT1878

Dear Ms. Suzuki,

We are writing to confirm your choice of a Primary Care Physician in NH. According to our records, you selected Lisa Giaimo, M.D. , as your Primary Care Physician.

It's important that you contact your Primary Care Physician to coordinate all your medical care. If you need to see a specialist, your Primary Care Physician will refer you to one who is affiliated with his or her hospital or medical group.

If the physician listed above is not the one you selected, please call Member Services at 1-800-555-1328.

Sincerely,

Your Name
Member Services

FIGURE F-19

Ms. Jenna Suzuki	Mr. Eric Jenkins	Ms. Eva Juarez
287 Mountain Rd.	289 Sugar Hill Rd.	73 Bay Rd.
Dublin, NH 03436	Franconia, NH 03632	Durham, NH 03814
Mr. Alex Field	Mr. Rich Sargent	
987 Ocean Rd.	34 Mill St.	
Portsmouth, NH 03828	Exeter, NH 03833	

Merging Word Documents

Independent Challenge 1

You work for Rocky Mountain Eye Care. Your office has designed a maintenance program for gas permeable (GP) contact lenses, and you want to send a letter introducing the program to all patients who wear GP lenses. You'll use Mail Merge to create the letter. If you are performing the ACE steps and are able to print envelopes on your printer, you will also use Word to print an envelope for one letter.

a. Start Word, then using either the Mailings tab or the Mail Merge task pane, create a letter main document using the file WMP F-3.docx from the drive and folder where you store your Data Files.

b. Replace Your Name with your name in the signature block, then save the main document as **WMP F-GP Letter Main**.

c. Use the file WMP F-4.mdb from the drive and folder where you store your Data Files as the data source.

d. Sort the data source by last name in alphabetical order, then filter the data so that only records with GP as the lens are included in the merge.

e. Insert an Address Block and a Greeting Line merge field in the main document, then preview the merged letters.

f. Merge all the records to a new document, then save it as **WMP F-GP Letter Merge**.

Advanced Challenge Exercise

- If you can print envelopes, select the inside address in the first merge letter, then click the Envelopes button in the Create group on the Mailings tab.
- On the Envelopes tab, verify that the Omit check box is not selected, then type your name in the Return address text box along with the address **Rocky Mountain Eye Care**, **60 Crandall Street**, **Boulder, CO 80306.**
- Click Options. On the Envelope Options tab, make sure the Envelope size is set to Size 10, then change the font of the Delivery address and the Return address to Times New Roman.
- On the Printing Options tab, select the appropriate Feed method for your printer, then click OK.
- Click Add to Document, click No if a message box opens asking if you want to save the new return address as the default return address, then print the envelope and submit it to your instructor.

g. Submit the file or a copy of the first merge letter per your instructor's directions, close all open Word files, saving changes, and then exit Word.

Independent Challenge 2

One of your responsibilities at Northwest Family Health, a growing family health clinic, is to create business cards for the staff. You use mail merge to create the cards so that you can easily produce standard business cards for future employees.

a. Start Word, then use the Mailings tab or the Mail Merge task pane to create labels using the current blank document.

b. Select Microsoft North American Size, which is described as Horizontal Card, 2" high × 3.5" wide. (*Hint*: Select the second instance of North American Size in the Product number list box.)

c. Create a new data source that includes the fields and records shown in Table F-3:

TABLE F-3

Title	First Name	Last Name	Phone	Fax	E-mail	Hire Date
Medical Director	Ruth	Harrington	(503) 555-3982	(503) 555-6654	rharrington@nwfh.com	1/12/10
Nurse Practitioner	Diego	Banks	(503) 555-2323	(503) 555-4956	dbanks@nwfh.com	3/18/11

d. Add six more records to the data source, including records for a Medical Assistant, an Immunization Coordinator, three Physicians, and an Administrative Assistant. Include your name in the record for the Administrative Assistant. (*Hint*: Be careful not to add a blank row at the bottom of the data source.)

e. Save the data source with the filename **WMP F-NWFH Employee Data** to the drive and folder where you store your Data Files, then sort the data by Title.

Independent Challenge 2 (continued)

f. In the first table cell, create the Northwest Family Health business card. Figure F-20 shows a sample business card, but you should create your own design. Include the clinic name, a street address, and the Web site address **www.nwfh.com**. Also include First Name, Last Name, Title, Phone, Fax, and E-mail merge fields. (*Hint*: If your design includes a graphic, insert the graphic before inserting the merge fields. Insert each merge field individually, adjusting the spacing between merge fields as necessary.)

FIGURE F-20

g. Format the business card with fonts, colors, and other formatting features. (*Hint*: Make sure to select the entire merge field, including the chevrons, before formatting.)

h. Update all the labels, preview the data, make any necessary adjustments, then merge all the records to a new document.

i. Save the merge document as **WMP F-NWFH Business Cards Merge** to the drive and folder where you store your Data Files, submit a copy to your instructor, then close the file.

j. Save the main document as **WMP F-NWFH Business Cards Main** to the drive and folder where you store your Data Files, close the file, then exit Word.

Independent Challenge 3

You need to create a class list for a fitness and nutrition class you teach for children who are overweight. You want the class list to include contact information for the children, as well as their age and Body Mass Index (BMI) at the time they registered for the class. You decide to use mail merge to create the class list. If you are completing the ACE steps, you will also use mail merge to create mailing labels.

a. Start Word, then use the Mailings tab or the Mail Merge task pane to create a directory using the current blank document.

b. Create a new data source that includes the following fields: First Name, Last Name, Age, BMI, Parent First Name, Parent Last Name, Address, City, State, ZIP Code, and Home Phone.

c. Enter the records shown in Table F-4 in the data source.

TABLE F-4

First Name	Last Name	Age	BMI	Parent First Name	Parent Last Name	Address	City	State	ZIP Code	Home Phone
Sophie	Wright	8	25.31	Kerry	Wright	58 Main St.	Camillus	NY	13031	555-2345
Will	Jacob	7	20.02	Bob	Jacob	32 North Way	Camillus	NY	13031	555-9827
Jackson	Rule	8	22.52	Sylvia	Rule	289 Sylvan Way	Marcellus	NY	13032	555-9724
Abby	Herman	7	21.89	Sarah	Thomas	438 Lariat St.	Marcellus	NY	13032	555-8347

d. Add five additional records to the data source using the following last names and BMIs:
O'Keefe, 24.03
George, 26.12
Goleman, 21.17
Siebert, 21.63
Choy, 23.45
Make up the remaining information for these five records.

e. Save the data source as **WMP F-Kids Fitness Class Data** to the drive and folder where you store your Data Files, then sort the records by last name.

f. Insert a table that includes six columns and one row in the main document.

g. In the first table cell, insert the First Name and Last Name merge fields, separated by a space.

h. In the second cell, insert the Age merge field.

i. In the third cell, insert the BMI merge field.

Merging Word Documents

Independent Challenge 3 (continued)

j. In the fourth cell, insert the Address and City merge fields, separated by a comma and a space.

k. In the fifth cell, insert the Home Phone merge field.

l. In the sixth cell, insert the Parent First Name and Parent Last Name merge fields, separated by a space.

m. Preview the merged data and make any necessary adjustments. (*Hint*: Only one record is displayed at a time when you preview the data.)

n. Merge all the records to a new document, then save the document as **WMP F-Kids Fitness Class List Merge** to the drive and folder where you store your Data Files.

o. Press [Ctrl][Home], press [Enter], type **Fitness and Nutrition for Children** at the top of the document, press [Enter], type **Instructor:** followed by your name, then center the two lines.

p. Insert a new row at the top of the table, then type the following column headings in the new row: **Name**, **Age**, **BMI**, **Address**, **Phone**, **Parent Name**.

q. Format the class list to make it attractive and readable, save your changes, submit a copy to your instructor, then close the file.

r. Close the main document without saving changes.

Advanced Challenge Exercise

- Open a new blank document, then use mail merge to create mailing labels using Avery US Letter 5162 Easy Peel Address labels.
- Use the WMP F-Kids Fitness Class Data data source you created, and sort the records first in zip code order, and then alphabetically by parent last name.
- In the first table cell, create your own address block using the Parent First Name, Parent Last Name, Address, City, State, and Zip Code merge fields. Be sure to include proper spacing and punctuation.
- Update all the labels, preview the merged data, merge all the records to a new document, then type your name centered in the document header.
- Save the document as **WMP F-Kids Fitness Class Labels Merge ACE** to the drive and folder where you store your Data Files, submit a copy to your instructor, close the file, then close the main document without saving changes.

s. Exit Word.

Real Life Independent Challenge

Mail merge can be used not only for mailings, but to create CD/DVD labels, labels for file folders, phone directories, business cards, and many other types of documents. In this independent challenge, you design and create a data source that you can use at work or in your personal life, and then you merge the data source with a main document that you create. Your data source might include contact information for your friends and associates, inventory for your business, details for an event such as a wedding (guests invited, responses, gifts received), data on one of your collections (such as music or photos), or some other type of information.

a. Determine the content of your data source, list the fields you want to include, and then determine the logical order of the fields. Be sure to select your fields carefully so that your data source is flexible and can be merged with many types of documents. Generally it is better to include more fields, even if you don't enter data in them for each record.

b. Start Word, start a mail merge for the type of document you want to create (such as a directory or a label), then create a new data source.

c. Customize the columns in the data source to include the fields and organization you determined in Step a.

d. Add at least five records to the data source, then save it as **WMP F-Your Name Data** to the location where you store your Data Files.

e. Write and format the main document, insert the merge fields, preview the merge, make any necessary adjustments, then merge the files to a document.

f. Adjust the formatting of the merge document as necessary, add your name to the header, save the merge document as **WMP F-Your Name Merge** to the drive and folder where you store your Data Files, submit a copy to your instructor, close the file, close the main document without saving changes, then exit Word.

Visual Workshop

Using mail merge, create the postcards shown in Figure F-21. Use Avery US Letter 3263 Postcard labels for the main document, and create a data source that contains at least four records, including your name. Save the data source as **WMP F-Patient Data**, save the merge document as **WMP F-Patient Reminder Card Merge**, and save the main document as **WMP F-Patient Reminder Card Main**, all to the drive and folder where you store your Data Files. (*Hints*: Notice that the postcard label main document is formatted as a table. To lay out the postcard, insert a nested table with two columns and one row in the upper-left postcard; add the text, graphic, and merge field to the nested table; and then remove the outside borders on the nested table. The clip art graphic uses the keyword "eye chart," and the fonts are Berlin Sans FB Demi and Calibri.) Submit a copy of the postcards to your instructor.

FIGURE F-21

Elizabeth B. Sloan, M.D.

974 West 96th Street, Suite 100
New York, NY 10025

Telephone: 212-555-8634

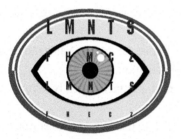

Our records indicate it is time for your
annual eye exam. Please call our office
to schedule an appointment.

Mr. Liam Geery

983 Broadway

Apt. 74

New York, NY 10025

Elizabeth B. Sloan, M.D.

974 West 96th Street, Suite 100
New York, NY 10025

Telephone: 212-555-8634

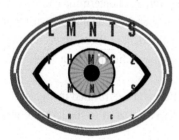

Our records indicate it is time for your
annual eye exam. Please call our office
to schedule an appointment.

Mr. Zeke Platte

234 W. 110th St.

Apt. 112

New York, NY 10027

Merging Word Documents

UNIT
G
Word 2010

Developing Multipage Documents

Files You Will Need:

WMP G-1.docx
WMP G-2.docx
WMP G-3.docx
WMP G-4.docx
WMP G-5.docx
WMP G-6.docx
WMP G-7.docx

Word includes many features designed to help you develop and format multipage documents, such as reports and manuals. Multipage documents can include cross-references, a table of contents, and even an index. You often create multipage documents in Outline view, where you can use headings and subheadings to organize the content. Once the document content is organized under headings and subheadings, you can use the Navigation pane to navigate to specific content to make changes and add new content. Finally, you can divide a multipage document into sections so that you can apply different formatting, such as headers, footers, and page numbers, to each section. Tony Sanchez, RN, the office manager at Riverwalk Medical Clinic, asks you to help him develop guidelines related to office management, filing procedures, and receptionist duties. Tony plans to use these documents as the basis for a Policy and Procedures Manual for the clinic. You start by working in Outline view to revise the structure for the guidelines, and then you use several advanced Word features to format the document for publication.

OBJECTIVES

Build a document in Outline view

Work in Outline view

Navigate a document

Generate a table of contents

Mark entries for an index

Generate an index

Insert footers in multiple sections

Insert headers in multiple sections

Finalize a multipage document

©Jeffrey Coolidge/Photodisc/Getty Images

Building a Document in Outline View

You work in Outline view to organize the headings and subheadings that identify topics and subtopics in multipage documents. In Outline view, each heading is assigned a level from 1 to 9, with Level 1 being the highest level and Level 9 being the lowest level. In addition, you can assign the Body Text level to each paragraph of text that appears below a document heading. Each level is formatted with one of Word's predefined styles. For example, Level 1 is formatted with the Heading 1 style, and the Body Text level is formatted with the Normal style. 🔲🔲🔲 You work in Outline view to develop the structure of the guidelines for Medical Office Management.

STEPS

1. **Start Word, click the** View tab, **then click the** Outline button **in the Document Views group**

   The document appears in Outline view. Notice that the Outlining tab is now active. Table G-1 describes the buttons on the Outlining tab.

TROUBLE
If the headings do not appear blue and bold, click the Show Text Formatting check box in the Outline Tools group to select it.

2. **Type** Management of the Medical Office

   Figure G-1 shows the text in Outline view. By default, the text appears at the left margin and is designated as Level 1. Also by default, Level 1 text is formatted with the Heading 1 style. You will work more with styles in the next unit.

3. **Press** [Enter], **click the** Demote button ⮕ **in the Outline Tools group to move to Level 2, then type** Introduction

   The text is indented, designated as Level 2, and formatted with the Heading 2 style.

4. **Press** [Enter], **then click the** Demote to Body Text button ⮕⮕ **in the Outline Tools group**

5. **Type the following text:** This report discusses the management of the medical office in terms of three activities: designating staff positions, creating a policy and procedures manual, and maintaining medical and office supplies., **then press** [Enter]

   The text is indented, designated as Body Text level, and formatted with the Normal style. Notice that both the Level 1 and Level 2 text are preceded by a plus symbol ⊕. This symbol indicates that the heading includes subtext, which could be another subheading or a paragraph of body text.

6. **Click the** Promote to Heading 1 button ⬅⬅ **in the Outline Tools group**

   The insertion point returns to the left margin and the Level 1 position.

7. **Type** Designating Staff Positions, **press** [Enter], **then save the document as** WMP G-Medical Office Management **to the drive and folder where you store your Data Files**

   When you create a long document, you often enter all the headings and subheadings first to establish the overall structure of your document before you enter body text.

QUICK TIP
You can press [Tab] to move from a higher level to a lower level, and you can press [Shift][Tab] to move from a lower level to a higher level.

8. **Use the** Promote ⬅, Demote ⮕, **and** Promote to Heading 1 ⬅⬅ **buttons to complete the outline shown in Figure G-2**

9. **Place the insertion point after Management of the Medical Office at the top of the page, press** [Enter], **click** ⮕⮕, **type** Prepared by Your Name, **save the document, submit it to your instructor, then close it**

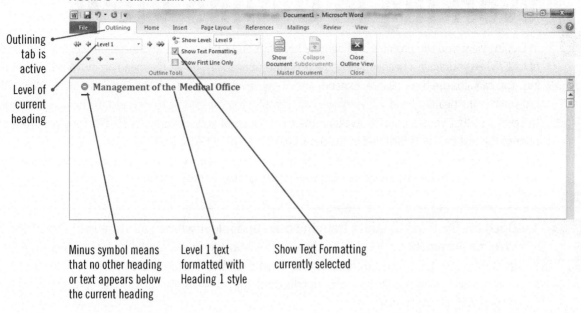

FIGURE G-1: Text in Outline view

Outlining tab is active

Level of current heading

Minus symbol means that no other heading or text appears below the current heading

Level 1 text formatted with Heading 1 style

Show Text Formatting currently selected

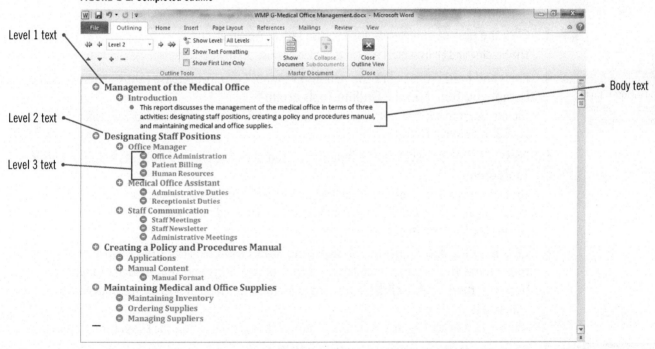

FIGURE G-2: Completed outline

Level 1 text

Level 2 text

Level 3 text

Body text

TABLE G-1: Outlining buttons on the Outlining tab

button	use to	button	use to
⟱	Promote text to Heading 1	▲	Move a heading and its text up one line
⟵	Promote text one level	▼	Move a heading and its text down one line
⟶	Demote text one level	✚	Expand text
⟹	Demote to body text	▬	Collapse text

Working in Outline View

In Outline view, you can promote and demote headings and subheadings and move or delete whole blocks of text. When you move a heading, all of the text and subheadings under that heading move with the heading. You can also use the Collapse, Expand, and Show Level commands on the Outlining tab to view all or just some of the headings and subheadings. For example, you can choose to view just the headings assigned to Level 1 so that you can quickly evaluate the main topics of your document. ▰▰▰ Tony has written a draft of the text he wants included in the guidelines for Medical Office Management. He created the document in Outline view so each heading is formatted with a heading style based on its corresponding outline level. You work with his document to reorganize the structure of the document.

STEPS

QUICK TIP
You can access the Outlining tab from the View tab or from the Outline button on the status bar.

1. **Open the file WMP G-1.docx from the drive and folder where you store your Data Files, save the document as WMP G-Medical Office Management Guidelines, scroll through the document to get a sense of its content, then click the Outline button 📄 on the status bar**

   The document changes to Outline view, and the Outlining tab opens. The image at the end of the document is not visible in Outline view.

2. **Click the Show Level list arrow in the Outline Tools group, then click Level 1**

   Only the headings assigned to Level 1 appear. All the headings assigned to Level 1 are formatted with the Heading 1 style. Notice that the title of the document, Management of the Medical Office, does not appear in Outline view because the title text is not formatted as Level 1.

3. **Click the plus outline symbol ⊕ to the left of Applications**

   The heading and all its subtext (which is hidden because the topic is collapsed) are selected.

QUICK TIP
You can use [Ctrl] to select multiple non-adjacent headings.

4. **Press and hold [Shift], click the heading Manual Content, release [Shift], then click the Demote button ➡ in the Outline Tools group**

   You use [Shift] to select several adjacent headings at once. The selected headings are demoted one level to Level 2, as shown in Figure G-3.

5. **Press [Ctrl][A] to select all the headings, then click the Expand button ➕ in the Outline Tools group**

   The outline expands to show all the subheadings and body text associated with each of the selected headings along with the document title. You can also expand a single heading by selecting only that heading and then clicking the Expand button.

6. **Click the plus sign ⊕ next to Designating Staff Positions, click the Collapse button ➖ in the Outline Tools group to collapse all the subheadings and text associated with the heading, then double-click ⊕ next to Maintaining Medical and Office Supplies to collapse it**

   You can double-click headings to expand or collapse them, or you can use the Expand or Collapse buttons.

QUICK TIP
You can also use your pointer to drag a heading up or down to a new location in the outline. A horizontal line appears as you drag to indicate the placement.

7. **Click the Move Up button 🔺 in the Outline Tools group once, then double-click ⊕ next to Maintaining Medical and Office Supplies**

   When you move a heading in Outline view, all subtext and text associated with the heading also move.

8. **Click the Show Level list arrow, click Level 3, double-click the plus sign ⊕ next to Managing Suppliers under the Maintaining Medical and Office Supplies heading, then press [Delete]**

   The Managing Suppliers heading and its associated subtext are deleted from the document. The revised outline is shown in Figure G-4.

9. **Click the Show Level list arrow, click All Levels, click the View tab, click the Print Layout button in the Document Views group, then save the document**

Developing Multipage Documents

FIGURE G-3: Level 1 headings demoted to Level 2

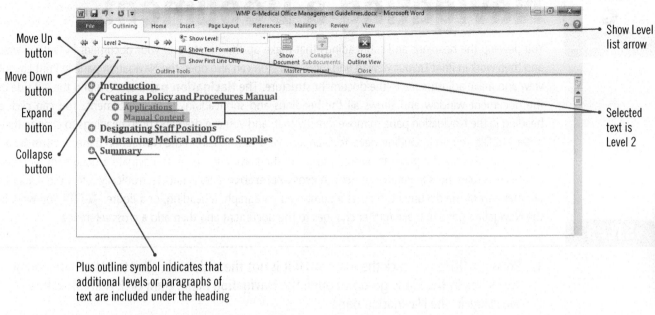

Move Up button

Move Down button

Expand button

Collapse button

Show Level list arrow

Selected text is Level 2

Plus outline symbol indicates that additional levels or paragraphs of text are included under the heading

FIGURE G-4: Revised outline

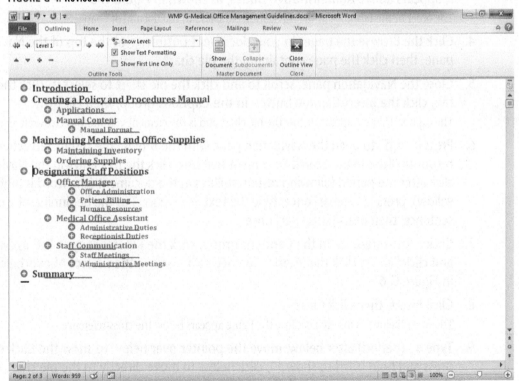

Word 2010

Developing Multipage Documents

Word 157

Navigating a Document

You develop the headings and subheadings that make up the structure of your document in Outline view and then work in Print Layout view to add more text. You can also open the Navigation pane in Print Layout view and make adjustments to the document structure. The **Navigation pane** opens along the left side of the document window and shows all the headings and subheadings in the document. You can click a heading in the Navigation pane to move directly to it, and you can drag and drop headings to change their order just like you do in Outline view. You can also view thumbnails in the Navigation pane. A **thumbnail** is a smaller version of a page. In addition to using the Navigation pane to navigate a document, you can create cross-references in your document. A **cross-reference** is text that electronically refers the reader to another part of the document, such as a numbered paragraph, a heading, or a figure. You work in the Navigation pane to make further changes to the document and then add a cross-reference.

STEPS

1. **Press [Ctrl][Home], click the View tab if it is not the active tab, click the Navigation Pane check box in the Show group to open the Navigation pane, then click Administrative Meetings in the Navigation pane**

   The Administrative Meetings subheading is selected in the Navigation pane, and the insertion point moves to the Administrative Meetings subheading in the document.

2. **Select week in the first line of text under the Administrative Meetings heading, then type month**

3. **Click Receptionist Duties in the Navigation pane, then drag Receptionist Duties up so that it appears above Administrative Duties, as shown in Figure G-5**

   The order of the headings in the Navigation pane and in the document change.

4. **Click the Browse the pages in your document button ⠿ at the top of the Navigation pane, then click the page containing the pie chart**

5. **Close the Navigation pane, scroll to and click the pie chart to select it, click the References tab, click the Insert Caption button in the Captions group, then click OK**

   The caption Figure 1 appears below the pie chart and is the element you want to cross-reference.

6. **Press [Ctrl][F] to open the Navigation pane with the Browse the results tab active, type responsibilities in the Search Document text box, click the first entry in the Navigation pane, click after the period following responsibilities in the document (the word is highlighted in yellow), press [Spacebar] once, type the text See Figure 1 as the beginning of a new sentence, then press [Spacebar] once**

7. **Click Cross-reference in the Captions group, click the Reference type list arrow, scroll to and click Figure, click the Insert reference to list arrow, then select Above/below as shown in Figure G-6**

8. **Click Insert, then click Close**

   The word "below" is inserted because the figure appears below the cross-reference.

9. **Type a . (period) after below, move the pointer over below to show the Click message, press and hold [Ctrl] to show ⠿, click below to move directly to the pie chart caption, close the Navigation pane, then save the document**

Developing Multipage Documents

FIGURE G-5: Changing the order of a subheading in the Navigation pane

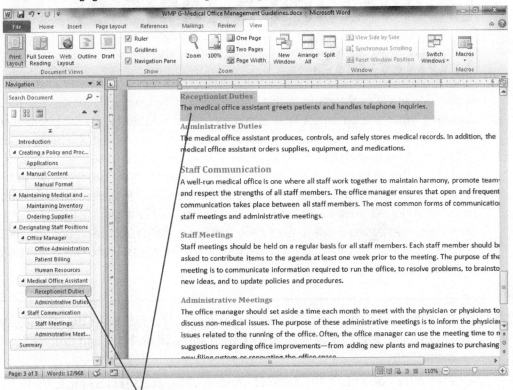

Receptionist Duties is moved above
Administrative Duties in the Navigation
pane and in the document

FIGURE G-6: Cross-reference dialog box

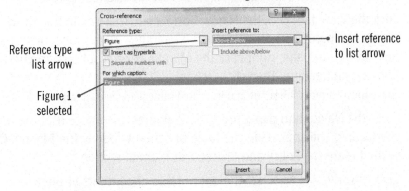

Reference type
list arrow

Figure 1
selected

Insert reference
to list arrow

Using bookmarks

A **bookmark** identifies a location or a selection of text in a document. To create a bookmark, you first move the insertion point to the location in the text that you want to reference. This location can be a word, the beginning of a paragraph, or a heading. Click the Insert tab, then click Bookmark in the Links group to open the Bookmark dialog box. In this dialog box, you type a name (which cannot contain spaces) for the bookmark, then click Add. To find a bookmark, press [Ctrl][G] to open the Find and Replace dialog box with the Go To tab active, click Bookmark in the Go to what list box, click the Enter bookmark name list arrow to see the list of bookmarks in the document, select the bookmark you require, click Go To, then close the Find and Replace dialog box.

Generating a Table of Contents

Readers refer to a table of contents to obtain an overview of the topics and subtopics covered in a multipage document. When you generate a table of contents, Word searches for headings, sorts them by heading levels, and then displays the completed table of contents in the document. By default, a table of contents lists the top three heading levels in a document. Consequently, before you create a table of contents, you must ensure that all headings and subheadings are formatted with the heading styles such as Heading 1, Heading 2, and Heading 3. When you work in Outline view, the correct heading styles are assigned automatically to text based on the outline level of the text. For example, the Heading 1 style is applied to Level 1 text, the Heading 2 style to Level 2 text, and so on. You are pleased with the content of the document and are now ready to create a new page that includes a table of contents. You use commands on the References tab to generate a table of contents.

STEPS

QUICK TIP
To apply formatting, use the Mini toolbar or the commands in the Font group and the Paragraph group on the Home tab.

1. **Click the Home tab, press [Ctrl][Home], press [Ctrl][Enter], press the [↑] once, type Table of Contents, select Table of Contents, then apply 18 pt, bold, and center alignment formatting**

2. **Click after Contents in the Table of Contents title, press [Enter] once, then click the Clear Formatting button ⌫ in the Font group**
   The insertion point is positioned at the left margin where the table of contents will begin.

3. **Click the References tab, then click the Table of Contents button in the Table of Contents group**
   A gallery of predefined, built-in styles for a table of contents opens.

4. **Click Insert Table of Contents to open the Table of Contents dialog box, click the Formats list arrow, click Formal, compare the dialog box to Figure G-7, then click OK**
   A table of contents that includes all the Level 1, 2, and 3 headings appears.

5. **Click the View tab, click the Navigation Pane check box in the Show group to open the Navigation pane, click the Browse the headings in your document button ▤ at the top of the Navigation pane, right-click the Manual Format subheading below the Manual Content subheading, then click Delete**
   The Manual Format subheading and its related subtext are deleted from the document.

6. **Close the Navigation pane, press [Ctrl][Home], then note that the Manual Format subheading still appears in the table of contents below the Manual Content subheading in the Creating a Policy and Procedures Manual section**

7. **Click Introduction to select the entire table of contents at once**
   When the table of contents is selected, you can update it to show changes.

8. **Right-click the table of contents, click Update Field, click Table in the Table of Contents title to deselect the table of contents, then scroll down so you can see the entire table of contents in the document window**
   The Manual Format subheading is removed, and the completed table of contents appears, as shown in Figure G-8. Each entry in the table of contents is a hyperlink to the entry's corresponding heading in the document.

9. **Move the pointer over the heading Staff Communication, press [Ctrl], click Staff Communication, then save the document**
   The insertion point moves to the Staff Communication heading in the document.

Developing Multipage Documents

FIGURE G-7: Table of Contents dialog box

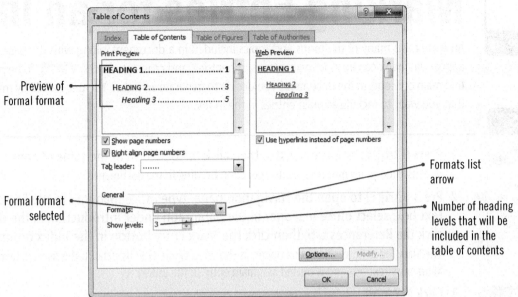

Preview of Formal format

Formal format selected

Formats list arrow

Number of heading levels that will be included in the table of contents

FIGURE G-8: Updated table of contents

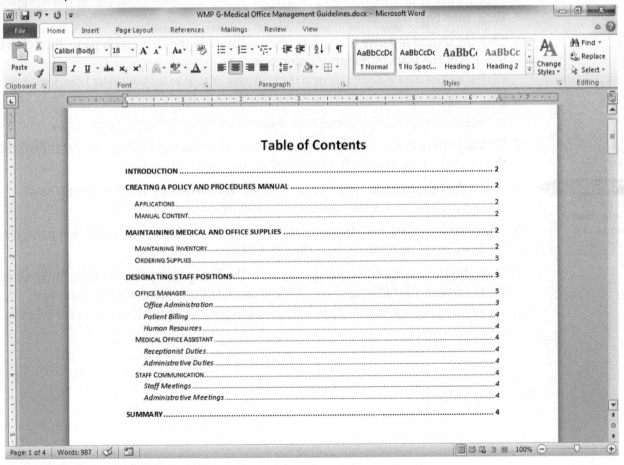

Marking Entries for an Index

An **index** lists many of the terms and topics included in a document, along with the pages on which they appear. An index can include main entries, subentries, and cross-references. To help readers quickly find main concepts in the document, you decide to generate an index. You get started by marking the terms that you want to include as main entries in the index.

STEPS

1. **Press [Ctrl][Home], press [Ctrl], then click** Introduction **in the table of contents**
   The insertion point moves to the Introduction heading in the document.

2. **Press [Ctrl][F] to open the Navigation pane, type** office manager **in the Search Document text box, select** office manager **in the paragraph under Introduction in the document, click the** References tab, **then click the** Mark Entry button **in the Index group**
   The Mark Index Entry dialog box opens, as shown in Figure G-9. By default, the selected text is entered in the Main entry text box and is treated as a main entry in the index.

3. **Click** Mark All
   Notice the term office manager is marked with the XE field code and the paragraph marks appear. **XE** stands for **Index Entry**. When you mark an entry for the index, the paragraph marks are turned on automatically so that you can see hidden codes such as paragraph marks, field codes, page breaks, and section breaks. These codes do not appear in the printed document. The Mark Index Entry dialog box remains open so that you can continue to mark text for inclusion in the index.

4. **Click anywhere in the document, click in the** Search Document text box **in the Navigation pane, then type** medical office assistant

5. **Click the second instance of** medical office assistant **in the Navigation pane, then click the** title bar **of the Mark Index Entry dialog box**
   The text medical office assistant appears in the Main entry text box in the Mark Index Entry dialog box.

6. **Click** Mark All
   All instances of medical office assistant in the document are marked for inclusion in the index.

7. **Click anywhere in the document, type** equipment **in the Search Document text box, click the** title bar **of the Mark Index Entry dialog box, then click** Mark All

8. **Follow the procedure in Step 7 to find and mark all instances of the following main entries:** orientation, budget, medications, **and** biologics

9. **Search for** Inventory, **click the second instance of** Inventory **in the Navigation pane, click the** Mark Index Entry dialog box, **then click** Mark

10. **Close the Mark Index Entry dialog box, close the Navigation pane, scroll up until you see the document title "Management of the Medical Office", then save the document**
    You see three entries marked for the index, as shown in Figure G-10. The other entries you marked are further down the document.

FIGURE G-9: Mark Index Entry dialog box

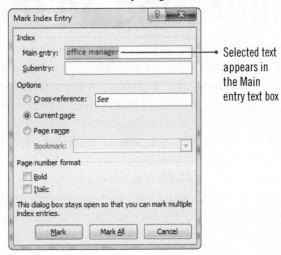

Selected text appears in the Main entry text box

FIGURE G-10: Index entries marked on the first page of the document text

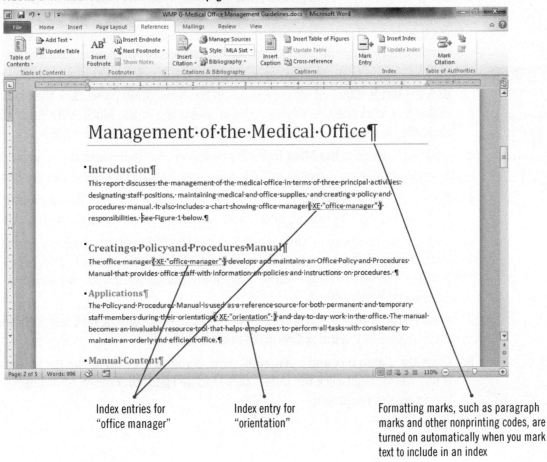

Index entries for "office manager"

Index entry for "orientation"

Formatting marks, such as paragraph marks and other nonprinting codes, are turned on automatically when you mark text to include in an index

Generating an Index

In addition to main entries, an index often includes subentries and cross-references. A **subentry** is text included under a main entry. For example, you could mark the text "stock control" as a subentry to appear under the main entry "Inventory." A **cross-reference** in an index refers the reader to another entry in the index. For example, a cross-reference in an index might read, "migraines. *See* headaches." Readers then know to refer to the "headaches" entry to find out more about migraines. Once you have marked all the index entries, you select a design for the index, and then you generate it. If you make changes to the document, you can update the index just like you update a table of contents when you add or remove content. ▓▓▓ You mark one subentry and one cross-reference for the index, create a new last page in the document, and then generate the index. You add one new main entry, and then update the index to reflect this change. The completed index contains all the main entries, the subentry, and the cross-reference you marked in this lesson and the previous lesson.

STEPS

1. **Press [Ctrl][F] to open the Navigation pane, type** stock control **in the Search Document text box, then click the** Mark Entry button **in the Index group on the References tab**
   The Mark Index Entry dialog box opens. The search term "stock control" is already entered into the Mark Index Entry dialog box.

2. **Select** stock control **in the Main entry text box, type** Inventory, **click in the Subentry text box, type** stock control **in the Subentry text box as shown in Figure G-11, then click** Mark
   The first and only instance of the text "stock control" is marked as a subentry to appear following the Main entry, Inventory. You use the Mark option when you want to mark just one occurrence of an item in a document.

QUICK TIP
If you cross-reference a term that is not already in the index, you can add the term as a main entry so that a page number is associated with the term.

3. **Click anywhere in the document, type** office supplies **in the Search Document text box, click the last instance of** office supplies **in the Navigation pane, click the** Mark Index Entry dialog box, **click the** Cross-reference option button **in the Mark Index Entry dialog box, click after** See, **type** Inventory **as shown in Figure G-12, then click** Mark

4. **Click** Close **to close the Mark Index Entry dialog box, then close the Navigation pane**
   Now that you have marked entries for the index, you can generate the index at the end of the document.

5. **Press [Ctrl][End], press [Ctrl][Enter], type** Index, **press [Enter], click the** Home tab, **select** Index **and apply** 18 pt, bold, **and** center alignment **formatting, then click below Index**

6. **Click the** References tab, **click** Insert Index **in the Index group, click the** Formats list arrow **in the Index dialog box, scroll down the list, click** Formal, **then click** OK
   Word has collected all the index entries, sorted them alphabetically, included the appropriate page numbers, and removed duplicate entries.

7. **Press [Ctrl][F], type** medical records **in the Search Document text box, click the** Mark Entry button **in the Index Group, then click** Mark All

8. **Close the dialog box and Navigation pane, scroll to the end of the document if the index is not visible, right-click the** index, **click** Update Field, **click** Index **to deselect the index, then save the document**
   The updated index appears, as shown in Figure G-13.

FIGURE G-11: Subentry in the Mark Index Entry dialog box

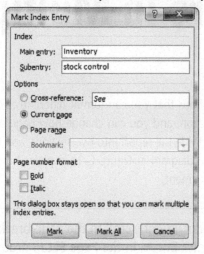

FIGURE G-12: Cross-reference in the Mark Index Entry dialog box

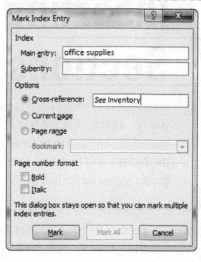

FIGURE G-13: Completed index

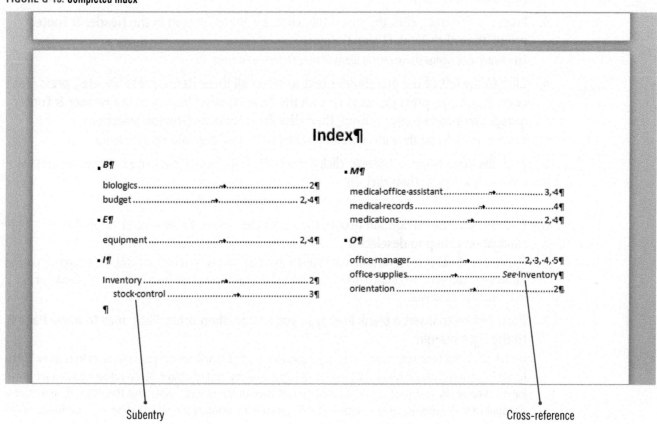

Subentry

Cross-reference

Inserting Footers in Multiple Sections

Multipage documents often consist of two or more sections that you can format differently. For example, you can include different text in the footer for each section, and you can change how page numbers are formatted from section to section. ░░░░░ You want to divide the report into two sections, and then format the headers and footers differently in each section. The diagram in Figure G-14 explains how the footer should appear on each of the first three pages in the document.

STEPS

QUICK TIP

You can also turn paragraph marks on or off by clicking the Show/Hide button ¶ in the Paragraph group on the Home tab.

1. **Press [Ctrl][Home] to move to the top of the document, scroll to the page break, click to the left of it, click the** Page Layout tab, **then click** Breaks **in the Page Setup group**

   You can see the page break because the paragraph marks were turned on when you marked entries for inclusion in the index. When you work with sections, you should leave paragraph marks showing so you can see the codes that Word inserts for section breaks and page breaks.

2. **Click** Next Page **under Section Breaks, press [Delete] to remove the original page break, then press [Delete] to remove the extra blank line**

   The document is divided into two sections. Section 1 contains the Table of Contents, and section 2 contains the rest of the document.

3. **Press [Ctrl][Home], click the** Insert tab, **click the** Footer button **in the Header & Footer group, then click** Blank (Three Columns)

   The footer area opens showing the Blank (Three Columns) format.

4. **Click to the left of the placeholder text to select all three items, press [Delete], press [Tab] once, type** Page, **press [Spacebar], click the** Page Number button **in the Header & Footer group, point to** Current Position, **then click** Plain Number **(the top selection)**

   The current footer for the entire document contains the word Page and a page number.

5. **Click the** Page Number button, **click** Format Page Numbers, **click the** Number format list arrow, **click i, ii, iii, then click** OK

   The page number in the footer area of the table of contents page is formatted as i.

6. **Click** Next **in the Navigation group, then click the** Link to Previous button **in the Navigation group to deselect it**

   You deselect the Link to Previous button to make sure that the text you type into the footer appears only in the footer in section 2. You must deselect the Link to Previous button each time you want the header or footer in a section to be unique.

7. **Press [Enter] to insert a blank line, type your name, then press [Tab] once to move Page 2 to the right margin**

   By default, Word continues numbering the pages in section 2 based on the page numbers in section 1. The footer in section 2 starts with Page 2 because section 1 contains just one page. You want section 2 to start with Page 1 because the first page in section 2 is the first page of the manual. Note also that the i, ii, iii format is not applied to the page number in section 2. Changes to page number formatting apply only to the section in which the change is made originally (in this case, section 1).

8. **Click the** Page Number button, **click** Format Page Numbers, **click the** Start at option button, **verify that 1 appears, click** OK, **then compare the footer to Figure G-15**

9. **Click the** Close Header and Footer button, **then save the document**

FIGURE G-14: Diagram of section formatting for footers

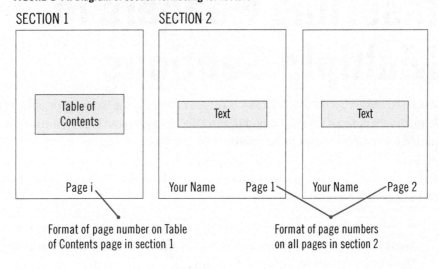

SECTION 1

Table of Contents

Page i

Format of page number on Table of Contents page in section 1

SECTION 2

Text

Your Name   Page 1

Text

Your Name   Page 2

Format of page numbers on all pages in section 2

FIGURE G-15: Completed footer

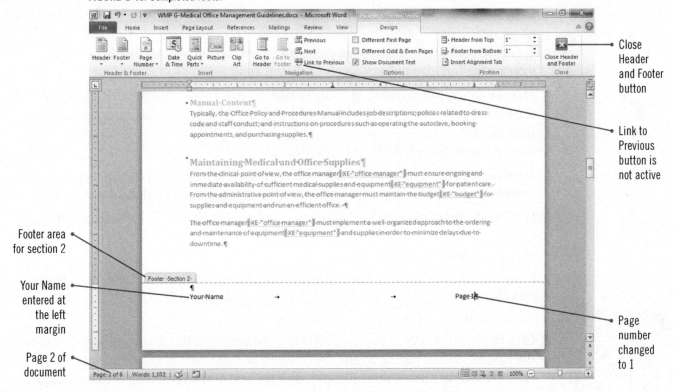

Close Header and Footer button

Link to Previous button is not active

Footer area for section 2

Your Name entered at the left margin

Page 2 of document

Page number changed to 1

Using text flow options

You adjust text flow options to control how text in a multipage document breaks across pages. To change text flow options, you use the Paragraph dialog box. To open the Paragraph dialog box, click the launcher in the Paragraph group on the Home tab, and then select the Line and Page Breaks tab. In the Pagination section, you can choose to select or deselect four text flow options. For example, you select the Widow/Orphan control option to prevent the last line of a paragraph from printing at the top of a page (a widow) or the first line of a paragraph from printing at the bottom of a page (an orphan). By default, Widow/Orphan is active. You can also select the Keep lines together check box to keep a paragraph from breaking across two pages.

Inserting Headers in Multiple Sections

When you divide your document into sections, you can modify the header to be different in each section. As you learned in the previous lesson, you must deselect the Link to Previous button when you want the text of a header (or footer) in a new section to be different from the header (or footer) in the previous section. ▓▓▓▓ The diagram in Figure G-16 shows that text will appear in the header on every page in section 2. You do not want any text to appear in the header on the table of contents page (section 1). You modify the headers in the two sections of the document and then add a cover page.

STEPS

1. **Press [Ctrl][Home] to move to the top of the document, then scroll up and double-click in the blank area above Table of Contents**

   The header area opens. The Header -Section 1- identifier appears along with the Header & Footer Tools Design tab. Refer to Figure G-16 and notice that you do not want text in the header in section 1.

2. **Click Next in the Navigation group, then click the Link to Previous button to deselect it**

   The identifier Header -Section 2- appears. You want text to appear on all the pages of section 2. You deselect the Link to Previous button so that the text you type appears only on this page and on subsequent pages.

3. **Type Riverwalk Medical Clinic, select the text, then use the Mini toolbar to center it, increase the font size to 14 pt, apply bold, and apply italic**

4. **Press [→] once, press [Enter], click the Header & Footer Tools Design tab if necessary, click the Close Header and Footer button, right-click the table of contents, click Update Field, then click OK**

   The page numbers in the table of contents are updated.

5. **Scroll through the document to verify that the header text does not appear on the table of contents page and does appear on the first and subsequent pages of the document text**

6. **Scroll to the Index page, right-click the index, then click Update Field to update the page numbers**

   The page numbers in the index are updated.

7. **Press [Ctrl][Home], click the Page Layout tab, click Breaks, click Next Page, press the [↑], click the Insert tab, click Cover Page in the Pages group, then click Conservative**

   A page appears that contains several content controls.

8. **Click the Subtitle content control (it includes the text Type the document subtitle), click the content control handle to select it (the handle turns dark gray and the text in the control turns dark blue), press [Delete], click the text at the bottom of the cover page, click Abstract, then press [Delete]**

9. **Enter text, as shown in Figure G-17, into the remaining four content controls**

   Some content controls may contain placeholder text. If a content control contains placeholder text that you do not want, select the placeholder text and then type the replacement text.

10. **Save the document**

Developing Multipage Documents

FIGURE G-16: Diagram of section formatting for headers

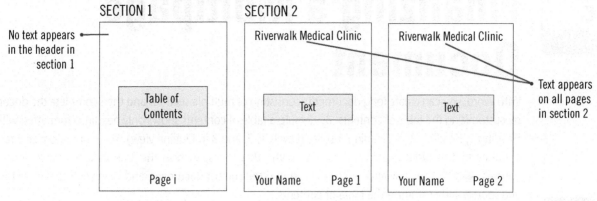

SECTION 1

SECTION 2

No text appears in the header in section 1

Table of Contents

Page i

Riverwalk Medical Clinic

Text

Your Name   Page 1

Riverwalk Medical Clinic

Text

Your Name   Page 2

Text appears on all pages in section 2

FIGURE G-17: Completed cover page

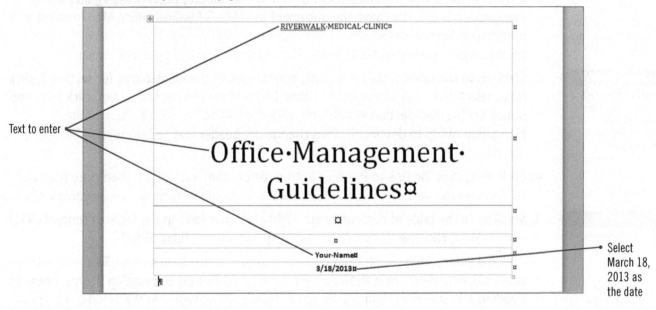

RIVERWALK·MEDICAL·CLINIC¤

Office·Management· Guidelines¤

Your·Name¤

3/18/2013¤

Text to enter

Select March 18, 2013 as the date

Understanding headers, footers, and sections

One reason you divide a document into sections is so that you can modify the page layout and the headers and footers differently in different sections. You can even modify the header and footer within a section because each section has two parts. The first part of a section is the first page, and the second part of the section is the remaining subsequent pages. This section structure allows you to omit the header on the first page of section 2, and then include the header on all subsequent pages in section 2. To do this, you place the insertion point in the section you want to modify, then you click the Different First Page check box in the Options group to specify that you wish to include a different header (or no header at all) on the first page of a section. In addition, you can also choose to format odd and even pages in a document in different ways by clicking the Different Odd & Even Pages check box in the Options group. For example, you can choose to left-align the document title on odd-numbered pages and right-align the chapter number on even-numbered pages.

Finalizing a Multipage Document

With Word, you can create long documents consisting of multiple sections and then complete the document by customizing the table of contents. By default, a table of contents shows only headings formatted with the Heading 1, Heading 2, or Heading 3 styles (Levels 1, 2, and 3 in Outline view). You can customize a table of contents so it includes headings formatted with other styles, such as the Title style or a style you create yourself. ▨▨▨ You copy and paste new text into the current document, and then you modify the headers and footers and customize the table of contents.

STEPS

1. Scroll to see the page break before the index, click to the left of the page break, click the Page Layout tab, click Breaks, click Next Page in the Section Breaks area, then press [Delete]

2. Open the file WMP G-2.docx from the drive and folder where you store your Data Files, press [Ctrl][A] to select all the text in the document, press [Ctrl][C], switch to the WMP G-Medical Office Management Guidelines document, press [Ctrl][V], add a Next Page section break, then save the document as WMP G-Medical Office Management and Information Session Guidelines

   The three pages of the Information Session Guidelines document appear in their own section.

   QUICK TIP
   QUICK TIP
   Make sure you click the Link to Previous button before you modify the header text.

3. Scroll up to the table of contents page, double-click in the header area for section 2, click Next, select Riverwalk Medical Clinic, type Office Management Guidelines, click Next and notice the Header –Section 4- indicator, click the Link to Previous button in the Navigation group to deselect it, then change the header text to Information Session Guidelines

4. Click Next, click the Link to Previous button, delete the header text, then close the header

   The document contains footers in four sections, and you have modified the header text in sections 3, 4, and 5.

   QUICK TIP
   By default, headings that use the Title style are not included in a table of contents. You need to assign the Title style a TOC level when you want to include headings that use the Title style in your table of contents.

5. Scroll up to the table of contents page, right-click anywhere in the table of contents, click Update Field, click the Update entire table option button, then click OK

6. Click the References tab, click the Table of Contents button, click Insert Table of Contents, click Options, select 1 next to Heading 1, type 2, type 3 next to Heading 2, type 4 next to Heading 3 as shown in Figure G-18, scroll down to Title, type 1 in the TOC level text box, click OK, click OK, then click Yes

   The Management of Information Sessions document starts at page 1 and you want page numbering to be consecutive.

7. Press [Ctrl], click Management of Information Sessions in the table of contents, scroll to the footer (you'll see Page 1), then double-click in the footer

8. Click the Page Number button in the Header & Footer group, click Format Page Numbers, click the Continue from previous section option button, then click OK

9. Click Next in the Navigation group, repeat Step 8, exit the footer area, view the document in One Page view, scroll up, then add a page break to the left of Office Manager on page 2

10. Update the table of contents page, update the index, save and close all documents, exit Word, then submit all files to your instructor

    Figure G-19 shows the first page of each of five sections in the document.

Developing Multipage Documents

FIGURE G-18: Table of Contents Options dialog box

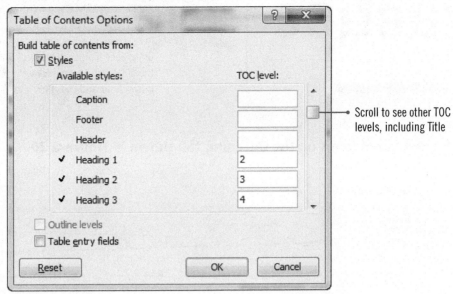

Scroll to see other TOC levels, including Title

FIGURE G-19: Selected pages of the completed document

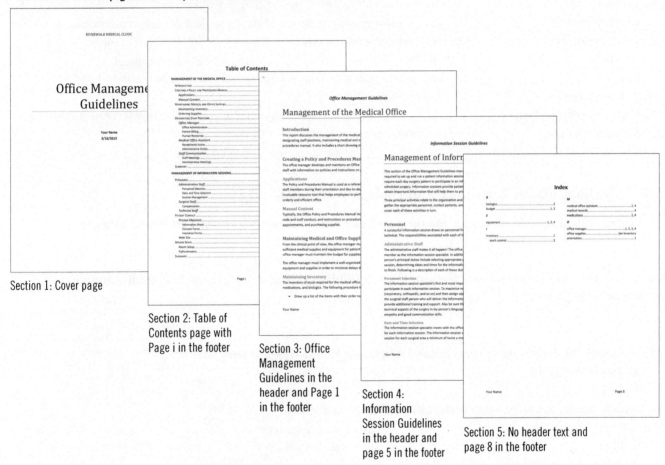

Section 1: Cover page

Section 2: Table of Contents page with Page i in the footer

Section 3: Office Management Guidelines in the header and Page 1 in the footer

Section 4: Information Session Guidelines in the header and page 5 in the footer

Section 5: No header text and page 8 in the footer

Modifying a table of contents

You can change how Word shows each heading and subheading level included in a table of contents. For example, you can choose to increase the indenting of a level 2 heading, or apply a new leader style to a level 3 heading. You use the Indent buttons in the Paragraph group on the Home tab to change the position of a table of contents entry, and you use the Tabs dialog box to modify the leader style applied to an entry in the table of contents.

Practice

Concepts Review

Label the numbered items on the Outlining tab shown in Figure G-20.

FIGURE G-20

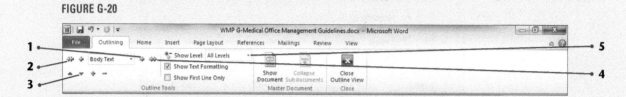

Match each term with the statement that best describes it.

6. Table of contents
7. Demote button
8. Mark Index Entry dialog box
9. Header
10. Cross-reference
11. Link to Previous button
12. Navigation pane

a. Used to enter a lower-level heading in Outline view
b. Text that appears at the top of every page in a document or section
c. Text that electronically refers the reader to another part of the document
d. Open to view the headings and subheadings in a document
e. List of topics and subtopics usually with page numbers, and shown at the beginning of a document
f. Deselect to create a header or footer in one section that is different from the header or footer in a previous section
g. Where you enter text for inclusion in an index

Select the best answer from the list of choices.

13. On the Outlining tab, which button do you click to move directly to Level 1 from any other level?
    a. ➡
    b. ⬇
    c. ⏪
    d. ➕

14. Which symbol in Outline view indicates that a heading includes subtext, such as subheadings or paragraphs of text?
    a. ➖
    b. ⊕
    c. ▲
    d. ➕

15. Which of the following options is not available in the Navigation pane?
    a. Browse headings
    b. Replace text
    c. Browse pages
    d. Find text

16. Which tab do you use to access the table of contents feature?
    a. Page Layout
    b. Insert
    c. References
    d. Review

17. Which index entry appears subordinate to a main entry?
    a. Cross-reference
    b. Next entry
    c. Mark place
    d. Subentry

Skills Review

1. **Build a document in Outline view.**
   a. Start Word, click the Show/Hide ¶ button in the Paragraph group to select it and turn on the display of paragraph marks if it is not active, then switch to Outline view.
   b. Type **Introduction by Your Name** as a Level 1 heading, press [Enter], type **Partnership Requirements** as another Level 1 heading, then press [Enter].
   c. Type **Background Information**, then use the Demote button to demote it to a Level 2 heading.
   d. Type the text shown in Figure G-21 as body text under Background Information.
   e. Use the Promote button to type the heading **Benefits** as a Level 2 heading, then complete the outline, as shown in Figure G-21.
   f. Turn off the display of paragraph marks, save the document as **WMP G-Partnership Agreement Outline** to the drive and folder where you store your Data Files, then close the document.

FIGURE G-21

```
⊖ Introduction·by·Your·Name¶
⊕ Partnership·Requirements¶
   ⊕ Background·Information¶
      ⊖ This·section·provides·background·information·about·Lakeview·Physiotherapy·
        Clinic·and·discusses·how·the·partnership·could·benefit·both·Evergreen·
        Naturopathy·Clinic·and·Lakeview·Physiotherapy·Clinic.¶
   ⊖ Benefits¶
   ⊖ Partnership·Need¶
⊕ Products·and·Services¶
   ⊖ Lakeview·Physiotherapy·Clinic·Services¶
   ⊖ Evergreen·Naturopathy·Clinic·Services¶
   ⊖ Package·Opportunities¶
⊕ Financial·Considerations¶
   ⊖ Projected·Revenues¶
   ⊖ Financing·Required¶
⊖ Conclusion¶
```

2. **Work in Outline view.**
   a. Open the file WMP G-3.docx from the drive and folder where you store your Data Files, save it as **WMP G-Partnership Agreement Proposal**, switch to Outline view, then show all Level 1 headings.
   b. Move the Financial Considerations heading below the Products and Services heading.
   c. Select the Partnership Requirements heading, click the Expand button twice, collapse Benefits, collapse Partnership Need, then move Benefits and its subtext below Partnership Need and its subtext.
   d. Collapse the Partnership Requirements section to show only the Level 1 heading.
   e. Show all levels of the outline, close Outline view, then save the document.

3. **Navigate a document.**
   a. Open the Navigation pane, show all the headings in the document if they are not displayed, then use the Navigation pane to navigate to the Financing Required heading in the document.
   b. Change "six months" to **year** in the paragraph below the Financing Required heading.
   c. Use the Navigation pane to navigate to the Package Opportunities heading in the document, then use the Navigation pane to delete the heading and its subtext.
   d. View thumbnails of the document pages in the Navigation pane, click the page containing the chart graphic, select the chart in the document, then insert **Figure 1** as a caption below the figure.
   e. Find the text **See Figure 1**, then insert a cross-reference to the figure using Above/below as the reference text.
   f. Insert a period after the word "below", test the cross-reference, scroll to see the chart, then save the document.

4. **Generate a table of contents.**
   a. Press [Ctrl][Home], insert a page break, press [Ctrl][Home], type **Table of Contents** at the top of the new first page, enhance the text with 18 pt and bold, center it, click after the title, press [Enter], then clear the formatting.
   b. Insert a table of contents using the Distinctive format.
   c. Use [Ctrl][click] to navigate to Partnership Need in the document, view the document headings in the Navigation pane, then delete the Partnership Need heading from the Navigation pane.
   d. Update the table of contents, then save the document.

Skills Review (continued)

5. **Mark entries for an index.**
   a. Find the words **sports medicine**, and mark all occurrences for inclusion in the index.
   b. Find and mark only the first instance of each of the following main entries: **Seattle**, **Olympic teams**, and **gym**. (*Hint*: Click Mark instead of Mark All.)
   c. Save the document.

6. **Generate an index.**
   a. Find **Personal Training Program**, click the Mark Index Entry dialog box, select Personal Training Program in the Main entry text box, type **Physiotherapy Services** as the Main entry and **personal training program** as the Subentry, then click Mark All.
   b. Repeat the process to insert **Pilates classes** as a subentry of **Lakeview Physiotherapy Clinic Services**.
   c. Find the text **teams**, then create a cross-reference in the Mark Index Entry dialog box to **sports medicine**.
   d. Close the Mark Index Entry dialog box and the Navigation pane.
   e. Insert a new page at the end of the document, type **Index** at the top of the page, and format it with bold and 18 pt and center alignment.
   f. Double-click below the index, and clear any formatting so the insertion point appears at the left margin, then insert an index in the Bulleted format.
   g. Find and mark the one instance of **Craniosacral Therapy**, update the index so it includes the new entry, close the Mark Index Entry dialog box and the Navigation pane, then save the document.

7. **Insert footers in multiple sections.**
   a. At the top of the document, click to the left of the page break below the Table of Contents, insert a Next Page section break, then remove the page break and the extra blank line.
   b. On the table of contents page, insert a footer using the Blank (Three Columns) format.
   c. Delete the placeholders, type your name, press [Tab] twice, type **Page**, press [Spacebar], then insert a page number at the current position using the Plain Number format.
   d. Change the format of the page number to i, ii, iii.
   e. Go to the next section, then deselect the Link to Previous button.
   f. Format the page number to start at 1 if necessary.
   g. Exit the footer area, scroll through the document to verify that the pages are numbered correctly, scroll to and update the page numbers in the table of contents, then save the document.

8. **Insert headers in multiple sections.**
   a. Move to the top of the document, then position the insertion point in the header area.
   b. Go to the next section, then deselect the Link to Previous button.
   c. Type **Evergreen Naturopathy Clinic**, center the text, then apply bold and italic.
   d. Exit the header area, then scroll through the document to verify that the header text does not appear on the first page of the document and that it does appear on all subsequent pages.
   e. At the top of the document, insert a Next Page section break, move to the top of the document, insert a cover page using the Pinstripes style, enter text and delete content controls as shown in Figure G-22, then save the document.

FIGURE G-22

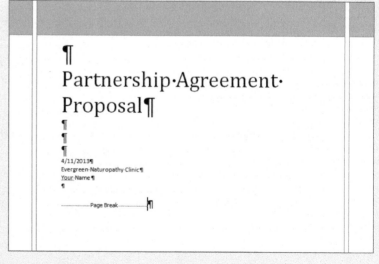

Developing Multipage Documents

Skills Review (continued)

9. **Finalize a multipage document.**

   a. Insert a Next Page section break between the last page of the text and the index page.

   b. Open the file WMP G-4.docx from the drive and folder where you store your Data Files, copy all the text, paste it into the Partnership Agreement Proposal document, then save the document as **WMP G-Partnership Agreements_ Lakeview Physiotherapy and First Fitness**.

   c. From the table of contents page, access the Header area, move to section 3, replace Evergreen Naturopathy Clinic with **Lakeview Physiotherapy Clinic**, move to section 4, click the Link to Previous button, then replace Lakeview Physiotherapy with **First Fitness**.

   d. Exit the header, insert a Next Page section break before the index and remove the page break if there is one, open the header area in section 5 (the index page), then deselect the Link to Previous button and remove the header from the index page.

   e. Check that the correct headers appear in sections 3, 4, and 5, then update the table of contents page (select the Update entire table option).

   f. Modify the table of contents options so that Heading 1 corresponds to Level 2 text, Heading 2 corresponds to Level 3 text, Heading 3 corresponds to Level 4 text, and Title text corresponds to Level 1 text.

   g. Modify the footers in sections 4 and 5 so that the page numbering is continuous. You should see page 7 on the index page.

   h. Scroll through the document and insert a page break to the left of Projected Revenues on page 2.

   i. Turn off the display of paragraph marks, update the index and table of contents pages, save the document, submit all files to your instructor, close them, then exit Word.

Independent Challenge 1

You work in the Finance Department of Body Fit, a successful fitness and spa facility in Philadelphia. Recently, the owners of Body Fit began selling franchises. Your supervisor asks you to format a report that details the development of these franchise operations.

   a. Start Word, open the file WMP G-5.docx from the drive and folder where you store your Data Files, then save it as **WMP G-Body Fit Franchises**.

   b. In Outline view, organize the document as shown in the following table, starting with Introduction, followed by Scope of the Report, and then moving column by column. Text that you designate as headings will be formatted with the blue font color.

heading	level	heading	level	heading	level
Introduction	1	Marianne Bennett	2	Milwaukee Clientele	3
Scope of the Report	2	Franchise Locations	1	Cleveland	2
Owner Information	1	Chicago	2	Cleveland Clientele	3
Gerry Grant	2	Chicago Clientele	3	Opening Schedules	2
Teresa Morales	2	Milwaukee	2		

   c. Switch the order of Cleveland and its accompanying subtext so it follows Chicago and its subtext.

Independent Challenge 1 (continued)

d. In Print Layout view and starting from the top of the document, find the text listed in column 1, and mark all instances of that text as Main entry or subentry for an index, based on the information in columns 2 and 3.

find this text	main entry	subentry
Chicago	Location	Chicago
Cleveland	Location	Cleveland
Milwaukee	Location	Milwaukee
Gerry Grant	Owner	Gerry Grant
Teresa Morales	Owner	Teresa Morales
Marianne Bennett	Owner	Marianne Bennett
Marketing Vice President	Marketing Vice President	
Mall	Mall	
Ohio	Ohio	

e. Insert a new page at the end of the document, type **Index** as the page title, format it with bold, a larger font size, and center alignment, then generate an index in the Modern format.

f. At the top of the document, insert a Next Page section break, then on the new first page, type **Table of Contents** as the page title, select the text, click Normal in the Styles group on the Home tab to remove the Heading 1 formatting, then format it with bold, a larger font size, and center alignnment. (*Hint*: If Table of Contents is formatted as Heading 1, it will appear in the Table of Contents, which you do not want.)

g. Generate a table of contents using the Classic format.

h. Add and format a header and footer so that the completed document appears as follows:

location	contents
Table of Contents page (section 1)	Footer containing your name at the left margin and **Page i** at the right margin
Page 1 and the following pages of the report (section 2)	Footer containing your name at the left margin and **Page 1** at the right margin Header containing the text **Body Fit Franchises**, centered, and bold and followed by a blank line (*Hint*: Press [Enter] at the end of the header text.)

i. Scroll through the document to ensure the headers and footers are correct, then add a page break before Franchise Locations so that it moves to page 2 of the document.

j. Turn off the display of formatting marks, then update the table of contents and index pages.

Advanced Challenge Exercise

- Use the Navigation pane to move directly to the Opening Schedules heading, then create a bookmark called **Dates** using the first of the three dates listed. (*Hint*: Select all or part of the first date—Chicago Franchise: April 22, 2013, click the Insert tab, click Bookmark in the Links group, type **Dates** as the bookmark name, then click Add.)
- Move to the beginning of the document, and go to your bookmark. (*Hint*: Press [Ctrl][G], click Bookmark, click Go To, then click Close.)
- Follow the same process to create a bookmark named **Location** that goes to the Franchise Locations heading, then close the Navigation pane. (*Hint*: Replace "Dates" with "Location" as the bookmark name, then click Add.)

k. Save the document, submit your file to your instructor, then close the document and exit Word.

Developing Multipage Documents

Independent Challenge 2

You assist several physicians at the Sunnydale Medical Clinic. One of the physicians, Dr. Martin, has asked you to create a document containing the History and Physical reports for three patients. Dr. Martin will be presenting a paper at a conference and will use the document as a handout.

a. Start Word, open WMP G-6.docx, then save it as **WMP G-History and Physical Reports**.

b. Use the Navigation pane to navigate to the heading HISTORY AND PHYSICAL: Harry Stein.

c. Insert a Next Page section break to the left of the heading HISTORY AND PHYSICAL: Harry Stein, then insert Next Page section breaks to the left of the patient report for Theresa Manzini and the patient report for Mark Hudson.

d. Show the paragraph formatting marks, move to the Patients heading in the Navigation pane, then make Harry Stein a cross-reference to the corresponding heading. (*Hint*: Select the text Harry Stein but not the paragraph mark following Stein, open the cross-reference dialog box, select Heading as the reference type, then select the HISTORY AND PHYSICAL: Harry Stein heading as the reference text.)

e. Follow the same process to cross-reference the other two patient names to their corresponding headings. Make sure you select only the name and not the paragraph mark following the name so that each entry appears on a separate line.

f. Test each cross-reference, using the Navigation pane to navigate back to the Patients heading.

g. Close the Navigation pane.

h. Insert a Next Page section break at the beginning of the document, move to the top of the new page 1, clear the formatting, type **Table of Contents** and format the text attractively, then generate a table of contents in the Formal style. (*Hint*: Make sure the text Table of Contents is not formatted as Heading 1.)

i. On the table of contents page, add your name centered in the footer. On the HISTORY AND PHYSICAL REPORTS (first page of section 2) page, add your name left-aligned in the footer and the page number 1 right-aligned in the footer. (*Hint*: Make sure you deselect the Link to Previous button before making changes to the footer in section 2.)

j. Exit the footer, go to the top of the document, add a Next Page section break, then in the new section, insert a cover page using the Cubicles style.

k. On the cover page, enter **Sunnydale Medical Clinic** as the company name, enter the title **History and Physical Reports**, then enter your name as the author. Remove any additional content controls.

l. From the table of contents page, enter the header area, then add headers to the sections of the document as shown below, formatting the header text with bold, italic, and centering. Make sure you deselect the Link to Previous button before typing new text in a header.

- Section 2. (contains the Table of Contents): no header
- Section 3: **Overview**
- Section 4: **Harry Stein**
- Section 5: **Theresa Manzini**
- Section 6: **Mark Hudson**

m. Update the table of contents, scroll through the document to verify that the headers and footers are correct in each section, then save the document.

Advanced Challenge Exercise

- On the table of contents page, increase the font size of each of the headings associated with Level 1 to 12 pt. (*Hint*: Use the selection pointer to click to the left of HISTORY AND PHYSICAL REPORTS to select it, increase the font size to 12 pt, then verify that the font size of the other Level 1 headings also increases.)
- On the table of contents page, increase the indent of the headings associated with Level 2 to .5 on the ruler bar. (*Hint*: Show the ruler bar if necessary (View tab, Ruler check box), use the selection pointer to click Past Medical History (the first Level 2 heading), then drag both of the indent markers on the ruler bar to the .5 mark.)
- Apply the Austin theme to the document. (*Hint*: Click the Page Layout tab, click Themes, then click Austin. The fonts and colors are changed to reflect the formatting associated with the Austin theme.) Scroll through the document to see how the headings and text appear.

n. Save the document, submit your file to your instructor, close the document, then exit Word.

Independent Challenge 3

As the program assistant in the Applied Business Technology Department at Highlands College in Nova Scotia, Canada, you are responsible for creating and formatting reports about programs at the college. You work in outline view to create a program report on the Medical Office Assistant program.

a. Create a new document and save it as **WMP G-Medical Office Assistant Program Report**.

b. In Outline view, enter the headings and subheadings for the report as shown in the table starting with **Program Overview**, followed by **Career Opportunities**. You need to substitute appropriate course names for Course 1, Course 2, and so on. For example, courses in the first term of the Medical Office Assistant program could be Medical Office Procedures, Medical Systems and Transcription, and so on. You choose the program and courses you want to include in the report.

heading	level	heading	level
Program Overview	1	[Enter name for Course 1]	3
Career Opportunities	2	[Enter name for Course 2]	3
Admission Requirements	2	Second Term	2
Program Content	1	[Enter name for Course 1]	3
First Term	2	[Enter name for Course 2]	3

c. Enter one paragraph of appropriate body text below each of the following headings in the outline: Program Overview, Career Opportunities, and Admission Requirements; then enter short course descriptions for each of the four courses included in the document. For ideas, refer to college Web sites and catalogs.

d. In Print Layout view, insert a Next Page section break at the top of the document, then add a cover page to the new section using the Puzzle style: include the name of the program as the title (for example, Medical Office Assistant Program), the name of the college (Highlands College, Nova Scotia) as the subtitle, and your name where indicated. Remove all other content controls.

e. Insert a Next Page section break to the left of Program Overview, then insert a page break in the body of the report to spread the report over two pages if it does not already flow to two pages.

f. Click in the header area for section 2, go to the header for section 3, deselect the Link to Previous button, then format the section 3 header with a right-aligned page number starting with Page 1 using the 1, 2, 3 format.

g. Go to the footer for section 2, format the section 2 footer with the name of the program left-aligned in the footer and your name right-aligned. Make sure you deselect Link to Previous.

h. Exit the footer area, scroll to the top of the blank page, clear the formatting, type **Table of Contents** as a title and format it attractively, insert a table of contents in the format of your choice, then save the document.

i. Customize the table of contents so that it includes only Heading 1 at TOC level 1 and Heading 3 at TOC level 2. None of the Heading 2 headings should appear in the revised table of contents.

j. Scroll through the document and verify that the header appears on both pages of the section 3 header and that the footer appears on all pages except the cover page.

k. Update the table of contents.

l. Save the document, close it, then submit your file to your instructor.

Developing Multipage Documents

Real Life Independent Challenge

This Independent Challenge requires an Internet connection.

Many hospitals and other medical establishments post job opportunities on their Web sites. You can learn a great deal about opportunities in a wide range of medical fields just by checking out the job postings on these Web sites. You decide to create a document that describes a selection of jobs available on an employment Web site of your choice.

a. Use your favorite search engine and the search phrase **health care jobs** to find Web sites that post jobs in the health care industry.

b. On the Web site you choose, identify two job categories (e.g., Nursing jobs and Lab Technician jobs) and then find two jobs that appeal to you and that you may even wish to apply for. You can choose to search for jobs in your home town or in another location.

c. Create a new document in Word, then save it as **WMP G-Online Job Opportunities**.

d. In Outline view, set up the document starting with the name of the employment Web site (e.g., monster.com), followed by Job Category 1, as shown in the table. (*Note*: You need to enter specific text for headings such as Nursing Jobs for Job Category 1 and Nursing-Acute Care for Job Posting.)

heading	level
Name of Web Site	1
Job Category 1	2
Job Name	3
Summary of Job Posting	Body Text
Job Category 2	2
Job Name	3
Summary of Job Posting	Body Text

e. Complete the Word document with information you find on the Web site. Include a short description of each job you select, and list some of the job duties. You do not need to include the entire job posting. If you copy selected text from a Web site, make sure you clear the formatting so that the text in the document is formatted only with the Normal style.

f. Format the document so that a header starts on page 1 and includes the text **Online Job Opportunities for Your Name**. Include a page number on each page of the document in the footer.

g. Save the document and submit the file to your instructor, then close the document.

Visual Workshop

Open the file WMP G-7.docx from the drive and folder where you store your Data Files, then save it as **WMP G-Medical Ethics Term Paper**. Modify the outline so that it appears as shown in Figure G-23. You need to change the order of some sections and delete one section. In Print Layout view, insert a Next Page section page break at the beginning of the document, go to the top of the page and clear the formatting, type **Table of Contents** and enhance the title so it appears similar to the title shown in Figure G-24, then generate a table of contents in the Fancy style. Insert a page break before Ethics Traditions in the text, create a footer in section 2 with a page number that starts with 1, reduce the zoom to 80%, then update the table of contents so that it appears as shown in Figure G-24. Be sure your name is on the document, save and close the document, then submit the file to your instructor.

FIGURE G-23

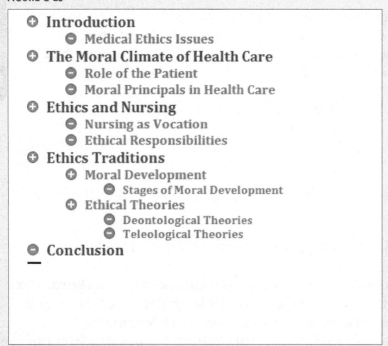

FIGURE G-24

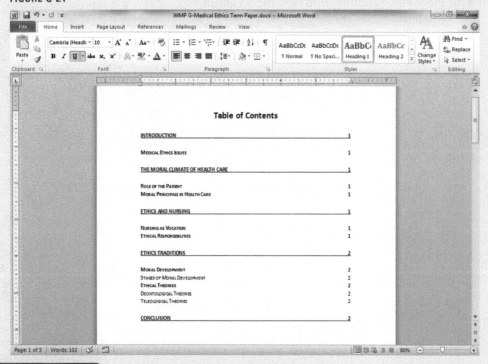

Developing Multipage Documents

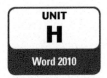

Working with Styles and Templates

You can use Word's predesigned Quick Style sets and templates to format your documents quickly, efficiently, and professionally. You can further customize your document-formatting tasks by creating your own Quick Style sets and templates. In this unit, you learn how to create new styles to format paragraphs, characters, lists, and tables, and how to save your newly created styles in a new Quick Style set. You also learn how to manage styles used in a document and how to create, apply, and revise a template. The Riverwalk Medical Clinic has hired you to produce profiles of clinic physicians for distribution to clinic patients. To save time, you create and apply styles in an existing profile, and then you develop a template on which to base each physician profile. This template includes a custom Quick Style set.

OBJECTIVES

Explore styles and templates

Modify predefined styles

Create paragraph styles

Create character and linked styles

Create custom list and table styles

Create a Quick Style set

Manage styles

Create a template

Revise and attach a template

©Jeffrey Coolidge/Photodisc/Getty Images

Exploring Styles and Templates

You use styles and templates to automate document-formatting tasks and to ensure consistency among related documents. A **style** consists of various formats such as font, font size, and alignment that you name and then save together as one set. For example, a style called "Main Head" might contain the following format settings: Arial font, 14-point font size, bold, and a bottom border. Each time you apply the Main Head style to selected text, all format settings included in the style are applied. A **template** is a file that contains the basic structure of a document, such as the page layout, headers and footers, styles, graphic elements, and boilerplate text.  You plan to use styles to format a physician profile and then create a template that you will use to develop a series of physician profiles. You start by familiarizing yourself with styles and templates.

DETAILS

Information about how you can use styles and templates to help you format documents quickly and efficiently follows:

- Using styles helps you save time in two ways. First, when you apply a style, you apply a set of formats all at once. You do not have to apply each format individually. Second, if you modify a style by changing one or more of the formats associated with that style, then all text formatted with that style is updated automatically. For example, suppose you apply a style named "Section Head" to each section head in a document. If you then modify the formatting associated with the Section Head style, Word automatically updates all the text formatted with the Section Head style to reflect the change. As discussed in Unit G, default heading styles are applied automatically to headings and subheadings when you work in Outline view to create the structure of a document. For example, the Heading 1 style is applied to text associated with Level 1, the Heading 2 style is applied to text associated with Level 2, and so on. You can modify a default heading style or you can create a new heading style.

- In Word, you can choose from 13 predefined Quick Style sets or you can create your own Quick Style set. Each **Quick Style set** contains **Quick Styles**, or simply **styles**, for a wide range of text elements such as headings, titles, subtitles, and lists. All of the styles associated with a Quick Style set are stored in the **Styles gallery**. Figure H-1 shows the list of predefined Quick Style sets, part of the Styles gallery, and styles in the Word 2010 Quick Style set applied to the document.

- Word includes five major style categories. A **paragraph style** includes font formats, such as font and font size, and paragraph formats, such as line spacing or tabs. You use a paragraph style when you want to format all the text in a paragraph at once. A **character style** includes character formats only, such as font, font size, and font color. You use a character style to apply character format settings only to selected text within a paragraph. A **linked style** applies either a character style or a paragraph style, depending on whether you click in a paragraph to select the entire paragraph or you select specific text. A **table style** specifies how you want both the table grid and the text in a table to appear. A **list style** allows you to format a series of lines with numbers or bullets and with selected font and paragraph formats. Figure H-2 shows a document formatted with the five style types. These styles have been saved in a new Quick Style set called Physician Profiles.

- Every document you create in Word is based on a template. Most of the time, this template is the **Normal template** because the Normal template is loaded automatically when you start a new document. The styles assigned to the Normal template, such as Normal, Title, Heading 1, Heading 2, and so on, are the styles you see in the Styles gallery when you open a new document.

- Word includes a number of predesigned templates. In addition, you can access a variety of templates online. You can also create a template that includes a custom Quick Style set. Finally, you can attach a template to an existing document and then apply the styles included with the template to text in the document.

FIGURE H-1: Predefined Quick Style set applied to a document

Quick Styles gallery

Click to open Quick Styles gallery

Click to access menu of Quick Style sets

List of Quick Style sets; your list may include additional Quick Style sets

Document formatted with the Word 2010 Quick Style set (the default)

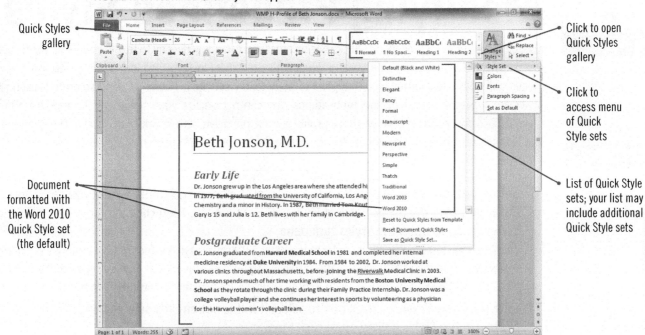

FIGURE H-2: New Quick Style set named Physician Profiles applied to a document

A paragraph style applies formatting to a paragraph, which might be one or more lines of text

A linked style applies formatting to text within a paragraph or to an entire paragraph depending on how text is selected

A character style applies formatting to text within a paragraph; this character style includes brown and italic

A list style adds bullets or numbers to a series of paragraphs

A table style applies formatting to the table grid and the table text

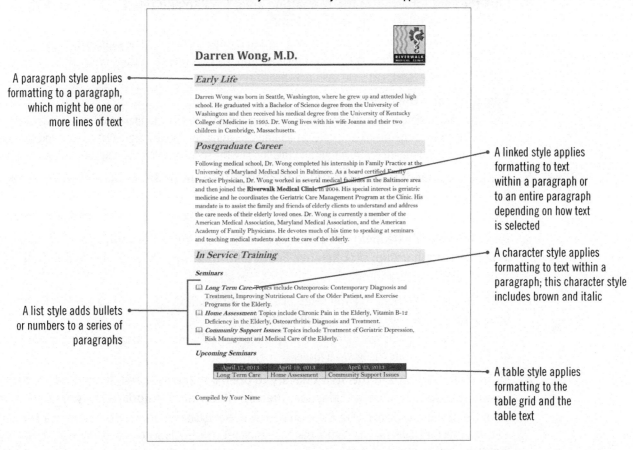

Understanding the Normal style

Text that you type into a blank document is formatted with the Normal style from the Word 2010 Quick Style set until you specify otherwise. By default, text formatted with the Normal style uses the 11-point Calibri font and is left-aligned, with a line spacing of 1.15 within a paragraph and 10 pt After Paragraph spacing. When you select a new Quick Style set, the styles associated with that Quick Style set are applied to the document.

Modifying Predefined Styles

Word 2010 includes 13 predefined Quick Style sets that you can apply directly to text in your document. Each Quick Style set has styles associated with it. Frequently used styles include the Normal, Title, Heading 1, and Heading 2 styles. The Normal style is applied to body text. Heading 1, Heading 2, and so on to Heading 9 styles are applied to headings and subheadings. You can personalize your documents by modifying any style. 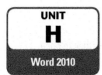 Your colleague has written a profile of clinic physician Beth Jonson, M.D. You decide to modify the Normal style currently applied to all body text in the document. You also modify the Heading 1 style.

STEPS

1. **Start Word, open the file WMP H-1.docx from the drive and folder where you store your Data Files, save the file as WMP H-Profile of Beth Jonson, then click the launcher 🔲 in the Styles group to open the Styles task pane**

   The **Styles task pane** lists all the styles in the Word 2010 Quick Style set and includes options for creating new styles, using the Style Inspector, and managing styles. The Title style is currently selected because the insertion point appears in the text "Beth Jonson", which is formatted with the Title style.

2. **Click the Show Preview check box to select it if it is not already selected, right-click Normal in the Styles gallery, then click Modify**

   The Modify Style dialog box opens, as shown in Figure H-3.

3. **Click the Font list arrow in the Formatting area, scroll to and select Bell MT, click the Font Size list arrow, select 12 pt, then click OK**

   The Modify Style dialog box closes, and all body text in the document is modified automatically to match the new settings for the Normal style. Text formatted with a style other than the Normal style, such as text formatted with the Heading 1 style, does not change.

4. **Select the Early Life heading**

   The Early Life heading is formatted with the Heading 1 style. You want to make formatting changes to the text formatted with the Heading 1 style. In addition to using the Modify Style dialog box, you can apply formatting to text formatted with a style and then update the style to match the new formatting.

5. **Use the commands in the Font group to change the font to Bell MT and the font color to Red, Accent 2, Darker 50%**

   You made changes to the character formatting. You continue by making changes to the paragraph formatting.

6. **With the Early Life heading still selected, click the Line and Paragraph Spacing button 📑 in the Paragraph group, click Remove Space Before Paragraph, click 📑 again, then click Add Space After Paragraph**

7. **With the Early Life heading still selected, click the Shading list arrow 🎨 in the Paragraph group, then click Red, Accent 2, Lighter 80%**

   You have made several changes to the selected text. You can update the style associated with the selected text to include the formatting changes you made.

8. **Right-click Heading 1 in the Styles gallery to open a menu as shown in Figure H-4, click Update Heading 1 to Match Selection, then scroll to view the updated headings**

   All of the headings formatted with the Heading 1 style are updated to match the formatting options you applied to the Early Life heading. Notice that the Heading 1 style in the Styles gallery shows a preview of the formatting associated with that style.

9. **Save the document**

   You have used two methods to modify the formatting attached to a style. You can modify the style using the Modify Styles dialog box, or you can make changes to text associated with a style and then update the style to match the selected text. You can use either of these methods to update any predefined style and any style you create yourself.

FIGURE H-3: Modify Style dialog box

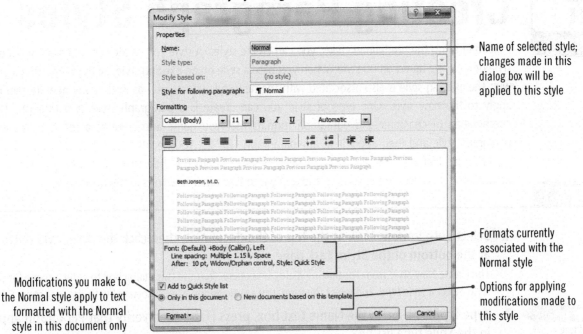

Name of selected style; changes made in this dialog box will be applied to this style

Formats currently associated with the Normal style

Modifications you make to the Normal style apply to text formatted with the Normal style in this document only

Options for applying modifications made to this style

FIGURE H-4: Updating the Heading 1 style with new formats

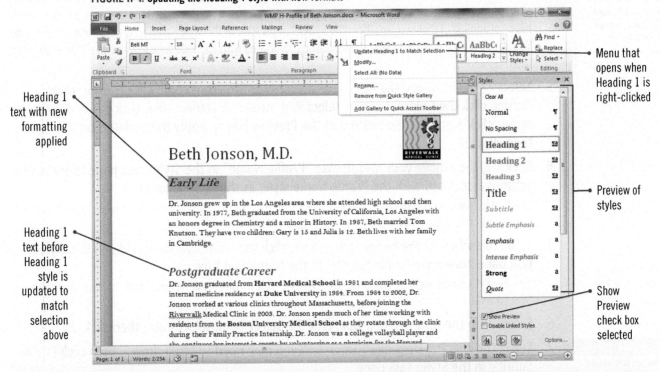

Menu that opens when Heading 1 is right-clicked

Heading 1 text with new formatting applied

Heading 1 text before Heading 1 style is updated to match selection above

Preview of styles

Show Preview check box selected

Revealing style formatting

Word includes two ways to quickly determine exactly what styles and formatting are applied to selected text. These methods are useful when you apply a style to text and not all the changes are made. To find out why, use the Style Inspector to open the Reveal Formatting task pane. To open the Style Inspector, click the text formatted with the style you want to investigate, then click the Style Inspector button at the bottom of the Styles task pane. The **Style Inspector** lists the styles applied to the selected text and indicates if any extra formats were applied that are not included in the style. For example, another user could apply formatting such as bold and italic that is not included in the style. You can clear these formats by clicking one of the four buttons along the right side of the Style Inspector or by clicking Clear All to remove all extra formats. If you need to investigate even further, you can click the Reveal Formatting button at the bottom of the Style Inspector to open the Reveal Formatting task pane. The **Reveal Formatting task pane** lists exactly which formats are applied to the character, paragraph, and section of the selected text.

Creating Paragraph Styles

Instead of using the predefined styles, you can create styles. A style you create can be based on an existing style or it can be based on no style. When you base a style on an existing style, all the formatting associated with the existing style is also associated with the new style you create, as well as any new formatting you apply to the new style. One type of style you can create is a paragraph style. A paragraph style is a combination of character and paragraph formats that you name and store as a set. You can create a paragraph style and then apply it to any paragraph. ▓▓▒▒▒ You decide to create a new paragraph style called Profile Name and apply it to the text formatted with the Title style, and then you create a new paragraph style called Profile Subtitle and apply it to two other headings in the document.

STEPS

1. **Select** Beth Jonson, M.D. **at the top of the document, then click the** New Style button ⊞ **at the bottom of the Styles task pane**

   The Create New Style from Formatting dialog box opens. You use this dialog box to enter a name for the new style, select a style type, and select the formatting options you want associated with the new style.

QUICK TIP
Any line of text followed by a hard return is considered a paragraph, even if the line consists of only one or two words.

2. **Type** Profile Name **in the Name text box, press** [Tab], **then verify that Paragraph appears in the Style type list box**

   The new style you are creating is based on the Title style because the Title style is applied to the currently selected text. When you create a new style, you can base it on the style applied to the selected text if a style has been applied to that text, another style by selecting a style in the Style based on list box, or no preset style. You want the new style to include the formatting associated with the Title style so you leave Title as the Style based on setting.

3. **Select** 22 pt, Bold, **and the** Red, Accent 2, Darker 50% **font color, click** Format, **click** Border, **click the** Color list arrow, **select** Red, Accent 2, Darker 50%, **click the** Width list arrow, **click** 3 pt, **click the bottom of the Preview box to apply the updated border style, then click** OK

4. **Click** OK, **then move your mouse over "Profile Name" in the Styles task pane to show the settings associated with the Profile Name style, as shown in Figure H-5**

   The Profile Name style is applied to the text Beth Jonson. The Profile Name style appears in the Styles task pane and in the Styles gallery. The Title style is also still available.

5. **Scroll to and select the heading** Seminars, **click the** New Style button ⊞ **on the Styles task pane, then type** Profile Subtitle **in the Name text box**

   The Profile Subtitle style is based on the Normal style because the selected text is formatted with the Normal style.

6. **Select** 12 **in the font size text box, type** 13, **select** Bold, **select** Italic, **then click** OK

QUICK TIP
You can also use the Format Painter to apply a style to text.

7. **Select the heading** Upcoming Seminars **(you may need to scroll down), then click** Profile Subtitle **in the Styles task pane**

   The new Profile Subtitle style is applied to two headings in the document.

8. **Compare the Styles task pane and document to Figure H-6, then save the document**

Working with Styles and Templates

FIGURE H-5: Formatting associated with Profile Name style

Profile Name style applied to text

Formats associated with Profile Name style

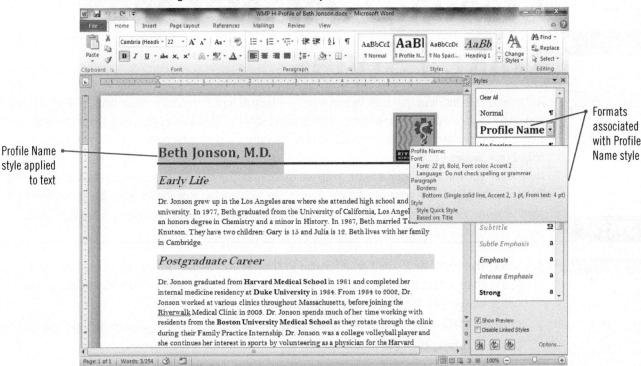

FIGURE H-6: Profile Subtitle style applied to text

Preview of Profile Subtitle style

Text formatted with the Profile Subtitle style

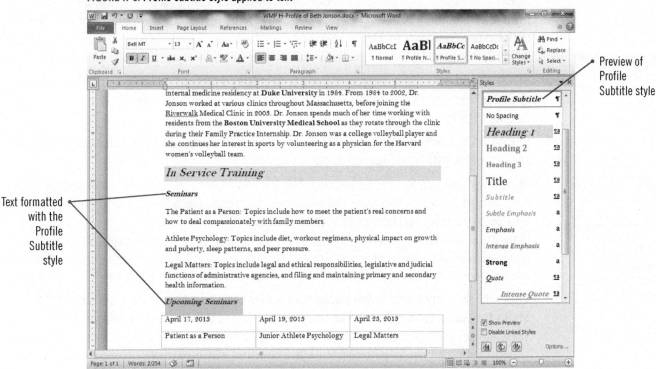

Creating Character and Linked Styles

A character style includes character format settings—such as font, font size, bold, and italic—that you name and save as a style. You apply a character style to selected text within a paragraph. Any text in the paragraph that is not formatted with the character style is formatted with the currently applied paragraph style. A linked style includes both character formats and paragraph formats, just like a paragraph style. The difference is that you can apply a linked style to an entire paragraph or to selected text within a paragraph. Linked styles are therefore very versatile. You create a character style called Seminars to apply to each seminar name and a linked style called Riverwalk to apply to each instance of Riverwalk Medical Clinic.

STEPS

QUICK TIP
You use [Ctrl] to select all the text you wish to format with a new style.

1. **Select the text** The Patient as a Person **in the section below Seminars, press and hold [Ctrl], then select the text** Athlete Psychology **at the beginning of the next paragraph and** Legal Matters **at the beginning of the next paragraph**

2. **Click the** New Style button 🔲 **at the bottom of the Styles task pane, type** Seminars **in the Name text box, click the** Style type list arrow, **then select** Character

3. **Select these character formatting settings: the** Bell MT font, 12 pt, Bold, Italic, **and the** Red, Accent 2, Darker 50% font color, **click** OK, **then click away from the text to deselect it**
   The text you selected is formatted with the Seminars character style. You can modify an existing character style in the same way you modify a paragraph style. You decide that you'd prefer the text to be formatted with a different color.

4. **Select** The Patient as a Person, **change the font color to** Blue, Accent 1, Darker 50%, **right-click** Seminars **in the Styles task pane to open the menu shown in Figure H-7, then click** Update Seminars to Match Selection
   All phrases formatted with the Seminars character style are updated. You can also create a linked style.

QUICK TIP
Mouse over the options in the Text Effects gallery, and then use the ScreenTips to help you make the correct selection.

5. **Scroll up and select** Riverwalk Medical Clinic **in the paragraph below Postgraduate Career, click the** Text Effects list arrow 🔲 **in the Font group, then select the** Gradient Fill – Blue, Accent 1 **(third row, fourth column)**

6. **Right-click the selected text, point to** Styles, **then click** Save Selection as a New Quick Style
   The Create New Style from Formatting dialog box opens.

QUICK TIP
You will only see the border when you apply the Riverwalk style to a paragraph because the border formatting applies only to paragraphs.

7. **Type** Riverwalk **as the style name, click** Modify, **click** Format, **click** Border, **set the color to** Red, Accent 2, Darker 50% **and the weight to** 3 pt, **click the** bottom border **in the Preview area to add a thick red border line, then click** OK
   In the Create New Style from Formatting dialog box, you see that the Linked (paragraph and character) style type is automatically assigned when you save a selection as a new Quick Style. The style you created includes character formatting (the text effect format) and paragraph formatting (the border line).

8. **Click** OK, **click anywhere in the paragraph under Early Life, then click** Riverwalk **in the Styles task pane (you may need to scroll up the Styles task pane to view Riverwalk)**
   The entire paragraph is formatted with the new Riverwalk style, as shown in Figure H-8. Notice that both the character formatting and the paragraph formatting associated with the Riverwalk linked style are applied to the paragraph, but that only the character formatting associated with the Riverwalk linked style is applied to selected text. You prefer to apply the Riverwalk style just to selected text within a paragraph.

9. **Click the** Undo button 🔲 **on the Quick Access toolbar, then save the document**

Working with Styles and Templates

FIGURE H-7: Updating the Seminars character style

New font color applied to selected text

Update Seminars to Match Selection option

Heads formatted with the original Seminars style

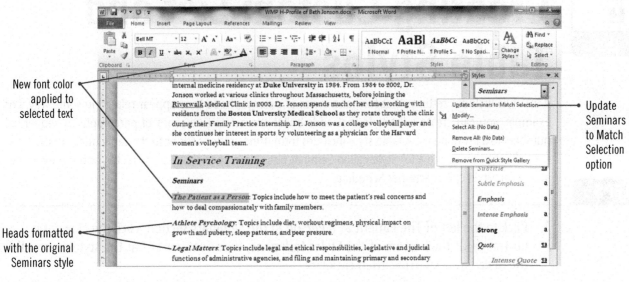

FIGURE H-8: Riverwalk linked style applied to a paragraph and to selected text

The Riverwalk linked style formats text with character and paragraph formats when applied to an entire paragraph

The Riverwalk linked style formats text with character formats only when applied to selected text within a paragraph

Paragraph style

Linked style can be applied to either selected text or a paragraph

Character style

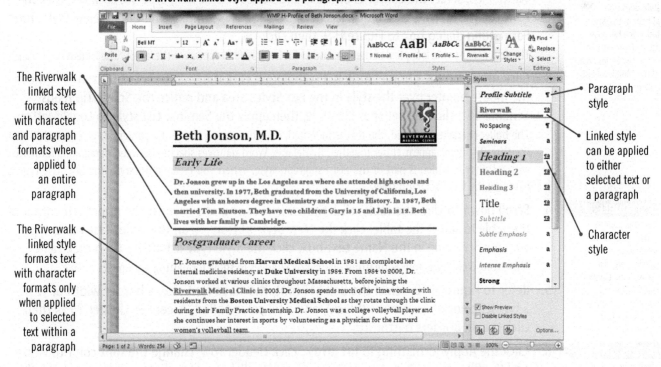

Identifying paragraph, character, and linked styles

Style types are identified in the Styles task pane by different symbols. Each paragraph style is marked with a paragraph symbol: ¶. You can apply a paragraph style just by clicking in any paragraph or line of text and selecting the style. The most commonly used predefined paragraph style is the Normal style. Each character style is marked with a character symbol: a. You can apply a character style by clicking anywhere in a word or by selecting a phrase within a paragraph. Predefined character styles include Emphasis, Strong, and Book Title. Each linked style is marked with both a paragraph symbol and a character symbol: ¶a. You can click anywhere in a paragraph to apply the linked style to the entire paragraph, or you can select text and then apply only the character formats associated with the linked style to the selected text. Predefined linked styles include Heading 1, Title, and Quote.

Creating Custom List and Table Styles

A list style includes settings that format a series of paragraphs so they appear related in some way. For example, you can create a list style that adds bullet characters to a series of paragraphs or sequential numbers to a list of items. A table style includes formatting settings for both the table grid and the table text. ▓▓▓▓ You create a list style called Seminar List with a special bullet character, and then you create a table style called Seminar Schedule.

STEPS

1. **Click to the left of The Patient as a Person in the Seminars section, click the** New Style **button 🔲 at the bottom of the Styles task pane, type** Seminar List **as the style name, click the** Style type list arrow, **then click** List

   You can also click the Multilevel List button in the Paragraph group on the Home tab, and then click Define New List Style to open the Define New List Style dialog box and create a new style.

2. **Click the** Bullets button 📋, **click the** Insert symbol button Ω, **click the** Font list arrow, **click** Wingdings, **select the contents of the** Character code text box, **type** 38, **click** OK, **click the** Font color list arrow, **click** Blue, Accent 1, Darker 50%, **compare the Create New Style from Formatting dialog box to Figure H-9, then click** OK

   The Seminar List style is applied to the text, and a blue book symbol appears to the left of "The Patient as a Person".

3. **Click** Athlete **in the phrase "Athlete Psychology", click the** Multilevel List button 📝, **move the mouse pointer over the style in the List Styles area and notice the ScreenTip reads Seminar List, click the** Seminar List style, **then apply the Seminar List style to** Legal Matters

   The bullet character is added, the text is indented, and the spacing above the paragraph is removed so that the three list items appear closer together. By default, Word removes spacing between paragraphs formatted with a list style, which is part of the List Paragraph style. When you create a list style, the List style type is based on the List Paragraph style.

4. **Scroll down to view the table, click the** table move handle ✛ **near the upper-left corner of the table to select the table, click the** New Style button 🔲 **on the Styles task pane, type** Seminar Schedule **in the Name text box, click the** Style type list arrow, **then click** Table

   The Create New Style from Formatting dialog box changes to show formatting options for a table.

5. **Refer to Figure H-10, select the** Bell MT font, **the** 12 pt font size, **a border width of** ½ pt, **a border color of** Automatic (black), **and a fill color of** Red, Accent 2, Lighter 80%, **then click the** All Borders button ⊞

6. **Click the** Apply formatting to list arrow, **click** Header row, **change the font color to** white **and the fill color to** Red, Accent 2, Darker 50%, **click the** Align button list arrow, **click the** Align Center button ▤, **then click** OK

   The table is formatted with the new Seminar Schedule table style, which includes a modified header row.

7. **Double-click the right edge of the table to adjust the column width**

   You want the table centered between the left and right margins of the page, and you want the centering format to be part of the Seminar Schedule style.

8. **Click the** Table Tools Design tab, **right-click the currently selected table style (far-left selection), click** Modify Table Style, **click** Format **in the lower-left corner of the dialog box, click** Table Properties, **click the** Center button **in the Alignment area, click** OK, **then click** OK

   The center format is part of the table style. The table appears as shown in Figure H-11.

9. **Click below the table to deselect it, then save the document**

Working with Styles and Templates

FIGURE H-9: Create New Style from Formatting dialog box

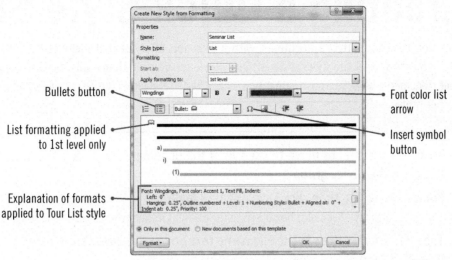

Bullets button

Font color list arrow

List formatting applied to 1st level only

Insert symbol button

Explanation of formats applied to Tour List style

FIGURE H-10: Table formatting selections

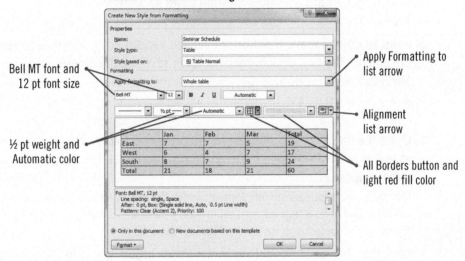

Bell MT font and 12 pt font size

Apply Formatting to list arrow

Alignment list arrow

½ pt weight and Automatic color

All Borders button and light red fill color

FIGURE H-11: Seminar List and Seminar Schedule styles applied

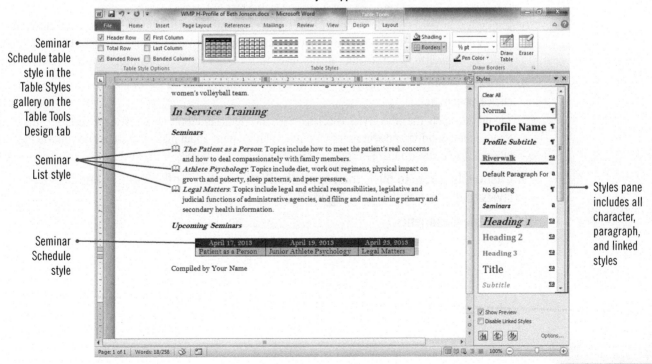

Seminar Schedule table style in the Table Styles gallery on the Table Tools Design tab

Seminar List style

Seminar Schedule style

Styles pane includes all character, paragraph, and linked styles

Working with Styles and Templates

Creating a Quick Style Set

Once you have formatted a document with a selection of styles that includes both new and existing styles, you can save all the styles as a new Quick Style set. You can then apply the Quick Style set to format other documents. ▓▓▓▓ You create a new Quick Style set called Physician Profiles, and then apply it to another profile.

STEPS

1. **Press [Ctrl][Home] to move to the top of the document, then click the** Change Styles button **in the Styles group**

2. **Point to** Style Set, **then click** Save as Quick Style Set

    The Save Quick Style Set dialog box opens to the default location where Quick Style sets are saved.

3. **Type** Physician Profiles **in the File name text box in the Save Quick Style Set dialog box, then click** Save

4. **Click the** Change Styles button, **then point to** Style Set

    The new Physician Profiles Quick Style set appears in the list of Style Sets, as shown in Figure H-12.

5. **Point to** Colors, **move the mouse over the various color schemes to see how the document changes, click** Hardcover, **then save the document**

    The color scheme has changed. You apply a new color scheme so the colors in that color scheme are available to you as you work on the document. You can apply the new Physician Profiles Quick Style set to a new document.

6. **Open the file** WMP H-2.docx **from the drive and folder where you store your Data Files, save it as** WMP H-Profile of Darren Wong, **then open the Styles task pane if it is not already open**

    Darren Wong's profile is currently formatted with the Formal Quick Style set, one of the 13 predefined style sets. The Title style is applied to "Darren Wong", and the Heading 1 style is applied to the "Early Life", "Postgraduate Career", and "In Service Training" headings.

7. **Click the** Change Styles button **in the Styles group, point to** Style Set, **then click** Physician Profiles

    The Physician Profiles Quick Style set is applied to the text in Darren Wong's profile, and all the new styles you created in previous lessons, except the Seminar List and Seminar Schedule styles, are available in the Styles gallery and the Styles task pane. Notice that the Hardcover color scheme you applied to Beth Jonson's profile is not applied. Color schemes are not saved with a Quick Style set. You must reapply the color scheme.

8. **Click the** Change Styles button **in the Styles group, point to** Colors, **then scroll to and click** Hardcover

    You need to apply the other styles associated with the Physician Profile Quick Style set, including the Profile Name, Profile Subtitle, and Seminars styles. You will learn more about managing styles and you will apply the Riverwalk style, the Seminar List style, and the Seminar Schedule style in the next lesson.

9. **Change the zoom to 60%, then apply the** Profile Name, Profile Subtitle, **and** Seminars **styles to the text as shown in Figure H-13**

10. **Save the document**

FIGURE H-12: Physician Profiles Quick Style set

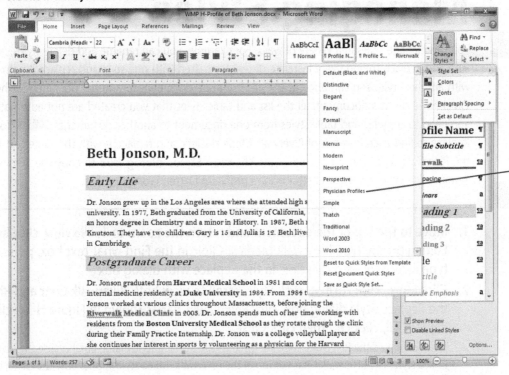

Physician Profiles listed in the selection of Quick Style sets; your list may include other Quick Style sets

FIGURE H-13: Applying styles from the Physician Profiles Quick Style set

Profile Name style applied to "Darren Wong, M.D."

Seminars style applied to "Long Term Care", "Home Assessment", and "Community Support Issues"

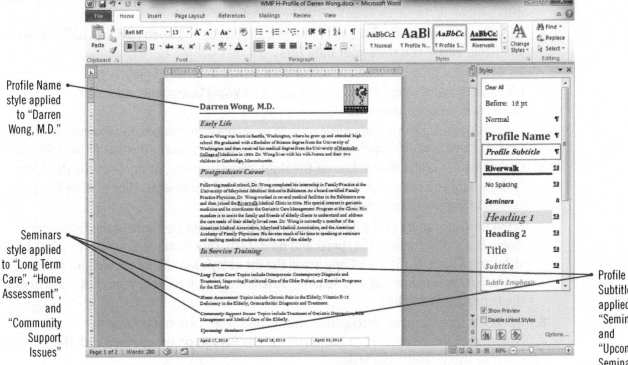

Profile Subtitle style applied to "Seminars" and "Upcoming Seminars"

Managing Styles

You can manage styles in a variety of ways. For example, you can rename and delete styles, and you can use Find and Replace to find every instance of text formatted with one style and replace it with text formatted with another style. You can also copy styles from one document to another document. When you apply a Quick Style set to a document, all the list and table styles that you created are not automatically available. You need to copy list and table styles from one document to another document. ▓▓▒▒▒ You use Find and Replace to find each instance of Riverwalk Medical Clinic and replace it with the same text formatted with the Riverwalk style. You then work in the **Manage Styles dialog box** to copy the Seminar List and the Seminar Schedule styles from Beth Jonson's profile to Darren Wong's profile.

STEPS

1. **Move to the top of the document and return the zoom to** 100% view, **click** Replace **in the Editing group, type** Riverwalk Medical Clinic **in the Find what text box, press [Tab], then type** Riverwalk Medical Clinic **in the Replace with dialog box**

2. **Click** More, **click** Format, **click** Style, **scroll to view both Riverwalk Char and Riverwalk in the Replace Style dialog box, click** Riverwalk Char **as shown in Figure H-14, click** OK, **click** Replace All, **click** OK, **then click** Close

   Two versions of the Riverwalk style are listed in the Replace Style dialog box because the Riverwalk style is a linked style. The Riverwalk Char version of the Riverwalk linked style applies only the character formats associated with the Riverwalk style to the selected text.

3. **Click the** Manage Styles button ⚙ **at the bottom of the Styles task pane, then click** Import/Export **to open the Organizer dialog box**

   You copy styles from the document shown in the left side of the Organizer dialog box to a new document that you open in the right side of the Organizer dialog box. The document in the left side is the source file because it contains the styles you want to copy. The document in the right side is the target file because it receives the styles you copy. By default, the target file is the Normal template.

4. **Click** Close File **under the list box on the left, click** Open File, **then navigate to the drive and folder where you store your Data Files**

   You do not see any Word documents listed because, by default, Word lists only templates.

5. **Click the** All Word Templates list arrow, **select** All Word Documents, **click** WMP H-Profile of Beth Jonson.docx, **then click** Open

   The styles assigned to Beth Jonson's profile appear in the list box on the left side. This document contains the Seminar List and Seminar Schedule styles and is the source document. You need to select the target document.

6. **Click** Close File **under the list box on the right, click** Open File, **navigate to the drive and folder where you store your Data Files, show all Word documents, click** WMP H-Profile of Darren Wong.docx, **then click** Open

7. **Scroll the list of styles in the Beth Jonson Profile document (left side of the Organizer dialog box), click** Seminar List, **press and hold [Ctrl], click** Seminar Schedule **to select both styles (see Figure H-15), click** Copy, **scroll the list of styles in the target file's list box to verify that the Seminar List and Seminar Schedule styles are listed, then click** Close **to exit the Organizer dialog box**

8. **Select the three seminar descriptions (from** Long Term Care **to** Community Support Issues), **click the** Multilevel List button ⸬▾ **in the Paragraph group, then click the** Seminar List style **shown under List Styles**

9. **Select the table, click the** Table Tools Design tab, **click the** Seminar Schedule table style, **double-click the right edge of the table, enter your name where indicated below the table, click** File, **click** Close, **click** Save, **then close the Styles task pane**

   The file WMP H-Profile of Beth Jonson is again the active document.

Working with Styles and Templates

FIGURE H-14: Selecting a style in the Replace Style dialog box

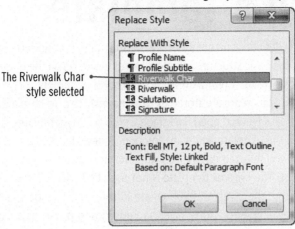

The Riverwalk Char style selected

FIGURE H-15: Managing styles using the Organizer dialog box

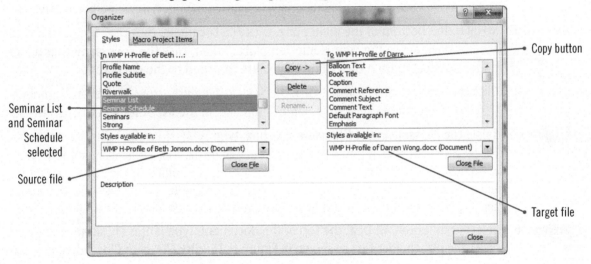

Seminar List and Seminar Schedule selected

Source file

Copy button

Target file

Renaming and deleting styles

To rename a style, right-click it in the Styles gallery, click Rename, type a new name, then press [Enter]. To delete a style from the Styles gallery, right-click the style, then click Remove from Quick Style Gallery. The style is deleted from the Styles gallery, but it is not deleted from your computer. You need to work in the Manage Styles

dialog box to delete a style from your system. Click the Manage Styles button at the bottom of the Styles task pane, select the style to delete, click Delete, then click OK to close the Manage Styles dialog box.

Creating a Template

A quick way to use all the styles contained in a document, including list and table styles, is to create a template. A template contains the basic structure of a document, including all the paragraph, character, linked, list, and table styles. You can create a template from an existing document, or you can create a template from scratch. Templates that you create are stored as **user templates**. To base a document on a user template, you click the File tab, click New to open Backstage view, click My templates in the Available Templates area, and then double-click the template you want to open. A new document that contains all the formats stored in the user template you selected opens. You can enter text into the document and then save it, just as you would any document. The original template is not modified. You create a new folder called Your Name Templates to store the templates you create in this unit, change the default location for user templates to the Your Name templates folder, save the Beth Jonson profile as a user template, modify the template, and then open the template as a new document.

1. **Click the** Start button ⊙ **on the taskbar, click** Computer, **navigate to the drive and folder where you store your Data Files, click** New folder, **type** Your Name Templates **as the folder name, then press** [Enter]

   You want the Your Name Templates folder to be the default location for user templates. Then, when you save a document as a template, it is saved to the Your Name Templates folder by default.

2. **Close** Explorer, **click the** File tab, **click** Options, **then click** Advanced

   The Advanced option provides you with numerous ways to customize how you work with Word.

3. **Scroll to the bottom of the dialog box, click** File Locations, **click** User templates, **click** Modify, **navigate to the Your Name Templates folder, click the** Your Name Templates folder **to select it, then click** OK **until you are returned to the document**

4. **Click the** File tab, **click** Save As, **click the** Save as type list arrow, **click** Word Template (*.dotx), **then double-click** Your Name Templates **in the list of folders to open the folder**

5. **Select the** filename **in the File name text box, type** WMP H-Profile Template, **then click** Save

   The file is saved as WMP H-Profile Template.dotx to your default template location, which is the folder you called Your Name Templates. The .dotx filename extension identifies this file as a template file. Word automatically includes two additional folders in the Your Name Templates folder—the Document Themes and Live Content folders. You do not need to access the files in these folders.

6. **Select** Beth Jonson, M.D. **at the top of the document, type** [Enter Physician Name Here], **enter the placeholder text as shown in Figure H-16, click** File, **click** Close, **then click** Save

   Now that you have created a template, you can use it to create a new document that contains all the styles and formatting you want.

7. **Click the** File tab, **click** New, **then click** My templates

   The Templates folder opens, and the template you saved is available.

8. **Select** WMP H-Profile Template.dotx **if it is not already selected, verify that the Document option button in the Create New section is selected, then click** OK

   The template opens as a new document. You can enter text into this document and then save the document just as you would any document.

9. **Select the text** [Enter Physician Name Here], **type** Jasmina Keyes, M.D., **type text in the table and resize the column widths as shown in Figure H-17, type your name where indicated, save the document as** WMP H-Profile of Jasmina Keyes **to the drive and folder where you store your Data Files (but not to the Your Name Templates folder), click** File, **then click** Close

Working with Styles and Templates

[Enter Physician Name Here]

Early Life

[Describe the early life]

Postgraduate Career

[Describe the postgraduate career]

In Service Training

Seminars

[Describe the three seminars, then format each seminar name with the Seminars style and each listing with the Seminar List style]

Upcoming Seminars

[Date]	[Date]	[Date]
[Seminar Name]	[Seminar Name]	[Seminar Name]

Compiled by Your Name

Adjust column widths if needed

FIGURE H-17: Table text for the new guide profile

Upcoming Seminars

May 5, 2013	May 12, 2013	May 25, 2013
Whole Health	Nutrition Tips	Therapeutic Massage

Default location for user templates

By default, user templates are stored in the My templates folder. The path for this folder is: C:\Users\Administrator\AppData\Roaming\Microsoft\Templates. Note that a different folder might appear for Administrator, depending on how your computer system is set up. If the default location where user templates are saved has been changed, you can change back to the default location by selecting the User Templates folder in the File Locations section of the Advanced Options in the Word Options dialog box and then changing the location. The AppData folder is a hidden folder by default, so if you do not see the AppData folder, then use the Control Panel to change your folder settings to show hidden folders.

You can also create templates to distribute to others. These templates are called **workgroup templates**. You navigate to and select the location of a workgroup template in the File Locations section of the Advanced Options in the Word Options dialog box in the same way you navigate to and select the location of a user template.

UNIT
H

Word 2010

Revising and Attaching a Template

You can modify a template just as you would any Word document. All new documents you create from the modified template will use the new settings. All documents that you created before you modified the template are not changed unless you open the Templates and Add-ins dialog box and direct Word to update styles automatically. 🔲🔳 You modify the Profile Name style in the Profile Template and then attach the revised template to a profile for Jeffrey Patrick. You then update the profiles for the other physicians with the revised template and delete the Physician Profiles style set.

STEPS

1. Click the File tab, click Open, navigate to and open the Your Name Templates folder, click WMP H-Profile Template.dotx, click Open, right-click Profile Name in the Styles gallery, click Modify, change the font to Arial Rounded MT Bold, change the font size to 18 pt, then click OK

2. Select Early Life, change the font to Arial Rounded MT Bold, open the Styles gallery, right-click Heading 1, then click Update Heading 1 to Match Selection
   You need to resave the Physician Profiles Quick Style set so that the new settings are available to new documents.

3. Click the Change Styles button, point to Style Set, click Save As Quick Style Set, click Physician Profiles.dotx, click Save, click Yes, click the File tab, click Close, then click Save

QUICK TIP
Colors schemes and Quick Style sets are not saved with templates.

4. Open the file WMP H-3.docx from the drive and folder where you store your Data Files, save the file as WMP H-Profile of Jeffrey Patrick, then apply the Hardcover color scheme and the Physician Profiles style set
   You need to attach the Profile Template to Jeffrey's profile so that you can apply all the new styles you created to the document. To do so you need to show the Developer tab.

5. Click the File tab, click Options, click Customize Ribbon, click the Developer check box in the list of Main Tabs as shown in Figure H-18, then click OK
   You use the Developer tab to work with advanced features such as form controls and templates.

6. Click the Developer tab on the Ribbon, click Document Template in the Templates group, click Attach, click WMP H-Profile Template.dotx, click Open, click the Automatically update document styles check box, then click OK
   The Profile Template file is attached to Jeffrey Patrick's profile.

TROUBLE
Apply the Seminar List style from the Multilevel List button, and apply the Seminar Schedule style from the Table Tools Design tab.

7. Click the Home tab, open the Styles task pane, apply styles as shown in Figure H-19, be sure your name is on the document, then save and close the document

8. Open the file WMP H-Profile of Beth Jonson.docx, click the Developer tab, click the Document Template button, click Attach, double-click WMP H-Profile Template.dotx, click the Automatically update document styles check box to select it, click OK, move the logo above the border line, enter your name where indicated, then save and close the document

9. Open the file WMP H-Profile of Darren Wong.docx, attach WMP H-Profile Template.dotx so Darren Wong's profile updates automatically, adjust the logo position, save and close the document, then repeat to update WMP H-Profile of Jasmina Keyes.docx

QUICK TIP
You delete the Physician Profiles style set from the list of style sets so only the default style sets appear for the next user of your computer system.

10. Open a new blank document, click the Change Styles button in the Styles group, point to Style Set, click Save as Quick Style Set, click Physician Profiles.dotx, press [Delete], click Yes, click Cancel, click the File tab, click Options, click Customize Ribbon, click the Developer check box to deselect it, click OK, exit Word, then submit all your files to your instructor

Working with Styles and Templates

FIGURE H-18: Adding the Developer tab to the ribbon

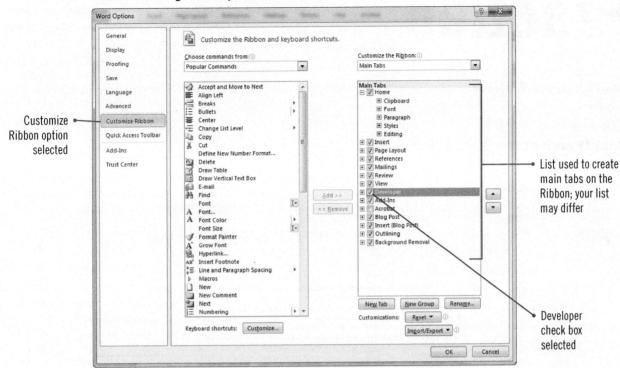

Customize Ribbon option selected

List used to create main tabs on the Ribbon; your list may differ

Developer check box selected

FIGURE H-19: Jeffrey Patrick, M.D., profile formatted with styles

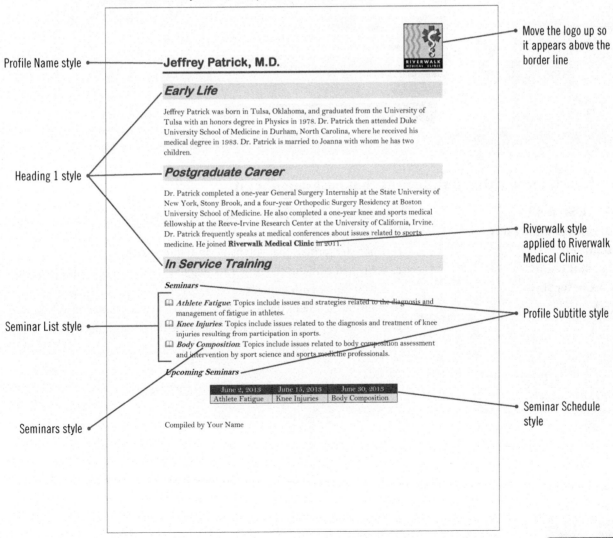

Profile Name style

Heading 1 style

Seminar List style

Seminars style

Move the logo up so it appears above the border line

Riverwalk style applied to Riverwalk Medical Clinic

Profile Subtitle style

Seminar Schedule style

Practice

Concepts Review

For current SAM information, including versions and content details, visit SAM Central (http://www.cengage.com/samcentral). If you have a SAM user profile, you may have access to hands-on instruction, practice, and assessment of the skills covered in this unit. Since various versions of SAM are supported throughout the life of this text, check with your instructor for the correct instructions and URL/Web site for accessing assignments.

Identify each of the items in Figure H-20.

FIGURE H-20

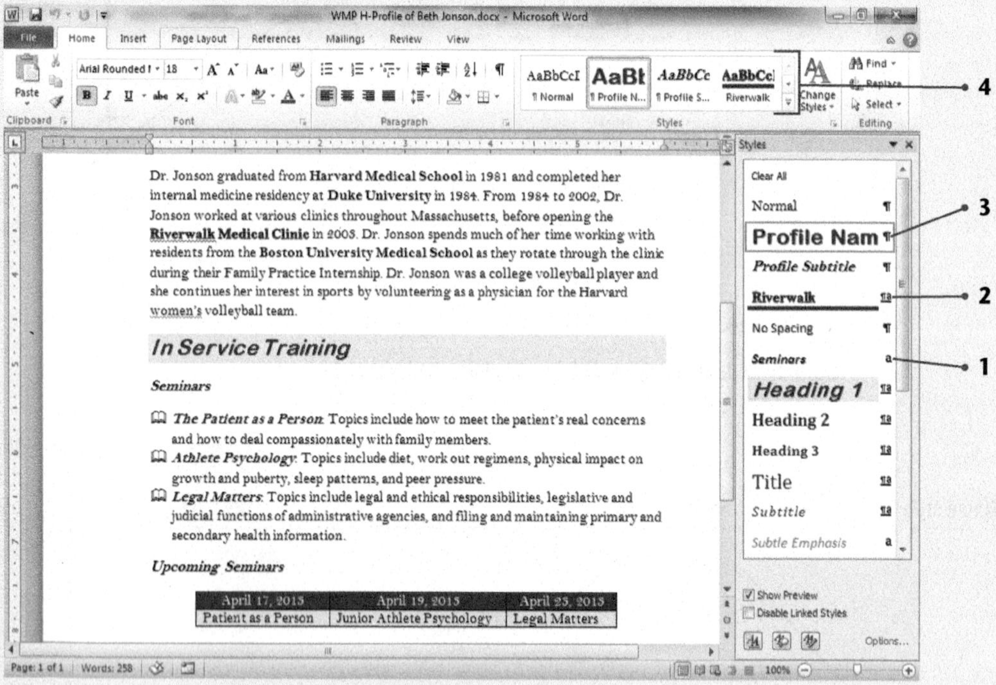

[Screenshot of Microsoft Word document titled "WMP H-Profile of Beth Jonson.docx - Microsoft Word" with callouts numbered 4, 3, 2, 1 pointing to the Styles pane on the right showing styles: Clear All, Normal, Profile Nam, Profile Subtitle, Riverwalk, No Spacing, Seminars, Heading 1, Heading 2, Heading 3, Title, Subtitle, Subtle Emphasis]

Match each term with the statement that best describes it.

5. **Quick Style set**

6. **Organizer dialog box**

7. **Template**

8. **Normal template**

9. **Character style**

a. A collection of character, paragraph, and linked styles that is named and available to all documents

b. Character formats that you name and store as a set

c. A file that contains the basic structure of a document in addition to selected styles; can be custom made

d. A file that contains the styles available to a new document in Word

e. Used to copy styles from a source document to a target document

Select the best answer from the list of choices.

10. **What is available in the Quick Style gallery?**
    a. Themes associated with a Quick Style set
    b. Styles associated with a Quick Style set
    c. Colors associated with a Quick Style set
    d. The Developer tab

11. **Which of the following definitions best describes a paragraph style?**
    a. Format settings applied only to selected text within a paragraph
    b. Format settings applied to a table grid
    c. Format settings applied to the structure of a document
    d. Format settings applied to all the text in a paragraph

12. **How do you modify a style?**
    a. Double-click the style in the Styles task pane.
    b. Right-click the style in the Styles gallery, then click Revise.
    c. Right-click the style in the Styles gallery, then click Modify.
    d. Click the style in the Styles task pane, then click New Style.

13. **Which dialog box do you use to copy styles from one document to another?**
    a. Organizer dialog box
    b. New Document dialog box
    c. Styles dialog box
    d. Modify Styles dialog box

14. **Which tab do you use to attach a template to an existing document?**
    a. Insert
    b. References
    c. Developer
    d. Page

Skills Review

1. **Modify predefined styles.**
   a. Start Word, open the file WMP H-4.docx from the drive and folder where you store your Data Files, save it as **WMP H-Conditions_Skin**, then open the Styles task pane.
   b. Modify the Normal style by changing the font to Times New Roman and the font size to 12 pt.
   c. Select the Contact Dermatitis heading, then change the font to Arial Black, the font size to 16 pt, and the font color to Purple, Accent 4, Darker 50%.
   d. Remove the Before paragraph spacing, add 6 pt After paragraph spacing, then add a 3 pt border line below the text in Purple, Accent 4, Darker 50%.
   e. Update the Heading 1 style so that it uses the new formats.

2. **Create paragraph styles.**
   a. Select the text "Allergic Skin Conditions" at the top of the document.
   b. Create a new style called **Condition** with the Arial Black font, 20 pt, and a bottom border of 3 pt, Purple, Accent 4, Darker 50%.
   c. Select "Summary of Treatments," then create a new paragraph style called **Treatment** that uses the Arial Black font, 18 pt, and bold, and changes the font color to Purple, Accent 4, Darker 50%.
   d. Save the document.

3. **Create character and linked styles.**
   a. Select "Irritant contact dermatitis" under the Contact Dermatitis heading, then create a new character style named **Condition Description** that uses the Arial Black font, 12 pt, and the Purple, Accent 4, Darker 50% font color.
   b. Apply the Condition Description style to "Allergic contact dermatitis," "Hives," and "Angioedema" in the body text.
   c. Select "immune system reaction" in the first paragraph, apply the Gradient Fill - Orange, Accent 6, Inner Shadow text effect, open the Create New Style from Formatting dialog box, then name the style **Feature** and verify the style type is set to the Linked style type.
   d. Apply the Feature style to the paragraph below the Contact Dermatitis heading, undo the application of the Feature style to the paragragh, then apply the Feature style just to the text "poison ivy, poison oak, or poison sumac" in the Allergic contact dermatitis paragraph.
   e. Save the document.

Skills Review (continued)

4. Create custom list and table styles.

  a. Click to the left of "Irritant contact dermatitis", then define a new list style called **Condition List**. (*Hint*: Click the Multilevel List button in the Paragraph group on the Home tab, then click Define New List Style.)

  b. Change the list style to Bullet, open the Symbol dialog box, verify the Wingdings character set is active, type **216** in the Character code text box, then change the symbol color by changing the font color to Purple, Accent 4, Darker 50%.

  c. Apply the Condition List style to each paragraph that describes condition. (*Hint*: You access the Condition List style by clicking the Multilevel List button.)

  d. Select the table at the bottom of the document, then create a new table style called **Treatment Table**.

  e. Select Purple, Accent 4, Lighter 80% for the fill color, change the border style to ½ pt and the border color to Automatic, then apply All Borders to the table.

  f. Format the header row with bold, the White font color, the Purple, Accent 4, Darker 50% fill color, and Center alignment.

  g. From the Table Tools Layout tab, modify the table properties of the current table so the table is centered between the left and right margins of the page, then save the document.

5. Create a Quick Style set.

  a. Save the current style set as **Health Conditions**, then view the Health Conditions style set in the list of Quick Style sets.

  b. Change the color scheme to Slipstream, then save the document.

  c. Open the file WMP H-5.docx from the drive and folder where you store your Data Files, then save it as **WMP H-Conditions_Heart**.

  d. Apply the Health Conditions Quick Style set to the document, then apply the Slipstream color scheme.

  e. Apply the Condition style to the title, then apply the Treatment style to "Summary of Treatments".

  f. Apply the Condition Description style to "Congenital abnormality", "Medical conditions", "Viral infection", and "Mechanical failure", then save the document.

6. Manage styles.

  a. Position the insertion point at the beginning of the document, open the Replace dialog box, enter **pump function** in the Find what text box, then enter **pump function** in the Replace with dialog box.

  b. Open the More options area, select the Style option on the Format menu, select the Feature Char style, then replace both instances of pump function with pump function formatted with the Feature Char style.

  c. Open the Manage Styles dialog box from the Styles task pane, then click Import/Export to open the Organizer dialog box.

  d. Close the file in the left of the Organizer dialog box, then open the file WMP H-Conditions_Skin.docx. (*Hint*: Remember to navigate to the location where you save files and to change the Files of type to Word documents.)

  e. Close the file in the right pane of the Organizer dialog box, then open the file WMP H-Conditions_Heart.docx.

  f. Copy the Condition List and Treatment Table styles from the WMP H-Conditions_Skin document to the WMP H-Conditions_Heart document, then close the Organizer dialog box and return to the document.

  g. In the file WMP H-Conditions_Heart.docx, apply the Condition List style to each of the four descriptions.

  h. Select the table, use the Table Tools Design tab to apply the Treatment Table style to the table, type your name where indicated at the end of the document, save the document, then close it.

  i. Close the Styles task pane.

Skills Review (continued)

7. **Create a template.**

   a. In Windows Explorer, create a new folder called **Your Name Skills Review** in the drive and folder where you store your Data Files.

   b. Change the file location for user templates to the new folder you named Your Name Skills Review.

   c. Save the current document (which should be WMP H-Conditions_Skin) as a template called **WMP H-Condition Descriptions.dotx** to the Your Name Skills Review folder.

   d. Select "Allergic Skin Conditions" at the top of the page, type **[Enter Condition Category Here]**, then delete text and enter directions so the document appears as shown in Figure H-21. (*Hint:* If new text is formatted with the Condition Description or Feature style, select the formatted text and click the Clear Formatting button in the Font group on the Home tab.)

FIGURE H-21

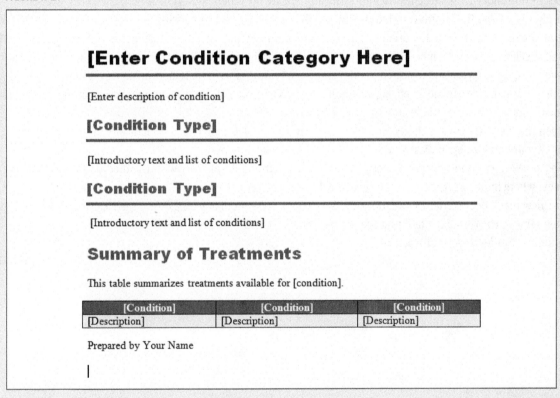

   e. Save and close the template.

   f. Create a new document based on the WMP H-Condition Descriptions template.

   g. Replace the title of the document with the text **Respiratory Conditions**, save the document as **WMP H-Conditions_Respiratory** to the drive and folder where you store your Data Files (but not to the Your Name Skills Review folder), then close it.

Skills Review (continued)

8. Revise and attach a template.

   a. Open the file WMP H-Condition Descriptions.dotx template from the Your Name Skills Review folder, then modify the Heading 1 style so that the font is Comic Sans MS, bold, italic. (*Note*: Be sure to open the template using the File and Open commands.)

   b. Modify the Condition style by changing the font to Comic Sans MS and applying bold, then modify the Treatment style by changing the font to Comic Sans MS.

   c. Resave the Health Conditions Quick Style set.

   d. Save and close the template.

   e. Open the file WMP H-6.docx from the drive and folder where your Data Files are located, save the file as **WMP H-Conditions_Knee**, then select the Slipstream color scheme and apply the Health Conditions Quick Style set.

   f. Show the Developer tab on the Ribbon, open the Templates and Add-ins dialog box, attach the WMP H-Condition Descriptions.dotx template, click the Automatically update document styles check box, then click OK.

   g. Apply styles from the Health Conditions Quick Style set that are associated with the WMP H-Condition Descriptions template so that the WMP H-Conditions_Knee document resembles the other documents you have formatted for this Skills Review. (*Hint*: Remember to apply the Condition, Condition Description, Treatment, Condition List, and Treatment Table styles, and to search for and apply the Feature Char style to both instances of "knee joint.")

   h. Enter your name where indicated, adjust column widths to ensure all text fits on one page, then save and close the document.

   i. Open the file WMP H-Conditions_Heart.docx, attach the updated template, automatically update document styles, enter your name where indicated, then save and close the document.

   j. Update WMP H-Conditions_Skin.docx and WMP H-Conditions_Respiratory with the modified template, enter your name where indicated, then save and close the documents.

   k. In a new blank document in Word, open the Save Quick Style Set dialog box, delete the Health Conditions style set, then remove the Developer tab from the Ribbon and exit Word.

   l. Submit your files to your instructor.

Working with Styles and Templates

Independent Challenge 1

You are the office manager of Evergreen Medical Clinic in Portland, Oregon. The annual clinic softball game is coming soon, and you need to inform the employees about the date and time of the game. To save time, you have already typed the text of the memo with some formatting. Now you need to change some of the styles, create a new Quick Style set, then use it to format another memo.

a. Start Word, open the file WMP H-7.docx from the drive and folder where you store your Data Files, then save it as **WMP H-Memo_Clinic Softball.**

b. Modify styles as shown in Table H-1.

TABLE H-1

style name	changes
Title	Berlin Sans FB font, 22-pt font size, Red, Accent 2, Darker 50%
Heading 1	Berlin Sans FB font, 14-pt font size, Red, Accent 2, Darker 25%

c. Change the color scheme to Module.

d. Save the style set as **Events**.

e. Select Your Name in the message header, then type your name. The completed memo is shown in Figure H-22.

FIGURE H-22

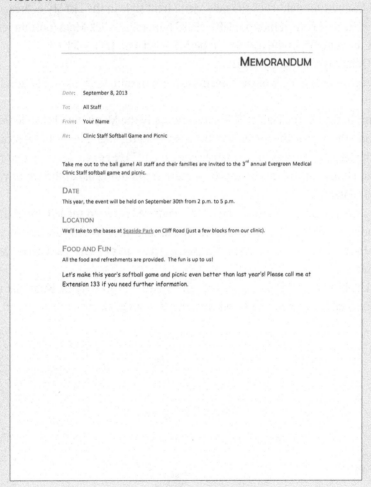

f. Save the document, then close it.

g. Open the file WMP H-8.docx, save the document as **WMP H-Memo_Holiday**, apply the Events Quick Style set, change the color scheme to Module, type your name where indicated, then save the document.

h. Remove the Events Quick Style set from the list of Quick Style sets, close the file and exit Word, then submit the files to your instructor.

Independent Challenge 2

You are in charge of the hospital cafeteria at Valley View Hospital in Toronto. Staff and hospital guests can choose entrees from either a winter menu or a summer menu, depending on the time of year. You have already created an unformatted version of the winter menu. Now you need to format text in the winter menu with styles, save the styles in a new Quick Style set called Menus, then use the Menus Quick Style set to format text in the summer version of the menu. You also need to work in the Organizer dialog box to copy the list and table styles you created for the Winter Menu to the summer version of the menu.

a. Start Word, open the file WMP H-9.docx from the drive and folder where you store your Data Files, then save it as **WMP H-Hospital Cafeteria Winter Menu**. Apply the Waveform color scheme.

b. Select the title "Valley View Hospital Cafeteria Winter Menu", and apply these formats: Arial, 18 pt, bold, a font color of Blue, Accent 1, Darker 50%, and Center alignment, then create a new style called **Menu Title** based on these formats. (*Hint*: Right-click the formatted text, point to Styles, click Save Selection as a New Quick Style, type Menu Title, then click OK.)

c. Select "On the Lighter Side", apply the formats Arial, 14 pt, bold, italic, a font color of Blue, Accent 1, Darker 25%, and a top and bottom border that has a 1 pt width with the same color as the text, then create a new paragraph style from the selection called **Menu Category**.

d. Click to the left of Camembert (the first selection in the On the Lighter Side section), then create a new list style called **Menu Item** that includes a bullet character from Wingdings symbol 84 (a stylized snowflake) that is colored Blue, Accent 1, Darker 50%.

e. Click the Multilevel List button, right-click the new Menu Item style in the List Styles area, click Modify, then in the Modify Style dialog box, click Format (bottom left), click Numbering, click More (bottom left), click the Add tab stop at: check box, select the contents of the text box, type **5.5**, click OK, then click OK.

f. Save the styles in a Quick Style set called **Menus**.

g. Apply the Menu Category style to each of the remaining main headings: Soups and Salads, Entrees, Desserts, and Dinner Times.

h. Select the menu items in the On the Lighter Side category, apply the Menu Item list style (remember to click the Multilevel List button), then apply the Menu Item list style to all the menu items in each category.

i. Click anywhere in the table, then create a new table style called **Cafeteria Hours** that fills the table cells with a light fill color of your choice and the header row with the corresponding dark fill color of your choice and the white font color, bold, and centering.

j. Modify the Cafeteria Hours table style so that the table is centered between the left and right margins of the page.

k. Type your name where indicated at the bottom of the document, then save the document and keep it open.

l. Open the file WMP H-10.docx, save it as **WMP H-Hospital Cafeteria Summer Menu**, then apply the Menus Quick Style set.

m. Format the appropriate headings with the Menu Title and Menu Category styles. Note that the Menu Items list style and the Cafeteria Hours table styles are not saved with the Menus Quick Style set. You need to copy them separately.

Working with Styles and Templates

Independent Challenge 2 (continued)

n. Change the color scheme to the color scheme of your choice. You do not need to select the same color scheme you applied to the winter menu.

o. Save the file, then open the Organizer dialog box from the Manage Styles dialog box. (*Hint*: Click Import/Export.)

p. In the Organizer dialog box, make WMP H-Hospital Cafeteria Winter Menu.docx the source file and WMP H-Hospital Cafeteria Summer Menu.docx the target file. Remember to select All Word Documents as the file type when opening the files.

q. Copy the Cafeteria Hours table style and the Menu Item list style from the file WMP H-Hospital Cafeteria Winter Menu.docx file to the WMP H-Hospital Cafeteria Summer Menu.docx file, then close the Organizer dialog box.

r. In the Summer menu document, apply the Menu Item list style to the first item (Goat cheeses).

s. Click the Multilevel List button, right-click the Menu Item style, click Modify, then change the bullet symbol for the Menu Item style to Wingdings 123 (a flower symbol).

t. Apply the updated Menu Item list style to all the menu items, apply the Cafeteria Hours table style to the table, then type your name where indicated at the bottom of the document.

Advanced Challenge Exercise

- In the Hospital Cafeteria Winter menu document, modify the Menu Title style so that it includes the Britannic Bold font and 20-point font size.
- Modify the Menu Category style so it includes the Gold, Accent 5, Darker 50% font color and a 1½ point top and bottom border in the same color.
- Modify the list style so that the bullet is diamond shape (character code 116) and Green, Accent 3, Darker 50%.
- Modify the table style so that the colors use variations on the Gold, Accent 5 color.
- Click text formatted with the Menu Category style, then change the name of the Menu Category style to **Category**. (*Hint*: Right-click the style name in the Styles gallery, click Rename, type the new name, then press [Enter].)

u. Remove the Menus style from the list of style sets.

v. Save the documents, submit all files to your instructor, then close all files.

Independent Challenge 3

As the Office Administrator at Sky Clinic, you are in charge of creating a design for a new staff newsletter that will be distributed to all clinic staff. Another colleague has already developed text for the first newsletter. First, you create a template for the newsletter, then you apply the template to the document containing the newsletter text.

a. Open a blank document in Word, modify the default location for user templates so that they are saved in the folder you created previously named Your Name Templates. This folder should be in the drive and folder where you store your Data Files.

b. Open the file WMP H-11.docx, save it as **WMP H-Newsletter Template.dotx** to the Your Name Templates folder. (*Hint*: You may need to navigate to the folder.) Then enter text and create styles as shown in Figure H-23. (*Note*: You will apply columns in a later step.)

FIGURE H-23

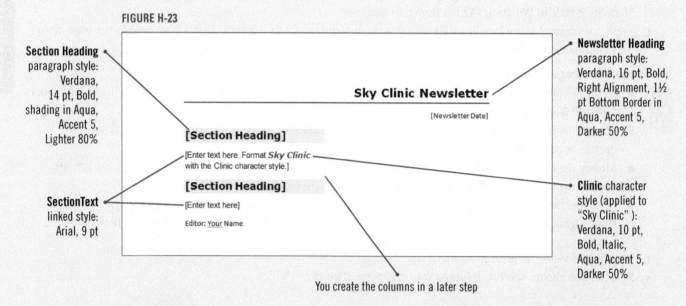

c. Save the style set as **Clinic**.

d. Click to the left of the first [Section Heading], then create two columns from this point forward. (*Hint*: Click the Page Layout tab, click the Columns list arrow in the Page Setup group, click More Columns, then in the Columns dialog box, click two in the Presets section, click the Apply to list arrow, select "This point forward", then click OK.)

e. Type your name where indicated, then save and close the template.

f. Start a new document based on the WMP H-Newsletter Template, type **October 2013** in place of [Newsletter Date], **Clinic Projects** in place of the first [Section Heading], and **Upcoming Events** in place of the next [Section Heading].

g. Save the document as **WMP H-Newsletter_October** to the drive and folder where you store your Data Files, then close the document.

h. Open the file WMP H-12.docx, save it as **WMP H-Newsletter_November**, show the Developer tab on the Ribbon, attach the WMP H-Newsletter Template.dotx to the document, apply the Clinic Quick Style set, then apply styles and formatting where needed. Make sure you apply the Section Text style to all paragraphs of text that are not headings, the date, and your name.

i. Use the Replace feature to find every instance of Sky Clinic (except Sky Clinic in the Newsletter Heading) and replace it with Sky Clinic formatted with the Clinic style. (*Hint*: Use the Find Next command, not the Replace All command.)

j. Apply the two-column format starting at the Work Schedule heading. (*Note*: You need to apply the two-column format because options related to the structure of a document saved with a template are lost when you attach the template to an existing document.)

k. Click at the end of the document (following your name), click the Page Layout tab, click Breaks, then click Continuous to balance the columns in the newsletter.

l. Modify the Section Text style so that the font size is 10 pt, then resave the Clinic Quick Style set.

Independent Challenge 3 (continued)

m. Save and close the document.

n. Open the file WMP H-Newsletter Template.dotx, reapply the Clinic Quick Style set so that the Section Text style changes, then modify the Newsletter Heading style so the font size is 22 pt.

o. Resave the Clinic Quick Style set, then save and close the template.

p. Open the file WMP H-Newsletter_October.docx, attach the updated template, then save and close the document.

q. Open the file WMP H-Newsletter_November.docx, then verify that the document is updated with the new style.

Advanced Challenge Exercise

- In the Work Schedule section, select the list of dates and topics from Day to Catherine Cassel, then convert the text to a table. (*Hint*: Click the Insert tab, click the Table list arrow, click Convert Text to Table, then click OK.)
- With the table selected, create a table style called **Schedule**.
- Change the fill color for the entire table to Blue, Accent 1, Lighter 80%, then adjust column width as needed so row text does not wrap to two lines.
- In the document, select Editor, open the Style Inspector, open the Reveal Formatting task pane, note the addition of Bold and 12 pt to the selected text as seen in the Reveal Formatting task pane Font area, click Clear All in the Style Inspector to remove this additional formatting, then close all open task panes.

r. Save the document, delete the Clinic Quick Style set, remove the Developer tab from the Ribbon, close the document and exit Word, then submit the files to your instructor.

Real Life Independent Challenge

This Independent Challenge requires an Internet connection.

From the Microsoft Office Templates Web site, you can access a variety of templates. You can import any template from the Web site directly into Word and then modify it for your own purposes. You decide to find and then modify a template for a letter related to health care.

a. Start Word, click the File tab, click New, scroll down and click Letters, then click Medical and healthcare letters.

b. Click the template Request for medical records, click Download, save the document as **WMP H-Request for Medical Records Letter.docx**, then click OK if prompted to close a warning message.

c. Read the text of the letter.

d. Modify the return address, recipient address, and content of the letter so it contains information relevant to you. If you wish, you can choose to enter fictional information.

e. Modify the Normal style by changing the font, font size, and color. You determine the settings.

f. Create a new style called **Name**, then apply it to each instance of your name in the letter.

g. Change the color scheme to view how the colors applied to the Normal and Name styles change, modify the Name style by changing the font size, then verify that all text formatted with the Name style is updated.

h. Save and close the document, exit Word, then submit the file to your instructor.

Visual Workshop

Create a new document, then type the text and create the tables shown in Figure H-24. Do not include any formatting. Select the Metro color scheme, apply the Title style to the title, then modify it so that it appears as shown in Figure H-24. Note that all the colors are variations of the Metro color theme, Turquoise, Accent 4, and the font style for the headings is Lucida Handwriting. Apply the Heading 1 style to the names of the price lists, then modify them so that they appear as shown in Figure H-24. Modify the Normal style so the font size is 14 pt. Create a table style called **Price List** that formats each table as shown in Figure H-24, then modify the column widths. Save the file as **WMP H-Massage Oils**, type **Compiled by Your Name** left aligned under the tables, submit a copy to your instructor, then close the document.

FIGURE H-24

Massage Oils

Massage Oils Price List

Product #	Massage Oil	Price
6590	Fir	$7.90
6592	Clove	$6.50
6593	Ginger	$8.00
6596	Lavender	$6.50

Perfume Oils Price List

Product #	Perfume Oil	Price
7880	Cinnamon	$7.00
7882	Jasmine	$7.50
7990	Marigold	$6.00
7995	Peppermint	$6.95
7998	Musk	$7.00

Compiled by Your Name

Working with Styles and Templates

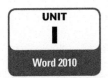

UNIT
I
Word 2010

Building Forms

Files You Will Need:

WMP I-1.jpg
WMP I-2.jpg
WMP I-3.docx
WMP I-4.jpg
WMP I-5.docx
WMP I-6.docx

Word provides the tools you need to build forms that users can complete within a Word document. A **form** is a structured document with spaces reserved for entering information. You create a form as a template that includes labeled spaces—called **content controls**—into which users type information. The form template can include a variety of content controls including Rich Text content controls, Building Block Gallery content controls, and even a Date Picker content control. Once you have created a form, you can protect it so that users can enter information into the form, but they cannot change the structure of the form itself. ▓▓▓ Tony Sanchez, RN, the office manager at Riverwalk Medical Clinic, has decided to create a Patient Summary Sheet. He wants you to create a form to collect the data. You start by creating the form template.

OBJECTIVES

Construct a form template

Add Text content controls

Add Date Picker and Check Box content controls

Add Drop-Down and Picture content controls

Add a Building Block Gallery content control

Insert Legacy Tools controls

Format and protect a form

Fill in a form as a user

Constructing a Form Template

A Word form is created as a **form template**, which contains all the components of the form. As you learned in an earlier unit, a **template** is a file that contains the basic structure of a document, such as the page layout, headers and footers, and graphic elements. The structure of a form template usually consists of a table that contains labels and two types of controls: content controls and Legacy Tools controls. A **label** is a word or phrase such as "Date" or "Patient Name" that tells people who fill in the form the kind of information required for a given field. A **control** is the placeholder that you, as the form developer, insert into the form. You insert a control to contain the data associated with the label. Figure I-1 shows a completed form template containing several different types of controls.  You need to create the basic structure of the form in Word, and then you save the document as a template to a new folder that you create.

STEPS

1. **Start Word, click the** File tab, **click** New, **then click** My templates **in the Available Templates section to open the New dialog box**

2. **Be sure** Blank Document **is selected in the Personal Templates section, click the** Template option button **in the Create New section, then click** OK
   A new document appears in the document window, and Template1 appears on the title bar.

QUICK TIP
To apply the Title style, click the More button ⬇ in the Styles group on the Home tab, then click Title.

3. **Click the** Page Layout tab, **click** Themes, **click** Concourse, **type** Patient Summary Sheet, **press** [Enter], **select the text, click the** Home tab, **then apply the Title style and center the text**

4. **Click below the title, click the** Insert tab, **click** Table, **click** Insert Table, **enter** 4 **for the number of columns and** 8 **for the number of rows, click** OK, **type** Patient Name, **press** [Tab] **twice, type** Family Physician, **select the** first three rows **of the table, then reduce the width of columns 1 and 3 as shown in Figure I-2**

QUICK TIP
To merge cells, select the cells to merge, click the Table Tools Layout tab, then click Merge Cells in the Merge group.

5. **Enter the remaining labels and merge cells to create the form shown in Figure I-3**
   Once you have created the structure for your form, you can save it as a template. First, you create a new folder to contain the template, and then you specify this folder as the location of user templates so that Word can find it.

6. **Click the** Start button **on the taskbar, click** Computer, **navigate to the drive and folder where you store your Data Files, click** New folder **on the menu bar, type** Your Name Form Templates **as the folder name, then press** [Enter]
   You set this new folder as the default location for user templates so all templates are stored automatically in the same location and so you do not need to navigate to the folder each time you save a template. A **user template** is any template that you create.

7. **Close Windows Explorer, return to Template1 in Word, click the** File tab, **click** Options, **click** Advanced, **then scroll to the bottom of the Word Options dialog box**

QUICK TIP
Write down the default location so you have the information available when you reset the File Location for User Templates to the default location.

8. **Click** File Locations, **click** User templates, **click** Modify, **navigate to the Your Name Form Templates folder, click the** Your Name Form Templates **folder, then click** OK **until you are returned to the document**

9. **Click the** Save button 🖫 **on the Quick Access toolbar, verify that "Patient Summary Sheet.dotx" appears in the File name text box, change the filename to** WMP I-Patient Summary Sheet.dotx, **then click** Save
   Word saves the template to the new folder you created.

FIGURE I-1: Form construction

Rich Text content control

Legacy Tools Text Form Field formatted to accept only an eight-digit number

Combo Box content control; a list arrow appears when users move to the field

Building Block Gallery content control contains text and a SmartArt graphic

Legacy Tools Text Form Field formatted for upper case and includes a Help message that appears on the status bar when a user moves to the field

Plain Text content control formatted with the Strong style

Date Picker content control; a calendar appears when users move to the field

Drop-Down List content control; a list arrow appears when users move to the field

Picture content control; a user can insert a picture file

Check Box content control; a check mark appears when a user clicks the box

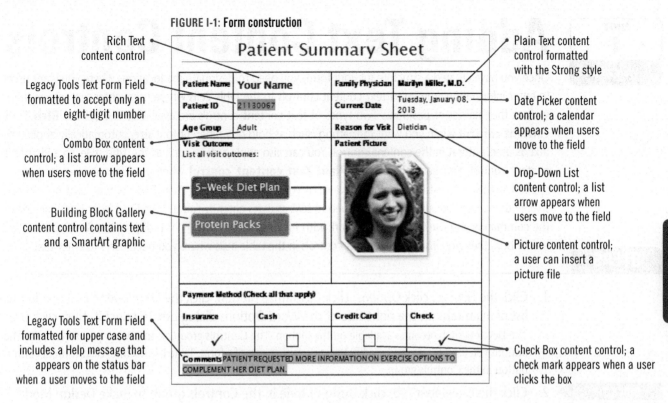

FIGURE I-2: Modifying column widths

Drag the border between columns 1 and 2 to the left

Drag the border between columns 3 and 4 to the left

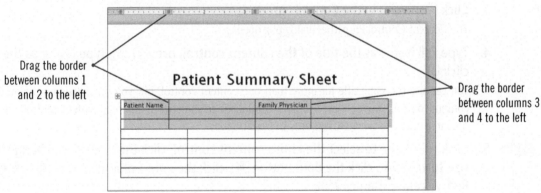

FIGURE I-3: Form with labels and merged cells

Merge cells

Merge cells

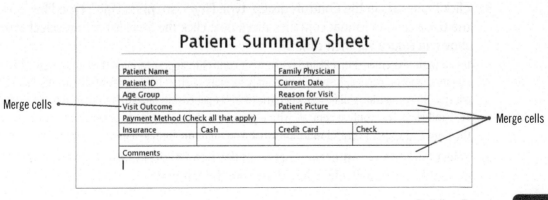

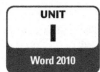

Adding Text Content Controls

Once you have created a structure for your form, you need to designate the locations where you want users to enter information. You insert text content controls in the table cells where users enter text information, such as their names or positions. Two types of text content controls are available. You use the **Rich Text content control** when you want formatting, such as bold or a different font size, automatically applied to text as users enter it in the content control. You can also apply a style, such as the Title style, to a Rich Text content control. You generally use the **Plain Text content control** when you do not need formatting applied to the text that users enter. However, if you want to format a Plain Text content control, you can specify that a style be automatically applied to text as users enter it. You use the Developer tab to access all the commands you use to create and work with forms in Word. You display the Developer tab on the Ribbon, then you insert text content controls in the table cells where you need users to enter text.

STEPS

1. **Click the** File tab, **click** Options, **click** Customize Ribbon, **click the** Developer check box **in the list of main tabs on the right side of the Word Options dialog box to select it, then click** OK

   The Developer tab becomes available on the Ribbon. The Controls group on the Developer tab contains the buttons you use to create and modify the various elements of a form. Table I-1 describes each content control button in the Controls group.

   QUICK TIP
   Design Mode must be active when you insert content controls, except Picture and Building Block Gallery content controls, into a form.

2. **Click the** Developer tab, **click** Design Mode **in the Controls group to make Design Mode active, click in the blank table cell to the right of Patient Name, then click the** Rich Text Content Control button Aa **in the Controls group**

   A Rich Text content control is inserted. When completing the form, the user will be able to enter text into this content control.

3. **Click** Properties **in the Controls group**

   The Content Control Properties dialog box opens.

4. **Type** Full Name **as the title of the content control, press** [Tab], **type** Name **as the tag, then click** OK

   You can use the same title for more than one content control, but you must assign a unique tag to each content control. The tag is used to help Word distinguish between different content controls that may have the same title. You can view tags only in Design Mode.

   QUICK TIP
   When the content control is selected, the title is dark blue and the rest of the control is shaded blue.

5. **Click** Full Name **to select the entire content control, click the** Home tab, **change the font size to** 16 point, **click the** Bold button B, **click the** Font Color list arrow A, **then select** Red, Accent 2, Darker 25%

6. **Click the** Developer tab, **select the text** Click here to enter text. **between the two tags, then type** Enter the patient's full name here. **as shown in Figure I-4**

7. **Press** [Tab] **two times to move to the blank cell to the right of Family Physician, then click the** Plain Text Content Control button Aa **in the Controls group**

8. **Click** Properties **in the Controls group, type** Physician, **press** [Tab], **type** Physician, **click the** Use a style to format contents check box, **click the** Style list arrow, **select** Strong **as shown in Figure I-5, then click** OK

   If you want text entered in a Plain Text content control to appear formatted when the user fills in the form, you must apply a paragraph style. If you apply formats, such as bold and font size, to the Plain Text content control, the formatting will be lost when the form is opened and filled in by a user. You can format both Rich Text and Plain Text content controls with a paragraph style. The Strong paragraph style that you applied to the Plain Text content control will show when you fill in the form as a user.

9. **Select** Click here to enter text. **between the two Physician tags, type** Enter N/A if the patient has no family physician, **then save the template**

Building Forms

FIGURE I-4: Rich Text content control

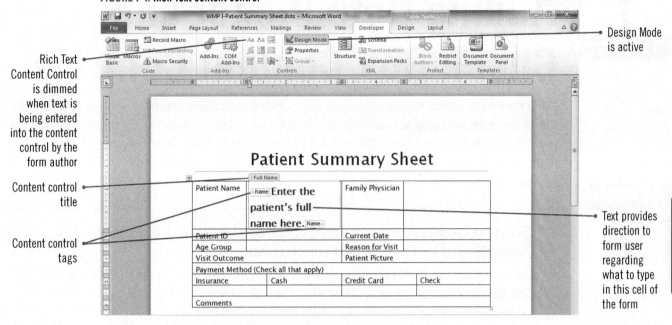

Design Mode
is active

Rich Text
Content Control
is dimmed
when text is
being entered
into the content
control by the
form author

Content control
title

Content control
tags

Text provides
direction to
form user
regarding
what to type
in this cell of
the form

Word 2010

FIGURE I-5: Content Control Properties dialog box

Title and Tag
can be the same
or different

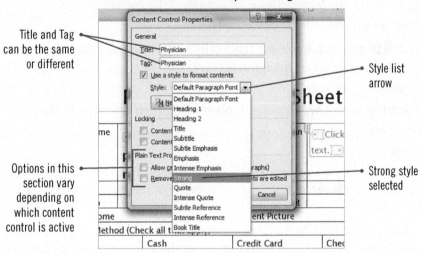

Style list
arrow

Strong style
selected

Options in this
section vary
depending on
which content
control is active

TABLE I-1: Buttons in the Controls group

button	use to
Aa	Insert a Rich Text content control when you want to apply formatting, such as bold, to text users type
Aa	Insert a Plain Text content control to apply a style to text users type or to display text as plain, unformatted text
	Insert a Picture content control when you want users to be able to insert a picture file
	Insert a Building Block Gallery content control when you want to insert a custom building block, such as a cover page or a SmartArt graphic
	Insert a Combo Box content control when you want users to select from a list or be able to add a new item
	Insert a Drop-Down List content control to provide users with a list of restricted choices
	Insert a Date Picker content control when you want to include a calendar control that users can use to select a specific date
	Insert a Check Box content control when you want to insert a check box that users can click to indicate a selection
	Insert controls from the Legacy Tools options when you want additional control over the content that can be entered into a control; if you have programming experience, you can insert ActiveX Controls into forms using the Legacy Tools button

Adding Date Picker and Check Box Content Controls

The **Date Picker content control** provides users with a calendar from which they can select a date. The **Check Box content control** inserts a check box that users can click to insert an "X" or another symbol of your choice such as a check mark. ▒▒▒▒ You want the form to include a Date Picker content control that users click to enter the current date and Check Box content controls that users can click to indicate their preferences among a selection of options.

1. **Click in the blank table cell to the right of Current Date, then click the** Date Picker Content Control button 📅 **in the Controls group**

2. **Click** Properties **in the Controls group, type** Current Date **as the title and** Date **as the tag, click the date format shown in Figure I-6, then click** OK
   You will see the calendar in a later lesson when you complete the form as a user.

3. **Select the contents of the Current Date content control, then type the message** Click the down arrow to show a calendar and select the current date.
   Users see this message when they fill in the form.

4. **Scroll to and click the blank table cell below Insurance, then click the** Check Box Content Control button ☑ **in the Controls group**
   A check box appears in the cell.

5. **Click** Properties, **type** Payment, **press [Tab], then type** Check Box

6. **Click the** Use a style to format contents check box, **click the** Style list arrow, **then select** Title
   If you want the check box to appear larger than the default size in the form, you need to modify it with a style that includes a large font size. You can also choose what character is inserted in the check box when a user clicks it.

7. **Click** Change **next to the Checked symbol label, click the** Font list arrow **in the Symbol dialog box, click** Wingdings **if that is not the active font, select the contents of the Character code text box, type** 252, **click** OK, **then click** OK
   A check mark symbol will appear in the check box when a user filling in the form clicks it.

8. **Click** Payment **to select the check box content control, press [Ctrl][C], press [→] to deselect the check box and move to the next cell (or press [→] once more if the insertion point did not move to the next cell), press [Ctrl][V], press [→], press [Ctrl][V], press [→], then press [Ctrl][V]**
   A check box appears under each of the four payment options.

9. **Use the selection pointer** ➹ **to click to the left of the row to select the entire row, press [Ctrl][E] to center each of the check boxes, click away from the selected row, then save the document**
   The Check Box and Date Picker content controls appear, as shown in Figure I-7.

Building Forms

FIGURE I-6: Selecting a date format

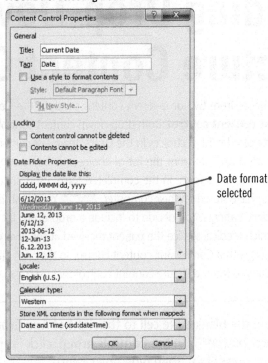

Date format
selected

FIGURE I-7: Form with the Date Picker and Check Box content controls added

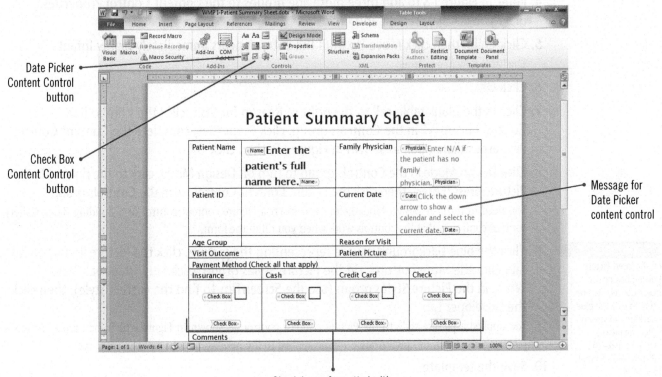

Date Picker
Content Control
button

Check Box
Content Control
button

Message for
Date Picker
content control

Check boxes formatted with
the Title style and centered

Adding Drop-Down and Picture Content Controls

You can choose from two drop-down content controls: the **Combo Box content control** and the **Drop-Down List content control**. Both drop-down content controls provide users with a list of choices. Users can only select from the list of choices in the Drop-Down List content control. In the Combo Box content control, users can select an item from the list of choices or they can type a new item. You can also insert a Picture content control into a form. In the completed form, users click the Picture content control and then insert a picture they have stored on their computer. You want to be able to identify the age range of Riverwalk Medical Clinic patients. You decide to include a drop-down list of age ranges on your form. You also want to identify which medical service the patient received at the Riverwalk Medical Clinic during his or her visit. You provide users with a Combo Box content control so they can either select an item from the list or enter a new item. Finally, you insert a Picture content control that users can use to insert a photograph of the patient.

STEPS

1. **Click in the blank table cell to the right of Age Group, click the Drop-Down List Content Control button ▦ in the Controls group, click Properties in the Controls group, type Age Group, press [Tab], then type Age Group**

2. **Click Add, type Infant, then click OK**
   "Infant" is the first choice, and it is the choice users see when they open the form.

3. **Click Add, type Teen, then click OK**

4. **Refer to Figure I-8 to add three more age groups to the Content Control Properties dialog box: Adult, Senior, and Child**

5. **Click Child, then click Move Up until the entry appears immediately below Infant**
   The list is now in age order.

6. **Click OK**

7. **Click in the blank table cell to the right of Reason for Visit, click the Combo Box Content Control button ▦ in the Controls group, click Properties, complete the Content Control Properties dialog box as shown in Figure I-9, then click OK**

8. **Click Design Mode in the Controls group to turn off Design Mode, click to the right of Patient Picture, press [Enter], then click the Picture Content Control ▤ in the Controls group**
   You need to turn off Design Mode before you insert a Picture content control or a Building Block Gallery content control so that the controls work when you fill in the form.

> **TROUBLE**
> If the Insert Picture dialog box opens, click Cancel, then be sure to click the blue background square (not the picture icon) to make the Picture Tools Format tab active.

9. **Click the blue background square representing the picture, click the Picture Tools Format tab, click the More button ▾ in the Picture Styles group, click Snip Diagonal Corner, White in the Picture Styles group (use the ScreenTips to find the correct style), then click the Developer tab**
   You applied a picture style to the Picture content control, as shown in Figure I-10. When a user inserts a picture in the form, this picture style will be applied to the inserted picture.

10. **Save the template**

FIGURE I-8: Entries for the Drop-Down List content control

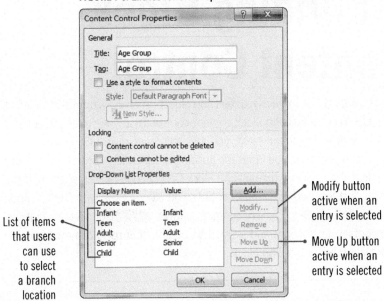

List of items
that users
can use
to select
a branch
location

Modify button
active when an
entry is selected

Move Up button
active when an
entry is selected

FIGURE I-9: Entries for the Combo Box content control

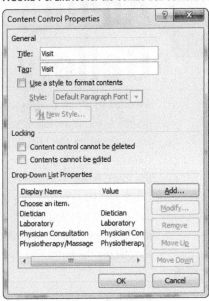

FIGURE I-10: Picture style selected

Design Mode
must be off
when inserting
a Picture
content control

Content control
tags are not
visible when
Design Mode is
turned off

Drop-Down List
content control

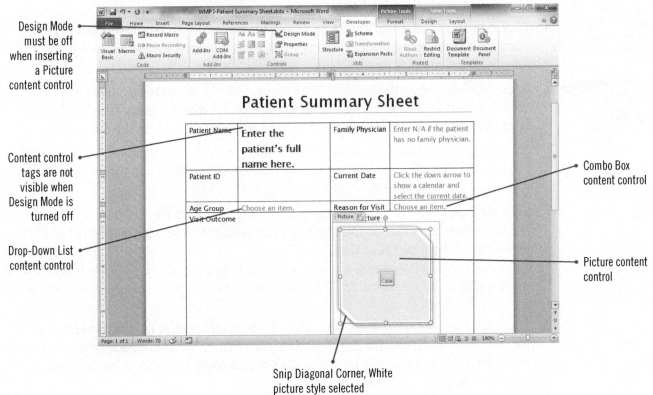

Combo Box
content control

Picture content
control

Snip Diagonal Corner, White
picture style selected

Adding a Building Block Gallery Content Control

A **Building Block Gallery content control** can contain both text and objects, such as pictures and SmartArt graphics. You must follow several steps to use a Building Block content control. First, you create the content you want to be the building block in a new document. Next, you save the content as a Quick Part to the General gallery (or any gallery of your choice). Then, you insert the Building Block Gallery content control into the form. Finally, you use the Quick Parts list arrow on the Building Block Gallery content control to insert the Quick Part you created into the form. Just like Picture content controls, you always work with Design Mode turned off when you are working with Building Block Gallery content controls. You create a Building Block Gallery content control that contains instructions and a SmartArt graphic that users can modify when they fill out the form. You start by creating a new building block.

STEPS

1. Click the File tab, click New, then click Create

   You create a new blank document that will contain the new building block you want to appear in the form.

2. Type the text List all visit outcomes:, press [Enter], click the Insert tab, click SmartArt in the Illustrations group, click List in the list of SmartArt types, click Vertical Box List as shown in Figure I-11, then click OK

   TROUBLE
   If the text pane is open, click the Text Pane button in the Create Graphics group to close the text pane.

3. Click the Change Colors button in the SmartArt Styles group, then select Colorful - Accent Colors (first selection in the Colorful section)

4. Click in the text above the SmartArt graphic, press [Ctrl][A] to select the contents of the document, click the Insert tab, click the Quick Parts list arrow in the Text group, then click Save Selection to Quick Part Gallery

   TROUBLE
   If a warning message opens, click Yes.

5. Type Visit Outcome as the building block name, click OK, save the document as WMP I-Patient Summary Building Block to the location where you save the files for this book (but *not* to the Your Name Form Templates folder), then close the document

6. Verify that WMP I-Patient Summary Sheet.dotx is the active document, click to the right of Visit Outcome, press [Enter], then verify that the Design Mode button in the Controls group on the Developer tab is not active

7. Click the Building Block Gallery Content Control button 🖼 in the Controls group, click the Quick Parts list arrow on the Building Block Gallery content control title tab as shown in Figure I-12, then click Visit Outcome

   Notice that a different color scheme is applied to the SmartArt graphic because you applied the Concourse theme to the form when you created it. The default Office theme was applied to the SmartArt graphic when you created it in a new document.

8. Click the white area just below List to select the SmartArt graphic (a gray box appears around the SmartArt graphic to indicate it is selected), scroll down if necessary, then drag the lower-right corner handle up and to the left to change the width of the SmartArt graphic to about 3" as shown in Figure I-13

9. Click outside the SmartArt graphic, then save the template

FIGURE I-11: Selecting the Vertical Box List SmartArt graphic

List type

Vertical Box List

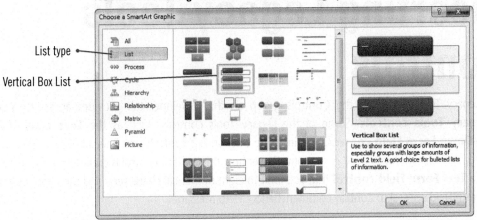

FIGURE I-12: Selecting the Visit Outcome building block

Design Mode must be turned off when inserting a Building Block content control

Quick Parts list arrow

Visit Outcome building block (you may see other building blocks in the General section)

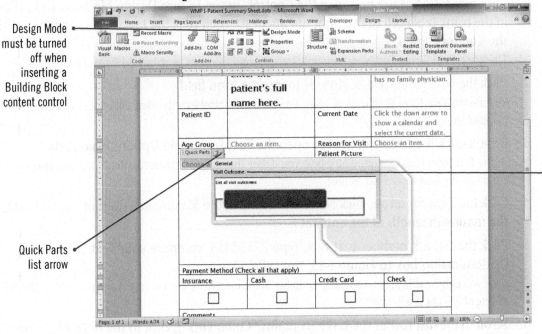

FIGURE I-13: Resizing the Visit Outcome building block

Drag the lower-right sizing handle up to reduce the size of the SmartArt graphic to about 3"

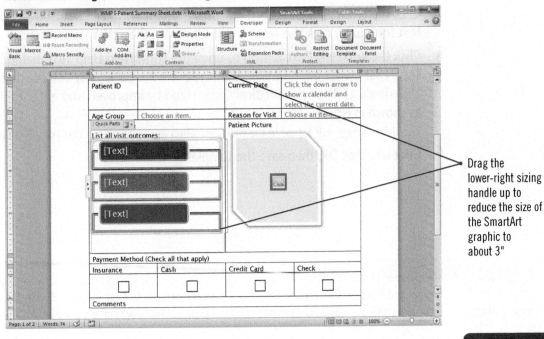

Inserting Legacy Tools Controls

The Legacy Tools button in the Controls group on the Developer tab provides access to a selection of **Legacy Tools controls**. Some of the Legacy Tools controls, such as the **Text control** and the **Drop-Down Form Field control**, are similar to the content controls you have already worked with. You use Legacy Tools when you need more control over how the content control is configured. First, you insert a **Text Form Field control** that you limit to eight numerical characters, and then you insert another Text Form Field control to contain comments and a Help message.

STEPS

1. **Click the** Design Mode button **in the Controls group to turn Design Mode back on, click in the blank table cell to the right of Patient ID, then click the** Legacy Tools button 🖳- **in the Controls group**

    The selection of Legacy Forms controls and ActiveX controls opens, as shown in Figure I-14.

2. **Click the** Text Form Field button abl **to insert a form field**

    You use the Text Form Field control when you need to control exactly what data a user can enter into the placeholder.

3. **Double-click the** text form field **to open the Text Form Field Options dialog box**

    In the Text Form Field Options dialog box, you define the type and characteristics of the data that users can enter into the Text Form Field control.

4. **Click the** Type list arrow, **click** Number, **then click the** Maximum length up arrow **to set the maximum length of the entry at** 8

5. **Click the** Default number text box, **type** 22334455, **compare your Text Form Field Options dialog box to Figure I-15, then click** OK

    Users will only be able to enter an 8-digit number in the form field. If users do not enter a number, the default setting of 22334455 will appear.

6. **Scroll to the last row of the table (contains "Comments"), click to the right of Comments, then press** [Spacebar]

7. **Click the** Legacy Tools button 🖳-, **click the** Text Form Field button abl, **double-click the** text form field, **click the** Text format list arrow, **then click** Uppercase

8. **Click the** Add Help Text button **to open the Form Field Help Text dialog box, click the** Type your own: option button, **then type** Ask the patient to describe how the patient experience at Riverwalk Medical Clinic could be improved and enter the comments here. **as shown in Figure I-16**

    The Help message will appear in the status bar when users click in the Text Form Field control.

9. **Click** OK, **click** OK, **then save the template**

ActiveX controls

The Legacy Tools button also provides you with access to ActiveX controls. You can use these controls to offer options to users or to run macros or scripts that automate specific tasks. You need to have some experience with programming to use most of the ActiveX controls.

FIGURE I-14: Inserting a Text Form Field control

Text Form
Field button

Legacy
Tools button

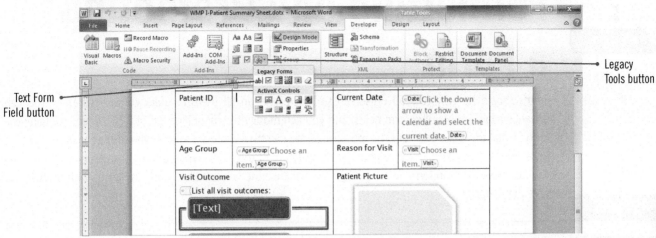

FIGURE I-15: Text Form Field Options dialog box

Type list arrow

Up arrow

22334455 entered as
the Default number

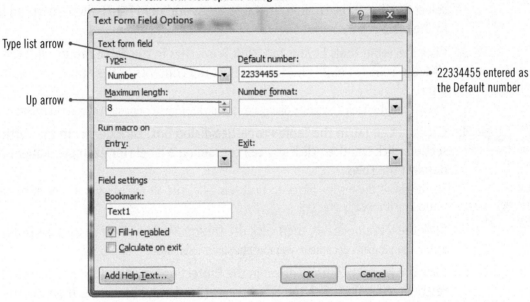

FIGURE I-16: Adding Help text

Type your own
option button

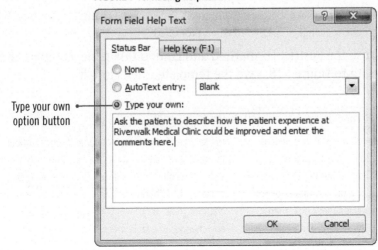

UNIT
I
Word 2010

Formatting and Protecting a Form

Forms should be easy to read on-screen so that users can fill them in quickly and accurately. You can enhance a table containing form fields, and you can modify the magnification of a document containing a form so that users can easily see the form fields. You can then protect a form so that users can enter only the data required but are *not* able to change the structure of the form. When a form is protected, information can be entered only in form fields. ▓▓▓ You enhance the field labels, modify the form, then protect and save the template.

STEPS

> **QUICK TIP**
> Instead of using the Format Painter, you can use the [Ctrl] key to select each label, then click the Bold button.

1. **Scroll up and select** Patient Name **in the first cell of the table, click the** Home tab, **click the** Bold button **B** **in the Font group, double-click the** Format Painter button ✒, **then use the Format Painter to enhance all the field labels with bold**

2. **Click the** Format Painter button ✒ **to turn off formatting, reduce the zoom to** 60%, **select the first three rows in the table, press and hold [Ctrl], then select the last four rows in the table**

3. **Click the** Table Tools Layout tab, **click** Properties **in the Table group, click the** Row tab, **click the** Specify height check box, **select the contents of the** Specify height text box, **then type** .45
   You work in the Table Properties dialog box to quickly format nonadjacent rows in a table.

> **TROUBLE**
> Don't worry that the table has extended to two pages. It will fit on one page when Design Mode is turned off.

4. **Click the** Cell tab **in the Table Properties dialog box, click** Center **in the Vertical alignment section, click** OK, **then click any cell containing a label (for example, Patient Name) to deselect the rows**
   The height of the rows is increased to at least .45", and all the labels and content controls are centered vertically within each table cell.

5. **Click the** Developer tab, **then click the** Design Mode button **to turn off Design Mode**
   Before you protect a document, you must be sure Design Mode is turned off.

6. **Click the** Restrict Editing button **in the Protect group, click the** check box **in the Editing restrictions section, click the** No changes (Read only) list arrow, **then click** Filling in forms **as shown in Figure I-17**

7. **Click** Yes, Start Enforcing Protection

8. **Type** cengage, **press [Tab], then type** cengage
   You enter a password so that a user cannot unprotect the form and change its structure. You can only edit the form if you enter the "cengage" password when prompted.

9. **Click** OK, **close the Restrict Formatting and Editing task pane, compare the completed form template to Figure I-18, save the template, then close it**

Protecting documents with formatting and editing restrictions

You protect a form so that users can enter data only in designated areas. You can also protect a document. To protect a document, click the Developer tab, click the Restrict Editing button, then choose the restriction settings you wish to apply. To restrict formatting, you click the Limit formatting to a selection of styles check box, then click Settings. You then choose the styles that you do not want users to use when formatting a document. For example, you can choose to prevent users from using the Heading 1 style or some of the table styles. For editing restrictions, you can specify that users may only make tracked changes or insert comments, or you can select No changes (read only) when you want to prevent users from making any changes to a document.

Building Forms

FIGURE I-17: Protecting a form

Design Mode must be turned off before protecting a form

Restrict Editing must be selected to protect a form

Filling in Forms selected

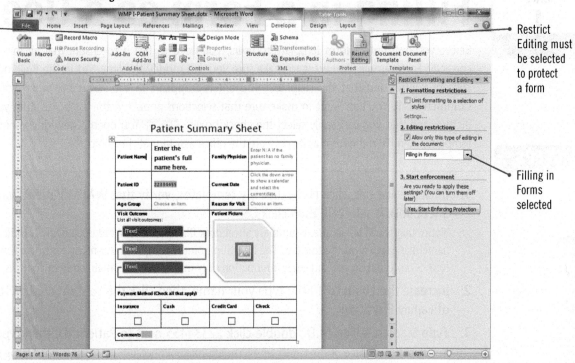

Word 2010

FIGURE I-18: Completed form template

Patient Summary Sheet

Patient Name	Enter the patient's full name here.	Family Physician	Enter N/A if the patient has no family physician.
Patient ID	22334455	Current Date	Click the down arrow to show a calendar and select the current date.
Age Group	Choose an item.	Reason for Visit	Choose an item.

Visit Outcome
List all visit outcomes:

[Text]

[Text]

[Text]

Patient Picture

Payment Method (Check all that apply)

Insurance	Cash	Credit Card	Check
☐	☐	☐	☐

Comments

Filling in a Form as a User

Before you distribute a form template to users, you need to test it to ensure that all the elements work correctly. For example, you want to make sure you can modify the SmartArt in the Building Block Gallery content control and that the Help text you entered appears in the status bar when you move to the Comments cell. You also want to make sure that selections appear in the list boxes, that you can insert a picture, and that you can easily select the check boxes. ▓▓▓▓ You open a new document based on the template, then fill in the form as if you were the office assistant at the clinic.

STEPS

1. **Click the File tab, click New, click My templates, verify that WMP I-Patient Summary Sheet.dotx is selected, then click OK**

   Notice that the WMP I-Patient Summary Sheet.dotx file opens as a Word document, as indicated by the filename that appears on the title bar. The insertion point highlights the content control following Name. The form is protected, so you can enter information only in spaces that contain content controls or check boxes.

2. **Increase the zoom to 100%, type your name, then click the content control to the right of Family Physician**

3. **Type Marilyn Miller, M.D., double-click 22334455 next to Patient ID, then type 21130067**

   Notice how the name of the family physician appears bold because you applied the Strong style when you inserted the Plain Text content control.

QUICK TIP
Users could also click the content control and type a new reason for visit because the content control is a Combo Box content control.

4. **Click the content control to the right of Current Date, click the down arrow, click the left arrow or right arrow to move to January 2013 as shown in Figure I-19, then click 8**

   The date of Tuesday, January 08, 2013, is entered.

5. **Click the content control to the right of Age Group, click the list arrow, click Adult, click the content control to the right of Reason for Visit, click the list arrow, then click Dietician**

TROUBLE
Be sure to click the frame of the blue box that contains the placeholder [Text] to select the entire box.

6. **Click the red box in the SmartArt graphic, type 5-Week Diet Plan, click the orange box, type Protein Packs, click the blue box frame, then press [Delete]**

   You can choose to remove boxes that you do not need for a particular patient. You can also add a new box by opening the text pane, clicking after a main entry, and then pressing [Enter].

7. **Click the picture icon 🖾 in the Picture content control in the Patient Picture cell, navigate to the drive and folder where you store your Data Files, then double-click WMP I-1.jpg**

8. **Click the check box below Insurance, click the check box below Check, verify that the insertion point appears next to Comments, note the message that appears on the status bar, then type the comment text shown in Figure I-20, noting that it will appear in lower case as you type**

9. **Press [Tab] to view the text in uppercase, switch to 60% view, compare the completed form to Figure I-21, save the document with the name WMP I-Patient Summary Sheet_Completed to the drive and folder where you save your files for this book, submit the file to your instructor, then close the document**

Editing a form template

Before you can edit a form template, you need to unprotect it. Open the form template, click the Developer tab, click the Restrict Editing button in the Protect group, click Stop Protection, then enter the correct password, if prompted. You can make changes to the structure of the form by inserting new controls and labels, and modifying the formatting. You protect the form again, and then save the template.

FIGURE I-19: Selecting the date

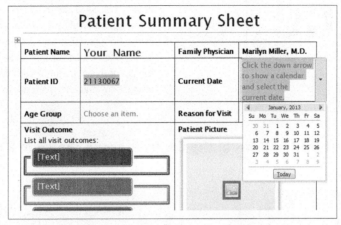

FIGURE I-20: Comment entry

Help text appears on the status bar

FIGURE I-21: Completed form

Patient Summary Sheet

Patient Name	Your Name	Family Physician	Marilyn Miller, M.D.
Patient ID	21130067	Current Date	Tuesday, January 08, 2013
Age Group	Adult	Reason for Visit	Dietician

Visit Outcome
List all visit outcomes:

5-Week Diet Plan

Protein Packs

Patient Picture

Payment Method (Check all that apply)

Insurance	Cash	Credit Card	Check
✓	☐	☐	✓

Comments PATIENT REQUESTED MORE INFORMATION ON EXERCISE OPTIONS TO COMPLEMENT HER DIET PLAN.

Practice

Concepts Review

For current SAM information, including versions and content details, visit SAM Central (http://www.cengage.com/samcentral). If you have a SAM user profile, you may have access to hands-on instruction, practice, and assessment of the skills covered in this unit. Since various versions of SAM are supported throughout the life of this text, check with your instructor for the correct instructions and URL/Web site for accessing assignments.

Identify each of the numbered buttons in the Controls group shown in Figure I-22.

FIGURE I-22

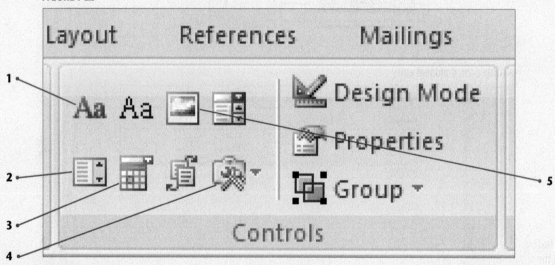

Match each term with the statement that best describes it.

6. **Rich Text content control**
7. **Design Mode**
8. **Date Picker content control**
9. **Combo box content control**
10. **Building Block Gallery content control**
11. **Drop-Down List content control**

a. Use to provide users with a list of items to click
b. Can be formatted with font and paragraph enhancements
c. Use to insert a calendar control
d. Deselect before protecting a document
e. Use to insert a document building block
f. Use to provide users with a list and space to type a new entry

Select the best answer from the list of choices.

12. **Which of the following statements best describes the purpose of a Rich Text or Plain Text content control?**
    a. A code visible only in Design Mode
    b. A placeholder for text such as a user's name
    c. A control that, when clicked, shows a list of options that the user can select
    d. A word or phrase such as "Name" or "Location" that tells users the kind of information required for a given field
13. **What happens when you click the list arrow next to a Date Picker content control in a form?**
    a. A blank box appears.
    b. A calendar grid appears.
    c. The current date appears.
    d. A dialog box opens where you can select a date.
14. **Which button do you click to open a task pane with options for protecting a form?**
    a. Protect Mode
    b. Restrict Editing
    c. Design Mode
    d. Form Design

Skills Review

1. Construct a form template.

a. Start Word, click the File tab, click Save As, click the Save as type list arrow in the Save As dialog box and select Word Template, navigate to the Your Name Form Templates folder, type **WMP I-Change of Grade Notification** as the filename, then click Save.

b. Refer to Figure I-23. Type **Change of Grade Notification**, press [Enter], enhance the text with the Title style, then change the Style Set to Formal.

c. Create a table that has 4 columns and 13 rows.

d. Type the text and merge cells as shown in Figure I-23, then save the template.

FIGURE I-23

CHANGE OF GRADE NOTIFICATION

Student Name		Student Picture	
Date			
Student Number			
Course Number			
Course Title			
Original Letter Grade	Revised Letter Grade	Program Profile	
A	A		
B	B		
C	C		
D	D		
F	F		
Grade Change Reason			
Comments			

2. Add Text content controls.

a. Show the Developer tab on the Ribbon if it is not already available, then turn on Design Mode.

b. Insert a Rich Text content control in the table cell to the right of Student Name.

c. In the Properties dialog box for the content control, type **First and Last Name** as the title and **Name** as the tag, exit the Properties dialog box, then click the Home tab.

d. Select the entire control, change the font size to 14 point, then change the font color to Blue, Accent 1, Darker 25%.

e. Between the two Name tags, enter **Type the student's full name here.** in the content control.

f. Click the Developer tab, click in the blank cell to the right of Grade Change Reason in the second to last row of the table, then insert a Plain Text content control.

g. In the Properties dialog box, enter **Description of Change** as the title and **Description** as the tag, then specify that the text be formatted with the Intense Emphasis style.

h. Between the two Description tags, type **Enter the reason for the grade change here.**, then save the template.

3. **Add Date Picker and Check Box content controls.**
   a. Insert a Date Picker content control in the blank cell to the right of Date.
   b. In the Properties dialog box, enter **Current Date** as the title and **Date** as the tag, then change the date format to the format that corresponds to March 18, 2013.
   c. Between the two Date tags, type the message **Click the down arrow to show a calendar, then select the date of the last day of term.**
   d. Insert a space and a Check Box content control to the right of "A" in the Original Letter Grade column, enter **Grade** for the Title and Tag, then apply the Heading 1 style to the Check Box content control.
   e. Change the Checked symbol to Character code 251 from the Wingdings font.
   f. Use Copy and Paste to insert a space and a Check Box content control to the right of each of the remaining letters in the Original Letter Grade and Revised Letter Grade columns.
   g. Select the cells containing the letter grade headings and grades, then center the contents.

4. **Add Drop-Down and Picture content controls.**
   a. Insert a Combo Box content control in the blank cell to the right of Course Title.
   b. In the Properties dialog box, enter **Course Title** as the title and **Title** as the tag.
   c. Add the following entries: **Medical Transcription**, **Clinical Procedures**, **Anatomy and Related Physiology**, **Computerized Medical Billing**, and **Pharmacology**.
   d. Use the Move Up and Move Down commands to put the list of courses in alphabetical order.
   e. Insert a Drop-Down List content control in the blank cell to the right of Course Number.
   f. In the Properties dialog box, enter **Course Number** as the title and tag, add the following entries: **100**, **150**, **200**, **220**, **300**, then save the template.
   g. Turn off Design Mode, then in the blank cell below Student Picture, insert a Picture content control.
   h. Click the picture placeholder, apply the Metal Frame picture style, then save the template.

5. **Add a Building Block Gallery content control.**
   a. Create a new blank document.
   b. Type **Enter the courses in the program in the spaces provided.**, then apply the Formal style set.
   c. On the next line, insert a SmartArt graphic using the Target List type from the List category (in the last line of the selection of graphics in the List category).
   d. Apply the Cartoon SmartArt style, then apply the Colorful Range - Accent Colors 4 to 5 color scheme.
   e. Click the text above the SmartArt graphic, then press [Ctrl][A] to select all the text and the SmartArt graphic.
   f. Save the selection to the Quick Parts gallery as a building block called **Program Profile**.
   g. Save the document as **WMP I-Medical Office Assistant Program Building Block** to the drive and folder where you save your files for this book (but *not* to the Your Name Form Template folder), then close the document.
   h. Verify that Design Mode is not active, then insert a Building Block Gallery content control in the blank cell below Program Profile in the form template.
   i. Use the Quick Parts list arrow to select Program Profile, then use your mouse to reduce the size of the SmartArt graphic. It should fit the space in column 3 so that the widths of column 1 and column 2 are similar. Be sure the form fits on one page. The SmartArt graphic will be approximately 3" wide and 1" high. You may need to reduce the zoom so that you can see and then resize the graphic.
   j. Save the template.

6. **Insert Legacy Tools controls.**
   a. Turn on Design Mode, then insert a Text Form Field control from the Legacy Tools in the blank cell to the right of Student Number.
   b. Double-click the control to open the Text Form Field Options dialog box, change the type to Number, change the Maximum length to **7**, then enter **1234567** as the default.
   c. Insert a Text Form Field control from the Legacy Tools in the blank cell to the right of Comments.
   d. Specify that the format should be uppercase, then add the help text: **Provide additional details if necessary.**
   e. Save the template.

Skills Review (continued)

7. **Format and protect a form.**
   a. Turn off Design Mode, then apply bold to all the labels in the form template.
   b. Change the view to 60%, select the table, then change the row height to at least .4".
   c. Vertically center text in all the cells. (*Hint*: Use the Cell tab in the Table Properties dialog box.)
   d. Protect the document for users filling in forms using the password **skills**, close the Restrict Formatting and Editing task pane, then save and close the template.

8. **Fill in a form as a user.**
   a. Start a new blank document based on the WMP I-Change of Grade Notification.dotx template, then complete the form as shown in Figure I-24. Insert WMP I-2.jpg (or your own picture if you wish) in the Picture content control. (*Hint*: To add a fourth bullet to the SmartArt graphic, type "Pharmacology" for the third bullet, open the text pane, click after "Pharmacology", press [Enter], then type "Anatomy".)
   b. Save the document as **WMP I-Change of Grade Notification_Completed** to the drive and folder where you store your files for this book, submit the file to your instructor, then close the document.

FIGURE I-24

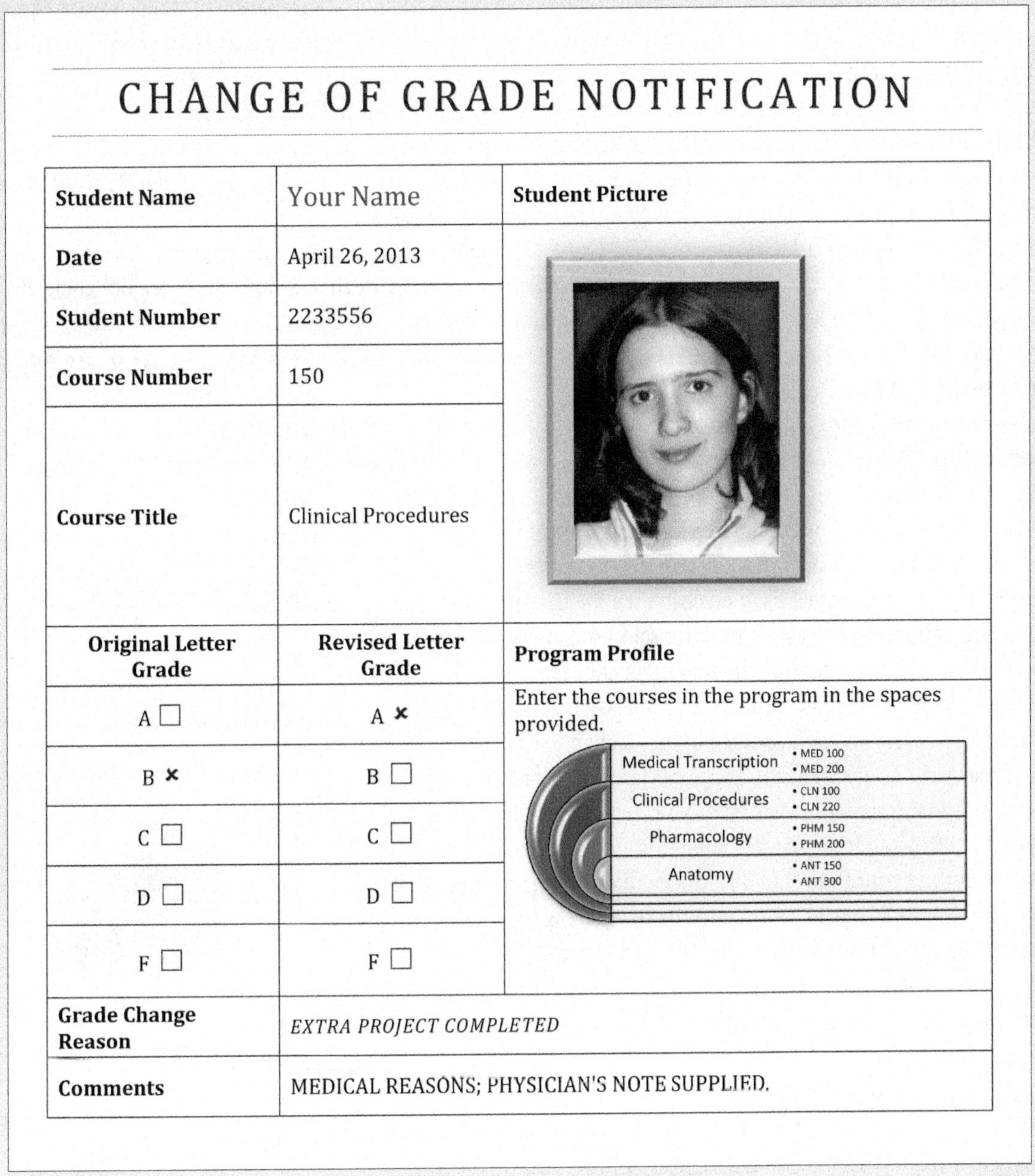

Independent Challenge 1

You work in the Administration Department at Maplewood General Hospital in Portland, Oregon. Several hospital administrators and senior medical staff have begun taking trips to hospitals around the world to investigate innovative programs in a variety of medical areas. Your supervisor asks you to create an itinerary form that administrators can complete online to help them keep track of their travel details.

a. Start Word and open the file WMP I-3.docx from the drive and folder where you store your Data Files. Save it as a template called **WMP I-Itinerary Form** to the Your Name Form Templates folder that you created when you completed the lessons in this unit. (Refer to the first lesson in this unit, if necessary.)

b. Make Design Mode on the Developer tab active, then insert a Rich Text content control in the blank table cell to the right of the Name label. Enter **Full Name** as the title and **Name** as the tag, then format the control with 14 pt, bold, and italic.

c. Insert a Date Picker control in the blank table cell to the right of Report Date. Enter **Date** as the title and tag, then select the date format that corresponds with June 30, 2013.

d. Click the Date content control title bar, then copy the content control to each of the seven cells in column 1 below the Date label.

e. Insert a Drop-Down List content control in the blank table cell to the right of Department. Enter **Department** as the title and tag, then add three selections: **Surgical**, **Research**, and **Human Resources**. Put the three entries in alphabetical order.

f. Insert a Text Form Field content control from the Legacy Tools in the blank table cell to the right of Extension. Specify the type as Number, a Maximum length of **3**, and **200** as the Default number.

g. Insert a Plain Text content control in the blank table cell to the right of Purpose of Travel. Enter **Travel Purpose** for the title and **Travel** for the tag, then apply the Intense Emphasis style.

h. Insert a Drop-Down List content control in the blank table cell to the right of Location. Enter **Location** as the title and tag, add three selections: **North America**, **Europe**, and **Asia**, then arrange them in alphabetical order.

i. Insert a Combo Box content control in the first cell below Category. Enter **Category** as the title and tag, then add three selections: **Transportation**, **Hotel**, and **Meeting**. Enter the text **Choose an item or type a new item** between the two tags.

j. Copy the content control, then paste it into each of the next six cells in the Category column.

k. Insert a Plain Text content control in the first cell below Details. Enter **Details** as the title and tag, change the style to Subtle Emphasis, then copy the control and paste it into each of the next six cells in the Details column.

l. Exit Design Mode, then insert a Picture content control in the blank cell to the right of Picture of Location. Apply the Drop Shadow Rectangle picture style.

m. Apply bold to all the form labels, then center the three labels: Date, Category, and Details.

n. Protect the form using the Filling in forms selection, enter **challenge1** as the password, then save and close the template.

o. Open a new document based on the template, then complete the form as if you were an administrator in the Human Resources department and had travelled to Paris on May 6, 2013, to explore French hospital funding models. Type your name in the Name content control and insert WMP I-4.jpg from the drive and folder where you store your Data Files into the Picture content control. Type any extension starting with 2. In the rows below the picture, enter details about transportation, hotels, and meetings for a trip to Paris. Type a least one category (for example, Food) that is not included in the list of Category options. You don't have to make an entry for each line.

p. Save the form as **WMP I-Itinerary_Paris**, submit a copy to your instructor, then close the document. An example of a completed Itinerary form is shown in Figure I-25.

FIGURE I-25

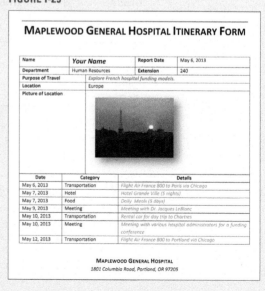

MAPLEWOOD GENERAL HOSPITAL ITINERARY FORM

Name	*Your Name*	Report Date	May 6, 2013
Department	Human Resources	Extension	240
Purpose of Travel	*Explore French hospital funding models.*		
Location	Europe		
Picture of Location			

Date	Category	Details
May 6, 2013	Transportation	*Flight Air France 800 to Paris via Chicago*
May 7, 2013	Hotel	*Hotel Grande Ville (5 nights)*
May 7, 2013	Food	*Daily Meals (5 days)*
May 9, 2013	Meeting	*Meeting with Dr. Jacques LeBlanc*
May 10, 2013	Transportation	*Rental car for day trip to Chartres*
May 10, 2013	Meeting	*Meeting with various hospital administrators for a funding conference*
May 12, 2013	Transportation	*Flight Air France 800 to Portland via Chicago*

MAPLEWOOD GENERAL HOSPITAL
1801 Columbia Road, Portland, OR 97205

Independent Challenge 2

You are the Office Manager for the Ontario Regional Health Center, a medical facility that has just instituted parking regulations for staff wanting to park in the new staff parking lot. Any staff member who wants to park in the lot must purchase a parking permit. You decide to create a Word form that staff members complete to purchase a parking permit. You create the form as a Word template saved on the company's network. Staffers can open a new Word document based on the template, then complete the form in Word, or they can print the form and fill it in by hand.

a. Start Word and open the file WMP I-5.docx from the drive and folder where you store your Data Files. Save it as a template called **WMP I-Parking Permit Requisition** to the Your Name Form Templates folder that you created when you completed the lessons in this unit. (Refer to the first lesson in this unit, if necessary.)

b. Be sure Design Mode on the Developer tab is active, then insert content controls with appropriate titles and tags (you choose) as follows:

Location	Content Control
Date	Date Picker content control using the 5-May-13 format
Name	Plain Text content control formatted with the style of your choice
Department	Drop-Down List content control with four entries (for example, Surgical, Outpatient) in alphabetical order
Extension	Plain Text content control formatted with the style of your choice
Staff, Administration, etc.	Check Box content control in each of the four Status cells formatted with the Heading 1 style and using the check mark symbol of your choice

c. Exit Design Mode, center the check boxes in all four of the Status cells, then apply bold to all the labels.

Advanced Challenge Exercise

- Add a new row at the bottom of the form, enter **Payment** in the first cell, then apply bold if necessary.
- Select the next four blank cells, click the Clear Formatting button on the Home tab, merge the four cells into one cell, then split the newly merged cell into three cells. (*Note*: This process creates three cells of equal width, independent of the cells above them.)
- Click in the second cell in the last row, click the Design Mode button on the Developer tab to turn it on, show the selection of Legacy Tools, then click the Option Button (ActiveX Control) button in the ActiveX Controls section. (*Note*: In a form containing a selection of option buttons, users can select just one button.)
- Click the Properties button, widen the Properties panel as needed to see all the text in column 2, select the OptionButton1 text next to Caption in the list of properties, then type **Payroll**.
- Repeat the procedure to insert two more ActiveX option button controls in cells 3 and 4 with the captions **Debit** and **Cash**.
- Close the Properties panel.
- Click the Design Mode button to exit design mode, save the template, then answer yes if a message regarding macros appears.
- Select the row containing the option buttons, then increase its height to .5" with center vertical alignment.

d. Protect the form for filling in forms, click OK to bypass password protection when prompted, then save and close the template.

e. Open a new document based on the template, then complete the form as a user with appropriate information you provide.

Independent Challenge 2 (continued)

f. Save the document as **WMP I-Parking Requisition_Completed** to the drive and folder where you store your files for this book, submit a copy to your instructor, close the document, then exit Word. Examples of completed Parking Requisition Forms are shown in Figure I-26.

FIGURE I-26

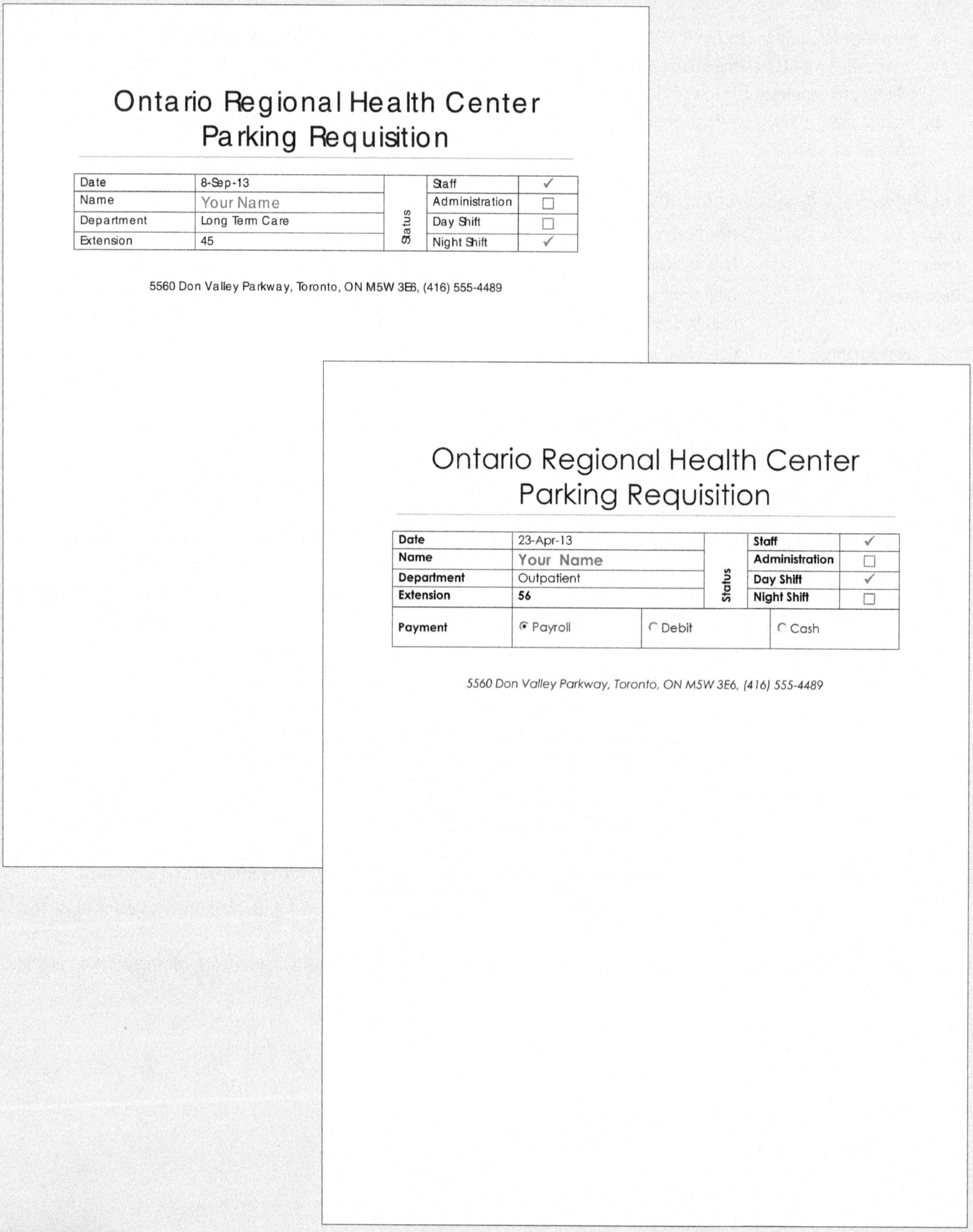

Ontario Regional Health Center
Parking Requisition

Date	8-Sep-13		Staff	✓
Name	Your Name		Administration	☐
Department	Long Term Care	Status	Day Shift	☐
Extension	45		Night Shift	✓

5560 Don Valley Parkway, Toronto, ON M5W 3E6, (416) 555-4489

Ontario Regional Health Center
Parking Requisition

Date	23-Apr-13		Staff	✓
Name	Your Name		Administration	☐
Department	Outpatient	Status	Day Shift	✓
Extension	56		Night Shift	☐
Payment	⊙ Payroll	○ Debit	○ Cash	

5560 Don Valley Parkway, Toronto, ON M5W 3E6, (416) 555-4489

Independent Challenge 3

You work as a Medical Office Assistant in the Reception area of Grace Hospital in Denver, CO. Your supervisor has asked you to create a form that you can use to collect information from patients about their experience at the hospital.

a. Start Word and open the file WMP I-6.docx from the drive and folder where your Data Files are located. Save it as a template called **WMP I-Feedback Form** to the Your Name Form Templates folder that you created when you completed the lessons in this unit. (Refer to the first lesson in this unit, if necessary.)

b. Switch to Design Mode, then insert and format controls as described below using titles and tags of your choice:

Location	Content Control
Name	Rich Text content control formatted with Heading 1
Current Date	Date Picker content control using the date format of your choice
Room #	Text Form Field content control from Legacy Tools that specifies Number as the type, a maximum length of 4 digits and a default number of **4455**.
Physician	Combo Box content control with the names of four physicians (for example, Mary Prentiss, M.D.; Doreen Jefferson, M.D; etc.), include the text **Select a physician or enter a new physician**. between the form tags as a direction to users.
Rankings	Check Box content control in each of the 16 blank cells for the ranking of course elements. Format the content controls with the Heading 1 style, and select the check mark character of your choice. (*Hint*: Insert and modify the first check box content control, then copy and paste it to the remaining table cells.)

c. Save the template, then create a new blank document.

d. Type the text: **Enter three words that summarize your experience at Grace Hospital.**

e. Press [Enter], then insert the Converging Radial SmartArt graphic from the Relationship category.

f. Type **Grace Hospital** in the circle shape, then apply the SmartArt style and color of your choice.

g. Select all the text and the SmartArt graphic, then save it as a building block called **Hospital Evaluation** in the Quick Parts gallery in the General category. (*Hint*: Be sure to click in the text above the SmartArt and use [Ctrl][A] to select all content for the building block.)

h. Save the Word document as **WMP I-Feedback Building Block** to the location where you save files for this book (but not to the Your Name Form Templates folder), then close the document.

i. In the form template, turn off Design Mode, insert a Building Block Gallery content control in the last row of the table, then select the Hospital Evaluation building block.

j. Reduce the size of the SmartArt graphic so it fills the row without overlapping the edges of the table and the entire form remains on one page.

k. Select the entire table, then change the cell alignment so all the text is centered vertically.

l. Use the Center button on the Home tab to center all the check boxes in relation to the numbers above them.

Advanced Challenge Exercise

- Turn on Design Mode, then delete one of the physicians from the Combo Box content control.
- Apply the table style of your choice to the entire table; experiment with the table style options (Header Row, Banded Columns, etc.) until you are satisfied with the appearance of your form.
- Turn off Design Mode, then make adjustments as needed to ensure the form remains on one page.

m. Protect the form for filling in forms, click OK to bypass password protection when prompted, then save and close the template.

n. Open a new document based on the template, then complete the form as a user with appropriate information you provide.

Independent Challenge 3 (continued)

o. Save the document as **WMP I-Feedback Form_Completed** to the drive and folder where you store the files for this book, submit it to your instructor, then close the document. Examples of completed Feedback Forms are shown in Figure I-27.

FIGURE I-27

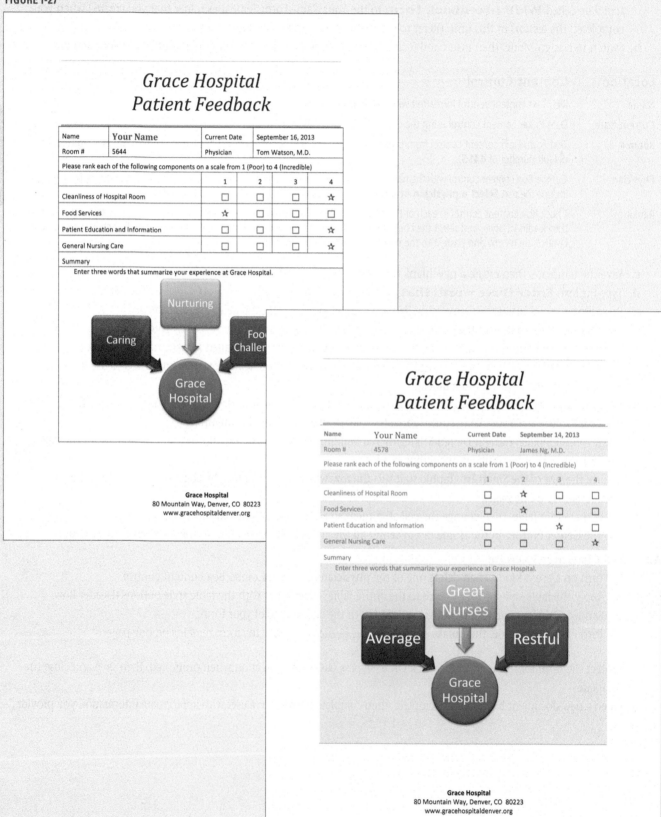

Building Forms

Real Life Independent Challenge

This Independent Challenge requires an Internet connection.

Microsoft Word includes a large number of healthcare form templates that you can adapt to meet the needs of your organization. You can learn a great deal about form design by studying how the form templates are constructed. To complete this independent challenge, you decide to find and complete one of the healthcare form templates included with Microsoft Word.

  a. Open Word, click the File tab, click New, click Forms in the list of document types in the Office.com Templates section, then explore the various categories and forms available.

  b. Click Medical and healthcare forms, scroll to and click the Medical office registration form (online), then click Download. The form was created with controls from the Legacy Tools selection. (*Note*: If the form you downloaded does not contain form fields, close the form without saving it, then download the online version of the Medical office registration form.)

  c. Enter the name of a practice or physician where indicated at the top of the document in the [Name of Practice] placeholder, then increase the font size to 16 point.

  d. Protect the form using the filling in forms setting, password protect the form or click OK to bypass password protection, then save the document as a template called **WMP I-Registration Form** to the Your Name Form Templates folder. Answer OK at the prompt.

  e. Close the template, then start a new document based on the template.

  f. Type your last name, first name, and middle name in the corresponding content controls, then complete the form with appropriate information (you can make up information and omit some information, but include your name in the Name fields). Save the form as **WMP I-Registration Form_Completed** and submit it to your instructor, then close the form. (*Note*: You can use the [Tab] key to move from field to field in a form created with Legacy Tools controls.)

Visual Workshop

You work in Laboratory Services at Deep Cove Medical Clinic. You create a simple form that hospital workers can complete online. Start Word, then save the document as a template named **WMP I-Film Request Form** to the Your Name Form Templates folder. Create and enhance the form shown in Figure I-28. Apply the Executive theme. The items in the drop-down list for Job Title are **ER Physician**, **Pediatric Nurse**, **Surgeon**, and **Triage Nurse**. The items in the drop-down list for Films are **CT Scan**, **MRI**, **Ultrasound**, and **X-rays**. Use the HH:mm format for the Time required field. (*Hint*: The field must be a Text Form Field content control from Legacy Tools. Select the Date type, and then select the HH:mm time format.) Select the Intense Emphasis style for the Special Instructions Plain Text content control. After inserting each check box content control, press the [Spacebar] once, then type the label ("Pick Up", "Delivery," etc.). Set the Before and After spacing for the entire table to 6 pt. Protect the form, close the template, then create a new document based on the template. Complete the form as shown in Figure I-29. Save the completed form as **WMP I-Film Request Form_Completed**, submit a copy to your instructor, then close the document.

FIGURE I-28

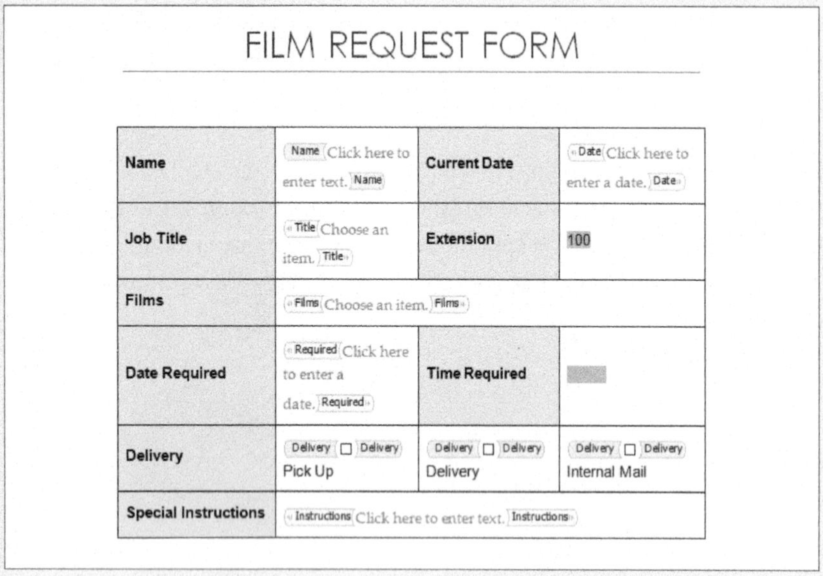

FILM REQUEST FORM

Name	Name Click here to enter text. Name	**Current Date**	Date Click here to enter a date. Date
Job Title	Title Choose an item. Title	**Extension**	100
Films	Films Choose an item. Films		
Date Required	Required Click here to enter a date. Required	**Time Required**	
Delivery	Delivery ☐ Delivery Pick Up	Delivery ☐ Delivery Delivery	Delivery ☐ Delivery Internal Mail
Special Instructions	Instructions Click here to enter text. Instructions		

FIGURE I-29

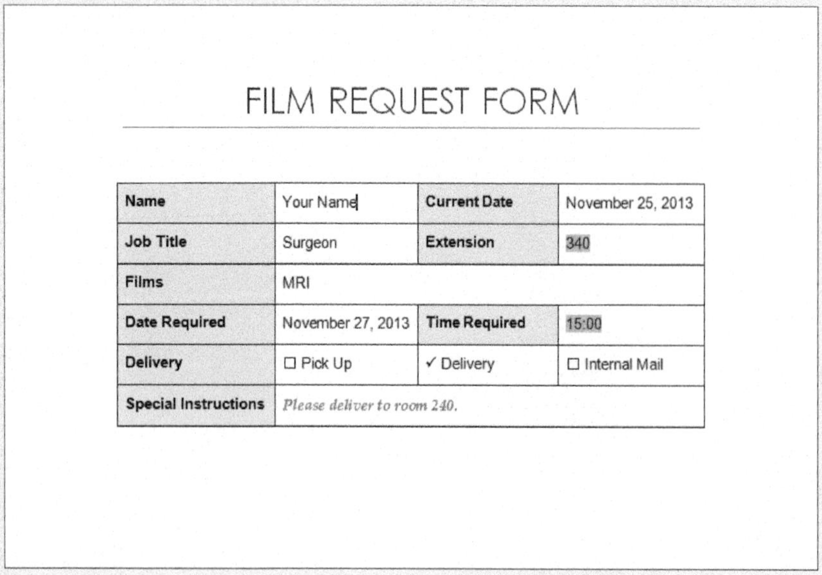

FILM REQUEST FORM

Name	Your Name	**Current Date**	November 25, 2013
Job Title	Surgeon	**Extension**	340
Films	MRI		
Date Required	November 27, 2013	**Time Required**	15:00
Delivery	☐ Pick Up	✓ Delivery	☐ Internal Mail
Special Instructions	*Please deliver to room 240.*		

Illustrating Documents with Graphics

Graphics can help illustrate the ideas in your documents, provide visual interest on a page, and give your documents punch and flair. In addition to clip art, you can add photos or graphics created in other programs to a document, or you can use the graphic features of Word to create your own images. In this appendix, you learn how to insert, modify, and position graphics, how to create and format a text box, and how to illustrate a document with charts. You are preparing materials for a staff meeting to discuss implementing a triage phone system at Riverwalk Medical Clinic. You use the graphic features of Word to illustrate a telephone triage form and a handout that describes the requirements for telephone etiquette and shows the distribution of incoming calls to the clinic by type.

OBJECTIVES

Insert a graphic

Size and position a graphic

Create a text box

Create a chart

Inserting a Graphic

Graphic images you can insert in a document include the clip art images that come with Word, photos taken with a digital camera, scanned art, and graphics created in other graphics programs. To insert a graphic file into a document, you use the Picture command in the Illustrations group on the Insert tab. Once you insert a graphic, you can apply a Picture style to it to enhance its appearance. ▰▰▰▰ You have formatted the text for a telephone triage form for potential urinary tract infections. You want to illustrate the form with the Riverwalk Medical Clinic logo, a graphic created in another graphics program. You insert the logo graphic file in the document, apply a shadow to the graphic, and then wrap text around it to make it a floating graphic.

STEPS

TROUBLE
This unit assumes rulers are displayed.

1. **Start** Word, **open the file** WMP 1-1.docx **from the drive and folder where you store your Data Files, save it as** WMP 1-UTI Triage Form, **click the** Show/Hide ¶ **button** ¶ **in the Paragraph group to display formatting marks, read the document to get a feel for its format and contents, then press** [Ctrl][Home]

   The form is divided into three sections and includes a table and columns of text.

2. **Click before the heading** Patient complains of... **under the table, click the** Insert tab, **then click the** Picture button **in the Illustrations group**

   The Insert Picture dialog box opens. You use this dialog box to locate and insert graphic files. Most graphic files are **bitmap graphics**, which are often saved with a .bmp, .png, .jpg, .tif, or .gif file extension. To view all the graphic files in a particular location, use the File type list arrow to select All Pictures.

TROUBLE
If you do not see All Pictures, click the File type list arrow, then click All Pictures.

3. **Verify that** All Pictures **appears in the File Type list box, navigate to the location where you store your Data Files, click the file** RMC Logo.jpg, **then click** Insert

   The logo is inserted as an inline graphic at the location of the insertion point, as shown in Figure 1-1. When a graphic is selected, white circles and squares, called **sizing handles**, appear on the sides and corners of the graphic, a green **rotate handle** appears, and the Picture Tools Format tab appears on the Ribbon. You use this tab to size, crop, position, wrap text around, format, and adjust a graphic.

4. **Click the** Picture Effects button **in the Picture Styles group on the Picture Tools Format tab, point to** Shadow, **move the pointer over the shadow styles in the gallery to preview them in the document, then click** Offset Diagonal Bottom Right **in the Outer section**

   A drop shadow is applied to the logo. You can use the Picture Effects button to apply other visual effects to a graphic, such as a glow, soft edge, reflection, or 3-D rotation.

QUICK TIP
Change a floating graphic to an inline graphic by changing the text wrapping style to In Line with Text.

5. **Click the** Picture Effects button, **point to** Shadow, **then click** Shadow Options

   The Format Picture dialog box opens. You use this dialog box to adjust the format settings applied to graphic objects.

6. **Click the** Distance up arrow **in the Shadow section four times until 7 pt appears, then click** Close

   The distance of the shadow from the picture is increased to 7 points. Notice that as you adjust the settings in the dialog box, the change is immediately applied to the logo.

QUICK TIP
To be able to position a graphic anywhere on a page, you must apply a text-wrapping style to it even if there is no text on the page.

7. **Click the** Wrap Text button **in the Arrange group, then click** Tight

   The text wraps around the sides of the graphic, as shown in Figure 1-2, making the graphic a floating object. A floating object is part of the drawing layer in a document and can be moved anywhere on a page, including in front of or behind text and other objects. Notice the anchor that appears in the upper-right corner of the logo next to the Patient complains of... paragraph. The anchor indicates the floating graphic is **anchored** to the nearest paragraph so that the graphic moves with the paragraph if the paragraph is moved. The anchor symbol appears only when formatting marks are displayed.

8. **Deselect the graphic, then click the** Save button 🖫 **on the Quick Access toolbar**

FIGURE 1-1: Inline graphic

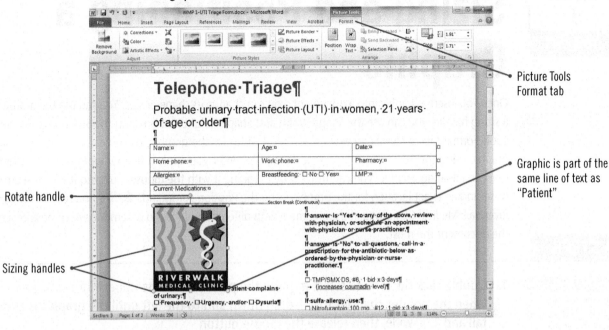

Picture Tools Format tab

Graphic is part of the same line of text as "Patient"

Rotate handle

Sizing handles

FIGURE 1-2: Floating graphic

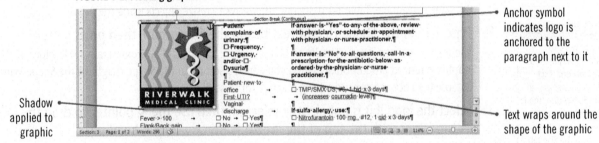

Anchor symbol indicates logo is anchored to the paragraph next to it

Shadow applied to graphic

Text wraps around the shape of the graphic

Correcting pictures, changing colors, and applying artistic effects

The Corrections command in the Adjust group allows you to adjust a picture's relative lightness (**brightness**), alter the difference between its darkest and lightest areas (**contrast**), and change the sharpness of an image. To make these adjustments, select the image and then click the Corrections button to open a gallery of percentages that you can preview applied to the picture. You can also fine-tune brightness, contrast, or sharpness by clicking Picture Corrections Options in the Corrections gallery, and then using the sliders in the Picture Corrections pane of the Format Picture dialog box to adjust the percentage.

The Color command in the Adjust group is used to change the vividness and intensity of color in an image (**color saturation**), and to change the "temperature" of a photo by bringing out the cooler blue tones or the warmer orange tones (**color tone**). The Color command is also used to recolor a picture to give it a stylized effect, such as sepia tone, grayscale, or duotone. To make changes to the colors in a picture, select it, click the Color button, and then select one of the color modes or variations in the gallery that opens.

The Artistic Effects command in the Adjust group allows you to make a photo look like a drawing, a painting, a photocopy, a sketch (see Figure 1-3), or some other artistic medium. To experiment with applying an artistic effect,

select a photo, click the Artistic Effects button, and then point to each effect to preview it applied to the photo.

After you edit a picture, you can undo any changes that you made by clicking the Reset Picture button in the Adjust group. This command also resets any changes you made to a picture's size, cropping, border, and effects.

FIGURE 1-3

Word 2010

Sizing and Positioning a Graphic

Once you insert a graphic into a document, you can change its shape or size. You can use the mouse to drag a sizing handle, you can use the Shape Width and Shape Height text boxes in the Size group on the Picture Tools Format tab to specify an exact height and width for the graphic, or you can change the scale of the graphic using the Size tab in the Layout dialog box. After you apply a text wrapping style to a graphic to make it a floating graphic, you can move it by dragging it with the mouse, nudging it with the arrow keys, or setting an exact location for the graphic using the Position command. ▧▧▧▧▧ You reduce the size of the Riverwalk Medical Clinic logo and experiment with different positions to determine which position enhances the document the most.

STEPS

1. **Double-click the logo to select it, place the pointer over the upper-right sizing handle, when the pointer changes to ⤢, drag down and to the left until the graphic is about 1½" tall and 1⅓" wide, then release the mouse button**
   As you drag, the transparent image indicates the size and shape of the graphic. You can refer to the ruler to gauge the measurements as you drag. When you release the mouse button, the image is reduced. Dragging a corner sizing handle resizes the logo proportionally so that its width and height are reduced or enlarged by the same percentage. Table 1-1 describes other ways to resize objects using the mouse.

2. **Type 1.15 in the Shape Height text box in the Size group, then press [Enter]**
   The logo is reduced proportionally to be precisely 1.15" tall and approximately 1.03" wide. In this case, the graphic is resized proportionally when you adjust a setting in the Shape Height or the Shape Width text box because the Lock aspect ratio setting is active for this graphic.

3. **Select the logo if it is not already selected, then use the ⛶ pointer to drag the logo up so its top aligns with the top of the Probable urinary tract... heading**
   As you drag, the transparent image indicates the position of the logo. When you release the mouse button, the logo is moved. Notice that the Probable urinary tract heading now wraps to the right of the logo and the table moves down.

4. **Click the Position button in the Arrange group, click Position in Top Right with Square Text Wrapping, then drag the anchor symbol next to the Telephone Triage paragraph**
   The graphic is aligned with the top and right margins. Moving an inline graphic using the Position button is a fast way to make it a floating graphic and position it so it is centered or aligned with the margins.

5. **Select the heading Telephone Triage and the subheading Probably urinary tract..., then click the Align Text Right button in the Paragraph group on the Home tab**
   The text is right-aligned and wraps to the left of the logo.

6. **Click the View tab, click the Gridlines check box in the Show/Hide group, select the logo, then press [→]**
   Non-printing drawing gridlines appear within the document margins in Print Layout view. You use drawing gridlines to help you size, align, and position objects. Pressing [→] nudges the logo right so its right edge aligns with the right edge of the drawing gridlines, as shown in Figure 1-4.

7. **Click the Gridlines checkbox to turn off the display of gridlines, click the Home tab, click ¶, press [Ctrl][End], type your name, save your changes, submit a copy to your instructor, then close the file**
   The completed document is shown in Figure 1-5.

Illustrating Documents with Graphics

FIGURE 1-4: Resized and repositioned logo

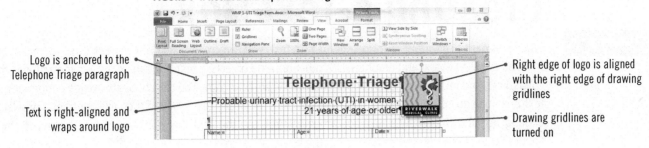

Logo is anchored to the Telephone Triage paragraph

Text is right-aligned and wraps around logo

Right edge of logo is aligned with the right edge of drawing gridlines

Drawing gridlines are turned on

FIGURE 1-5: Completed form

TABLE 1-1: Methods for resizing an object using the mouse

do this	to
Drag a top or bottom square sizing handle	Change the height of a graphic object
Drag a side square sizing handle	Change the width of a graphic object
Drag a corner sizing handle	Resize a clip art or bitmap graphic and maintain its proportions
Press [Shift] and drag a corner sizing handle	Resize any graphic object and maintain its proportions
Press [Ctrl] and drag a side, top, or bottom sizing handle	Resize any graphic object vertically or horizontally while keeping the center position fixed
Press [Ctrl] and drag a corner sizing handle	Resize any graphic object diagonally while keeping the center position fixed
Press [Shift][Ctrl] and drag a corner sizing handle	Resize any graphic object while keeping the center position fixed and maintaining its proportions

Cropping graphics

If you want to use only part of a picture in a document, you can **crop** the graphic to trim the parts you don't want to use. To crop a graphic, select it, then click the Crop button in the Size group on the Picture Tools Format tab. Cropping handles (solid black lines) appear on all four corners and sides of the graphic. To crop one side of a graphic, drag a side cropping handle inward to where you want to trim the graphic. To crop two adjacent sides at once, drag a corner cropping handle inward to the point where you want the corner of the cropped image to be. When you finish adjusting the parameters of the graphic, click the Crop button again to turn off the crop feature.

You can also crop a graphic to fit a shape, such as an oval, a star, a sun, or a triangle, or you can crop a graphic to conform to a certain aspect ratio, so that its height and width are proportionate to a ratio, such as 3:5. To apply one of these cropping behaviors to a graphic, select it, click the Crop list arrow in the Size group, point to Crop to Shape or to Aspect Ratio on the menu that opens, and then select the option you want.

Creating a Text Box

When you want to illustrate your documents with text, you can create a text box. A **text box** is a container that you can fill with text and graphics. Like other drawing objects, a text box can be resized, formatted with colors, lines, and text wrapping, and positioned anywhere on a page. You can choose to insert a preformatted text box that you customize with your own text, draw an empty text box and then fill it with text, or select existing text and then draw a text box around it. You use the Text Box button in the Text group or the Shapes button in the Illustrations group on the Insert tab to create a text box. ▰▰▰ You have drafted the text for a handout on telephone etiquette and want to format some of the information in the handout in a text box. You select the text you want to include in the text box, insert the text box, resize and position the text box on the page, and then format it using a text box style.

To draw an empty text box, click the Text Box button, click Draw Text Box, then click and drag with the + pointer to create the text box.

Always verify that a text box is sized so that all the text fits.

1. **Open the file** WMP 1-2.docx **from the drive and folder where you store your Data Files, save it as** WMP 1-Telephone Calls, **click the** Show/Hide ¶ **button** ¶ **in the Paragraph group to display formatting marks, then read the document to get a feel for its format**

2. **Scroll down, click before the heading** Telephone Etiquette, **then drag to select the heading and all the text below the heading, excluding the last paragraph mark in the document**
   The heading and the text below the heading are selected.

3. **Click the** Insert tab, **then click the** Text Box button **in the Text group**
   A gallery of preformatted text boxes and sidebars opens.

4. **Click** Draw Text Box
   The selected text is formatted as a text box, as shown in Figure 1-6. When you draw a text box around existing text or graphics, the text box becomes part of the drawing layer (a floating object) and can be resized and moved anywhere on the page.

5. **Click the** Drawing Tools Format tab, **click the** Size button **if you do not see the Shape Width and Shape Height text boxes, type** 2.6 **in the Shape Width text box in the Size group, then press** [Enter]
   The text box is resized to be 2.6" wide and 5.48" tall.

6. **Click the** Position button **in the Arrange group, then click** Position in Middle Right with Square Text Wrapping
   The text box is moved to the middle right side of the page and text wraps around the text box.

7. **Scroll up, drag the anchor symbol next to the "Excellence in…" paragraph, move the pointer over the text box border until the pointer changes to** ⬥, **then drag the text box straight up until its top aligns with the top of the first line of body text and its right border aligns with the right margin**
   The text box is top-aligned with the body text.

8. **Deselect the text box, click the** Home tab, **click** ¶ **in the Paragraph group, click in the text box, then double-click the** text box frame **with the** ⬥ **pointer**
   Clicking inside a text box with the I pointer moves the insertion point inside the text box so the text can be edited. Double-clicking the text box frame selects the text box and activates the Drawing Tools Format tab.

9. **Click the** More button ▾ **in the Shape Styles group, then click** Subtle Effect – Olive Green, Accent 3
   A quick style that includes subtle olive green shading, a thin green border, and a slight shadow is applied to the text box, as shown in Figure 1-7. You can also create your own designs using the Shape Fill and Shape Outline buttons in the Shape Styles group.

10. **Save your changes**

Illustrating Documents with Graphics

FIGURE 1-6: Text box

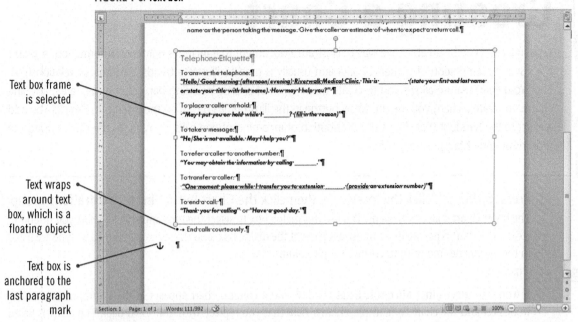

Text box frame is selected

Text wraps around text box, which is a floating object

Text box is anchored to the last paragraph mark

FIGURE 1-7: Formatted text box

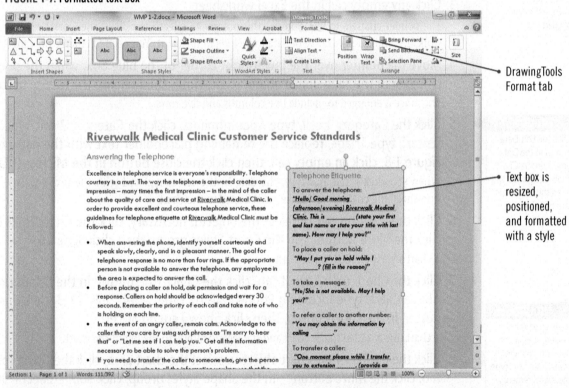

DrawingTools Format tab

Text box is resized, positioned, and formatted with a style

Linking text boxes

If you are working on a longer document, you might want text to begin in a text box on one page and then continue in a text box on another page. By creating a **link** between two or more text boxes, you can force text to flow automatically from one text box to another, allowing you to size and format the text boxes any way you wish. To link two or more text boxes, you must first create the original text box, fill it with text, and then create a second, empty text box. Then, to create the link, select the first text box, click the Create Link button in the Text group on the Drawing Tools Format tab to activate the pointer, and then click the second text box with the pointer. Any overflow text from the first text box flows seamlessly into the second text box. As you resize the first text box, the flow of text adjusts automatically between the two linked text boxes. If you want to break a link between two linked text boxes so that all the text is contained in the original text box, select the original text box, and then click the Break Link button in the Text group.

Creating a Chart

Adding a chart can be an attractive way to illustrate a document that includes numerical information. A **chart** is a visual representation of numerical data and usually is used to illustrate trends, patterns, or relationships. The Word chart feature allows you to create many types of charts, including bar, column, pie, area, and line charts. To create a chart, you use the Chart button in the Illustrations group on the Insert tab. You add a chart to the handout that shows the distribution of incoming phone calls, by type, to the clinic during the months of April, May, June, and July.

STEPS

1. **Press [Ctrl][End], click the Insert tab, then click the Chart button in the Illustrations group**

   The Insert Chart dialog box opens. You use this dialog box to select the type and style of chart you intend to create. The chart types are listed in the left pane of the dialog box, and the styles for each chart type are listed in the right pane. You want to create a simple column chart.

2. **Click OK**

   A worksheet opens in a Microsoft Excel window and a column chart appears in the Word document. The worksheet and the chart contain placeholder data that you replace with your own data. The chart is based on the data in the worksheet. Any change you make to the data is made automatically to the chart.

3. **Click any empty cell in the Excel worksheet**

   The pointer changes to ✛. You use this pointer to select the cells in the worksheet. The blue lines in the worksheet indicate the range of data to include in the chart. You need to enlarge the range.

4. **Move the pointer over the lower-right corner of the blue box, when the pointer changes to ↘, drag the range one column to the right, then release the mouse button**

   The range is enlarged to include five columns and five rows.

5. **Click the Category 1 cell, type Appointments, click the Category 2 cell, type Refills, press [Enter], type Triage, replace the remaining placeholder text with the data shown in Figure 1-8, click an empty cell, then click the close button in the Microsoft Excel window**

   When you click a cell and type, the data in the cell is replaced with the text you type. As you edit the worksheet, the changes you make are reflected in the chart.

6. **Click the chart border to select the object if necessary, click the Chart Tools Design tab, click the More button ⊽ in the Chart Styles group, then click Style 26**

   A chart style is applied to the chart.

7. **Click the Chart Tools Layout tab, click the Chart Title button in the Labels group, click Above Chart, type Incoming Phone Calls by Type, April – July 2013, click the Legend button in the Labels group, then click Show Legend at Left**

   A chart title is added to the chart and the legend moves to the left of the chart.

8. **Click the border of the chart object to select the chart area, click the Chart Tools Format tab, click the More button ⊽ in the Shape Styles group, click Subtle Effect – Blue, Accent 1, type 2.7 in the Shape Height text box in the Size group, type 7.1 in the Shape Width text box in the Size group, press [Enter], then scroll up as needed to see the chart**

   A style is applied to the chart area and the chart is resized so that it fits at the bottom of page 1.

9. **Right-click Triage to select the Horizontal axis, click the Bold button B on the Mini toolbar, click the Grow Font button A˘, right-click the legend, click B, then click A˘, right click the chart title, then click the Shrink Font button A˘**

   The text in the horizontal axis and the legend is enlarged and formatted with bold, and the font size of the chart title is reduced. The completed handout is shown in Figure 1-9.

10. **Press [Ctrl][End], type your name in the footer, save your changes, submit a copy to your instructor, close the file, then exit Word**

QUICK TIP
Click the Change Chart Type button in the Type group on the Chart Tools Design tab to change the type of chart.

TROUBLE
Click the Edit Data button in the Data group on the Chart Tools Design tab to open the worksheet and edit the chart data.

TROUBLE
If the chart is not resized, drag a corner sizing handle to resize it slightly, type the measurements as noted in Step 8, then press [Enter].

QUICK TIP
To format any chart element, select it, then click the Format Selection button in the Current Selection group on the Chart Tools Format tab to open the Format dialog box.

Illustrating Documents with Graphics

FIGURE 1-8: Chart object in Word and worksheet in Excel

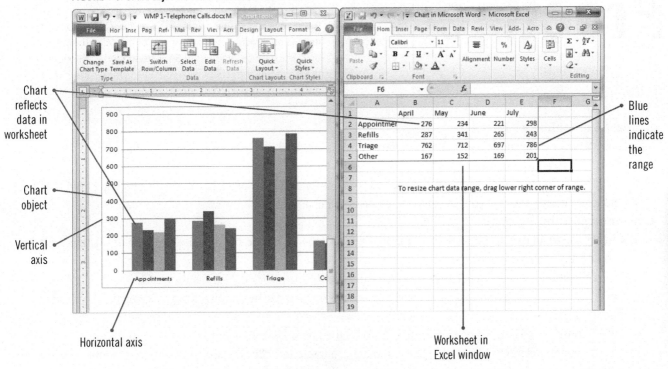

Chart reflects data in worksheet

Chart object

Vertical axis

Horizontal axis

Blue lines indicate the range

Worksheet in Excel window

FIGURE 1-9: Completed handout with chart

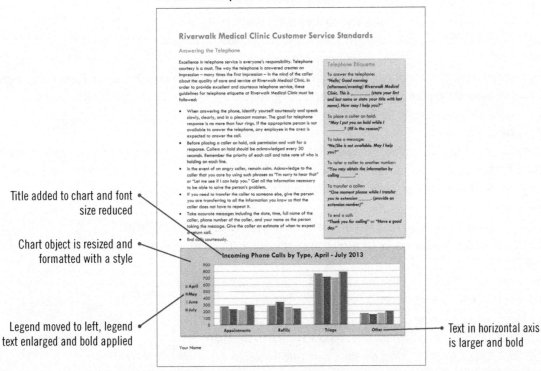

Title added to chart and font size reduced

Chart object is resized and formatted with a style

Legend moved to left, legend text enlarged and bold applied

Text in horizontal axis is larger and bold

Creating SmartArt graphics

Diagrams are another way to illustrate concepts in your documents. The powerful Word **SmartArt** feature makes it easy for you to quickly create and format many types of diagrams, including pyramid, target, cycle, and radial diagrams, as well as lists and organization charts. To insert a SmartArt graphic in a document, click the SmartArt button in the Illustrations group on the Insert tab to open the Choose a SmartArt Graphic dialog box. In this dialog box, select a diagram category in the left pane, select a specific diagram layout and design in the middle pane, preview the selected diagram layout in the right pane, and then click OK. The SmartArt object appears in the document with placeholder text, and the SmartArt Tools Design and Format tabs are enabled. These tabs contain commands and styles for customizing and formatting the SmartArt graphic and for sizing and positioning the graphic in the document.

Practice

1. **Insert a graphic.**
   a. Start Word, open the file WMP 1-3.docx from the drive and folder where you store your Data Files, and save it as **WMP 1-Sun Safety Handout**.
   b. Read the document to get a feel for its format and contents, press [Ctrl][Home], insert the file Beach.jpg from the drive and folder where you store your Data Files, then save your changes.

2. **Size and position a graphic.**
   a. Change the zoom level to 50%, select the photo, then click the Crop button in the Size group on the Picture Tools Format tab.
   b. Drag the right-middle cropping handle left approximately ½", then click the Crop button again.
   c. Reduce the size of the photo to approximately 75% of the original size by dragging a corner sizing handle toward the middle of the photo.
   d. Type **3** in the Shape Height text box in the Size group, then press [Enter].
   e. Change the zoom level to 100%, select the photo if it is not selected, click the More button in the Picture Styles group, move the pointer over each style in the Picture Styles gallery to preview the style applied to the photo, then apply the Soft Edge Oval style.
   f. Use the Position command to move the photo to the middle center of the page.
   g. Turn on the display of drawing gridlines, then drag the photo straight up so its top is aligned with the top of the first line of body text and the photo is centered between the margins.
   h. Apply Tight text wrapping to the photo, use the arrow keys to adjust the position of the photo if necessary so the text wraps smoothly around the photo, turn off the display of gridlines, then save your changes. (*Hint*: Press [Ctrl] as you press an arrow key to nudge the photo in small increments.)

3. **Create a text box.**
   a. Scroll to page 2, select the heading Being a Good Role Model and the paragraph below it, then insert a text box.
   b. Scroll to locate the text box, then use the Position command to move the text box to the upper-right corner of the page.
   c. Apply the – Subtle Effect – Orange, Accent 6 shape style to the text box, then save your changes.

4. **Create a chart.**
   a. Press [Ctrl][End], insert a chart, scroll down the list of chart types, then create a pie chart.
   b. Click the Sales cell, type **Sunscreen Usage**, replace the data in the worksheet with the data shown in Figure 1-10, then close Excel.
   c. Click the Chart Tools Design tab, click the More button in the Chart Styles group, then apply Style 32 to the chart.
   d. Click the More button ⊡ in the Chart Layouts group, experiment by applying several different chart layouts, then apply Layout 6 to the chart.
   e. Click the Chart Tools Layout tab, then use the Chart Title button to remove the chart title.
   f. Use the Legend button to add a legend above the chart.
   g. Click the Chart Tools Format tab, then resize the chart to be 4.3" tall and 7" wide.
   h. Select the chart area if necessary, use the Shape Outline button in the Shape Styles group to remove the border from the chart object, then deselect the chart object.
   i. Type **Prepared by** followed by your name in the document footer, save your changes, submit a copy to your instructor, close the file, then exit Word.

FIGURE 1-10

⊿	A	B	C
1		Sunscreen Usage	
2	Always	41	
3	Often	34	
4	Sometimes	15	
5	Rarely	6	
6	Never	4	
7			

Illustrating Documents with Graphics

Collaborating on Documents

Files You Will Need:

WMP 2-1.docx

WMP 2-2.docx

WMP 2-3.docx

WMP 2-4.docx

Several Word features make it easier to create and edit documents in cooperation with other people. The Track Changes, Comment, and Compare features in Word facilitate collaboration when two or more people are working on the same document. In this appendix, you learn how to track and review changes to a document, how to insert and work with comments, and how to compare two documents by combining changes from two reviewers into a single document. ▦▦▦▦ You have circulated a draft of the Influenza Information Sheet to two colleagues for feedback. You use the Track Changes, Comment, and Compare features to review their suggestions for changes and to combine their feedback into a final document.

OBJECTIVES

Track changes

Insert, view, and edit comments

Compare and combine documents

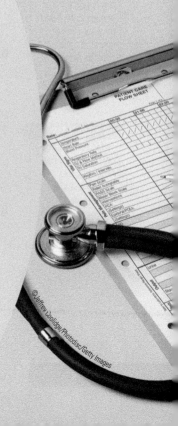

Tracking Changes

A **tracked change** is a mark that shows where an insertion, deletion, or formatting change has been made in a document. When the Track Changes feature is turned on, each change that you or another reviewer makes to a document is tracked. Text that is inserted in a document is displayed as colored, underlined text. Deleted text is shown as colored strikethrough. Formatting changes and comments are shown in balloons in a markup area on the right side of the document. As you review the tracked changes in a document, you can choose to accept or reject each change. When you accept a change it becomes part of the document. When you reject a change, the text or formatting is restored to its original state. To turn tracked changes on and off, you use the Track Changes button in the Tracking group on the Review tab. ▨▨▨▨ The office manager Tony Sanchez, R.N., has used the Track Changes feature to suggest revisions to the draft of the Influenza Information Sheet. You review Tony's tracked changes, accepting or rejecting them as you go, and then edit the document with your additional changes.

STEPS

QUICK TIP
To change the way revisions are displayed in the document, click the Show Markup button in the Tracking group, point to Ballons, and then select from the options.

1. **Start Word, open the file WMP 2-1.docx from the drive and folder where you store your Data Files, save it as WMP 2-Flu Draft 1, then click the Review tab**
   The document contains tracked changes, as shown in Figure 2-1. Notice that the Track Changes button in the Tracking group on the Review tab is enabled, indicating that tracked changes are turned on in the document. Any change you make to the document will be marked as a tracked change.

2. **Click the Next button in the Changes group**
   The insertion point moves to the first tracked change in the document, in this case, a sentence inserted in the introductory paragraph.

3. **Click the Accept button in the Changes group**
   The sentence becomes part of the document and the insertion point moves to a balloon containing a comment. You will work with comments in the next lesson, so you skip over the comment for now.

4. **Click the Next button in the Changes group**
   The insertion point moves to the deleted text "virus".

QUICK TIP
To quickly restore a line of text to its original state, select the entire line of text, and then click the Reject button.

5. **Click the Reject button in the Changes group, then click the Reject button again**
   The deleted word "virus" is restored to the document, the insertion point moves to the inserted word "germ", then "germ" is removed from the document, returning the text to its original state, as shown in Figure 2-2. The insertion point moves to the next tracked change in the document.

6. **Right-click the selected text that begins It is also…, then click Accept Insertion on the shortcut menu**
   The sentence becomes part of the document text. You can accept or reject any tracked change by right-clicking it, then selecting the appropriate command on the shortcut menu.

QUICK TIP
To facilitate collaboration with several reviewers, the tracked changes made by each reviewer are displayed in a different color.

7. **Scroll down until the heading When To Be Vaccinated on page 2 is at the top of your screen, select September in the first sentence under the heading, type October, place the insertion point before the period at the end of that same paragraph, then type , usually April**
   Your tracked changes are added to the document using a different color, as shown in Figure 2-3.

8. **Click the Track Changes button in the Tracking group to turn off the Track Changes feature, press [Ctrl][Home], replace Your Name with your name at the top of the document, then click the Save button 🖫 on the Quick Access toolbar to save your changes**

Collaborating on Documents

FIGURE 2-1: Tracked changes and comments in the document

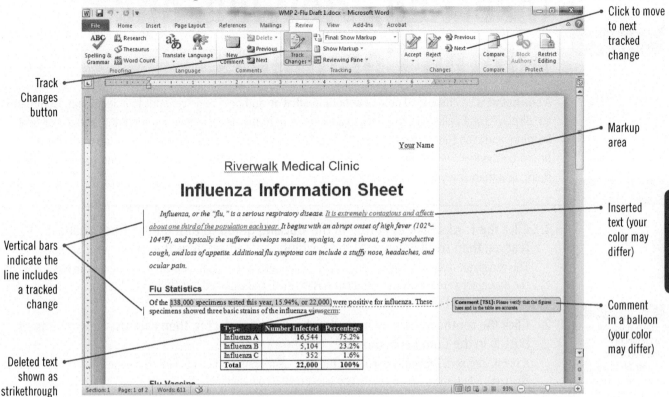

Track Changes button

Vertical bars indicate the line includes a tracked change

Deleted text shown as strikethrough

Click to move to next tracked change

Markup area

Inserted text (your color may differ)

Comment in a balloon (your color may differ)

FIGURE 2-2: Text restored to its original state

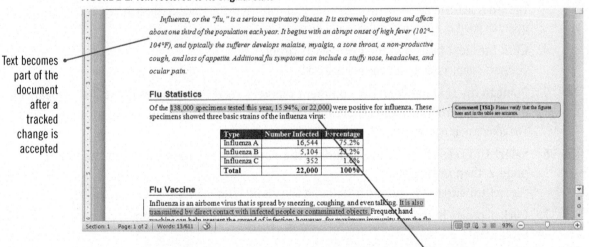

Text becomes part of the document after a tracked change is accepted

Text is restored to the original state after rejecting the deleted and inserted text

FIGURE 2-3: New tracked changes in the document

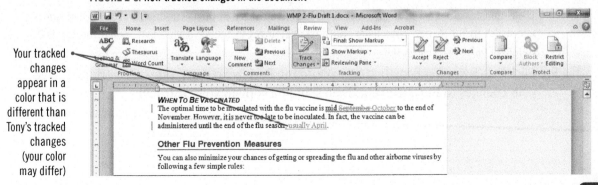

Your tracked changes appear in a color that is different than Tony's tracked changes (your color may differ)

Inserting, Viewing, and Editing Comments

A **comment** is an embedded note or annotation that an author or reviewer adds to a document. Comments are displayed in a balloon in the markup area in the right margin of a document in Print Layout, Full Screen Reading, and Web Layout views. To insert a comment, you use the New Comment button in the Comments group on the Review tab. ▨▨▨▨ You review the comments in the document, respond to them or delete them, and then add your own comments.

STEPS

1. **Click the Track Changes button in the Tracking group to turn on the Track Changes feature, then scroll down until the heading Flu Statistics is at the top of your screen**

   The paragraph under the Flu Statistics heading contains a comment. Notice that comment marks appear in the document at the point the comment was inserted, and a dashed line leads from the right comment mark to the comment balloon in the markup area.

2. **Click the comment balloon in the markup area to select it, then click the New Comment button in the Comments group**

   A blank comment balloon is inserted in the document using a different color (the same color as your tracked changes). You respond to a comment by selecting the comment and then inserting your own comment.

3. **Type The numbers are correct., then click outside the comment balloon to deselect the comment**

   The text is added to the comment balloon, as shown in Figure 2-4. You can edit comment text by placing the insertion point in a comment balloon and then typing.

4. **Click the Next button in the Comments group**

   The next comment in the document is selected.

5. **Point to the text between the comment markers, read the comment text that appears in a ScreenTip, then click the Delete button in the Comments group**

   The comment is removed from the manuscript.

6. **Select Egg-related allergies. (including the paragraph mark) in the list at the top of page 2, then press [Delete]**

   "Egg-related allergies." is removed from the list and the list is renumbered.

7. **Click allergies in the deleted Step 3, click the New Comment button, then type This is redundant.**

   A new comment is inserted in the document, as shown in Figure 2-5. The deleted text to which the comment refers is shown as strikethrough in the document and is shaded in the same color as the comment.

8. **Click the Reviewing Pane list arrow in the Tracking group, then click Reviewing Pane Vertical**

   The comments and tracked changes in the document are listed in the Reviewing pane on the left side of the screen. It's useful to view comments and tracked changes in the Reviewing pane when the full text of a comment or tracked change does not fit in the balloon.

9. **Click the Reviewing Pane button to close the Reviewing pane, press [Ctrl][Home], save your changes to the document, then submit a copy to your instructor**

FIGURE 2-4: Response comment in the document

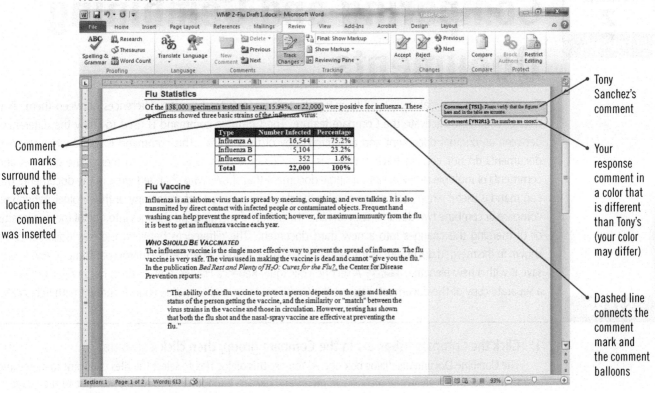

Comment marks surround the text at the location the comment was inserted

Tony Sanchez's comment

Your response comment in a color that is different than Tony's (your color may differ)

Dashed line connects the comment mark and the comment balloons

Word 2010

FIGURE 2-5: New comment in the document

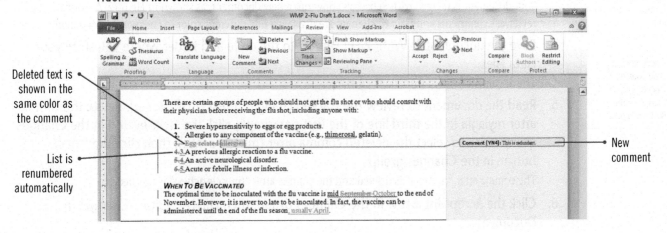

Deleted text is shown in the same color as the comment

List is renumbered automatically

New comment

Comparing and Combining Documents

The Word Compare feature is used to merge two documents to show the differences between them. Two distinct commands activate the Compare feature. The Compare command is used to show the differences between an original document and an edited copy of the original. This command is useful when the two documents do not contain tracked changes. The Combine command is used to merge the changes and comments of multiple reviewers into a single document that shows who changed what in the document. This command is useful when each reviewer edits the document using a separate copy of the original. When you compare or combine two documents, you have the option of merging the changes into one of the documents or of merging the changes into a new third document. The differences between the two documents are shown in the merged document as tracked changes. You can then examine the merged document, edit it, and save it with a new filename. ⬛⬛⬛⬛ A second colleague, Rebecca Haines, R.N., returns her revisions to you in a separate copy of the document. You use the Combine command to merge your document with Rebecca's.

STEPS

1. **Click the Compare list arrow in the Compare group, then click Combine**
   The Combine Documents dialog box opens. You use this dialog box to select the files you want to merge and to indicate which elements, such as comments and headers and footers, you want to include in the merge.

2. **Click the Original document list arrow, click Browse, navigate to the drive and folder where you store your Data Files, double click the file WMP 2-2.docx, click the Revised document list arrow, click Browse, navigate to the drive and folder where you store your Data Files, then double click the file WMP 2-Flu Draft 1.docx**
   The file WMP 2-2.doc is the file that contains Rebecca's comments and tracked changes. The Combine Documents dialog box is shown in Figure 2-6.

> **TROUBLE**
> If several panes open, click the Compare list arrow in the Compare group, point to Show Source Documents, click Hide Source Documents, then close the Reviewing pane.

3. **Make sure the settings in your dialog box match the settings in Figure 2-6, including the Word level option button and the New document option button, then click OK**
   Your document is merged with Rebecca's copy into a new document, as shown in Figure 2-7. Notice that each reviewer's comments and tracked changes are displayed in a different color in the merged document.

4. **Save the document as WMP 2-Flu Draft 2 to the drive and folder where you store your Data Files**
   The document is saved with a new filename.

5. **Read the document to review the tracked changes, press [Ctrl][Home], delete the comma after mylagia in the third line of the first paragraph, click the Next button in the Changes group twice to select the deleted comma after (muscle aches), then click the Reject button in the Changes group**
   The comma after "mylagia" is deleted and the comma after "(muscle aches)" is restored.

6. **Click the Accept list arrow in the Changes group, then click Accept All Changes in Document**
   All the tracked changes are accepted and become part of the document.

7. **Click the first comment to select it, click the New Comment button in the Comments group, type Yes, then click outside the comment balloon to deselect it**
   A new comment is added to the document, as shown in Figure 2-8.

8. **Scroll to page 2, right-click the comment on page 2, then click Delete Comment**
   The comment is deleted.

9. **Save your changes to the document, submit a copy, close all open files, then exit Word**

Collaborating on Documents

FIGURE 2-6: Combine Documents dialog box

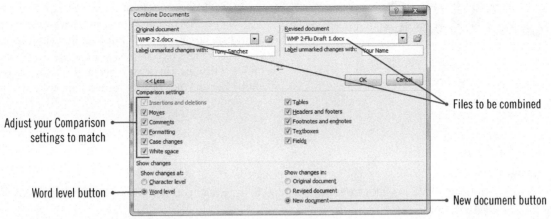

Adjust your Comparison settings to match

Word level button

Files to be combined

New document button

FIGURE 2-7: Combined document showing changes from each reviewer

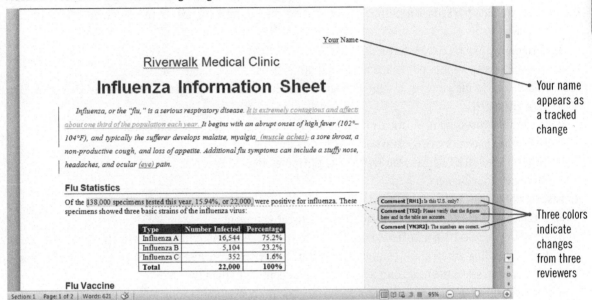

Your name appears as a tracked change

Three colors indicate changes from three reviewers

FIGURE 2-8: New comment

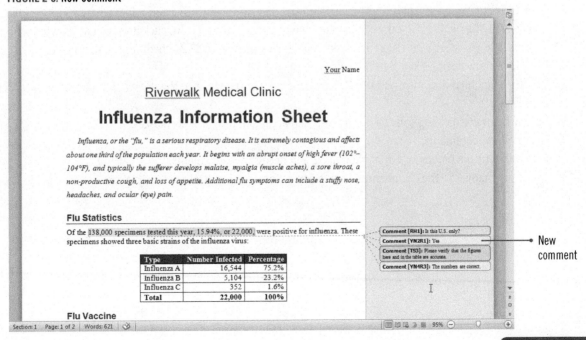

New comment

Practice

For current SAM information, including versions and content details, visit SAM Central (http://www.cengage.com/samcentral). If you have a SAM user profile, you may have access to hands-on instruction, practice, and assessment of the skills covered in this unit. Since various versions of SAM are supported throughout the life of this text, check with your instructor for the correct instructions and URL/Web site for accessing assignments.

Skills Review

1. **Track changes.**
   a. Start Word, open the file WMP 2-3.docx from the drive and folder where you store your Data Files, then save it as **WMP 2-Scheduling Draft 1**.
   b. Using the Next button in the Changes group on the Review tab, review the tracked changes in the document, then press [Ctrl][Home] to return to the beginning of the document.
   c. Reject the first tracked change, then accept all remaining tracked changes in the document. Skip over the comments for now.
   d. Turn on the Track Changes feature.
   e. In the Five-step approach to scheduling appointments heading, change Five to **Six**.
   f. Add the following sentence as item number 4 in the numbered list: **Repeat the agreed-upon time to the patient.**
   g. Under the Processing new patients heading at the bottom of page 2, delete the sentence **All patient information is confidential.**, including the bullet.
   h. Turn off the Track Changes feature, press [Ctrl][Home], replace Your Name with your name at the top of the document, then save your changes.

2. **Insert, view, and edit comments.**
   a. Scroll down, select the first comment, then delete the comment.
   b. Scroll down, select **The following table** in the last sentence of the first paragraph under the Determining the time... heading, insert a new comment, then type **Should we create a table for each physician?**
   c. Scroll down, select the next comment, insert a new comment, then type **Yes**.
   d. Press [Ctrl][Home], save your changes to the document, then submit a copy to your instructor.

3. **Compare and combine documents.**
   a. Open the Combine Documents dialog box.
   b. Click the Original document list arrow, click Browse, navigate to the drive and folder where you store your Data Files, double-click the file WMP 2-4.docx, click the Revised document list arrow, click Browse, navigate to the drive and folder where you store your Data Files, then double-click the file WMP 2-Scheduling Draft 1.docx.
   c. Choose to show changes in a New document, then click OK.
   d. Save the combined document as **WMP 2-Scheduling Draft 2** to the drive and folder where you store your Data Files.
   e. Review the tracked changes in the document, then accept all the tracked changes.
   f. Delete all the comments.
   g. Proof-read the document for errors, then make any necessary adjustments.
   h. Save your changes to the document, submit a copy, close all open files, then exit Word.

Working with Windows Live and Office Web Apps

If the computer you are using has an active Internet connection, you can go to the Microsoft Windows Live Web site and access a wide variety of services and Web applications. For example, you can check your e-mail through Windows Live, network with your friends and coworkers, and use SkyDrive to store and share files. From SkyDrive, you can also use Office Web Apps to create and edit Word, PowerPoint, Excel, and OneNote files, even when you are using a computer that does not have Office 2010 installed. ▤▤▤▤ You work in the Vancouver branch of Quest Specialty Travel. Your supervisor, Mary Lou Jacobs, asks you to explore Windows Live and learn how she can use SkyDrive and Office Web Apps to work with her files online.

(*Note*: SkyDrive and Office Web Apps are dynamic Web pages, and might change over time, including the way they are organized and how commands are performed. The steps and figures in this appendix were accurate at the time this book was published.)

OBJECTIVES

Explore how to work online from Windows Live

Obtain a Windows Live ID and sign in to Windows Live

Upload files to Windows Live

Work with the PowerPoint Web App

Create folders and organize files on SkyDrive

Add people to your network and share files

Work with the Excel Web App

Exploring How to Work Online from Windows Live

You can use your Web browser to upload your files to Windows Live from any computer connected to the Internet. You can work on the files right in your Web browser using Office Web Apps and share your files with people in your Windows Live network. ▆▆▆ You review the concepts and services related to working online from Windows Live.

DETAILS

- **What is Windows Live?**

  Windows Live is a collection of services and Web applications that you can use to help you be more productive both personally and professionally. For example, you can use Windows Live to send and receive e-mail, to chat with friends via instant messaging, to share photos, to create a blog, and to store and edit files using SkyDrive. Table WEB-1 describes the services available on Windows Live. Windows Live is a free service that you sign up for. When you sign up, you receive a Windows Live ID, which you use to sign in to Windows Live. When you work with files on Windows Live, you are cloud computing.

- **What is Cloud Computing?**

  The term **cloud computing** refers to the process of working with files online in a Web browser. When you save files to SkyDrive on Windows Live, you are saving your files to an online location. SkyDrive is like having a personal hard drive in the cloud.

- **What is SkyDrive?**

  SkyDrive is an online storage and file sharing service. With a Windows Live account, you receive access to your own SkyDrive, which is your personal storage area on the Internet. On your SkyDrive, you are given space to store up to 25 GB of data online. Each file can be a maximum size of 50 MB. You can also use SkyDrive to access Office Web Apps, which you use to create and edit files created in Word, OneNote, PowerPoint, and Excel online in your Web browser.

- **Why use Windows Live and SkyDrive?**

  On Windows Live, you use SkyDrive to access additional storage for your files. You don't have to worry about backing up your files to a memory stick or other storage device that could be lost or damaged. Another advantage of storing your files on SkyDrive is that you can access your files from any computer that has an active Internet connection. Figure WEB-1 shows the SkyDrive Web page that appears when accessed from a Windows Live account. From SkyDrive, you can also access Office Web Apps.

- **What are Office Web Apps?**

  Office Web Apps are versions of Microsoft Word, Excel, PowerPoint, and OneNote that you can access online from your SkyDrive. An Office Web App does not include all of the features and functions included with the full Office version of its associated application. However, you can use the Office Web App from any computer that is connected to the Internet, even if Microsoft Office 2010 is not installed on that computer.

- **How do SkyDrive and Office Web Apps work together?**

  You can create a file in Office 2010 using Word, Excel, PowerPoint, or OneNote and then upload the file to your SkyDrive. You can then open the Office file saved to SkyDrive and edit it using your Web browser and the corresponding Office Web App. Figure WEB-2 shows a PowerPoint presentation open in the PowerPoint Web App. You can also use an Office Web App to create a new file, which is saved automatically to SkyDrive while you work. In addition, you can download a file created with an Office Web App and continue to work with the file in the full version of the corresponding Office application: Word, Excel, PowerPoint, or OneNote. Finally, you can create a SkyDrive network that consists of the people you want to be able to view your folders and files on your SkyDrive. You can give people permission to view and edit your files using any computer with an active Internet connection and a Web browser.

FIGURE WEB-1: SkyDrive on Windows Live

Browser window

SkyDrive - Windows Live tab

By default, one folder is available on SkyDrive; you can create additional folders

The name of the person who signed into Windows Live and SkyDrive appears here

Monitors the amount of space still available on your SkyDrive

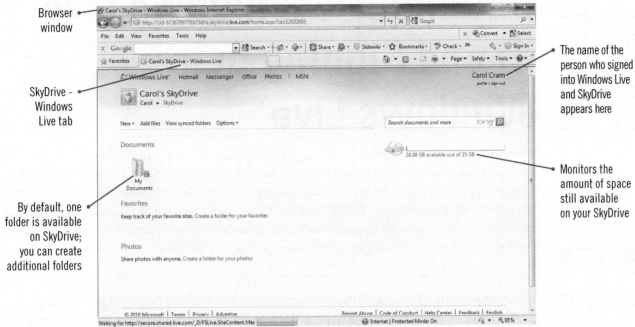

FIGURE WEB-2: PowerPoint presentation open in the PowerPoint Web App

Browser window

Ribbon available in PowerPoint Web App

The presentation in PowerPoint Web App maintains the same look and feel as the same presentation in the desktop version of PowerPoint

Name of PowerPoint presentation open in PowerPoint Web App

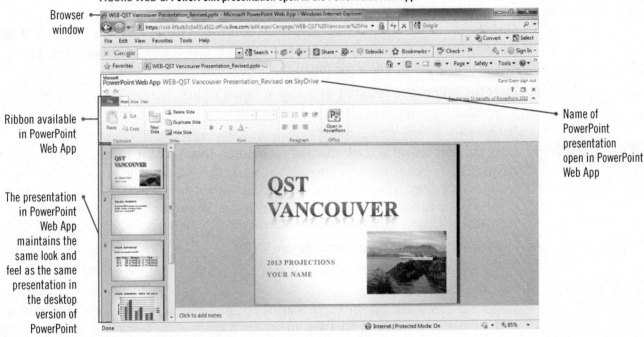

TABLE WEB-1: Services available via Windows Live

service	description
E-mail	Send and receive e-mail using a Hotmail account
Instant Messaging	Use Messenger to chat with friends, share photos, and play games
SkyDrive	Store files, work on files using Office Web Apps, and share files with people in your network
Photos	Upload and share photos with friends
People	Develop a network of friends and coworkers, then use the network to distribute information and stay in touch
Downloads	Access a variety of free programs available for download to a PC
Mobile Device	Access applications for a mobile device: text messaging, using Hotmail, networking, and sharing photos

Obtaining a Windows Live ID and Signing In to Windows Live

To work with your files online using SkyDrive and Office Web Apps, you need a Windows Live ID. You obtain a Windows Live ID by going to the Windows Live Web site and creating a new account. Once you have a Windows Live ID, you can access SkyDrive and then use it to store your files, create new files, and share your files with friends and coworkers. ⬛⬛⬛⬛ Mary Lou Jacobs, your supervisor at QST Vancouver, asks you to obtain a Windows Live ID so that you can work on documents with your coworkers. You go to the Windows Live Web site, create a Windows Live ID, and then sign in to your SkyDrive.

STEPS

QUICK TIP
If you already have a Windows Live ID, go to the next lesson and sign in as directed using your account.

1. **Open your Web browser, type home.live.com in the Address bar, then press [Enter]**

   The Windows Live home page opens. From this page, you can create a Windows Live account and receive your Windows Live ID.

2. **Click the Sign up button** *(Note: You may see a Sign up link instead of a button)*

   The Create your Windows Live ID page opens.

3. **Click the Or use your own e-mail address link under the Check availability button or if you are already using Hotmail, Messenger, or Xbox LIVE, click the Sign in now link in the Information statement near the top of the page**

4. **Enter the information required, as shown in Figure WEB-3**

   If you wish, you can sign up for a Windows Live e-mail address such as yourname@live.com so that you can also access the Windows Live e-mail services.

TROUBLE
The code can be difficult to read. If you receive an error message, enter the new code that appears.

5. **Enter the code shown at the bottom of your screen, then click the I accept button**

   The Windows Live home page opens. The name you entered when you signed up for your Windows Live ID appears in the top right corner of the window to indicate that you are signed in to Windows Live. From the Windows Live home page, you can access all the services and applications offered by Windows Live. See the Verifying your Windows Live ID box for information on finalizing your account set up.

6. **Point to Windows Live, as shown in Figure WEB-4**

   A list of options appears. SkyDrive is one of the options you can access directly from Windows Live.

TROUBLE
Click I accept if you are asked to review and accept the Windows Live Service Agreement and Privacy Statement.

7. **Click SkyDrive**

   The SkyDrive page opens. Your name appears in the top right corner, and the amount of space available is shown on the right side of the SkyDrive page. The amount of space available is monitored, as indicated by the gauge that fills with color as space is used. Using SkyDrive, you can add files to the existing folder and you can create new folders.

8. **Click sign out in the top right corner under your name, then exit the Web browser**

   You are signed out of your Windows Live account. You can sign in again directly from the Windows Live page in your browser or from within a file created with PowerPoint, Excel, Word, or OneNote.

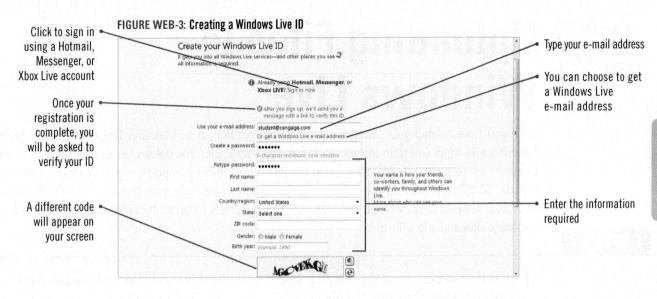

FIGURE WEB-3: Creating a Windows Live ID

Click to sign in using a Hotmail, Messenger, or Xbox Live account

Once your registration is complete, you will be asked to verify your ID

A different code will appear on your screen

Type your e-mail address

You can choose to get a Windows Live e-mail address

Enter the information required

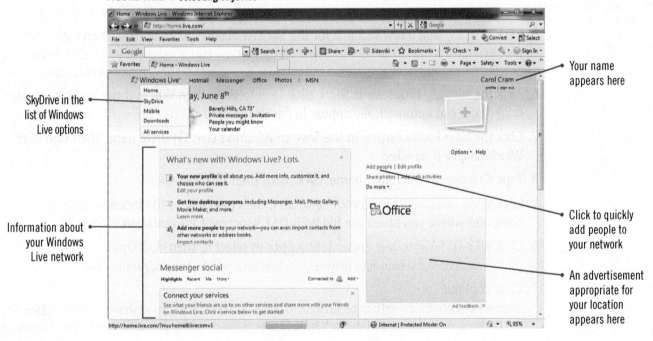

FIGURE WEB-4: Selecting SkyDrive

SkyDrive in the list of Windows Live options

Information about your Windows Live network

Your name appears here

Click to quickly add people to your network

An advertisement appropriate for your location appears here

Verifying your Windows Live ID

As soon as you accept the Windows Live terms, an e-mail is sent to the e-mail address you supplied when you created your Windows Live ID. Open your e-mail program, and then open the e-mail from Microsoft with the Subject line: Confirm your e-mail address for Windows Live. Follow the simple, step-by-step instructions in the e-mail to confirm your Windows Live ID. When the confirmation is complete, you will be asked to sign in to Windows Live, using your e-mail address and password. Once signed in, you will see your Windows Live Account page.

Web Apps

Uploading Files to Windows Live

Once you have created your Windows Live ID, you can sign in to Windows Live directly from Word, PowerPoint, Excel, or OneNote and start saving and uploading files. You upload files to your SkyDrive so you can share the files with other people, access the files from another computer, or use SkyDrive's additional storage. ░░░░░ You open a PowerPoint presentation, access your Windows Live account from Backstage view, and save a file to SkyDrive on Windows Live. You also create a new folder called Cengage directly from Backstage view and add a file to it.

STEPS

1. **Start PowerPoint, open the file** WEB-1.pptx **from the drive and folder where you store your Data Files, then save the file as** WEB-QST Vancouver Presentation

2. **Click the** File tab, **then click** Save & Send

   The Save & Send options available in PowerPoint are listed in Backstage view, as shown in Figure WEB-5.

3. **Click** Save to Web

QUICK TIP

Skip this step if the computer you are using signs you in automatically.

4. **Click** Sign In, **type your e-mail address, press [Tab], type your** password, **then click** OK

   The My Documents folder on your SkyDrive appears in the Save to Windows Live SkyDrive information area.

5. **Click** Save As, **wait a few seconds for the Save As dialog box to appear, then click** Save

   The file is saved to the My Documents folder on the SkyDrive that is associated with your Windows Live account. You can also create a new folder and upload files directly to SkyDrive from your hard drive.

6. **Click the** File tab, **click** Save & Send, **click** Save to Web, **then sign in if the My Documents folder does not automatically appear in Backstage view**

7. **Click the** New Folder button **in the Save to Windows Live SkyDrive pane, then sign in to Windows Live if directed**

8. **Type** Cengage **as the folder name, click** Next, **then click** Add files

9. **Click** select documents from your computer, **then navigate to the location on your computer where you saved the file WEB-QST Vancouver Presentation in Step 1**

10. **Click** WEB-QST Vancouver Presentation.pptx **to select it, then click** Open

    You can continue to add more files; however, you have no more files to upload at this time.

11. **Click** Continue

    In a few moments, the PowerPoint presentation is uploaded to your SkyDrive, as shown in Figure WEB-6. You can simply store the file on SkyDrive or you can choose to work on the presentation using the PowerPoint Web App.

12. **Click the** PowerPoint icon 🔲 **on your taskbar to return to PowerPoint, then close the presentation and exit PowerPoint**

FIGURE WEB-5: Save & Send options in Backstage view

PowerPoint file

Save & Send area
in Backstage view

Save to Web
option

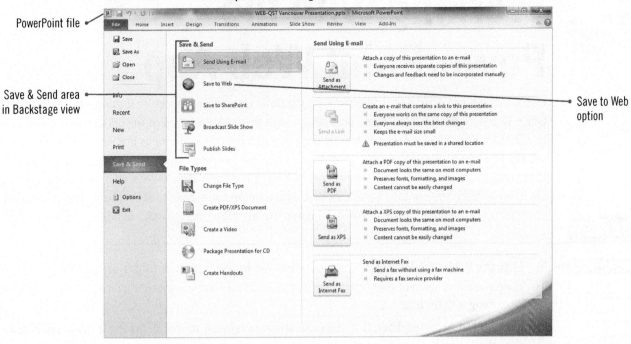

FIGURE WEB-6: File uploaded to the Cengage folder on Windows Live

Browser
window

Path to file

Current folder
menu bar

Uploaded file

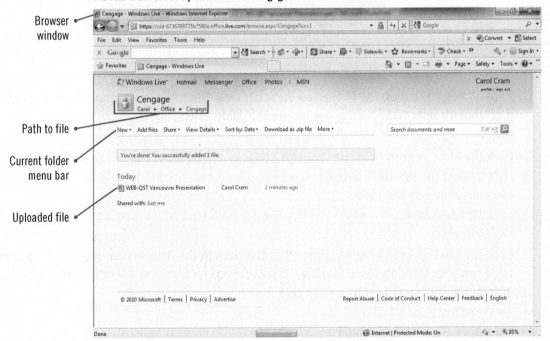

Working with the PowerPoint Web App

Once you have uploaded a file to SkyDrive on Windows Live, you can work on it using its corresponding Office Web App. **Office Web Apps** provide you with the tools you need to view documents online and to edit them right in your browser. You do not need to have Office programs installed on the computer you use to access SkyDrive and Office Web Apps. From SkyDrive, you can also open the document directly in the full Office application (for example, PowerPoint) if the application is installed on the computer you are using. ▰▰▰ You use the PowerPoint Web App to make some edits to the PowerPoint presentation. You then open the presentation in PowerPoint and use the full version to make additional edits.

STEPS

1. **Click the WEB-QST Vancouver Presentation file in the Cengage folder on SkyDrive**

   The presentation opens in your browser window. A menu is available, which includes the options you have for working with the file.

2. **Click Edit in Browser, then if a message appears related to installing the Sign-in Assistant, click the Close button ✖ to the far right of the message**

   In a few moments, the PowerPoint presentation opens in the PowerPoint Web App, as shown in Figure WEB-7. Table WEB-2 lists the commands you can perform using the PowerPoint Web App.

3. **Enter your name where indicated on Slide 1, click Slide 3 (New Tours) in the Slides pane, then click Delete Slide in the Slides group**

   The slide is removed from the presentation. You decide to open the file in the full version of PowerPoint on your computer so you can apply WordArt to the slide title. You work with the file in the full version of PowerPoint when you want to use functions, such as WordArt, that are not available on the PowerPoint Web App.

4. **Click Open in PowerPoint in the Office group, click OK in response to the message, then click Allow if requested**

   In a few moments, the revised version of the PowerPoint slide opens in PowerPoint on your computer.

5. **Click Enable Editing on the Protected View bar near the top of your presentation window if prompted, select QST Vancouver on the title slide, then click the Drawing Tools Format tab**

6. **Click the More button ▾ in the WordArt Styles group to show the selection of WordArt styles, select the WordArt style Gradient Fill - Blue-Gray, Accent 4, Reflection, then click a blank area outside the slide**

   The presentation appears in PowerPoint as shown in Figure WEB-8. Next, you save the revised version of the file to SkyDrive.

7. **Click the File tab, click Save As, notice that the path in the Address bar is to the Cengage folder on your Windows Live SkyDrive, type WEB-QST Vancouver Presentation_Revised. pptx in the File name text box, then click Save**

   The file is saved to your SkyDrive.

8. **Click the browser icon on the taskbar to open your SkyDrive page, then click Office next to your name in the SkyDrive path, view a list of recent documents, then click Cengage in the list to the left of the recent documents list to open the Cengage folder**

   Two PowerPoint files now appear in the Cengage folder.

9. **Exit the Web browser and close all tabs if prompted, then exit PowerPoint**

FIGURE WEB-7: Presentation opened in the PowerPoint Web App from Windows Live

Browser window

Name of Web App

PowerPoint Web App Ribbon

URL is the file location

FIGURE WEB-8: Revised PowerPoint presentation

PowerPoint title bar

PowerPoint Ribbon

Presentation title enhanced using full version of PowerPoint

Name added using PowerPoint Web App

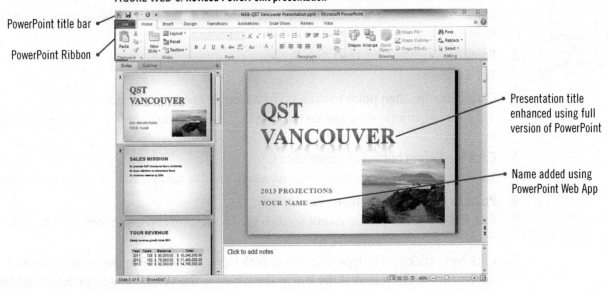

TABLE WEB-2: Commands on the PowerPoint Web App

tab	commands available
File	• Open in PowerPoint: select to open the file in PowerPoint on your computer • Where's the Save Button?: when you click this option, a message appears telling you that you do not need to save your presentation when you are working on it with PowerPoint Web App. The presentation is saved automatically as you work. • Print • Share • Properties • Give Feedback • Privacy • Terms of Use • Close
Home	• Clipboard group: Cut, Copy, Paste • Slides group: Add a New Slide, Delete a Slide, Duplicate a Slide, and Hide a Slide • Font group: Work with text: change the font, style, color, and size of selected text • Paragraph group: Work with paragraphs: add bullets and numbers, indent text, align text • Office group: Open the file in PowerPoint on your computer
Insert	• Insert a Picture • Insert a SmartArt diagram • Insert a link such as a link to another file on SkyDrive or to a Web page
View	• Editing view (the default) • Reading view • Slide Show view • Notes view

Creating Folders and Organizing Files on SkyDrive

As you have learned, you can sign in to SkyDrive directly from the Office applications PowerPoint, Excel, Word, and OneNote, or you can access SkyDrive directly through your Web browser. This option is useful when you are away from the computer on which you normally work or when you are using a computer that does not have Office applications installed. You can go to SkyDrive, create and organize folders, and then create or open files to work on with Office Web Apps. ▰▰ You access SkyDrive from your Web browser, create a new folder called Illustrated, and delete one of the PowerPoint files from the My Documents folder.

STEPS

TROUBLE
Go to Step 3 if you are already signed in.

1. **Open your Web browser, type** home.live.com **in the Address bar, then press** [Enter]
   The Windows Live home page opens. From here, you can sign in to your Windows Live account and then access SkyDrive.

TROUBLE
Type your Windows Live ID (your e-mail) and password, then click Sign in if prompted to do so.

2. **Sign into Windows Live as directed**
   You are signed in to your Windows Live page. From this page, you can take advantage of the many applications available on Windows Live, including SkyDrive.

3. **Point to** Windows Live, **then click** SkyDrive
   SkyDrive opens.

4. **Click** Cengage, **then point to** WEB-QST Vancouver Presentation.pptx
   A menu of options for working with the file, including a Delete button to the far right, appears to the right of the filename.

5. **Click the** Delete button ☒, **then click** OK
   The file is removed from the Cengage folder on your SkyDrive. You still have a copy of the file on your computer.

6. **Point to** Windows Live, **then click** SkyDrive
   Your SkyDrive screen with the current selection of folders available on your SkyDrive opens, as shown in Figure WEB-9.

7. **Click** New, **click** Folder, **type** Illustrated, **click** Next, **click** Office **in the path under Add documents to Illustrated at the top of the window, then click** View all **in the list under Personal**
   You are returned to your list of folders, where you see the new Illustrated folder.

8. **Click** Cengage, **point to** WEB-QST Vancouver Presentation_Revised.pptx, **click** More, **click** Move, **then click the** Illustrated folder

9. **Click** Move this file into Illustrated, **as shown in Figure WEB-10**
   The file is moved to the Illustrated folder.

FIGURE WEB-9: Folders on your SkyDrive

Current location

Folders currently available

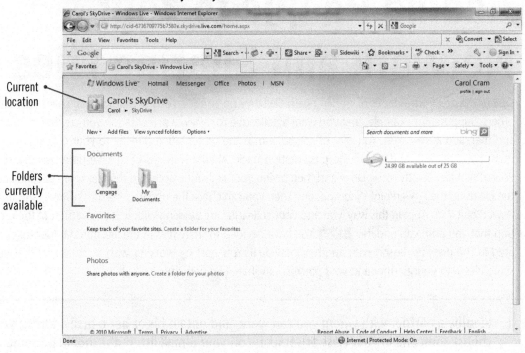

FIGURE WEB-10: Moving a file to the Illustrated folder

Click to move file to this location

Be sure to rename a file before moving it if you are moving it to a location where another copy of the same file exists

Name of file to be moved

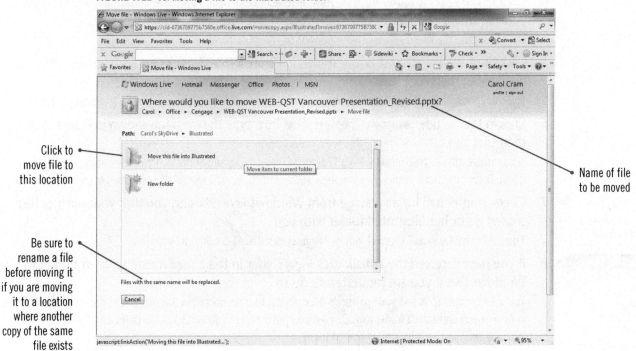

Adding People to Your Network and Sharing Files

One of the great advantages of working with SkyDrive on Windows Live is that you can share your files with others. Suppose, for example, that you want a colleague to review a presentation you created in PowerPoint and then add a new slide. You can, of course, e-mail the presentation directly to your colleague, who can then make changes and e-mail the presentation back. Alternatively, you can save time by uploading the PowerPoint file directly to SkyDrive and then giving your colleague access to the file. Your colleague can edit the file using the PowerPoint Web App, and then you can check the updated file on SkyDrive, also using the PowerPoint Web App. In this way, you and your colleague are working with just one version of the presentation that you both can update. ⬛⬛⬛ You have decided to share files in the Illustrated folder that you created in the previous lesson with another individual. You start by working with a partner so that you can share files with your partner and your partner can share files with you.

STEPS

TROUBLE
If you cannot find a partner, read the steps so you understand how the process works.

1. **Identify a partner with whom you can work, and obtain his or her e-mail address; you can choose someone in your class or someone on your e-mail list, but it should be someone who will be completing these steps when you are**

2. **From the Illustrated folder, click Share**

3. **Click Edit permissions**

   The Edit permissions page opens. On this page, you can select the individual with whom you would like to share the contents of the Illustrated folder.

4. **Click in the Enter a name or an e-mail address text box, type the e-mail address of your partner, then press [Tab]**

   You can define the level of access that you want to give your partner.

5. **Click the Can view files list arrow shown in Figure WEB-11, click Can add, edit details, and delete files, then click Save**

   You can choose to send a notification to each individual when you grant permission to access your files.

TROUBLE
If you do not receive a message from Windows Live, your partner has not yet completed the steps to share the Illustrated folder.

6. **Click in the Include your own message text box, type the message shown in Figure WEB-12, then click Send**

   Your partner will receive a message from Windows Live advising him or her that you have shared your Illustrated folder. If your partner is completing the steps at the same time, you will receive an e-mail from your partner.

7. **Check your e-mail for a message from Windows Live advising you that your partner has shared his or her Illustrated folder with you**

   The subject of the e-mail message will be "[Name] has shared documents with you."

QUICK TIP
You will know you are on your partner's SkyDrive because you will see your partner's first name at the beginning of the SkyDrive path.

8. **If you have received the e-mail, click View folder in the e-mail message, then sign in to Windows Live if you are requested to do so**

   You are now able to access your partner's Illustrated folder on his or her SkyDrive. You can download files in your partner's Illustrated folder to your own computer where you can work on them and then upload them again to your partner's Illustrated shared folder.

9. **Exit the browser**

FIGURE WEB-11: Editing folder permissions

Folder permissions will be changed for the Illustrated folder

Click to select network permission options

Type email address to continue to add people

Person whose permission status will change

Click to select person from list of contacts

Click to select permission option

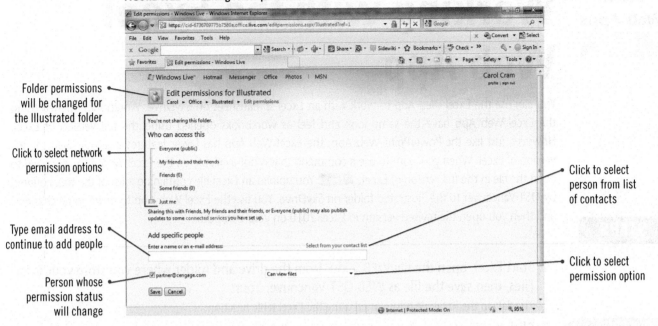

FIGURE WEB-12: Entering a message to notify a person that file sharing permission has been granted

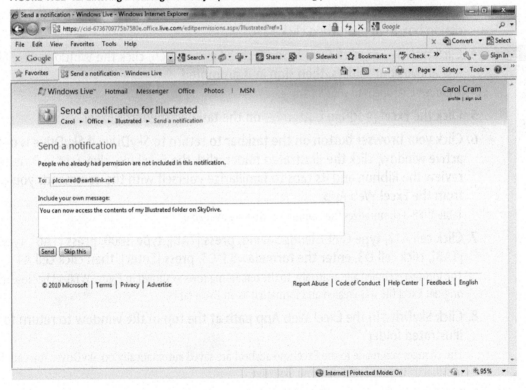

Sharing files on SkyDrive

When you share a folder with other people, the people with whom you share a folder can download the file to their computers and then make changes using the full version of the corresponding Office application.

Once these changes are made, each individual can then upload the file to SkyDrive and into a folder shared with you and others. In this way, you can create a network of people with whom you share your files.

Working with the Excel Web App

You can use the Excel Web App to work with an Excel spreadsheet on SkyDrive. Workbooks opened using the Excel Web App have the same look and feel as workbooks opened using the full version of Excel. However, just like the PowerPoint Web App, the Excel Web App has fewer features available than the full version of Excel. When you want to use a command that is not available on the Excel Web App, you need to open the file in the full version of Excel. ░░░░░ You upload an Excel file containing a list of the tours offered by QST Vancouver to the Illustrated folder on SkyDrive. You use the Excel Web App to make some changes, and then you open the revised version in Excel 2010 on your computer.

STEPS

1. **Start Excel, open the file WEB-2.xlsx from the drive and folder where you store your Data Files, then save the file as WEB-QST Vancouver Tours**

   The data in the Excel file is formatted using the Excel table function.

2. **Click the File tab, click Save & Send, then click Save to Web**

   In a few moments, you should see three folders to which you can save spreadsheets. My Documents and Cengage are personal folder that contains files that only you can access. Illustrated is a shared folder that contains files you can share with others in your network. The Illustrated folder is shared with your partner.

3. **Click the Illustrated folder, click the Save As button, wait a few seconds for the Save As dialog box to appear, then click Save**

4. **Click the File tab, click Save & Send, click Save to Web, click the Windows Live SkyDrive link above your folders, then sign in if prompted**

   Windows Live opens to your SkyDrive.

5. **Click the Excel program button ▓ on the taskbar, then exit Excel**

6. **Click your browser button on the taskbar to return to SkyDrive if SkyDrive is not the active window, click the Illustrated folder, click the Excel file, click Edit in Browser, then review the Ribbon and its tabs to familiarize yourself with the commands you can access from the Excel Web App**

   Table WEB-3 summarizes the commands that are available.

7. **Click cell A12, type Gulf Islands Sailing, press [TAB], type 3000, press [TAB], type 10, press [TAB], click cell D3, enter the formula =B3*C3, press [Enter], then click cell A1**

   The formula is copied automatically to the remaining rows as shown in Figure WEB-13 because the data in the original Excel file was created and formatted as an Excel table.

8. **Click SkyDrive in the Excel Web App path at the top of the window to return to the Illustrated folder**

   The changes you made to the Excel spreadsheet are saved automatically on SkyDrive. You can download the file directly to your computer from SkyDrive.

9. **Point to the Excel file, click More, click Download, click Save, navigate to the location where you save the files for this book, name the file WEB-QST Vancouver Tours_Updated, click Save, then click Close in the Download complete dialog box**

   The updated version of the spreadsheet is saved on your computer and on SkyDrive.

10. **Exit the Web browser**

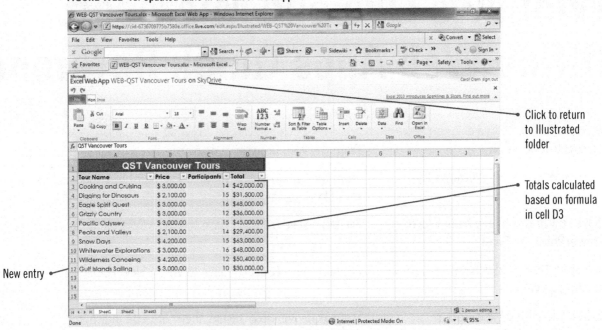

Click to return
to Illustrated
folder

Totals calculated
based on formula
in cell D3

New entry

TABLE WEB-3: Commands on the Excel Web App

tab	commands available
File	• Open in Excel: select to open the file in Excel on your computer • Where's the Save Button?: when you click this option, a message appears telling you that you do not need to save your spreadsheet when you are working in it with Excel Web App; the spreadsheet is saved automatically as you work • Save As • Share • Download a Snapshot: a snapshot contains only the values and the formatting; you cannot modify a snapshot • Download a Copy: the file can be opened and edited in the full version of Excel • Give Feedback • Privacy Statement • Terms of Use • Close
Home	• Clipboard group: Cut, Copy, Paste • Font group: change the font, style, color, and size of selected labels and values, as well as border styles and fill colors • Alignment group: change vertical and horizontal alignment and turn on the Wrap Text feature • Number group: change the number format and increase or decrease decimal places • Tables: sort and filter data in a table and modify Table Options • Cells: insert and delete cells • Data: refresh data and find labels or values • Office: open the file in Excel on your computer
Insert	• Insert a Table • Insert a Hyperlink to a Web page

Exploring other Office Web Apps

Two other Office Web Apps are Word and OneNote. You can share files on SkyDrive directly from Word or from OneNote using the same method you used to share files from PowerPoint and Excel. After you upload a Word or OneNote file to SkyDrive, you can work with it in its corresponding Office Web App. To familiarize yourself with the commands available in an Office Web App, open the file and then review the commands on each tab on the Ribbon. If you want to perform a task that is not available in the Office Web App, open the file in the full version of the application.

In addition to working with uploaded files, you can create files from new on SkyDrive. Simply sign in to SkyDrive and open a folder. With a folder open, click New and then select the Web App you want to use to create the new file.

Windows Live and Microsoft Office Web Apps Quick Reference

To Do This	Go Here
Access Windows Live	From the Web browser, type **home.live.com**, then click Sign In
Access SkyDrive on Windows Live	From the Windows Live home page, point to Windows Live, then click SkyDrive
Save to Windows Live from Word, PowerPoint, or Excel	File tab | Save & Send | Save to Web | Select a folder | Save As
Create a New Folder from Backstage view	File tab | Save & Send | Save to Web | New Folder button
Edit a File with a Web App	From SkyDrive, click the file, then click Edit in Browser
Open a File in a desktop version of the application from a Web App: Word, Excel, PowerPoint	Click Open in [Application] in the Office group in each Office Web App
Share files on Windows Live	From SkyDrive, click the folder containing the files to share, click Share on the menu bar, click Edit permissions, enter the e-mail address of the person to share files with, click the Can view files list arrow, click Can add, edit details, and delete files, then click Save

Glossary

Active The currently available document, program, or object; on the taskbar, the button of the active document appears in a darker shade while the buttons of other open documents are dimmed.

Alignment The position of text in a document relative to the margins.

Anchored When a floating graphic is associated with a paragraph so that it moves with the paragraph if the paragraph is moved; an anchor symbol appears next to the paragraph when the floating graphic is selected and formatting marks are displayed.

Ascending order Lists data alphabetically or sequentially (from A to Z, 0 to 9, or earliest to latest).

AutoComplete A feature that automatically suggests text to insert.

AutoCorrect A feature that automatically detects and corrects typing errors, minor spelling errors, and capitalization, and inserts certain typographical symbols as you type.

Automatic page break A page break that is inserted automatically at the bottom of a page.

Backstage view The set of commands related to managing files and the information about them, including opening, printing, and saving a document, creating a new document, and protecting a document before sharing it with others.

Backward-compatible Software feature that enables documents saved in an older version of a program to be opened in a newer version of the program.

Bibliography A list of sources that you consulted or cited while creating a document.

Bitmap graphic A graphic that is composed of a series of small dots called "pixels" and often saved with a .bmp, .png, .jpg, .tif, or .gif file extension.

Blog An informal journal that is created by an individual or a group and available to the public on the Internet; short for weblog.

Blogger The person who creates and maintains a blog.

Boilerplate text Text that appears in every version of a merged document.

Bold Formatting applied to text to make it thicker and darker.

Bookmark Text that identifies a location, such as the beginning of a paragraph or a selection of text in a document.

Border A line that can be added above, below, or to the sides of a paragraph, text, or table cell; a line that divides the columns and rows of a table. Also refers to a window's edge; drag to resize the window.

Brightness The relative lightness of a photograph.

Building block A reusable piece of formatted content or document part that is stored in a gallery.

Building Block Gallery content control A reusable piece of formatted content or a document part that is stored in a gallery. The Building Block Gallery content control often contains text and objects, such as pictures and SmartArt graphics, into which users can enter content when completing a form.

Bullet A small graphic symbol used to identify an item in a list.

Cell The box formed by the intersection of a table row and a table column.

Cell reference A code that identifies a cell's position in a table. Each cell reference contains a letter (A, B, C, and so on) to identify its column and a number (1, 2, 3, and so on) to identify its row.

Center Alignment in which an item is centered between the margins.

Character spacing Formatting that changes the width or scale of characters, expands or condenses the amount of space between characters, raises or lowers characters relative to the line of text, and adjusts kerning (the space between standard combinations of letters).

Character style A named set of character format settings that can be applied to text to format it all at once; you use a character style to apply format settings only to select text within a paragraph.

Chart A visual representation of numerical data, usually used to illustrate trends, patterns, or relationships.

Check Box content control A content control that inserts a check box. You click a Check Box content control to insert a symbol, such as an "X" or a check mark.

Check Box form field control A legacy tool that inserts a check box, similar to a Check Box content control, but that is inserted using the Legacy Tools command in the Controls group on the Developer tab.

Citation A parenthetical reference in the document text that gives credit to the source for a quotation or other information used in a document.

Click and Type A feature that allows you to automatically apply the necessary paragraph formatting to a table, graphic, or text when you insert the item in a blank area of a document in Print Layout or Web Layout view.

Click and Type pointer A pointer used to move the insertion point and automatically apply the paragraph formatting necessary to insert text at that location in the document.

Clip A media file, such as a graphic, photograph, sound, movie, or animation, that can be inserted into a document.

Clip art A collection of graphic images that can be inserted into documents, presentations, Web pages, spreadsheets, and other Office files.

Clip Organizer A library of the clips that come with Word.

Clipboard A temporary storage area for items that are cut or copied from any Office file and are available for pasting. *See* Office Clipboard and System Clipboard.

Cloud computing When data, applications, and resources are stored on servers accessed over the Internet or a company's internal network rather than on users' computers.

Color saturation The vividness and intensity of color in a photograph.

Color tone The relative warmth or coolness of the colors in a photograph.

Column break A break that forces text following the break to begin at the top of the next column.

Combo Box content control One of the two Drop-Down content controls. To use a Combo Box content control, you select an item from a list of choices or type in a new item.

Comment An embedded note or annotation that an author or a reviewer adds to a document; appears in a comment balloon, usually to the right of the document text.

Compatible The capability of different programs to work together and exchange data.

Content control An interactive object that is embedded in a document you create from a template and that expedites your ability to customize the document with your own information.

Contextual tab Tab on the Ribbon that appears when needed to complete a specific task; for example, if you select a graphic, the Picture Tools Format tab appears.

Contrast The difference in brightness between the darkest and the lightest areas of a photograph.

Control A placeholder that the form developer inserts in a form; it is used to contain the data associated with the label.

Copy To place a copy of an item on the Clipboard without removing it from a document. Also, to make a duplicate copy of a file, folder, or other object that you want to store in another location.

Copy and paste To move text or graphics using the Copy and Paste commands.

Crop To trim away part of a graphic. The act of making a picture smaller by taking away parts of the top, bottom, and sides.

Cross-reference Text that electronically refers the reader to another part of the document; you click a cross-reference to move directly to a specific location in the document.

Cut To remove an item from a document and place it on the Clipboard.

Cut and paste To move text or graphics using the Cut and Paste commands.

Data field A category of information, such as last name, first name, street address, city, or postal code.

Data record A complete set of related information for a person or an item, such as a person's contact information, including name, address, phone number, e-mail address, and so on.

Data Source In mail merge, the file with the unique data for individual people or items; the data merged with a main document to produce multiple versions.

Date Picker content control A content control that provides you with a calendar you can use to select a specific date.

Delete To permanently remove an item from a document.

Descending order Lists data in reverse alphabetical or sequential order (from Z to A, 9 to 0, or latest to earliest).

Dialog box launcher An icon available in many groups on the Ribbon that you can click to open a dialog box or task pane, offering an alternative way to choose commands. *Also called* launcher.

Document The electronic file you create using Word.

Document properties Details about a file, such as author name or the date the file was created, that are used to describe, organize, and search for files.

Document window The portion of a program window in which you create the document; displays all or part of an open document.

Draft view A view that shows a document without margins, headers and footers, or graphics.

Drag and drop To use a pointing device to move or copy a file or folder to a new location.

Drawing gridlines A grid of nonprinting lines that appears within the margins in Print Layout view to help you size, align, and position graphics. *See also* Gridlines.

Drop cap A large dropped initial capital letter that is often used to set off the first paragraph in a document.

Drop-Down Form Field content control A content control that provides users with a list of choices. Two drop-down content controls are available: the Drop-Down List content control and the Combo Box content control.

Drop-Down List content control One of the two Drop-Down content controls. To use a Drop-Down List content control, you select an item from a list of choices.

Endnote Text that provides additional information or acknowledges sources for text in a document and that appears at the end of a document.

Figure Any object such as a chart, a picture, an equation, or an embedded object to which a caption can be added.

File An electronic collection of stored data that has a unique name, distinguishing it from other files, such as a letter, video, or program.

File tab Provides access to Backstage view and the Word Options dialog box.

Filename A unique, descriptive name for a file that identifies the file's content.

Filter In a mail merge, to pull out records that meet specific criteria and include only those records in the merge.

First line indent A type of indent in which the first line of a paragraph is indented more than the subsequent lines.

Floating graphic A graphic to which text wrapping has been applied, making the graphic independent of text and able to be moved anywhere on a page.

Font The typeface or design of a set of characters (letters, numbers, symbols, and punctuation marks).

Font effect Font formatting that applies a special effect to text, such as small caps or superscript.

Font size The size of characters, measured in points (pts).

Footer Information, such as text, a page number, or a graphic, that appears at the bottom of every page in a document or a section.

Footnote Text that provides additional information or acknowledges sources for text in a document and that appears at the bottom of the page on which the note reference mark appears.

Form A structured document with spaces reserved for entering information.

Form template A file that contains the structure of a form. You create new forms from a form template. Changes made to new forms based on a form template, such as changing labels, do not affect the structure of the form template file.

Format Painter A feature used to copy the format settings applied to the selected text to other text you want to format the same way.

Formatting marks Nonprinting characters that appear on screen to indicate the ends of paragraphs, tabs, and other formatting elements.

Full Screen Reading view A view that shows only the document text on screen, making it easier to read and annotate.

Gallery A visual collection of choices you can browse through to make a selection. Often available with Live Preview.

Gridlines Nonprinting lines that appear on screen to show the boundaries of table cells or to help you size, align, and position graphics. *See also* Table gridlines or Drawing gridlines.

Group In a Microsoft program window's Ribbon, a section containing related command buttons.

Gutter Extra space left for a binding at the top, left, or inside margin of a document.

Hanging indent A type of indent in which the second and subsequent lines of a paragraph are indented more than the first.

Hard page break *See* Manual page break.

Header Information, such as text, a page number, or a graphic, that appears at the top of every page in a document or a section.

Header row The first row of a table that usually contains the column headings.

Highlighting Transparent color that can be applied to text to call attention to it.

Horizontal ruler A ruler that appears at the top of the document window in Print Layout, Draft, and Web Layout view.

Horizontal scroll bar *See* Scroll bar.

Hyperlink Text or a graphic that opens a file, Web page, or other item when clicked. *Also called* link.

I-beam pointer The pointer used to move the insertion point and select text.

Indent The space between the edge of a line of text or a paragraph and the margin.

Indent marker A marker on the horizontal ruler that shows the indent settings for the active paragraph.

Index Text, usually appearing at the end of a document, that lists terms and topics in a document that you have marked for inclusion in the index, along with the pages on which they appear.

Inline graphic A graphic that is part of a line of text.

Insertion point The blinking vertical line that shows where text will appear when you type in a document.

Integrate To incorporate a document and parts of a document created in one program into another program; for example, to incorporate an Excel chart into a PowerPoint slide, or an Access table into a Word document.

Interface The look and feel of a program; for example, the appearance of commands and the way they are organized in the program window.

Italic Formatting applied to text to make the characters slant to the right.

Justify Alignment in which an item is flush with both the left and right margins.

Keyboard shortcut A combination of keys or a function key that can be pressed to perform a command.

Label (form) A word or phrase such as "Date" or "Location" that tells you the kind of information required for a given area in a form.

Landscape orientation Page orientation in which the page is wider than it is tall.

Launch To open or start a program on your computer.

Launcher *See* Dialog box launcher.

Left-align Alignment in which the item is flush with the left margin.

Left indent A type of indent in which the left edge of a paragraph is moved in from the left margin.

Legacy Tools controls Form controls used when the form designer requires more control over the type of content entered into the form than is available with content controls. Legacy Tools controls include Text form field controls and Check Box form field controls.

Line spacing The amount of space between lines of text.

Linked style A named set of format settings that are applied either to characters within a paragraph or to the entire paragraph, depending on whether the entire paragraph or specific text is selected.

Link (text box) A connection between two or more text boxes so that the text flows automatically from one text box to another.

List box A box that displays a list of options from which you can choose (you may need to scroll and adjust your view to see additional options in the list).

List layout A SmartArt graphic used to show information that is non-sequential. Variations include Vertical Bullet List, Stacked List, Horizontal Picture List, and Trapezoid List.

List style A named set of format settings, such as indent and outline numbering, that you can apply to a list to format it all at once.

Live Preview A feature that lets you point to a choice in a gallery or palette and see the results in the document without actually clicking the choice.

Mail merge To merge a main document that contains boilerplate text with a file that contains customized information for many individual items to create customized versions of the main document.

Main document In a mail merge, the document with the boilerplate text.

Manage Styles dialog box A dialog box used to change options for working with styles (for example, rename and delete styles) and to copy styles between documents.

Manual page break A page break inserted to force the text following the break to begin at the top of the next page.

Margin The blank area between the edge of the text and the edge of a page.

Merge To combine adjacent cells into a single larger cell. *See also* Mail merge.

Merge field A placeholder that you insert in the main document to indicate where the data from each record should be inserted when you perform a mail merge.

Merged document In a mail merge, the document that contains customized versions of the main document.

Microsoft Word Help button A button used to access the Word Help system.

Mini toolbar A toolbar that appears faintly above text when you first select it and includes the most commonly used text and paragraph formatting commands.

Mirror margins Margins used in documents with facing pages, where the inside and outside margins are mirror images of each other.

Multilevel list A list with a hierarchical structure; an outline.

Navigation pane A pane showing the headings and subheadings as entries that you can click to move directly to a specific heading anywhere in a document. The Navigation pane opens along the left side of the document window.

Negative indent A type of indent in which the left edge of a paragraph is moved to the left of the left margin.

Nested table A table inserted in a cell of another table.

Normal style The paragraph style that is used by default to format text typed in a blank Word document.

Normal template The template that is loaded automatically when a new document is created in Word.

Note reference mark A mark (such as a letter or a number) that appears next to text to indicate that additional information is offered in a footnote or endnote.

Nudge To move a graphic a small amount in one direction using the arrow keys.

Office Clipboard A temporary storage area shared by all Office programs that can be used to cut, copy, and paste multiple items within and between Office programs. The Office Clipboard can hold up to 24 items collected from any Office program. *See also* System Clipboard.

Office Web App Versions of the Microsoft Office applications with limited functionality that are available online from Windows Live SkyDrive. Users can view documents online and then edit them in the browser using a selection of functions. Office Web Apps are available for Word, PowerPoint, Excel, and One Note.

Online collaboration The ability to incorporate feedback or share information across the Internet or a company network or intranet.

Open To use one of the methods for opening a document to retrieve it and display it in the document window.

Option button A small circle in a dialog box that you click to select only one of two or more related options.

Orphan The first line of a paragraph when it appears alone at the bottom of a page.

Outdent *See* Negative indent.

Outline view A view that shows the headings of a document organized as an outline.

Paragraph spacing The amount of space between paragraphs.

Paragraph style A named set of paragraph and character format settings that can be applied to a paragraph to format it all at once.

Password A special sequence of numbers and letters known only to selected users, that users can create to control who can access the files in their user account area; helps keep users' computer information secure.

Paste To insert items stored on the Clipboard into a document.

Picture content control A content control used in forms that provides a placeholder for a picture; you can insert a picture in a Picture content control in a form.

Plain Text content control A form control used when you do not need formatting applied to text when users complete a form and enter text in the form control. You can also specify that a style be applied to text entered in a Plain Text content control when form users enter text in the form.

Point (n.) The unit of measurement for text characters and the space between paragraphs and characters; 1/72 of an inch.

Portrait orientation Page orientation in which the page is taller than it is wide.

Previewing Viewing a document on screen to see exactly how it will look when printed.

Print Layout view A view that shows a document as it will look on a printed page.

Print Preview A view of a file as it will appear when printed.

Quick Access toolbar A small toolbar on the left side of a Microsoft application program window's title bar, containing icons that you click to perform common actions quickly, such as saving a file.

Quick Part A reusable piece of content that can be inserted into a document, including a field, document property, or a preformatted building block.

Quick Style A set of format settings that can be applied to text or an object to format it quickly and easily; Quick Styles appear in galleries. *See also* Style.

Quick Style set A group of paragraph and character styles that share common fonts, colors, and formats, and are designed to be used together in a document to give it a cohesive look.

Reveal Formatting task pane A pane that shows in a list all the formatting applied to selected text, including Font, Paragraph, and Section formatting.

Ribbon In many Microsoft application program windows, a horizontal strip near the top of the window that contains tabs (pages) of grouped command buttons that you click to interact with the program.

Rich Text content control A form control used when you want the content entered in the Rich Text content control by a user to be formatted with specific font and paragraph formats. You can also specify that a style be applied to text when form users enter text in the Rich Text content control.

Right-align Alignment in which an item is flush with the right margin.

Right indent A type of indent in which the right edge of a paragraph is moved in from the right margin.

Rotate handle A green circle that appears above a graphic when the graphic is selected; drag the rotate handle to rotate the graphic.

Sans serif font A font (such as Calibri) whose characters do not include serifs, which are small strokes at the ends of letters.

Save To store a file permanently on a disk or to overwrite the copy of a file that is stored on a disk with the changes made to the file.

Save As Command used to save a file for the first time or to create a new file with a different filename, leaving the original file intact.

Scale To resize a graphic so that its height to width ratio remains the same.

Screen capture A snapshot of your screen, as if you took a picture of it with a camera, which you can paste into a document.

ScreenTip A label that appears when you position the mouse over an object; identifies the name of a button or feature, briefly describes its function, conveys any keyboard shortcut for the command, and includes a link to associated help topics, if any.

Scroll To use the scroll bars or the arrow keys to display different parts of a document in the document window.

Scroll arrow The arrow at the end of a scroll bar that is clicked to scroll a document one line at a time, or to scroll a document left and right in the document window.

Scroll bar The bar on the right edge (vertical scroll bar) or bottom edge (horizontal scroll bar) of the document window that is used to display different parts of the document in the document window.

Scroll box A box in a scroll bar that you can drag to display a different part of a window; indicates your relative position within a document.

Section A portion of a document that is separated from the rest of the document by section breaks.

Section break A formatting mark inserted to divide a document into sections.

Select To change the appearance of an item by clicking, double-clicking, or dragging across it, to indicate that you want to perform an action on it.

Serif font A font (such as Times New Roman) whose characters include serifs, which are small strokes at the ends of letters.

Shading A background color or pattern that can be applied to text, tables, or graphics.

Shortcut key *See* Keyboard shortcut.

Sizing handles The white circles that appear around a graphic when it is selected; used to change the size or shape of a graphic.

SkyDrive An online storage and file sharing service. Access to SkyDrive is through a Windows Live account. You can store up to 25 GB of data in a personal SkyDrive, with each file a maximum size of 50 MB.

SmartArt graphic A diagram, list, organizational chart, or other graphic created using the SmartArt command and used to provide a visual representation of data. Eight layout categories of SmartArt graphics are available in Word: List, Picture, Process, Cycle, Hierarchy, Relationship, Matrix, and Pyramid.

Soft page break *See* Automatic page break.

Sort (data) To organize data, such as table rows, items in a list, or records in a mail merge, in ascending or descending order.

Split To divide a cell into two or more cells, or to divide a table into two tables.

Status bar The bar at the bottom of the Word program window that shows information about the document, including the current page number, the total number of pages in a document, the document word count, and the on/off status of spelling and grammar checking, and contains the view buttons, the Zoom level button, and the Zoom slider.

Style A named collection of character and paragraph formats that are stored together and can be applied to text to format it quickly. *See also* Quick Style.

Style Inspector Shows the Paragraph and Text level formatting applied to selected text; used to reset paragraph and text formatting to the default formats and to clear formatting.

Styles Gallery Location where all the styles associated with a Quick Style set are stored; you access the Style Gallery by clicking the More button in the Styles group on the Home tab.

Styles task pane Contains all the styles available to the current document and the buttons to access the Style Inspector, the Reveal Formatting task pane, and the Manage Styles dialog box.

Subentry Text included under a main entry in an index.

Subscript A font effect in which text is formatted in a smaller font size and placed below the line of text.

Suite A group of programs that are bundled together and share a similar interface, making it easy to transfer skills and program content among them.

Superscript A font effect in which text is formatted in a smaller font size and placed above the line of text.

Symbol A special character that can be inserted into a document using the Symbol command.

System Clipboard A clipboard that stores only the last item cut or copied from a document. *See also* Clipboard and Office Clipboard.

Tab A part of the Ribbon or a dialog box that includes groups of buttons for related commands.

Tab (ruler) A location on the horizontal ruler that indicates where to align text. *See also* Tab stop.

Tab leader A line that appears in front of tabbed text.

Tab stop A location on the horizontal ruler that indicates where to align text.

Table A grid made up of rows and columns of cells that can contain text and graphics.

Table gridlines Nonprinting blue dotted lines that show the boundaries of table cells. *See also* Gridlines.

Table style A named set of table format settings that can be applied to a table to format it all at once. The Table style includes settings for both the table grid and the table text.

Template A formatted document that contains placeholder text you can replace with new text. A file that contains the basic structure of a document including headers and footers, styles, and graphic elements.

Text box (document) A container that you can fill with text and graphics; created from the Insert tab in Word.

Text control A Legacy Tool. *Also called* Text Form Field control.

Text effect Formatting that applies a visual effect to text, such as a shadow, glow, outline, or reflection.

Text Form Field control A Legacy Tool used when the form developer requires more control over how the content control is configured than is possible when using a Rich Text content control or a Plain Text content control. A Text Form Field control is inserted using the Legacy Tools command in the Controls group on the Developer tab.

Theme A set of unified design elements, including theme colors, theme fonts for body text and headings, and theme effects for graphics that can be applied to a document all at once.

Thumbnail Smaller version of a page that appears in the Navigation pane when you select the Browse pages in your document tab on the Navigation pane.

Title bar The bar at the top of the program window that indicates the program name and the name of the current file.

Toggle button A button that turns a feature on and off.

User interface A collective term for all the ways you interact with a software program.

User template Any template created by the user.

Vertical alignment The position of text in a document relative to the top and bottom margins.

Vertical ruler A ruler that appears on the left side of the document window in Print Layout view.

Vertical scroll bar *See* Scroll bar.

View A way of displaying a document in the document window; each view provides features useful for editing and formatting different types of documents. Views include Print Layout (the default), Full Screen Reading, Web Layout, Outline, and Draft.

View buttons Buttons on the status bar that you use to change document views.

Web Layout view A view that shows a document as it will look when viewed with a Web browser.

Widow The last line of a paragraph when it is carried over to the top of the following page, separate from the rest of the paragraph.

Windows Live A collection of services and Web applications that people can access through a login. Windows Live services include access to e-mail and instant messaging, storage of files on SkyDrive, sharing and storage of photos, networking with people, downloading software, and interfacing with a mobile device.

Word processing program A software program that includes tools for entering, editing, and formatting text and graphics.

Word program window The window that contains the Word program elements, including the document window, Quick Access toolbar, Ribbon, and status bar.

Word wrap A feature that automatically moves the insertion point to the next line as you type.

WordArt A drawing object that contains text formatted with special shapes, patterns, and orientations.

Workgroup Template A template created for distribution to others.

Works cited A list of sources that you cited while creating a document.

XE **(Index Entry)** Field code inserted next to text marked for inclusion in an index.

XML Acronym that stands for eXtensible Markup Language, which is a language used to structure, store, and send information.

XML format New file format for Word documents beginning with Word 2007.

Zoom level button A button on the status bar that you use to change the zoom level of the document in the document window.

Zoom slider An adjustment on the status bar that you use to enlarge or decrease the display size of the document in the document window.

Zooming in A feature that makes a document appear bigger but shows less of it on screen at once; does not affect actual document size.

Zooming out A feature that shows more of a document on screen at once but at a reduced size; does not affect actual document size.

Index

M

Mail Merge feature, WD 2, 130–131
Mail Merge Recipients dialog box, WD 136–137, 144
mail merge templates, WD 132
mailing labels, WD 142–143
Mailings tab, WD 141
main documents, WD 130, 132–133
Manage Styles dialog box, WD 194
Manage versions option, Info tab, WD 40
managing styles, WD 194–195
manual page break, WD 106–107
margins, WD 102–103
Mark Index Entry dialog box, WD 162–165
Match Fields command, WD 141
merge fields, WD 130, 138–139, 145
merged document, WD 130
merging
  cells, WD 86–87, 212
  data, WD 140–141
merging documents, WD 129–152
  data sources, designing, WD 134–135
  labels, creating, WD 142–143
  mail merge, WD 130–131
  main documents, creating, WD 132–133
  merge fields, adding, WD 138–139
  merging data, WD 140–141
  overview, WD 129
  records
    editing, WD 136–137
    entering, WD 136–137
    filtering, WD 144–145
    sorting, WD 144–145
Microsoft Access, OFF 2, 5
Microsoft Excel. *See* Excel
Microsoft Office, OFF 1–16
  closing files, OFF 14–15
  creating files, OFF 8–9

exiting programs, OFF 4–5
Help system, OFF 14–15
opening files, OFF 10–11
overview, OFF 2–3
saving files, OFF 8–11
starting programs, OFF 4–5
user interface, OFF 6–7
viewing and printing documents, OFF 12–13
Microsoft Office Web Apps. *See* Web Apps
Microsoft Outlook, WD 135
Microsoft PowerPoint, OFF 2
Microsoft Windows Live. *See* Windows Live
Microsoft Word. *See* Word
Microsoft Word Help button, WD 4–5
Mini toolbar, WD 12–13
mirror margins, WD 103
mobile devices, Windows Live apps for, WEB 3
Modify Style dialog box, WD 184–185
modifying
  columns, WD 82–83
  predefined styles, WD 184–185
  rows, WD 82–83
mouse pointers, WD 5
moving
  columns, WD 81
  rows, WD 81
multilevel lists, WD 62
multipage documents, WD 153–180
  creating in Outline view, WD 154–155
  finalizing, WD 170–171
  generating
    indexes, WD 164–165
    table of contents, WD 160–161
  inserting footers in multiple sections, WD 166–167
  inserting headers in multiple sections, WD 168–169
  marking entries for indexes, WD 162–163

navigating, WD 158–159
overview, WD 153
working in Outline view, WD 156–157
My templates folder, WD 197

N

navigating
  documents, WD 16–17, 33
  multipage documents, WD 158–159
Navigation pane, Print Layout view, WD 158
negative indent, WD 61
nested tables, WD 91
networks
  adding people to, WEB 12–13
  sharing files on, WEB 12–13
  via Windows Live, WEB 3
New Address List dialog box, WD 134–135
next page section breaks, WD 104
No Spacing style, WD 6
Normal style, WD 6, 183
Normal template, WD 182
numbering, WD 62–63
Numbering Library, WD 62–63

O

odd page section breaks, WD 104
Office Clipboard, OFF 9, 13, WD 26, 30–31
Office Web Apps, Microsoft. *See* Web Apps, Microsoft Office
OneNote Web App, WEB 15
online collaboration, OFF 2
Open as Copy option, Open dialog box, OFF 11
Open dialog box, Excel, OFF 10–11
Open Read Only option, Open dialog box, OFF 11
Organizer dialog box, WD 194–195

creating documents with, WD 14–15

defined, WD 182, 212

exploring, WD 182–183

form, WD 212–213

mail merge, WD 132

overview, WD 181

revising, WD 198–199

workgroup, WD 197

testing forms, WD 226–227

text. *See also* formatting

bold, WD 12, 52

converting to tables, WD 79

copying and pasting, WD 28–29

cross-references, WD 158–159

cutting and pasting, WD 26–27

finding and replacing, WD 32–33

formatting using Mini toolbar, WD 12–13

highlighting, WD 65

inserting with AutoCorrect, WD 35

italics, WD 52

selecting in documents, WD 10–11

underlining, WD 53

text content controls, WD 214–215

Text control, WD 222

text flow options, WD 167

Text Form Field control, WD 222

Text Form Field Options dialog box, WD 222–223

text wrapping breaks, WD 107

themes

defined, WD 50

formatting using, WD 57

overview, OFF 2–3

thesaurus, WD 36

thumbnails, WD 158

title bar, OFF 6–7, WD 4

Title style, WD 170, 212

toggle button, WD 10

U

underlining text, WD 53

Undo button, WD 10, 15

Update Labels command, WD 141

uploading files to Windows Live, WEB 6–7

user interface, OFF 6–7

user templates, WD 196–197, 212

V

verifying Windows Live ID, WEB 5

vertical rulers, WD 4–5

vertical scroll bar, WD 4–5

view buttons, WD 4–5

View tab, PowerPoint Web App, WEB 9

viewing documents, WD 16–17

views, OFF 12, WD 17

W

Web Apps, Microsoft Office

Excel Web App, WEB 14–15

overview, OFF 5, WD 8, WEB 2, 8

PowerPoint Web App, WEB 8–9

quick reference to, WEB 16

Web Layout view, OFF 12–13, WD 17

Web sources, WD 118

widows, WD 106

Windows Live, WEB 1–16

creating folders and organizing files on SkyDrive, WEB 10–11

Excel Web App, WEB 14–15

obtaining IDs, WEB 4–5

overview, OFF 5, WD 8

PowerPoint Web App, WEB 8–9

quick reference, WEB 16

sharing files, WEB 12–13

signing in to, WEB 4–5

uploading files to, WEB 6–7

working online from, WEB 2–3

Word

Help window, OFF 14–15

overview, OFF 2

printing documents, OFF 12

Save As dialog box, OFF 9

themes, OFF 2–3

viewing documents, OFF 12

Word Count dialog box, WD 36–37

word processing software, WD 2–3

Word Web App, WEB 15

word-wrap feature, WD 6

workgroup templates, WD 197

works cited list, WD 118

X

XE (Index Entry), WD 162

Z

Zoom feature, WD 16

Zoom level button, WD 4–5

Zoom slider, WD 4–5, 16–17

Zoom tools, OFF 6